AF816800

Assessment of Earning Capacity

Fourth Edition

Michael Shahnasarian, Ph.D.

Lawyers & Judges Publishing Company, Inc.
Tucson, Arizona

This publication is designed to provide accurate and authoritative information in regard to the subject matter covered. It is sold with the understanding that the publisher is not engaged in rendering legal, accounting, or other professional service. If legal advice or other expert assistance is required, the services of a competent professional person should be sought.

—From a Declaration of Principles jointly adopted by
a Committee of the American Bar Association
and a Committee of Publishers and Associations.

The publisher, editors and authors must disclaim any liability, in whole or in part, arising from the information in this volume. The reader is urged to verify the reference material prior to any detrimental reliance thereupon. Since this material deals with legal, medical and engineering information, the reader is urged to consult with an appropriate licensed professional prior to taking any action that might involve any interpretation or application of information within the realm of a licensed professional practice.

Copyright ©2015 by Lawyers & Judges Publishing Co., Inc. All rights reserved. All chapters are the product of the Authors and do not reflect the opinions of the Publisher, or of any other person, entity, or company. No part of this book may be reproduced in any form or by any means, including photocopy, or electronic use, without permission from the Publisher's representative at the Copyright Clearance Center, Inc. (CCC) at www.copyright.com.

Lawyers & Judges Publishing Company, Inc.

P.O. Box 30040 • Tucson, AZ 85751-0040
(800) 209-7109 • FAX (800) 330-8795
e-mail: sales@lawyersandjudges.com
www.lawyersandjudges.com

Library of Congress Cataloging-in-Publication Data

Shahnasarian, Michael, author.
Assessment of earning capacity / Michael Shahnasarian, Ph.D. -- Fourth Edition.
pages cm
Includes bibliographical references and index.
ISBN 978-1-936360-35-2 (alk. paper) -- ISBN 1-936360-35-7 (alk. paper)
1. Evidence, Expert--United States. 2. Wages--Estimates--United States. 3. Work capacity evaluation--United States. I. Title.
KF8961.S53 2015
347.73'67--dc23

2014030366

ISBN 13: 978-1-936360-35-2
ISBN 10: 1-936360-35-7
Printed in the United States of America
10 9 8 7 6 5 4 3 2 1

online
www.lawyersandjudges.com

Contents

Part II
Conducting Vocational Assessments

Part III
Forensic Practice Issues

Preface

Initially published in 2001 (Shahnasarian, 2001), Lawyers & Judges Publishing Company released the second edition of *Assessment of Earning Capacity* in 2004 (Shahnasarian, 2004a) and the third edition in 2011 (Shahnasarian, 2011). This fourth edition aims to build on its predecessors' foundations – namely, promoting precision and objectivity in matters involving the valuation of earning capacity. To this end, *Assessment of Earning Capacity, 4th Edition,* provides new and updated information on the art and science of assessing earning capacity and communicating expert opinions in forensic settings.

The primary audiences I intended to address in the first edition and subsequent editions of Assessment of Earning Capacity have been (a) vocational rehabilitation experts, those involved in applying the mechanics and principles necessary to offer opinion testimony on earning capacity, and (b) lawyers, those involved in prosecuting earning capacity claims. Over the years, and as the book evolved, other audiences – including economists and accountants, insurance adjusters, and those undergoing assessments of earning capacity – demonstrated interest in the book. Each audience has a different perspective and reason for reading it.

- Vocational rehabilitation experts keep abreast of their profession's literature to remain current on developments and techniques necessary to perform their work. They aim to refine applications of the mechanics undergirding their assessments and the manner in which to best communicate and defend their findings. Mindful that lawyers will carefully scrutinize, challenge, and criticize their work, experts seek to develop and present unassailable opinions. This involves applying the science of their profession to address pending vocational questions, and aptly communicating and defending opinions.
- Lawyers' motivations in books of this sort range from a desire to become educated in the rubrics of earning capacity assessment to generating fodder to impeach an expert retained by opposing counsel. Not surprisingly, many lawyers have purchased editions of *Assessment of Earning Capacity* solely to prepare for cross-examining me! By extension, they tend to focus on methodologies employed, and bases and grounds for opinions rendered. Additionally, lawyers' evaluations of opinions on earning capacity often concentrate on an expert's ability to credibly communicate opinions in both written and testimonial formats.
- Economists and accountants focus on the outputs of vocational experts' opinions. These can include assessments of an individual's employability; past, present, and future earning capacity; work-life expectancy; and other vocational factors necessary to value a claim.
- Insurance adjusters, with responsibility to manage a claim for earning capacity damages and with settlement authority, consider both case-specific and ancillary factors including values of comparable cases, costs associated with a case's defense versus the value of claimed damages, and the deterrent value associated with aggressively defending a case with an aim to thwart the onset of other like claims. They focus primarily on economic risk factors, although the merits of a pending case also concern them, especially when threats of a bad faith claim and associated punitive damages claims loom.
- Those undergoing assessments of earning capacity generally have less interest in the technical elements vocational rehabilitation professionals, economists and accountants, insurance adjusters, and lawyers apply to value a claim. Their objectives focus on understanding the damages assessment process and being able to adeptly communicate the merits of their claims. To more fully address claimants' interests in the valuation of their damages claims, including loss of earning capacity damages, I wrote *A Claimant's Guide to Understanding and Presenting Injury Damages* (Shahnasarian, 2012), pub-

lished by the American Bar Association. Ceaser (2014) reviewed this work.

Assessment of earning capacity in forensic forums continues to be an evolving art and science. It is multifaceted and complex, often requiring analysis and synthesis of legal, medical, psychological, vocational, economic, and other factors. New audiences, each with their own perspectives and interests, will likely continue to emerge. Accordingly, and as new research, methodologies, and techniques advance, I expect books like *Assessment of Earning Capacity, Fourth Edition,* will continue to evolve indefinitely.

This edition of *Assessment of Earning Capacity* enfolds in three parts: Part I, foundation issues; Part II, conducting vocational assessments; and Part III, forensic practice issues. Readers of prior editions will find new and expanded discussions throughout the book. Additionally, this edition includes all new sample reports, clinical interview excerpts, case studies, and proposed trial questions, along with updated sample retention letters, retention agreement information, intake forms, and other administrative documents essential to practice as a vocational rehabilitation expert.

The *Earning Capacity Assessment Form* (Shahnasarian, 2004a; 2010b), the only standardized measure developed to facilitate vocational experts' evaluations of claims of loss of earning capacity, was introduced in the inaugural issue of *Assessment of Earning Capacity.* Like its second and third editions, this edition expounds on the instrument's underlying theory (Shahnasarian, 2010b) and updated research.

Neulicht (2011) and Slesnick (2012) reviewed the last (third) edition of *Assessment of Earning Capacity* (Shahnasarian, 2011). Other relevant reviews appear in Fields (2012), and Gibbs and Crtalic (2013), which focus on the *Earning Capacity Assessment Form – 2.*

My approximately 30 years' experience with the judicial system allowed me to gain insight into its behind-the–scenes happenings and inspired me to write a fictional story, *Justice Indicted* (Shahnasarian, 2013). This novel, a social commentary, chronicles a young person who acquired disabling problems and unwillingly became involved in a lawsuit in which his earning capacity, among other things, is controverted.

As in prior editions of *Assessment of Earning Capacity,* I am grateful to Steve Weintraub, president of Lawyers & Judges Publishing Company, for the opportunity to publish this fourth edition. Additionally, many thanks to Todd A. Wilber for his technical writing assistance—he has been my rock in all four editions of this work. Finally, without the support and patience of my wife, Jeannie, I would not have been able to complete this fourth edition.

Michael Shahnasarian, Ph.D.

Part I

Foundation Issues

Chapter 1

Vocational Expert Consultation

1.1 Vocational Expert Consultation

The greatest economic asset most people possess is their earning capacity—a measure of past, present, and future ability to earn employment income with respect to maximum capacity. Vocational evaluators, at the request of lawyers and judges, frequently assess claims of loss of earning capacity propounded in litigated matters. In these instances, a claimant typically asserts that some event—such as a motor vehicle accident, product malfunction, medical mishap, work-related incident, or wrongful termination—caused him to experience present and/or future damage to earn money through work activity. While these events often have physical and/or psychological bases driving the claims, there are also events requiring vocational evaluators' analyses that sometimes do not involve these bases. Examples include employment law disputes in which claimants allege wrongful termination and cases involving marriage dissolution in which a trier of fact imputes earning capacity to a spouse as part of an overall disposition on an alimony decision.

An evaluator's analysis of potential loss of earning capacity should, when relevant, include assessments of voluntary and involuntary reasons an individual may not have been fully participating in vocational activities or otherwise realizing her career development potential. For example, an individual may have abstained from employment for reasons related to pursuing childcare or eldercare activities, or lack of financial need. Among other things, this analysis may be relevant when discerning differentials between a subject's *earnings* and *earning capacity.*

Earnings refers to a demonstrated, historical record of generating compensation through employment activity. *Earning capacity* refers to the ability to optimize employment efforts and realize earning potential. Individuals do not always convert their earning capacity, and sometimes an earnings record can understate or overstate earning capacity.

Lack of financial need to aggressively pursue career development is a common reason some underachieve their earning capacity. Deductions about loss of earning capacity that give significant weight to earnings records in these cases could cause gross underestimation of earning capacity. Similarly, a case involving an earnings record of an heir to a lucrative family business, extended an inflated level of compensation, could be an artifact of nepotism. Here, relying on demonstrated earnings as an index of earning capacity could also lead to spurious deductions.

Generally, when available, an analysis of an individual's demonstrated earnings history helps construct a baseline for establishing an earning capacity when an event, such as an accident or an abrupt job termination, intervened and altered opportunities for career development. Earnings and earning capacity, however, are distinct concepts, and vocational evaluators should assess their nuances. While synonymous in some cases, they are not overlapping concepts.

As an economic asset, earning capacity is quite often underappreciated and not fully understood. For many persons, work and other vocational activities consume approximately one-half of their waking hours during two-thirds of their lifetimes. These activities provide means for financial subsistence and influence fulfillment and personal adjustment. Psychologically, work greatly affects self-concept and self-worth. These noneconomic damages elements also merit vocational evaluators' attention when considering claims of loss of earning capacity.

Assessing claims of loss of earning capacity involves a complex, systematic process incorporating many factors including the maximum amount of employment income an individual is capable of generating given his vocational profile, workplace conditions, specified industry and/or locale, and other relevant factors. The process may involve reviewing records to determine demonstrated and potential capabilities, interviewing a claimant, administering standardized tests, conducting labor market research, and evaluating collateral information including, at times, information from healthcare providers, family members, coworkers, and others capable of providing insight on capacities and limitations related to issues in dispute.

The complexity of deriving, within a reasonable degree of vocational rehabilitation probability, opinions on claims of loss of earning capacity that are admissible as evidence in a court of law varies. For example, when a long-term employee is dismissed and a question about the propriety of the severance is challenged, questions posed to a vocational evaluator include a reasonable length of time for the claimant to find new employment, the claimant's current earning capacity, and differentials between pretermination earning capacity and future earning capacity.

For a young person with an acquired disability, premorbid and latent earning capacity are of prime interest. In injury cases in which physical and psychological problems arguably prevent a claimant from returning to prior work, evaluators assess residual skills and ability to pursue alternate employment or otherwise resume vocational rehabilitation such as through retraining. Examinations involving individuals suspected of underachieving their earning capacity frequently include assessment of indicia such as inconsistencies between scholastic records and work accomplishments, along with opinions regarding true earning capacity. Myriad factors could be germane in a given case, and skilled evaluators cull them, assign appropriate weight, and apply scientific bases of vocational rehabilitation when performing analyses.

Earning capacity may be undeveloped or underdeveloped in cases, for example, involving a child, college student, young professional, an entrepreneur early in establishing a business, or someone not fully pursuing career development. Occasionally, earning capacity is latent—or not being applied to earn income—as in the case of a 30-year-old homemaker choosing to remain home to raise young children, or as in the case of an individual choosing to perform missionary work rather than enter the workplace. In other cases, earnings an individual generates may not accurately benchmark earning capacity. Examples can include cases in which an assessment of earning capacity is conducted at a time an individual forsakes employment to pursue education, or a person starts a new business after years of success as a business professional. Measuring earning capacity is even more complex when injuries interfere with a person's ability to work, psychological factors influence vocational behavior, work nuances govern work opportunities, or social stigmatization is somehow a factor in a person's career development.

Lost wages constitute a significant element of damages in many types of litigation. Qualified, scientifically derived vocational opinions assist triers of fact to render dispositions in:

- Matters involving disability
- Claims related to the Americans with Disabilities Act
- Employment law disputes
- Family law
- Long-term disability insurance

A brief discussion about vocational experts' typical involvement in litigation follows. Readers may also be interested in Dunn's (2014) comments on the American legal system and recitation of the *Rules of Civil Procedure*.

Disputes about wage claims often involve issues such as career development potential, earning capacity before an event in question, earnings and earning capacity, and technical questions related to transferable skills, reasonableness of a subject's mitigation efforts, and actual damages sustained. Examiners must also consider secondary gain when evaluating a loss of earning capacity claim's merit.

A. Matters Involving Acquired Disabilities

Vocational evaluators address loss of earning capacity allegations—both present and future—attributable to an acquired disability. The disabilities and associated problems onset through mechanisms such as personal injury, a medical event, product malfunction, and industrial accident. These analyses focus on quantifying claims of lost earning capacity.

B. Claims Related to the Americans with Disabilities Act

In cases related to the Americans with Disabilities Act, vocational evaluators address questions about reasonable workplace accommodations and provide opinions about earning capacity damages secondary to an employer's alleged failure to extend reasonable accommodations.

C. Employment Law Disputes

Among the most common employment law disputes involving earning capacity opinions are wrongful termination claims stemming from alleged sexual harassment and discrimination based on, for example, age, gender, or place of origin. Common questions vocational consultants encounter relate to a plaintiff's earning capacity after job displacement, reasonable length of time to secure employment after transitioning to a new job, and future earnings losses attributable to differentials between earning capacity before termination and future earning capacity. Opinions about the reasonableness of a plaintiff's job search and other mitigation efforts are sometimes also solicited.

D. Family Law

Vocational issues in family law cases often relate to a trier of fact's decision on how to impute alimony; either spouse's earning capacity may be at issue and may influence the disposition. Sometimes, after a marriage dissolves, either spouse may seek to adjust alimony payments. This request usually presumes one of the spouse's earning capacities has changed since the disposition on alimony, which can suffice to argue the merits of an alimony adjustment.

E. Long-Term Disability Insurance

Many individuals opt for income protection through long-term disability insurance policies. Claims for this insurance emanate when policyholders profess to have acquired physical and/or mental impairments that prohibit them from resuming their own occupation, and in some cases any occupation; qualification standards are typically policy specific. Vocational evaluators' assessments address issues specific to the pending claim.

F. Other Matters Involving Vocational Opinions

Assessment of earning capacity can also be material in many other cases including those involving decedents. In a wrongful death claim involving a thirty-eight-year-old computer programmer, for example, the decedent's estate asserted an earning capacity standard the defendant insurance company recognized. Another interesting case involved a doctoral student who was accused of plagiarism and dismissed from a graduate institution. She litigated for economic damages she alleged were caused by a wrongful dismissal, and she calculated an earning capacity claim in terms of the educational equivalent she associated with her planned studies.

Occasionally, an industry regulatory body gives rise to the need for a vocational expert's opinion. For instance, wrongful termination disputes involving wage claims sometimes present to industry arbitration panels such as the National Association of Securities Dealers. Additionally, insurance companies use vocational experts to assess individuals' abilities to return to prior work or to pursue retraining necessary to qualify for alternate occupations. Questions about claims of loss of earning capacity sometimes also arise in Jones Act (maritime law) and whistleblower litigation. In all of these cases, vocational analyses and opinion testimony aid triers of fact.

1.2 Vocational Expert Services

A vocational expert's engagement in a litigated matter depends on whether the expert serves as a consulting expert or a testifying expert. Additionally, the vocational issues in dispute and other case-specific issues dictate the types of referral questions and method of inquiry afforded the expert.

A. Scope of Involvement

Table 1.1 compares vocational experts' participation, depending on their retention: consulting expert or testifying expert. The vocational expert's best use, as conveyed in Table 1.1, figures in lawyers' overall analyses of a case at hand.

An attorney's decision to retain a vocational expert as either a consulting expert or a testifying expert depends on many factors including the facts in dispute, available evidence, and trial strategy. Often, the vocational expert is initially retained as a consulting expert, and, as the case develops, the expert's status is converted to testifying expert.

Table 1.1
Case Participation of a Consulting Expert versus a Testifying Expert

	Consulting Expert	Testifying Expert
Expert examination of plaintiff	Not conducted	May or may not be conducted (Typically is conducted)
Disclosure of vocational expert's involvement	May or may not be disclosed (Typically not disclosed)	Always disclosed
Discoverability of expert's analysis and opinions	Not discoverable	Fully discoverable
Deposition or trial testimony of expert	Not provided	May or may not be provided

For example, a consulting expert may initially be retained to review an opposing vocational expert's opinions based on a review of records and independent research, and to advise the attorney on matters such as questioning the opposing expert at deposition and trial, and preliminarily appraising the value of claimed loss of earning capacity damages.

Attorneys sometimes hire vocational experts as consulting experts to develop analyses that are undiscoverable by opposing counsel. If an attorney determines, however, that a case could be better leveraged for settlement or argued at trial with a testifying expert, the attorney may decide to convert the status of the consulting expert to testifying expert before the end of the case's discovery phase. When an expert's status changes to testifying expert, the expert's methods, research, and opinions become discoverable—subject to review and analysis by opposing counsel, experts, and the court, as well as interrogation via deposition and cross-examination at trial.

Often, lawyers defending cases that involve risk of significant damage awards avoid disclosing their damages expert's assessments. In these occasions, a desire to avoid establishing a "floor," or minimum amount, for damages undergirds defense lawyers' rationales. For example, if the value of damages in a given case that a defense expert computes is $5 million compared to a $5.5 million or even up to a $10 million damages assessment that a plaintiff expert computed, defense lawyers weigh the following questions in their decisions to present their expert's opinion:

- Does the $5 million damages assessment set a "floor" for the jury to award the plaintiff that exceeds the amount defense counsel believes is tenable to argue against?
- What is the risk triers of fact, persuaded by some or all of plaintiff counsel's arguments, will view the $5 million damages assessment as a "starting point" and adjust this value upwards, giving increased credence to the plaintiff expert's damages assessment?
- Is it better, in terms of suppressing a damages award, not to disclose the defense expert's damages assessment and, instead, concentrate on attacking the plaintiff expert's opinions?

As the discussion above suggests, case-specific strategic issues tend to dictate lawyers' decisions on a vocational expert's involvement and best use. An expert's role often evolves over a claim's life span.

B. Responding to Vocational Questions

While vocational experts frequently assess earning capacity, several secondary issues often merit investigation. Figure 1.1 shows the two-phase process vocational experts apply to identify and evaluate vocational issues. Phase I focuses on assessing potential past and present earnings damages. Phase II focuses on assessing potential future earning capacity damages. The diagram provides a superstructure for framing vocational questions and planning a method of inquiry. Often, new questions arise during the evaluation process. Chapter 4, *Processes Undergirding the Assessment of Earning Capacity,* includes a more comprehensive discussion about issues vocational experts frequently address, along with appropriate responses to vocational questions.

1.3 Bases for Earning Capacity Opinions

Assessing earning capacity is often complex and involves multifactorial analyses. At a general level, competent vocational experts undertake a hierarchical process that involves assessing and building on a foundation of extant evidence, developing new evidence, and synthesizing information to formulate a vocational opinion. Figure 1.2 identifies the bases for developing a sound opinion on earning capacity and related issues.

A. Analysis of Existing Evidence

The following information is necessary for a vocational expert to assess earning capacity:

- Medical issues related to career development
- Psychological issues related to career development
- Education (including prior scholastic performance), training, credentialing, and specialty skills
- Work history, experience, and earnings record

After evaluating these pertinent data, vocational experts examine individual traits, such as age, need and capacity for retraining, and potential vocational handicaps. Chapter 5, *Earning Capacity and Loss of Earning Capacity,* discusses these subject-specific factors.

B. Development of New Evidence

Vocational experts develop supplemental information, for example, by examining claimants and conducting case-specific research. A vocational examination is typically twofold, and involves a clinical interview and administration of a battery of standardized tests. Experts often conduct labor market research as the evaluation process unfolds. New evidence to facilitate an analysis can also emanate from consultations with those who have knowledge of a claimant, including healthcare experts, employers, and family

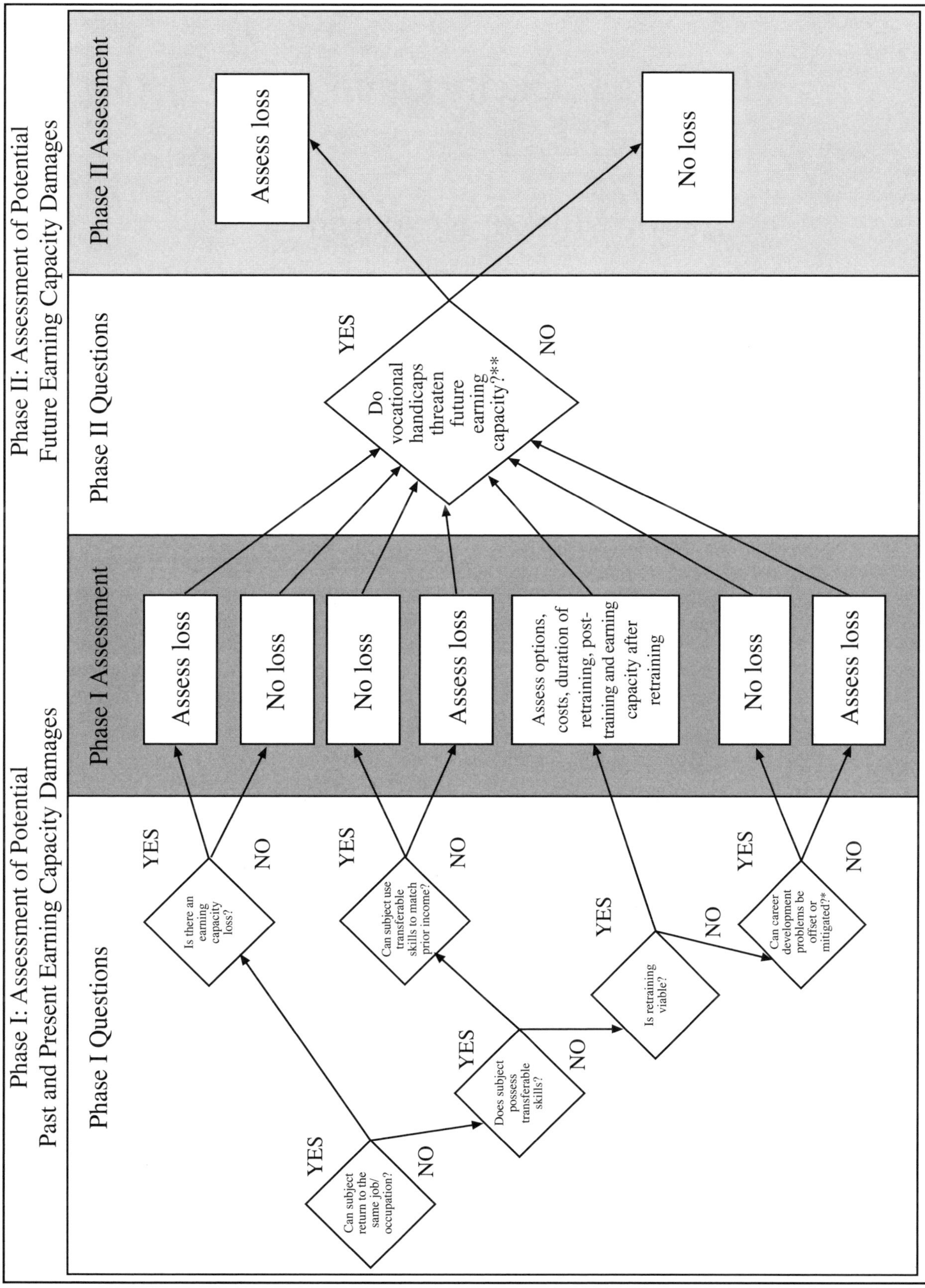

* Resources could include ergonomic devices, workplace reengineering, and vocational guidance services.
** Vocational handicaps include diminished access to work opportunities, need for workplace accomodations, employer bias in hiring and advancement, and diminished earning capacity.

***Figure 1.1** Sequential assessment of vocational alternatives and earning capacity damages*

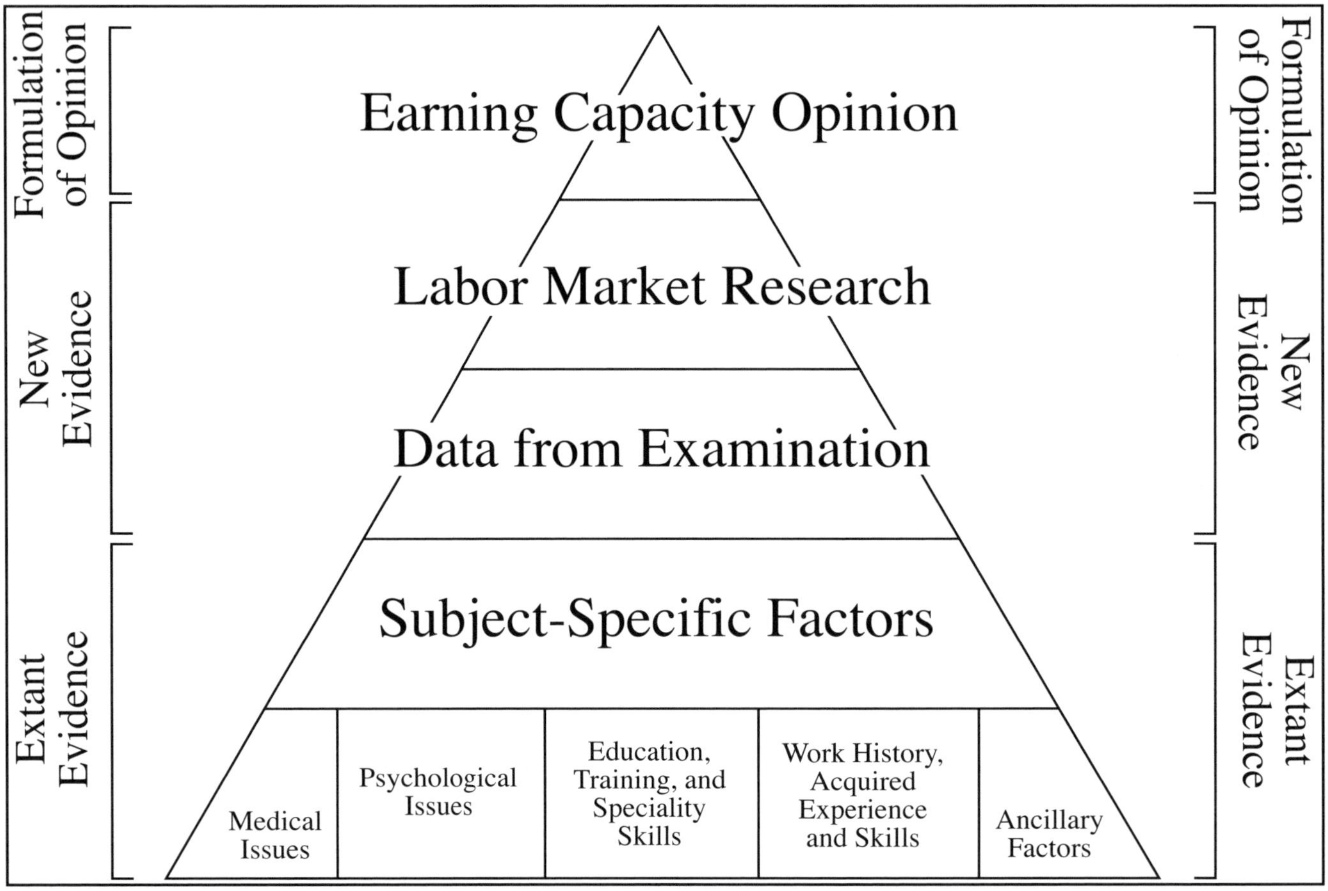

Figure 1.2 *Basis of an earning capacity opinion*

members. Chapter 4 presents a model to assess earning capacity.

C. Formulating an Opinion

To form an opinion about a subject's earning capacity, vocational experts must consider pertinent facts and variables. When cases have scarce or conflicting information and an expert cannot ascribe more weight to any particular opinion on which she is dependent—such as disparate physician opinions about an individual's functional capacities—a vocational expert may outline multiple scenarios, each contingent on the varying underlying assumptions.

Over the course of an assessment, a vocational expert evaluates the interface between a job's requirements—both exertional and nonexertional—and an individual's capacities—again, both exertional and nonexertional. Presuming viable job/person matches arise, subsequent analyses may include identifying the availability of current job opportunities and rates of pay.

1.4 Selecting a Vocational Expert

The selection of a vocational expert as a consultant and potential expert witness should be carefully undertaken. In addition to developing evidence and providing counsel about the merits and deficiencies of an attorney's damages theory, vocational experts, as a matter of course, may become the voice of the attorney. This voice—both directly and vicariously—may present evidence to persons involved in the settlement process, opposing counsel, other experts, judges, and triers of fact. As such, this voice is subject to intense scrutiny, challenge, and evaluation.

An individual perceived as marginally qualified or unqualified, biased, ill-prepared, or lacking in credibility does not add value to the judicial process. Perceptions of these types will likely undermine rather than aid a lawyer's efforts.

Those weighing the value of an expert opinion tend to consider an expert's qualifications, methods, professional demeanor, and presentation compared to other experts. During settlement negotiations, an expert's reputation, quality of analysis, and performance during a deposition contribute to the opposing counsel's assessment of the expert. An expert witness who communicated poorly during a deposition—for example, by appearing unprepared, defensive, or aloof—may embolden an opposing lawyer who is strategizing on ways to dispel damages arguments.

If a dispute is not resolved before trial, the attorney presenting the testifying expert must qualify the individual as an expert in whom the trier of fact can trust. Ideally, an expert's qualifications and professionalism are beyond reproach. A well-respected vocational expert with a reputation for making objective, reasonable, and credible presentations before triers of fact can be instrumental in helping to resolve a dispute.

Vocational experts should hold a graduate degree—preferably a doctorate—in rehabilitation counseling, psychology, or an allied discipline. Other credentials that help qualify practitioners include a state license to practice psychology or mental health counseling, and certification as a rehabilitation counselor, vocational evaluator, or career counselor. Individuals who focus on earning capacity assessments of people with disabilities and related problems such as future rehabilitation care needs often hold certifications related to life care planning and case management. The following factors should also be considered when retaining a prospective vocational expert:

- Professional experience
- Prior expert witness experience
- Publications
- Involvement in related professional and community activities
- Professional presentations
- Professional recognition
- Involvement in professional associations
- Service on pertinent editorial boards
- Contributions to the profession
- Reputation within both the legal community and the expert's professional community

A word of caution about credentials is in order. Like many professions, the behavioral sciences, including vocational guidance, have several designations that purport expertise. Unfortunately, many impressive-sounding credentials are little else; credentials may connote competence, but they do not ensure competence. An individual with many initials after his name may seem well qualified, but investigation may find unaccredited institutions granted the credentials, or that the credentials require little more than a fee and minimal set of qualifications to obtain.

Any case in which an expert is later perceived as marginally qualified will suffer. Regardless of a case's merits, arguments about vocational damages will weaken from suspect expert evidence. Further, a negative impression that an ill-qualified expert casts may poorly reflect on the retaining attorney, adversely affecting other case aspects.

While credentials are essential to consider when selecting a vocational expert, attorneys should also learn about the expert's standards as a practitioner and her presentation style. Further, knowledge of an expert's prior testimony experience and reputation within the legal community helps determine which vocational expert to retain.

Case-specific facts can also affect a decision on vocational expert selection. As an example, consider a case involving an incident in which a person, while incarcerated, made a claim of loss of earning capacity based on disabling problems acquired during a cell house altercation. Plaintiff's counsel chose to retain a vocational rehabilitation expert who had previously worked in a maximum-security prison. The assumption underlying the case, partly, was that the expert's experience in corrections—supplemented with vocational rehabilitation training and experience—would enhance credibility among triers of fact.

Before retaining an expert, lawyers should request and review the practitioner's curriculum vita. Questioning members of the community about the practitioner's reputation and performance as an expert witness also constitutes due diligence. Lawyers can render the ostensibly best-qualified experts ineffective if the expert communicates poorly or is easily manipulated. For instance, a pithy message culled from keen insight and analysis could be lost to a jury if it is conveyed via boring, verbose, overly technical, or incomprehensible testimony. Additionally, an expert who is unyielding, even when presented with compelling evidence that contradicts him, could be perceived as dogmatic, closed-minded, or biased.

Effective experts make appropriate concessions during cross-examination, yet remain resolute in expressing their conviction about their overarching opinions. Of course, if a vocational expert appears argumentative, evasive, or arrogant, he will likely offend a trier of fact. More discussion about a vocational expert's testimony appears in Chapter 11, *Testimony*.

An experienced vocational expert can greatly assist a case's presentation by integrating vocational opinions and case-specific details. She can also provide a professional evaluation of theories advanced by the opposition, research the merits of opposing theories, propose alternate theories, and refer other professionals who can further assist the attorney.

Van de Bittner, Wallace, Cottle, and Simon (2012) discussed qualifications for vocational experts. They also compared recommended qualifications as specified in eight published, peer-reviewed professional journals and related texts.

Geographic considerations can also affect selection decisions. Generally, lawyers prefer to retain experts either near the court's jurisdiction or from the original locale of the claimant. Unless one can provide a justifiable reason for using an expert from afar—such as the expert's unique credentials or particularly qualified ability to address issues at hand—the opposition may insinuate that a far-reaching search was necessary to locate an expert willing to offer farfetched opinions.

1.5 Conclusion

A vocational consultant provides professional opinions about earning capacity and related issues to all parties in a disputed matter. This both illuminates the true measure of the damages in question and promotes resolution of disputes. Attorneys who seek a consultant's input should investigate the consultant's qualifications, methods of inquiry, and presentation style to ensure maximum benefit to their cases.

Chapter 2

Logistical and Contextual Considerations

2.1 Litigation Phases and Expert Involvement

In most cases, vocational evaluators become involved in litigation at the request of an attorney—either plaintiff or defense. Infrequently, counsel representing both parties stipulate to a single vocational expert. Also infrequently, a party in dispute initiates a request for vocational evaluation services.

Typically, counsel representing claimants first retain a vocational evaluator to assess damages and, if necessary, provide expert witness services. Vocational evaluators that defense counsel employ typically review their counterparts' assessments and opinions, and, if necessary, rebut assessments of claimed damages. They sometimes also critique opposing experts' analyses—for example, by pointing out methodological and/or technical deficiencies—and propose questions to their retaining lawyer that are intended to dispel less-than-robust opinions.

Vocational issues in dispute may include:

- Capacity to perform various occupations
- Lost earnings
- Earning capacity and lost earning capacity
- Merits of job search
- Need and capacity for retraining
- Accessibility to jobs
- Need for accommodations
- Feasibility of implementing accommodations
- Impact of labor market and industry trends
- Acquired vocational handicaps
- Vocational rehabilitation plans

Lawyers enlist vocational evaluators' services at various phases of the dispute resolution process. Shahnasarian (2015) outlined vocational expert roles and activities over the course of a claim. A vocational evaluator can become involved in one or more of the following phases: presuit phase, discovery phase, or trial phase.

A. Presuit Phase

In some cases, evaluators become involved during the presuit phase—the phase before plaintiff's counsel files a Complaint. This document asserts another party's liability and announces intent to pursue compensation for alleged damages.

The presuit phase culminates with the presentation of a demand and subsequent settlement discussions between lawyers. Vocational evaluators contribute to the demand by evaluating and quantifying vocational damages; lawyers incorporate this assessment in their overall demand, which may also include assessments of medical expenses—both past and future—and intangible damages such as mental anguish and loss of services of a spouse.

As an example of a typical presuit demand for alleged vocational damages, the following excerpts appeared in a demand letter involving a thirty-seven-year-old certified public accountant who reduced her work schedule by forty percent while her daughter was an infant. According to her lawyer: "Ms. West's plans were to return [to work] full time as a CPA/partner in her firm, once her daughter enrolled in school. This would have been in 2013. Unfortunately, this 2011 accident and the chronic pain and limitations she suffers as a result of it have limited her ability to return full time to work." Citing various medical records, impairment ratings, physician restrictions, and a vocational evaluator's assessment that "Ms. West will experience a 10% to 25% reduction in her earning capacity, and up to a 5-year reduction in her work-life expectancy," the plaintiff's lawyer then referenced an economist's report, attached as an appendix to the demand letter. The economist applied the claimant's historical earnings record while incorporating the vocational evaluator's assessment of vocational damages, ultimately quantifying claimed past lost wages and anticipated lost future wages.

During the presuit phase, depositions have yet to be taken, and the claimant has yet to respond to interrogatory questions. If the case does not settle, claimant's counsel will file a Complaint, the discovery phase begins, and then the claimant becomes a claimant/plaintiff.

B. Discovery Phase

Once a Complaint has been filed, litigation commences and continues through the end of trial, unless the case is dismissed, settlement occurs, or the case goes into appeal. If the vocational evaluator did not examine the plaintiff during the presuit phase, this may occur on one or more occasions during the discovery phase. When serving as consulting experts rather than testifying experts, vocational evaluators' analyses focus on records reviews, research, and consulting with other experts.

After an expert's opinions have been disclosed to counsel opposing the lawyer who retained the expert, the expert, in most cases, is subject to a deposition. During this process, experts can expect to be questioned on numerous topics including:

- Retention details
- Qualifications
- History with the retaining lawyer
- Practice details (including percentage of time spent performing expert witness work, fees derived from expert witness work, and percentage of time retained by defense/plaintiff counsel)
- Fees
- Methodology employed
- Records reviewed
- Communications (including those with lawyers, other experts, and collateral sources)
- Examination procedures
- Tests administered, along with results and interpretations
- Clinical interview subject matter
- Research conducted to develop opinions
- Report details
- Bases for opinions
- All opinions developed
- Planned future work on the case
- Exhibits planned for use at trial

Additionally, during a deposition, attorneys customarily review the vocational evaluator's file and often request copies, which become exhibits to the deposition transcript. Vocational evaluators have the right to review and make changes to their testimony once the deposition has been transcribed; changes are recorded on an errata sheet.

The most common reasons to make changes to testimony via an errata sheet include:

Correcting the record if information is incorrect
Supplementing responses if information has been omitted or is incomplete
Providing information that was not recalled at the time of the deposition but has since been recollected

When experts or others raise their right hand and take an oath administered by a court-appointed officer to tell the truth, the whole truth, and nothing but the truth, they oblige themselves to do so. Those who fall short are subject to perjury.

While responding to deposition questions, it is essential to listen carefully and provide careful, thoughtful responses. Avoid succumbing to duress accompanying a lawyer's mode of questioning, such as rapid-fire questions, hostile and accusatory innuendo, bullying, badgering, and out-of-context misrepresentations. Of course, sound preparation before the deposition is essential. Vocational evaluators should always read their deposition testimony before testifying at trial, as part of their trial preparation. More information on expert witness depositions is in Chapter 11.

Other activities in which vocational evaluators sometimes participate during the discovery phase include evidentiary hearings, mediations, and mock trials. Evidentiary hearings occur when counsel opposing the lawyer disputes an expert's planned examination procedures—such as a test protocol the lawyer finds objectionable—and the court addresses the objection. In these cases, vocational experts may write an affidavit citing rationale for the planned methodology and/or provide testimony on this topic at a hearing; after the hearing, the court's ruling binds the expert.

Mediations involve off-the-record discussions and negotiations, facilitated by a mediator, during which parties with an interest in the litigation—including named parties, family members, lawyers, and adjusters—attempt to resolve the pending dispute. Representations of expert opinions and sometimes expert reports are disclosed. Occasionally, vocational experts attend portions of the mediation, and explain complex vocational issues and associated damages assessments.

Mock trials involve truncated presentations of a case's highlights to individuals presumed to simulate jury characteristics. Like mediations, mock trials are off the record, although lawyers sometimes relate selected information to their opponents, as well as to their retained experts and others with an interest in a dispute's outcome. A mock trial allows attorneys, among other things, to gauge prospective juror receptivity to evidence and arguments being contemplated to present at trial.

Based on a mock trial's outcome and information learned through the process, lawyers thereafter make adjustments and hone their trial strategies. Like a mediation, portions of a vocational evaluator's assessment may be presented, and experts sometimes participate in the simulation.

C. Trial Phase

The testimony a vocational expert provides at trial has three parts: direct examination, cross-examination, and redirect examination. In some jurisdictions, jurors also have a right to propose questions; this occurs at the judge's discretion after redirect examination.

First, during direct examination, counsel who retained the expert elicits testimony on credentialing that qualifies him to render expert analysis, the methodology implemented to assess pending vocational issues, and the arrived-at opinions. In some cases, after the retaining lawyer has presented the vocational evaluator as an expert, opposing counsel may voir dire the witness. A voir dire is an examination of a purported expert's competence to provide expert opinions.

Second, during cross-examination, the opposing lawyer questions the expert. While opposing lawyers' tenors of cross-examinations vary, experts can generally expect this questioning to be far less amicable—typically aggressive and hostile—than questioning during direct examination. Generally, the cross-examining lawyers aim to a) persuade triers of fact to discount or dismiss the expert's testimony, and b) appropriate portions of the expert's analysis that bolster their damages theories.

Third, during redirect examination, the retaining lawyer again questions the expert. If concerned that cross-examination denigrated the expert's credibility, the retaining lawyer will attempt to "rehabilitate" the expert. For example, if cross-examination elicits testimony that more than two years have elapsed since an expert examined the plaintiff and innuendo has been cast that the expert has remote knowledge of the plaintiff's current condition, the retaining lawyer may elicit testimony about the expert's continued review of updated records and assessment that an updated examination was unnecessary. Other redirect examination objectives include providing experts opportunities to expound on testimony helpful to the retaining lawyer's case that the cross-examining attorney may have inadvertently elicited.

After evidence has been presented and both sides rest their case, jurors deliberate the merits of the evidence and arguments, and eventually respond to questions in dispute. In anticipation of juror deliberations, opposing counsel prepares a form for jurors to record their decisions. The court has final decision-making authority on the contents of the jury verdict form.

Figure 2.1 presents a completed jury verdict form used in a case in which a man experienced an above-knee amputation because of a motorcycle versus motor vehicle accident. The forms typically pose specific questions related to liability and damages. At the end of a trial, a jury-appointed jury foreperson announces the jury's decision and presents the jury verdict form to the court.

When disputes are settled by a bench trial rather than a jury trial, the court makes findings of fact and conclusions. As an example, after a five-day bench trial in a maritime case involving a marine biologist/university professor who lost all functional use of his left, dominant upper extremity because of a mishap while aboard a research vessel, a US district judge rendered a final judgment. Below is the court's conclusions related to the plaintiff's claims of lost wages and profits from a consulting business he operated.

Lost Wages and Lost Profits

Damages for lost wages and lost profits must be established with reasonable certainty. See Benjamin v. Deal, 831 So. 2d 1227, 1229 (Fla. 4th DCA 2002); see also Hale Container Line, Inc. v. Houston Sea Packing Co., Inc., 137 F.3d 1455, 1474 (11th Cir. 1998) ("under general maritime law, damages for lost profits against the tortfeasor are allowed only when the amount of such profit is proven with reasonable certainty.")

XYZ University Wage Loss Claim

The court finds that plaintiff suffered no loss of past XYZ wages as a result of the accident. Plaintiff's tax returns for the five years prior to the accident (2004-2008) show plaintiff's XYZ Social Security wages to be $77,683, $83,524, $89,296, $93,130, and $45,497, respectively. Plaintiff's Social Security wages from XYZ in 2009 and 2010 were $85,702 and $85,209, respectively. Plaintiff re-

IN THE CIRCUIT COURT, NINTH JUDICIAL CIRCUIT, IN AND FOR POLK COUNTY, FLORIDA
CASE NO: 2007-CA-012345

AARON MICHAEL FRANK,
Plaintiff,

vs.

POLK COUNTY BOARD OF
COUNTY COMMISSIONERS,
Defendants.
________________________________/

VERDICT FORM

We, the jury, return the following verdict:

1. Was there negligence on the part of JANE AUSTEN/POLK COUNTY which was a legal cause of loss, injury, or damage to AARON FRANK?

YES _X_ NO ___

If your answer to question one is no, your verdict is for POLK COUNTY, and you should not proceed further except to date and sign this verdict form and return it to the courtroom. If your answer to question one is YES, please answer question 2.

2. Was there negligence on the part of AARON FRANK which was a legal cause of his injury, loss, or damage?

YES _X_ NO ___

If your answer to question 2 is no, skip question 3 and continue on to question 4. If your answer to question 2 is yes, please answer question 3.

3. State the percentage of any negligence which was a legal cause of loss, injury, or damage to AARON FRANK that you charge to:

JANE AUSTEN/POLK COUNTY
___67___%

AARON FRANK
___33___%

TOTAL MUST BE 100%

In determining the amount of damages, do not make any reduction because of the negligence, if any, of AARON FRANK. If you find that AARON FRANK was negligent, the court, in entering judgment, will make an appropriate reduction in the damages awarded.

Please answer question 4.

4. What is the total amount of AARON FRANK'S damages for lost earnings in the past?

a) In the past?
$ 137,280

5. What is the total amount of AARON FRANK'S damages for medical expenses incurred in the past and medical expenses to be incurred in the future?

a) In the past?
$ 551,527.37

b) In the future?
$ 2,376,000

c) What is the number of years over which those future damages are intended to provide compensation? _____40____
years

d) What is the present value of those future medical expenses? $
2,376,000

6. What is the total amount of AARON FRANK'S damages for pain and suffering, disability, physical impairment, disfigurement, mental anguish, inconvenience, aggravation of a disease or physical defect, and loss of capacity for the enjoyment of life sustained in the past and to be sustained in the future?

a) In the past?
$ 228,258

b) In the future?
$ 1,521,720

TOTAL DAMAGES OF AARON FRANK $ 4,814,785.37
(add lines 4a, 5a, 5d, 6a and 6b)

SO SAY WE ALL, this ___day of July 2014.

____
FOREPERSON

Figure 2.1 *Jury Verdict Form*

ceived his full XYZ salaries in 2009 and 2010. Plaintiff's tax records showed no loss in his XYZ wages following the accident. Therefore, the court awards plaintiff $0 in past lost income for his XYZ wages.

Further, the court finds that plaintiff failed to establish with reasonable certainty any loss of future wages from XYZ. Plaintiff contends that he will not be promoted to full professorship as a result of the accident and will therefore forfeit an increase in salary. The court finds this claim to be speculative. The determination of full professorship is based on a number of factors including sufficient publications, speaking engagements, and obtaining research grants. Further, plaintiff applied for full professorship before the accident and was advised by the Dean to withdraw his application for lack of sufficient publications. Plaintiff is still able to conduct research and publish and may still be promoted to full professorship. The court is mindful of the limitations plaintiff might face with regards to traveling and self-care needs; however, there is no evidence the plaintiff will not be promoted to full professorship as a result of these limitations or that any failure to be promoted would be proximately caused by the accident and resulting injuries. The court also finds plaintiff's testimony that he will no longer be able to secure grants to pay for his summer salary to be speculative. Therefore, the court awards plaintiff $0 for future lost wages and XYZ salary.

ABC Consulting Business

Plaintiff fails to provide enough evidence to allow the court to discern, with a reasonable degree of certainty, plaintiff's loss of profits from ABC. Plaintiff committed to XYZ, pursuant to his "outside activities" reports, that he would devote an average of eight (8) hours per week on ABC related work; however, with the exception of two postaccident ABC statements, there is no evidence on the record as to the actual number of hours per month plaintiff expended on ABC work before and after the accident. There is also no evidence on the record reflecting a decline in the number of hours plaintiff expended on ABC work as a result of the accident. The two postaccident statements show that plaintiff performed twenty-six (26) hours of work for ABC in November 2009, merely two months before the accident, and thirty-three (33) hours of ABC work in March 2010.

A review of ABC's tax records reveals the net profit per books of $1,926 for 2007 and $18,362 in 2008. From 2009 through 2011, ABC reported net profit per books of $21,087, $12,623, and $9,505, respectively. There is no evidence on this record to suggest that any decline in net profits from 2009 to 2011 was due to a decline in hours expended on ABC work by plaintiff because of the accident. Thus, the evidence is insufficient to allow the court to conclude that plaintiff experienced any loss from ABC as a result of the accident. Therefore, the court awards plaintiff $0 in past and future loss income for ABC.

Detailed information on the evolution of a claim appears in *A Claimant's Guide to Understanding and Presenting Injury Damages: A Damages Expert's Perspective* (Shahnasarian, 2012).

2.2 Administrative Issues

A vocational expert's involvement in a case typically begins with a request for a curriculum vitae and retention information, along with a request for assurance that the expert's potential involvement would not pose a conflict. Next, a lawyer or paralegal contacts the expert and provides general information about the case for which the expert's services are being sought. Other subject matter of this conversation typically includes various logistical details such as report deadline dates, and deposition and trial schedules. Experts should document this communication as well as subsequent substantive communications, as they are invariably questioned during depositions and trials about when they initially became involved in a case, what they were told, and what they were asked to do.

2.3 Expert Retention

In anticipation of requests for retention information, experts should maintain a current curriculum vitae, a letter specifying retention procedures and requirements, and a retention agreement form. A sample retention letter appears in Appendix 2.1. Typical retention letters include the following information:

- Fees and billing details
- Documents requested
- Examination procedures
- Cancellation policies

At the onset of an engagement, most experts require lawyers to sign a retention agreement and pay a retainer fee, which is then applied toward fees as they are accrued. This document denotes a contractual agreement and, along with a retention letter, can be helpful if disputes about scope of services or fees arise. A sample retention agreement appears in Appendix 2.2.

Without a signed retainer agreement and retainer fee payment, most vocational experts do not consider themselves engaged and eschew contrary representations. Sometimes unscrupulous lawyers pirate experts—that is, represent to an opposing lawyer an expert's retention without formally having consummated a retention. This allows the lawyer to avoid paying a retainer fee and accruing expert fees, and is typically done early in the litigation process; it also effectively disallows the opponent to retain the named expert.

Of course, disclosing an expert as having been retained before retention has been consummated is misrepresentation. Most experts view pirating practices with the same disdain a celebrity likely would display after learning a product manufacturer publicly represented his endorsement without obtaining consent and providing payment.

Along with retention letters that specify the scope of examinations, it is also helpful for vocational evaluators to develop written policies on the presence of third parties—especially nonparticipants—at vocational rehabilitation examinations, and to present this policy before an exam, when a third party's presence is announced and/or anticipated. Among the third parties who sometimes attend examinations are lawyers, court reporters, videographers, interpreters, family members, friends, and caregivers.

2.4 Maintaining an Examination's Integrity

Unless a court order specifying modifications to examination protocol is presented before an exam, vocational examiners typically adhere to a generally accepted vocational rehabilitation methodology (please reference Chapter 10) and employ consistent procedures across exams. Occasionally, counsel representing an examinee will object to a vocational evaluator's planned examination protocol. These objections invariably are voiced when the evaluator has been retained by the opposing lawyer, and are grounded in concerns that planned exam procedures could develop evidence not in concert with the examinees objectives. Examples of issues giving rise to protestations of examination protocols vocational evaluators encounter include the planned administration of various tests, and examinees' need to complete intake forms and other documents without lawyers' advance review.

Regulations that test publishers impose, codes of ethics, and standards of practice govern evaluators' handling and transmittal of standardized tests and related information. Appendix 2.3 includes a sample letter apprising interested parties about covenants binding evaluators in how they can transmit this type of data. In addition to restrictions of the sorts specified, evaluators' concerns about departures from standard examination protocols relate to marginalizing the validity of examination results.

Evaluators are wardens of an examination's proper conduct. Outside interference—for example, a lawyer's coaching—can render an examination invalid. Evaluators should take preemptive measures to prohibit the corruption of examination protocols.

Preferably, opposing parties reach agreement on any departure from standard examination procedures before an exam begins. When this cannot be accomplished between the opposing parties, they usually seek the court's intervention, and a hearing regarding an evaluator's procedures will ensue. Evaluators sometimes provide an affidavit and/or testimony addressing examination issues in dispute. The court's ruling ultimately binds the evaluator in conducting an exam. Appendix 2.4 includes an example of a court order specifying the scope of the vocational rehabilitation evaluation.

Ensuring that third parties do not overly interfere with an examination can be challenging. When third parties attend, evaluators can preserve an examination's dignity by:

- Making procedures and policies explicit before the examination
- Coordinating logistics, such as tape changes with videographers, so interruptions will not occur at inopportune times (e.g., during the administration of an in-progress timed test)
- Situating seating to prohibit verbal and nonverbal communications between those in attendance
- Controlling the input of collateral information from third parties as needed (e.g., clarifying comments)
- Referencing pertinent rulings that place parameters on third parties' attendance. For instance, in *Bacallo v. Dauphin,* 963 So.2d 962 (Florida 3rd District Court of Appeals, 2007), the court ruled, "A third party's presence, particularly an attorney's presence, during a medical examination is premised upon a requirement that the third party will not interfere with the doctor's examination."

Occasionally, despite an examiner's best efforts, outside interference arises. Typically, this occurs when a defense lawyer requests an examination and unsolicited input emanates from a plaintiff lawyer in attendance. Quite often, lawyers' unwanted involvement is a product of their overzealous advocacy; however, at other times the interference is calculated and can have motives that include intimidating and provoking an examiner, along with testing an examiner's limits.

In one case, a plaintiff arrived at a vocational rehabilitation evaluation with his lawyer and a court reporter. The lawyer demanded at the onset to review an intake form his client would be required to complete; the evaluator complied with this request. Then the lawyer announced he was instructing his client not to respond to questions about education and work history, among other things, since this information was available in records produced. The evaluator cited the relevance of this information in a vocational rehabilitation evaluation and lack of a court order restricting the scope of her examination. Confronted with an impasse and unwilling to yield to the plaintiff lawyer's edict, the evaluator sought assistance from the defense lawyer who retained her.

Lengthy delays ensued, and the opposing lawyers eventually discussed the dispute about information the examiner was attempting to obtain; also in attendance during this telephone conference were the examiner, examinee, and court reporter. While explaining his objection to the evaluator's intake form, plaintiff's counsel used an expletive to describe it. Interestingly, the court reporter whom plaintiff's counsel commissioned did not record the telephone conference. The opposing lawyers failed to arrive at a resolution and agreed to pursue the dispute with the judge presiding over the case.

After the aborted examination, the vocational evaluator provided in a letter to the defense lawyer a full account of events that occurred, including mention of the expletive plaintiff's counsel used in the examinee's presence to describe the intake form. The defense lawyer subsequently published the letter to the court, and the plaintiff's lawyer disagreed with the information the vocational evaluator documented—including use of an expletive. Further, plaintiff's counsel filed a lawsuit against the vocational evaluator, alleging libel and slander, and moved to strike her as an expert witness. In retrospect, the vocational evaluator suspected this had been the motive of plaintiff's counsel all along—to prohibit development of evidence not consistent with the lawyer's theory and to extract the vocational evaluator from the case.

If unforeseen interference during an examination occurs and the examiner cannot satisfactorily reconcile it, examiners should suspend the examination and seek assistance from the retaining lawyer. Additionally, as in the case cited above, careful documentation of events is necessary, as is enlisting witnesses who can verify events that later may be controverted.

2.5 Video Recording of Examinations

Video recording vocational rehabilitation evaluations is becoming increasingly common, and, like interference from a lawyer, can also prove unnerving and can invalidate an examination. The equipment, logistics, and need to coordinate recording details with a videographer, along with the visual presence of electronic equipment of all sorts—including cameras on tripods, microphones, monitors, back drops, and special lighting—interject in a clinical interview an artificial ambiance that threatens to undermine an evaluator's efforts to maintain standardization protocols.

Shahnasarian (2009a) noted examiners' challenges when video recording accompanies an evaluation are twofold: Comply with an examinee's right to have the examination event recorded, and preserve an examination's integrity by prohibiting the video-recording process from overly contaminating it. Among the recommendations Shahnasarian presented were to develop and present in advance a position statement on video recording, and document—both in writing and photographically—matters related to the video recording. Appendix 2.5 includes a sample position statement on video-recording evaluations, and Figure 2.2 is a photograph of video-recording equipment that was part of an attorney-commissioned examination environment.

(please insert previously used pics, page 18 from 3rd edition, plus additional pic we will send)

2.6 The Litigation Environment

Examinations conducted in forensic cases are far from akin to those conducted in a clinical context, devoid of litigation. As vocational experts, evaluators must understand and appreciate the adverse, manipulative, and scrutiny-laden litigation environment in which they will be performing their expert witness work. While the judicial process may superficially appear ordained to find the truth, those involved in its inner workings soon learn that self-serving aims abound and crafty sabotage—perpetrated by any number of sources and often lawyer-engineered—is de rigueur. Shahnasarian (2009b) commented on this.

Clearly, employment as an expert witness requires a skill set and vocational profile different from what is required of those who practice in nonlitigation settings. Even the best clinicians may lack the skills, disposition, and mettle necessary for this practice specialization. Those who choose to pursue expert witness work—which, when performed aptly, is vital to the adjudication process—should do so with understanding and forbearance. For example, although competent clinicians who are not experienced in forensic ways would likely take umbrage when lawyers aggressively and unfairly attack their credentials, methodologies, and opinions, a seasoned expert witness will negotiate these challenges with perspective and insight on underlying intentions, motives, and predatory lawyer tactics.

Intimidation, bullying, embedding half-truths in deposition and trial questions, and taking information out of context are but a few of the tactics expert witnesses routinely encounter. Unfortunately, these types of lawyer-inspired artifacts of the judicial process permeate the fact-finding process. Shahnasarian (2012) described common plaintiff and defense lawyer strategies.

After consenting to serve as an expert witness, be as prepared as possible to confront an onslaught of creative, unforeseen, never-ending subterfuge—ranging from defamation of your professionalism to innuendo that your opinions are bought and you are akin to a prostitute—perpetrated by counsel and experts averse to counsel that has retained you. Field (2014) discussed adverse situations vocational and economic experts encounter. While noting filing a lawsuit and pursuing compensation for damages is among the most aggressive actions an individual can legally undertake, one lawyer likened pursuing litigation to the dropping of an atomic bomb: After an action of this type, rules of fair play no longer exist.

Vocational experts cannot fully insulate and protect themselves from the goings-on of the legal process. Adhering to standards of practice, maintaining dignity and decorum, seeking assistance when events go awry, and not deviating from areas of expertise hallmark experts who remain above the fray. Additionally, in objectively stated terms, carefully document troubling events you encounter. Appendix 2.5 features as an example a memorandum a vocational rehabilitation expert wrote after receiving a threatening, innuendo-laced telephone call from a lawyer who formerly retained him as an expert witness.

2.7 Conclusion

Effective vocational evaluators understand the dispute resolution process, litigation environment, and their contributions to just adjudication. Attention to administrative details, such as clearly specifying retention parameters and examination protocols, can help preempt problems that range from an expert's scope of involvement in pending litigation to controlling third party interference during a vocational rehabilitation evaluation. Further, while appreciating the challenges of conducting valid examinations in an adversarial environment, competent vocational experts are mindful of undermining efforts that are common in adversarial proceedings.

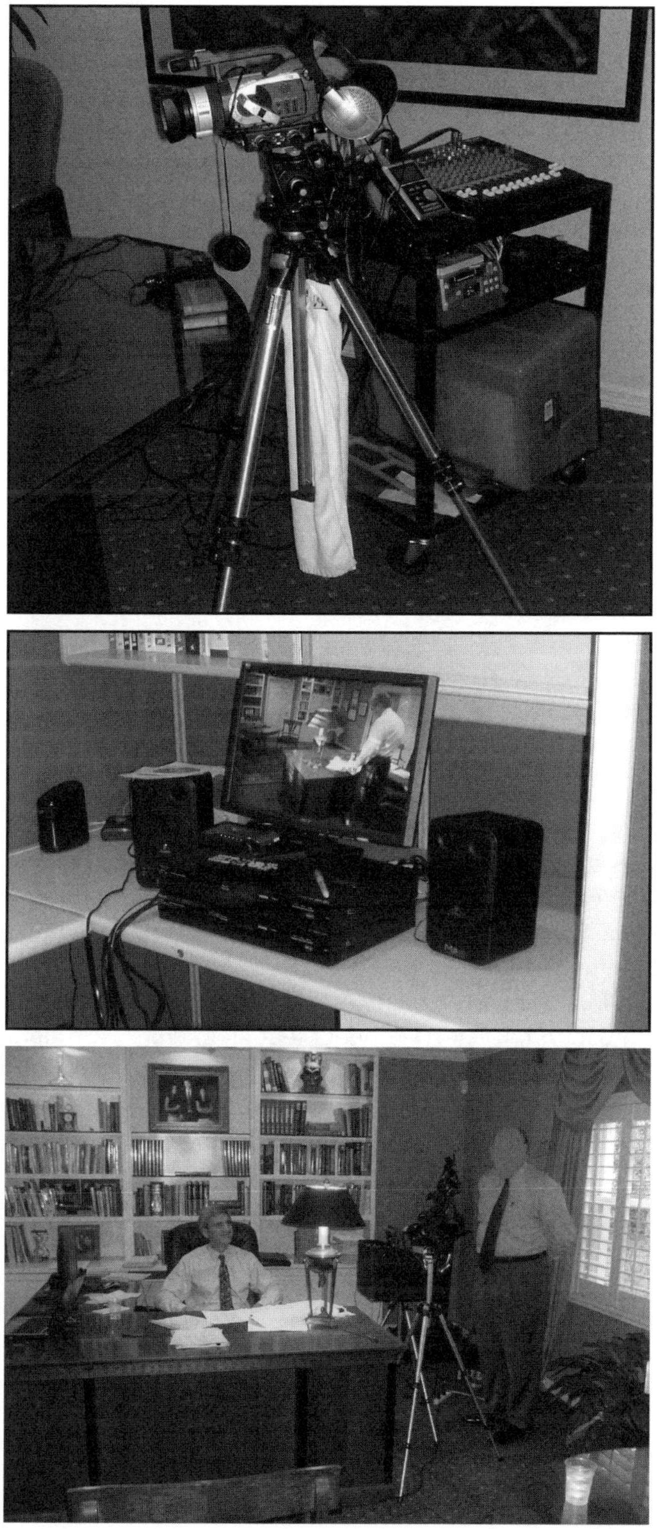

Figure 2.2 *Photographs that a vocational evaluator used to provide visual documentation of an examination environment counsel representing an examinee commissioned. Descriptions and visual images of specially placed lights, multiple microphones, video monitors, electrical cords and digital equipment strewn about, and a videographer wearing headphones and operating a high-tech control panel in view of an examinee will help dispel the notion that a discretely placed camera recorded an examination. These photographs appeared in an appendix of an examiner's report.*

Appendix 2.1
Sample Retention Letter

Career Consultants of America
11019 N. Dale Mabry Hwy.
Tampa, FL 33618
Tel: (813) 265-9262 Fax: 265-4226

Michael Shanasarian, Ph.D.

March 11, 2014

James Jones, Esquire

Re: Heath Puskarich

Dear Mr. Jones:

Thank you for your interest in my rehabilitation consultation services. The areas that I am asked to address most frequently relate to vocational rehabilitation and future medical needs (e.g., developing a life care plan or treatment plan). I have attached a copy of my curriculum vita for your reference.

Vocational Rehabilitation Evaluations

My typical procedures in conducting a vocational rehabilitation evaluation include first reviewing pertinent records, detailed below, and then conducting a comprehensive examination. My examination has two parts: a clinical interview and administration of various tests. The entire exam takes approximately 6 to 8 hours to complete. Of course, the examinee is extended opportunities to take breaks as needed, including a lunch break.

I conduct my examinations in English. If English is not the examinee's first language, please notify me in advance and arrange for an interpreter. Examinations that involve an interpreter typically take longer, and I will need to plan accordingly. I also attempt to accommodate the examinee as requested (e.g., seating preferences, special equipment needs, meal service, etc.). Again, please notify me in advance.

While I prefer to conduct my examination in my office, I can, if necessary, conduct it at an alternate location. Please provide as much advance notice as possible for out-of-town examinations. Members of my staff provide support assistance as needed.

Typically, I request to review the following records before my examination:

- Complaint
- Responses to Interrogatories
- Deposition of Plaintiff
- Depositions of Physicians
- Depositions of Employers
- Medical Records (including reports of diagnostic evaluations, hospital admission and discharge reports, operative reports, assessments, and available preinjury medical records)
- Psychological Records
- Employment Records
- School Records
- Tax Returns

Of course, I am interested in new records that may have been generated after my examination. Please keep me abreast of any information concerning my area of inquiry.

The clinical interview generally requires 3 to 4 hours to complete. During this time, the examinee will be asked detailed questions about presenting problems, treatment, limitations and capabilities, medical history, activities of

Vocational Testing

The vocational tests that I prescribe, and members of my staff usually administer, typically require between 4 and 5 hours for an examinee to complete. While I generally vary the battery of tests prescribed depending on the examinee's background, I administer tests that assess mental functioning (including intelligence testing and aptitude testing), occupational interests, and personality. The following tests are among those that I frequently prescribe:

- Wahler Physical Symptoms Inventory
- Beck Depression Inventory
- Wide Range Achievement Test—Revision 3
- Shipley Institute of Living Scale
- Multidimensional Aptitude Battery
- Minnesota Multiphasic Personality Inventory—II
- Self-Directed Search—Form R or Form E
- Purdue Pegboard
- Strong Interest Inventory
- Campbell Interest and Skills Inventory
- Wechsler Memory Scale
- Wechsler Adult Intelligence Scale—3
- Grooved Pegboard

Life Care Planning

If significant future care is anticipated for an examinee, I will, on request, prepare a life care plan that identifies future care needs and associated costs. My practice in developing a life care plan is to consult with other practitioners—who have treated or evaluated the examinee—to obtain comprehensive, multidisciplinary recommendations for future care. Of course, I add my own recommendations when appropriate. Then, I determine future care costs by contacting service providers and vendors. Finally, I assemble a report and invite those who have made recommendations to review it. Suggested revisions are subsequently incorporated and, if necessary, I will author additional drafts.

After I complete my examination, I provide a written report of my vocational rehabilitation evaluation that includes opinions on vocationally relevant matters. I usually complete this report within 30 business days after my examination.

Retention

To formally retain me, I require a nonrefundable retainer in the amount of $3,500. I do not consider myself engaged in a matter until my office has received a signed retainer. Monies from the retainer are applied to costs as they accrue.

Fee Schedule

	Michael Shahnasarian, Ph.D.	*Associate Expert*
In-Office Assessment: *Includes interviewing examinee, testing instruments, test administration and scoring, test interpretation, consultations, and other services.*	$480 per hour *(assessments typically require 6 to 8 hours)*	$250 per hour *(assessments typically require 6 to 8 hours)*
In-Office Assessment Cancellation Fee: *(no cancellation fee if 48 hours or more in advance; one half if canceled 24 to 48 hours in advance; full fee for less than 24 hours in advance)*	$2,750.00	$1,750.00

*Hourly Rates: *Standard 30-day report turnaround*	$480 per hour	$250 per hour
**Expedited:* *Less than 30-day report turnaround* **Hourly rates will be charged for additional interviewing, reviewing records, conducting research, consulting, preparing reports, preparing for deposition or trial testimony, casework, and traveling.*	$520 per hour	$350 per hour
Testing beyond initial assessment: *Includes testing instruments, test administration and scoring, and test interpretation.*	$300 per hour	$300 per hour
Out-of-Office Assessment: *Includes testing instruments, test administration and scoring, test interpretation, consultations, trial testimony, and other related services.*	$5,000 per day	$2,500 per day
Weekend Examination Rate:	$6,000 per day	$3,000 per day
Life Care Plans		
Standard:	$ 5,000.00	
Catastrophic:	$ 8,000.00	
International:	$10,000.00	
Deposition Fee: *Unless notified otherwise, a 2-hour minimum will apply*	$500 per hour	$350 per hour

Rates remain in effect for 6 months from the date retainer is received. Thereafter, our fees will be billed at the prevailing rate, not to exceed an increase of 10% per year for the duration of the agreement.

Generally, a vocational rehabilitation evaluation includes a review of records, a rehabilitation examination (clinical interview and testing administration), scoring and interpreting testing, labor market research, and report writing. Considering these services, an in-office vocational rehabilitation evaluation typically costs from $5,000 to $8,000, depending upon the complexity of the case.

Since a full day is commonly required to conduct a rehabilitation examination, compliance with scheduled appointments is important in the management of the overall responsibilities associated with my practice. Consequently, I enforce the following cancellation policy for scheduled examinations: no cancellation fee if the appointment is canceled 48 hours or more in advance, one-half of the examination fee is billed for appointments canceled 24 hours to 48 hours in advance, and the full fee is billed for no-show appointments and appointments canceled less than 24 hours in advance.

Trial Testimony

If a trial date is scheduled in Hillsborough County or an adjacent county and I am notified that my testimony is anticipated, I will required a $1,000 deposit applied towards preparation for trial, trial appearance and testimony, travel and other costs incurred. I will reserve 4 hours, charged at my rate of $480 per hour, to ensure availability on the appointed trial date. I will block a full day, billed at my daily rate of $5,000 to ensure availability upon notification of anticipated testimony at other locales. It should be noted that these funds will be applied to actual testimony time.

Invoicing

Billing for any services provided will be done semimonthly. Payment is due upon receipt of an invoice and shall be directed to Career Consultants of America at its offices in Tampa. Expenses incurred with my services, such as travel expenses will be billed at cost.

If payment is not received within 30 days of receipt of invoice, interest shall accrue at the rate of one and one-half percent per month until paid. If it becomes necessary to retain the services of an attorney to collect any balance due, you agree to pay all attorney fees and costs associated with the collection of this account. You also agree to waive trial by jury. Legal proceedings resulting from nonpayment of fees related to my services shall be conducted in Hillsborough County, Florida.

Videographers

If a videographer is requested to be present, please notify my office at least 48 hours in advance so that we can prepare. Only certified videographers will be permitted to set up equipment in our offices. He/she should arrive between 15 and 30 minutes before the appointed interview time to set up equipment and to prevent any delay in the examination. No interference by the videographer during the examination will be tolerated, and the videographer may not remain in the room during the examination. The camera should be unattended once set up is completed. The videographer should not interact with the examinee or with my staff members. If a tape requires changing, a member of my staff should be notified—the videographer should not enter the interview room unescorted. At least 10 minutes advance notice should be provided for changing a videotape.

Mobile Telephone Usage

I ask that the use of mobile telephones be limited by the examinee. Mobile telephones must be set to vibrate mode or turned off completely.

Location

Career Consultants of America, Inc., is located in a busy, suburban area of Tampa that is approximately 15 minutes northeast of Tampa International Airport. Three restaurants are less than one-half block from my office and many others are within a short drive.

I do not permit smoking or soliciting in my office. Since examinations commonly last up to a full day, please do not bring children to my office if they are not involved in the examination. Guests in my office are asked to remain in designated areas, and respect the privacy of others they may encounter.

Please sign the attached form, and return it to my office with the appropriate retainer fee. Of course, let me know if you have any further questions. I look forward to working with you.

Sincerely,

Michael Shahnasarian, Ph.D.
Certified Rehabilitation Counselor, #3701
Certified Vocational Evaluator, #58360
Certified Life Care Planner #258
Licensed Psychologist, PY5644
Fellow, National Career Development Association
Fellow, International Academy of Life Care Planners

Enclosures
Dictated by Dr. Shahnasarian and signed in his absence to avoid delay.

Appendix 2.2
Sample Retention Agreement

Career Consultants of America
11019 N. Dale Mabry Hwy.
Tampa, FL 33618
Tel: (813) 265-9262 Fax: 265-4226

Michael Shanasarian, Ph.D.

TAX ID # XX-26-XXXXX

March 11, 2010
James Jones, Esquire
Fax: 813-555-1234
Re:

Terms: Due Upon Receipt
To retain Dr. Shahnasarian, the nonrefundable fee indicated below is required. Dr. Shahnasarian is not officially retained until our office has received a retainer fee. This fee will be applied to services as they are provided. Promulgation of Dr. Shahnasarian as an expert before official retention is misrepresentation.

Retainer Fee	**$3,500**
Balance due	**$3,500**

Career Consultants of America
11019 N. Dale Mabry Hwy.
Tampa, FL 33618
Tel: (813) 265-9262 Fax: 265-4226

Michael Shanasarian, Ph.D.

Retention Agreement

I would like to retain Dr. Shahnasarian's services in the case of ________________________ .

I have read Dr. Shahnasarian's letter dated ________________, and I understand that signing this agreement shall acknowledge the fees associated with conducting a vocational rehabilitation evaluation in connection with this matter and that I and my client shall be jointly and severally responsible for the payment of all fees as explained in the letter.

Signature________________________________ Date ____________

Print complete name and title__________________________
Firm____
Mailing address____________________________________
Telephone No._____________________________________
E-mail____

Appendix 2.3
Sample Letter Regarding Covenants Binding Evaluators in Transmitting Standardized Tests and Related Information

Career Consultants of America
11019 N. Dale Mabry Hwy.
Tampa, FL 33618
Tel: (813) 265-9262 Fax: 265-4226

Michael Shanasarian, Ph.D.

TAX ID # XX-26-XXXXX

March 11, 2010
Re: Margaret Curtin

Dear Mr. R. Miller:

This letter is in response to your request for copies of all raw data and test results from my examination of Margaret Curtin. Accordingly, I have enclosed a copy of documents completed by Ms. Curtin, a copy of my clinical interview notes, and test results that are non-psychological in nature. Please note that the Florida Administrative Code (Chapter 64B19.18.004) addresses the use of psychological test instruments and states, "A psychologist who uses test instruments may not release test data, such as test protocols, test questions, or written answer sheets, except (1.) through a licensed psychologist, or (2.) after complying with the procedure set forth in Rule 64B19.005, FAC, and obtaining an order from a court of other tribunal or competent jurisdiction, or (3.) when the release of the material is otherwise required by law." Accordingly, I will release the psychological test results to a licensed psychologist you identify.

Please do not hesitate to contact me if you have any further questions.

Sincerely,

Michael Shahnasarian, Ph.D.
President

Enclosures

Appendix 2.4: Sample Court Order Specifying Scope of Vocational Rehabilitation

IN THE CIRCUIT COURT OF THE SIXTH JUDICIAL CIRCUIT
IN AND FOR PASCO COUNTY, FLORIDA

IN RE: THE MARRIAGE OF:
HAROLD JULIUS WARD,

Petitioner/Husband

v.

CASE NO: 01-2014-DR-2345-ES

DIVISION: "K"
BETTY DOROTHY WARD,

Respondent/Wife.

__________________________/

ORDER GRANTING PETITIONER/HUSBAND'S VERIFIED MOTION FOR VOCATIONAL EVALUATION AND LABOR MARKET SURVEY

THIS CAUSE came on to be heard on Thursday, September 26, 2014, upon the Petitioner/Husband's Verified Motion for Vocational Evaluation and Labor Market Survey. The Court having heard the argument of counsel for the respective parties, reviewed the Petitioner/Husband's Verified Motion for Vocational Evaluation and Labor Market Survey and being otherwise fully advised in the premises, it is therefore

ORDERED AND ADJUDGED as follows:

1. This Court has jurisdiction over the parties and the subject matter herein.
2. The Petitioner/Husband's Verified Motion for Vocational Evaluation and Labor Market Survey is hereby GRANTED as I do find that good cause has been shown, but I do find a very good argument for not doing it. In the long run, I am going to err on the side of caution. I am going to allow the examination and grant the motion because in the grand scheme of things I think it would be much more detrimental to have to come back on the back end or all things considered, I can just picture a final hearing where that has not been done, and I think it would be safer on that.
3. Michael Shahnasarian, Ph.D., of Career Consultants of America located at 11019 N. Dale Mabry Highway, Tampa, Florida 33618-3801, is approved to conduct a full vocational evaluation and labor market survey of the Respondent/Wife, including, but not limited to, testing, and the Respondent/Wife shall cooperate with the process. The expert shall travel to Respondent/Wife's place of residence or her counsel's office, at their option, for the purposes of conducting this evaluation.
4. The initial costs of said evaluation shall be paid by the Petitioner/Husband without prejudice for this Court's final determination.
5. Upon completion of the expert's evaluation counsel shall be provided with the expert evaluation and/ or experts reports.
6. That this Court retains jurisdiction of this cause of action and of the parties hereto for the purpose of enforcing the executory provisions of this order, as well as for entry of such other orders as might be deemed just or appropriate. Further, both parties are Ordered to take whatever action is reasonable

and necessary to, and conduct themselves in a manner conducive with, carrying out the intent and purpose of said order.

DONE AND ORDERED in Chambers, Dade City, Florida, this _____ day of _______, 2014.

____

JANICE DIONISIO
Judge, Circuit Court

COPIES FURNISHED TO:

Attorney for Petitioner/Husband

Attorney for Respondent/Wife

Appendix 2.5
Position Statement on Recording Rehabilitation Evaluations
Michael Shahnasarian, Ph.D.

I have been performing rehabilitation examinations for cases in litigation for approximately 20 years, and I respect the right of the subject of the examination to have the examination recorded. Additionally, I do not object to the presence of others, besides the examinee during my examination, provided the individuals do not interfere with the examination process and conduct themselves professionally. This includes not participating in the examination, remaining out of eyesight of the examinee while the examination is in progress, minimizing equipment-related interruptions, not interfering with the operations of my practice outside the examination room, respecting the privacy of other patients and individuals in my office, remaining in designated areas within my office when not in the examination room, and interacting with my staff professionally and courteously. Further, I request that any third party present abide by the 2007 Florida 3rd District Court ruling, which states, "A third party's presence, particularly an attorney's presence, during a medical exam is premised upon a requirement that the third party will not interfere with the doctor's examination (*Bacallo vs. Dauphin*, 963 So.2d 962)."

The examinations I conduct do not involve a physical examination. Information is gathered through a clinical interview and various forms and tests the examinee completes. The examinee is welcome to take breaks as needed, and my staff and I make every attempt to accommodate an examinee's requests.

If a videographer will be at an examination I conduct, I require 48 hours advance notice. My office space is limited, and my staff will need to ensure an appropriate examination room and additional space is available to accommodate the extra individuals in attendance. Also, I request that the videographer arrive at my office before the examination to set up equipment, so as not to delay the examination schedule.

I will make every attempt to accommodate those in my office to record an examination. This includes cooperating with videographers to make tape changes and to configure the examination room as requested to facilitate recording quality. Especially close coordination is necessary during portions of my examination that involve the administration of timed tests; those recording the examination are not permitted to interrupt the process to change tapes or for any other reason. I request that only certified videographers perform the videotaping.

I prefer that the camera used to videotape my examination be unattended. Further, during portions of my examination when my staff or I are not present with the examinee (e.g., during standardized testing), I require that outside parties, likewise, remain out of the examination room. Of course, the unattended camera can continue running.

If an exam I conduct is videotaped, the videographer does not have the right to include me or my staff in the videotaping picture without obtaining prior consent. Of course, audio recording via the videotaping is permissible, and my staff will cooperate with wearing microphones and/or using other audio-recording equipment. The videotaping, however, is to be of the subject of the exam only, similar to the type of recording made when a deposition is videotaped. My rationale for this policy includes the following:

1. My staff and I have a right to privacy. We will fully cooperate with recording efforts that provide an avenue to verify that information I report comports with actual information and events that occurred during my exam—namely, by allowing all audiotaping and videotaping of the examinee.
2. The psychological literature is rife with empirical studies and analyses of how any outside observation affects an event (e.g., Hawthorne Effect, Yerkees-Dodson Law). A camera aimed at a nonconsenting professional attempting to perform his or her job, in particular, adds unnecessary stress, compromises the individual's ability to perform her or his job, and is a violation of privacy.

Career Consultants of America, founded in 1986, is a respected practice that takes pride in its tradition of professionalism and courteous service to patients and others. We request that outside guests comply with the guidelines set forth in this policy statement so as to ensure the recording of an examination will respect the rights of all involved and maintain the integrity of my examination as much as possible.

Appendix 2.6
Memo to file

MEMORANDUM

CONFIDENTIAL

Date: May 3, 2014

To: File

From: Michael Shahnasarian, Ph.D.

Subject: **Telephone Conversation with Timothy A. Smith, Esquire**

I had a telephone consultation with Timothy A. Smith about several pending cases in which he retained me as an expert witness. During this discussion, Mr. Smith also made some unrelated comments.

While we did not specifically discuss the pending case in which I was retained by defense counsel and Mr. Smith represents the plaintiff, Deborah Jones, Mr. Smith did reference the case by name, and he said he believes I "tried to help the defense out a little bit too much." He suggested that I had been less than objective. His tone was amicable, and he presented his comments avuncularly, stating, "I like you."

Mr. Smith went on to reference his "inner circle" of approximately 20 lawyers in the State of Florida, who he suggested were well networked and superior trial attorneys. He went on to state our conversation was "off the record," and he said he does not want to get me "Fryed (i.e., the victim of a Frye hearing), because then I can't use [retain] you." He implicitly suggested I control my retentions, dissuading me from accepting retentions from defense counsel.

Upon further discussion, Mr. Smith made comments implying that he and his "inner circle" are skilled at obtaining and presenting information about experts that will discredit them and seriously threaten the viability of their continued expert-witness practices. He specifically referenced numerous radiologists who he implied he is in the process of debilitating, referencing Frye hearings in which allegations of applications of "junk science" will be tested. Mr. Smith elaborated how his loyalty to his clients supersedes professional and personal relationships he has with me, and he indicated that, in pursuing his clients' best interests, he would deal aggressively with me in cases in which I was retained by opposing counsel. While making these latter comments, Mr. Smith said, "I may talk slow but I can think pretty fast," and he again referenced Frye hearings, along with his skill and presenting evidence in a manner that is favorable to positions he advocates—regardless of the validity and merits of his arguments.

In response to Mr. Smith's comment, I cited my longevity as an expert witness—approximately 25 years. Also, I noted that my expert retentions are evenly divided among plaintiff and defense counsel. Finally, I indicated that I have taken pride in attempting to remain objective and to apply practice standards in my work.

Chapter 3

Expert Evidence

Synopsis

3.1 Expert Evidence

Federal Rule of Evidence 702 states: "If scientific, technical or other specialized knowledge will assist the trier of fact to understand the evidence or to determine a fact in issue, a witness qualified as an expert by knowledge, skill, experience, training, or education, may testify thereto in the form of an opinion or otherwise, if 1) the testimony is based upon sufficient facts and data, 2) the testimony is the product of reliable principles and methods, and 3) the witness has applied the principles and methods reliably to the facts of the case."

The Supreme Court has rendered decisions emphasizing rigorous methods and reasoning must undergird expert opinions and testimony. *Daubert v. Merrell Dow Chemical Pharmaceuticals, Inc.*, and *Kumho Tire Co. v. Carmichael* are two landmark cases in which courts focused on admissibility of scientific expert testimony. In essence, expert witnesses must prove their methods have been tested, subjected to peer review and publication, evaluated for error, reasoned scientifically to the facts, and held generally acceptable by the scientific community.

In traditional clinical settings outside litigation, clients seeking services and guidance for vocational issues typically acquiesce or at least cooperate with qualified practitioners. This premise does not always hold in situations in which claimed vocational damages are at issue. In fact, the converse is often the rule-of-thumb: Counsel opposing an expert's referral source, regardless of an opinion's validity, typically rejects opposing expert opinions as being biased. Further, regardless of expert opinion validity, opposing counsel—in the course of their client advocacy roles—often employ any legal or theatrical means to dispense with expert opinions, averse to their objectives, from becoming evidence.

The implications of statements in the paragraph above are profound and include the following:

- In a forum explicitly intended to discern the truth (i.e., our society's justice system), individuals—including lawyers, judges, and triers of fact—who are typically far less technically competent and not legally qualified to address pending vocational issues in dispute, address them anyway. To wit:
  (a.) Lawyers argue the merits of anything from the questions an expert plans to ask during a clinical interview to the types of assessment measures an expert plans to administer, and then attempt to disqualify opinions contrary to their objectives while appropriating—often through clever spinning—information helpful to their causes.
  (b.) Judges rule on a myriad of evidentiary issues including the efficacy of expert methodologies and opinions.
  (c.) Ultimately, triers of fact weigh evidence, including expert evidence, while deliberating a verdict.
- Expert opinions, over the course of discovery and presentation at trial, are morphed vis-à-vis and among other things: lawyer reframings of expert evidence; filtering of evidence from both the court and, selectively, by opposing counsel; and trier-of-fact perceptions.

- Most disputes settle before trial, and, in these cases, tortfeasors, insurance adjusters, trial consultants, and others with a stake in a dispute's outcome evaluate expert opinions. Their criteria, ironically but not surprisingly, does not necessarily focus on the technical merits of an expert's opinion. Rather, it focuses on factors that include risk assessment; potential to undermine, impeach, or otherwise dispel or neutralize expert opinions (again, regardless of whether or not opinions are valid); and self-interests including potential to profit from ceding, negotiating, or aggressively pursuing a claim of loss of earning capacity.

For better or worse, there are many unique dynamics and artifacts of the justice system that conflict with the manner in which scientific inquiry and service delivery outside litigation evolves. Regardless of a vocational evaluator's competency, the robustness undergirding methods upon which analyses are derived, and the presentation of opinions—not to mention a professional's regard among peers outside a litigation setting—are all subject to intense and sometimes unfair challenge when part of dispute resolution processes.

Welcome to the justice system. It is not suited for potential expert witnesses who become easily offended, intimidated, or defensive when aggressively and unfairly questioned by laypeople about the efficacy of their opinions—lest the weak-at-heart or those with Pollyannaish views that believe, in the end, the justice system produces outcomes that invariably yield the truth.

What does this portend for those who choose to hold themselves out as expert witnesses and participate in resolving matters where questions of earning capacity are in dispute? Briefly, the implications are threefold: (1.) astute experts are aware of the manipulative nature of the litigation environment; (2.) they are technically competent, thorough in their analyses, and prepared to undergo intense and sometimes unfair scrutiny; and (3.) in all communications, including documentary and testimonial communications, they anticipate and artfully fend challenges intended to undermine their opinions.

Adherence to generally accepted vocational rehabilitation evaluation methodologies and standards of practice are the bedrock upon which vocational experts can withstand challenges to their assessments. Valuing claims of loss of earning capacity and assessing related issues are evolving arts/sciences, and vocational experts should have a solid grounding in their discipline's theories and methods. Knowledge of both generally accepted vocational rehabilitation methodologies and forensic mandates is essential.

3.2 Methodologies for Evaluating Claims of Loss of Earning Capacity

Many methodologies for conducting a vocational rehabilitation evaluation have been proposed (e.g., Parker and Schaller, 1996; Shahnasarian, 2001; Sleister, 2000; Tate, Heinrich, Paasuke, and Anderson, 1998; Weed, 1999). This section summarizes the most common mainstream methodologies practitioners apply in their analyses of claims of loss of earning capacity.

Dillman (1998) specified four factors central to assessing earning capacity: reduction in labor market access, reduction in the average pay for the residual jobs available to the individual, reduction in work life or hours available for work, and reduction in the ability to compete for employment. Field (2008) identified four contemporary methodologies to evaluate loss of earning capacity claims:

- The Deutsch/Sawyer (1986) Model. Underlying assumptions include the premise that preinjury and postinjury earnings are not necessarily accurate indices of an individual's wage-earning capacity. The model emphasizes career goals and age, and assumes that potential to earn should be a focal point when evaluating a claim of loss of earning capacity. Other factors the model considers are education, intellectual development, academic development, work history, and transferable skills.
- Labor Market Access/Wage Loss (Field and Field, 2001). This methodology emphasizes analyzing lost wage claims with respect to labor market conditions. It involves two steps. First, preinjury levels of examinee vocational functioning are compared to job and corresponding statistical data in a specified geographic area. Second, an examinee's postinjury level of functioning is compared to job data in the same geographical area. The model presumes that comparisons of worker preinjury and postinjury levels of functioning to people employed in a geographic area can be made to deduce percentage losses on measures such as employability in a given economy, based on an examinee's residual level of functioning.
- The RAPEL Method (Weed, 1999). RAPEL is an acronym for Rehabilitation plan, Access to the labor market, Placeability, Earnings capacity, and Labor force participation. These evaluation activities involve assessment of several factors both specific and extrinsic to the examinee. The acronym is

intended to cue examiners on important evaluation criteria.

- A "Practical Approach" (Shahnasarian, 2001; 2004a). While deeming the methodology prescribed in the first and second editions of *Assessment of Earning Capacity* as "a practical approach," Field (2008) cited elements of the evaluation process that lend to sequential analysis and formulation of an opinion on loss of earning capacity claims. After synthesizing subject-specific and relevant labor market information, the process culminates with an evaluation of the 14 ECAF factors. Shahnasarian (2010a) elaborated on earning capacity assessment theory (ECAT), the theoretical bases undergirding the ECAF and ECAF-2.

Robinson and Pomeranz (2011) recently introduced the Vocational and Rehabilitation Assessment Model (VRAM). This method incorporates three sequential components: records review and rehabilitation interview, labor market research and inquiry, and rehabilitation analysis and opinion formulation. The investigative methods and analytical processes incorporated in the VRAM are similar to those specified in the four methodologies described above. Robinson (2014) provided a recent review of forensic rehabilitation and vocational earning capacity models.

Vocational experts' analyses often focus on two overarching referral questions: Is a claim of loss of earning capacity merited? If so, what is the loss? Shahnasarian developed the Earning Capacity Assessment Form (Shahnasarian, 2004c) and the Earning Capacity Assessment Form-2 (ECAF-2) (Shahnasarian, 2010b) to operationalize the methodology undergirding his approach to assessing claims of loss of earning capacity. The ECAF aims to facilitate evaluators' analyses of these questions through systematic analysis and appraisal; it is not intended to serve as a self-standing outcome measure. More information about the ECAF appears in Chapter 5.

In a review of four mainstream methods to evaluate earning capacity, Field (2008) referred to the method incorporating the ECAF as a "practical" approach that is a "rather straightforward and commonsense method" (p. 28). While recommending standards for vocational rehabilitation experts in California, the International Association of Rehabilitation Professionals—Diminished Future Earning Capacity Work Group relied, in part, on Shahnasarian's (2004a) methodology for assessment of earning capacity (Austin et al., 2009). Robinson, Young, and Pomeranz (2009) conducted a content analysis of factors identified in vocational evaluation analyses and concluded that greater standardization, empirically grounded in vocational evaluation theory, is needed. The authors cited the 14 ECAF factors as a means to accomplish this.

Shahnasarian (2008) found a paucity of empirically based studies in the forensic vocational rehabilitation literature, and concluded a more highly evolved literature base would help curtail the emergence of greatly divergent expert opinions that derive from the same fact pattern. More information about methodologies used to assess claims of loss of earning capacity appears in Robinson (2014).

3.3 Presenting Expert Evidence

A. Consulting Experts

Consulting experts typically are not disclosed to parties opposing the retaining lawyer. They sometimes, upon request, prepare reports or analyses referenced, for example, at mediations and settlement conferences; adjusters are often particularly interested in these analyses.

Reports a consulting expert prepares are rarely distributed to counsel opposing the lawyer who retained the consulting expert, and, unless the reports are proffered as expert evidence for intended use at trial, consulting experts are not subject to deposition and/or trial testimony. The services consulting experts may provide include:

- Performing initial assessments from reviews of records and research
- Evaluating counterpart reports and methods used to develop opinions, ultimately providing second opinions
- Assisting lawyers in deposing and cross-examining counterpart experts
- Developing theories, supported by extant information and/or research, which the retaining lawyer can further pursue
- Conferring on how to best pursue issues in dispute, given facts in evidence and expert analysis

B. Testifying Experts

Informally, vocational experts—as either consulting or testifying experts—make their opinions known through consultations (telephonic, in-person, or via electronic communications, for example) and sometimes in informal written reports to retaining sources. Formally, their opinions are typically disclosed through three means: their vocational rehabilitation report(s), deposition testimony, and trial testimony. Testifying experts should expect to present their opinions through all of these means.

Disclosures of expert opinions are governed both by court calendars, which mandate dates associated with presenting expert evidence, and lawyer strategies and tactics that sometimes range from highly aggressive to dilatory. Most judges will not allow into evidence at trial opinions not disclosed during the pending litigation's discovery phase (please refer to Chapter 2 for a review of the phases of litigation). It is critical, therefore, that vocational experts commemorate the opinions they intend to present at trial in synch with the court's calendar.

At times, new evidence developed after a vocational expert examined a claimant may cause the expert to revise her opinions. Surveillance showing a claimant performing activities the expert previously believed to be beyond a claimant's functional capacities and viewed after a report's publication, for example, may cause revision of opinions formulated before this evidence emerged. Again, experts should be mindful that, unless they disclose opinions during the litigation's discovery phase, new opinions will likely be inadmissible at trial. For this reason—along with other reasons that include providing triers of fact with accurate expert analyses—vocational experts must both keep abreast of claimants they have evaluated after formal examinations have transpired, and make known new and amended opinions, based on new evidence.

Occasionally, in addition to reviewing updated records, vocational experts may find performing additional work after rendering an initial report helpful when preparing to present final opinions. This could include conducting an updated examination as well as updating labor market research and information gained through consultations.

It should be noted that a change in an expert's opinion may trigger additional discovery via deposition, as opposing lawyers have a right to investigate the bases for any changed or new opinions. Vocational experts, of course, should remain objective and receptive to all new evidence they consider after developing their initial opinions, including evidence presented during a trial.

More discussion on the type of information vocational experts generally provide in their reports and testimonies follows. More information on these topics appears throughout this book.

C. Expert Interrogatories

Quite often, expert witnesses must respond to interrogatory questions; their responses are usually written and sometimes notarized. The interrogatories typically inquire about the expert's background including education, training, and work experience; general litigation experience; fees; testimonial history; and services as an expert witness, including proportion of work performed at the request of counsel representing plaintiffs compared to counsel representing defendants. Occasionally, depending on when the interrogatories are propounded, questions may address case-specific issues such as when records were received, methods of analysis, reports generated, opinions developed, and bases for opinions. Appendix 3.1 is an example of expert interrogatories.

Of course, experts must respond to interrogatory questions to the best of their ability, fully and accurately disclosing requested information; however, if they do not maintain information requested, they are not obligated to create it. For example, if an interrogatory question asks about total fees a retaining law firm has paid an expert during the past 10 years and the expert does not maintain this data as a regular course of business, the expert is not obligated to research and compute the requested information. On occasions like this, experts should note the requested information is not available, and, if possible, estimate as accurately as possible to respond to the question.

Experts' interrogatory responses are often the first evidence they contribute to a case. Most often, lawyers averse to the lawyer who retained the expert use bias-related information from experts' interrogatory responses at trial to dissuade triers of fact from accepting an expert's testimony. Longstanding relationships with referral sources, high billing rates, and proclivity to perform disproportionate amounts of expert services at the request of defendant or plaintiff counsel are among the types of information from interrogatory answers with which lawyers confront experts at trial.

Experts, when possible and under appropriate conditions, should provide perspective through their testimony on information from interrogatory responses lawyers attempt to present out of context. When confronted with a cross-¬examination question such as, "Isn't it true that you bill $300 an hour for traveling from your office to the courthouse, and while you wait outside the courtroom to testify?" for example, an appropriate response may be: "Yes. I bill at my hourly relate regardless of the service I am asked to provide and for the time I am away from my office—not seeing patients and still incurring costs associated with operating my practice, including wages I pay my employees, rent, and other overhead costs." A simple "Yes/No" response to the question posed can mislead triers of fact and play into the averse lawyer's agenda to cast the expert in an unfavorable light.

Experts who do not submit to lawyers' half-truth representations—which can be difficult in the heat of intense, rapid-fire cross-examination and dramatic lawyer behavior—stand to preserve their credibility and expose cheap manipulation tactics. When explanation is needed, experts have the right to provide information triers of fact require to evaluate evidence fairly. Astute experts avoid being bullied into giving yes/no answers when elaboration is needed to provide appropriate context and perspective.

D. Affidavits

At times, experts draft an affidavit, a written sworn statement. Affidavits address specific, controverted issues. For example, counsel representing a plaintiff may take the position that a defense expert does not have the right to conduct a vocational rehabilitation evaluation, or to administer various tests. If the defense-retained expert, on the other hand, believes that information emerging from these methods of inquiry would facilitate an analysis of a claim of loss of earning capacity, the defense lawyer could ask the expert to draft an affidavit specifying this, along with the rationale.

The court typically considers affidavits, opposing lawyers' arguments, and other evidence at evidentiary hearings. Occasionally, experts testify. Experts are bound to the court's ruling and should request a copy of the court's disposition. An example of a court ruling after a hearing on the scope of a vocational rehabilitation evaluation in a marriage dissolution case appears as Appendix 3.2. The vocational expert testified in the hearing and specifically addressed how planned standardized testing was essential to the evaluation process. Counsel representing the wife objected, unsuccessfully, to the planned assessment measures.

E. The Vocational Rehabilitation Report

After completing a vocational rehabilitation evaluation, vocational experts often generate written reports that review information amassed during their evaluations—such as records reviewed and a summary of pertinent information from these records, interview information, test data, and results from any independent research—along with findings and opinions addressing referral questions.

Typically, an expert who examined a claimant at the request of a defense lawyer is obligated to produce a report. In some cases, when counsel representing a plaintiff requests a vocational rehabilitation evaluation, the lawyer may instruct the vocational evaluator not to write a report. Reasons for this include preferences some lawyers have for an oral briefing before deciding whether to create written evidence and the desire to conserve costs.

Occasions also arise when lawyers—representing plaintiffs and defendants—request that a vocational expert draft a report from records and research only, providing a preliminary analysis for the benefit of those litigating a case and determining its strategy.

A vocational expert's report may be used for informational purposes by the retaining attorney, or it could be disclosed to others who have an interest in a pending claim, including lawyers, adjusters, experts retained to rebut the vocational expert who authored a report, other experts in related damages areas, and claimants. Of course, in some cases, an expert's report can become evidence. Depending on the forum in which a vocational rehabilitation evaluation was initiated, an expert's report may be used in any of the following contexts:

- Reference in a demand package distributed to lawyers, insurance adjusters, or defendants
- Reference material in a settlement video recording
- Evidence distributed to counsel opposing the lawyer who retained the vocational expert
- Reference material in a mock trial
- Reference material presented at a mediation
- Trial exhibit

The contents of a report of a vocational rehabilitation evaluation vary and correspond to, among other things, the forum in which a dispute is tried, facts specific to a pending case, and specific referral questions. Vocational issues germane in the following forums are delineated in later chapters of this book: acquired disabilities (Chapter 6), the Americans with Disabilities Act (Chapter 7), employment law (Chapter 8), family law (Chapter 9), and long-term disability disputes (Chapter 10). Each of these chapters includes a sample report of a vocational rehabilitation evaluation.

A vocational expert's opinion usually begins with an assessment of an individual's career development. This assessment typically includes analyses of acquired skills, demonstrated earnings, and career-related activities after an incident in dispute. Depending on the facts of a case and pending referral questions, a vocational expert may render opinions on several factors including but not limited to:

- Assessment of past, present, and future earning capacity
- Degree to which alleged career disruption, physical problems, and psychological problems may impair earning capacity and career development
- Skills and abilities, along with capacities to augment these
- Appropriateness of mitigation efforts (e.g., job search, retraining)
- Identification and assessment of vocational handicaps vocational handicaps
- Recommendations for vocational rehabilitation
- Evidence of secondary gain or malingering

If appropriate, and assuming they possess the requisite qualifications, vocational experts often note in their reports when a case merits a life care plan—a document that delineates current and future care needs along with associated costs reasonably anticipated for an examinee due to issues in dispute. Life care plans typically constitute separate reports and are discussed in more detail later in this book.

Vocational experts should be mindful that all of their reports, as well as other information generated during the course of expert witness involvement in pending and other cases, may be obtained by parties with interests adverse to those who retained the expert. A vocational expert's report will be closely scrutinized and critiqued by counsel opposing the retaining party, as well as by experts retained by opposing counsel retains. The review by opposing parties is typically undertaken to criticize the vocational expert's methods or conclusions, and to develop rebuttal strategies.

Comparisons of an expert's opinions rendered in prior cases and pending cases sometimes uncover inconsistencies between cases, despite similar underlying facts; lawyers use information of this type to impeach witnesses. This is accomplished by referencing an expert's prior analyses and implying the expert provides biased opinions, depending on the referral source. If confronted with this situation, ask to read the documents containing the alleged inconsistencies before responding. Experts who are under pressure and/or respond prematurely, relying solely on memory, increase risk of providing inaccurate or incomplete information. This can further complicate the situation and detract from the expert's credibility. Of course, when possible and if appropriate, an expert's response to an allegation of giving inconsistent opinions should include an explanation of how the cases in question differ, and why, therefore, varying conclusions are in order.

After litigation has concluded, attorneys often retain and circulate vocational experts' reports for future reference. Experts should assume that their reports will survive the instant litigation, and, once memorialized, statements made and inferences drawn will years later be culled by numerous readers. Regardless of how reports are used in conjunction with pending referral questions, experts should remain consistent and objective in all matters related to conducting and reporting the results and conclusions from a vocational rehabilitation evaluation.

F. Deposition and Trial Testimony

Testimony offered during depositions and trials provides vocational experts opportunities to explain methods employed and bases for conclusions developed. These events also offer lawyers opposing the lawyer who retained the vocational expert to challenge the expert.

Vocational experts' testimonial evidence typically involves inferences from records, observations and clinical impressions, and information generated from examinations (including interviews and testing), consultations, and research. While vocational experts should be familiar with all evidence upon which they have relied in the process of developing opinions, they should be especially familiar with evidence they independently developed—including interviews, testing, labor market research, consultations, and other independent inquiry. Experts can be certain that opposing attorneys will challenge and juxtapose this evidence with other evidence—particularly evidence inconsistent with the expert's evidence and analyses. Unprepared experts risk loss of credibility and, correspondingly, degradation of the opinions they ultimately offer.

Vocational experts should always presume lawyers who cross-examine them have full access to all of the evidence they have evaluated. Further, experts should assume opposing lawyers have the benefit of expert advice vis-à-vis counterpart experts they retained, and other vast resources—including colleagues solicited via listserv posts and other sources—to dispel the expert's opinions and to discredit testimonial evidence. Failure to do so and to adequately prepare for adverse assaults when testifying can be a vocational rehabilitation expert's *fait accompli*.

Questions lawyers opposing an expert's referral source propound during depositions and trial often highlight facts supportive to their cases, and sometimes intend to enhance and exploit these facts. Among lawyers' aims are to use opposing experts to support their cases. Evidence extracted from an opposing expert who is supportive to a lawyer's arguments is immensely powerful, and crown jewels they invariably attempt to conquer. Opposing lawyers typically restate sound bites, either verbatim or paraphrased, of any concession an opposing expert has made during closing arguments—their time of crescendo.

As an example, consider a marriage dissolution case in which counsel representing the husband retained a vocational rehabilitation expert to assess the wife's earning capacity. The wife held a bachelor's degree in systems management and demonstrated an impressive work and earnings history before she withdrew from the workplace approximately two years before the couple's separation. Counsel representing the wife provided several defenses about why the wife was unable to realize her prior earnings levels, including a psychologist's diagnosis of "depression." The diagnosis lacked further elaboration, and no treatment for any mental health problems evidenced.

The wife's lawyer deposed the vocational expert at

length, first generally and then case-specifically, about the ill effects of depression on vocational functioning. The general questions included the likes of: "Isn't it true that many people who have depression are so debilitated that they neglect their hygiene and become reclusive?" "Depression can cause some people to almost become immobile—isn't that right?" And, "In extreme situations, isn't it true that some people with depression become so hopeless and despondent that they see no way out of their situations other than suicide?"

One answer to the three questions posed, of course, is "Yes." A better answer is: "In some limited cases, that's true; in most cases that's not true. It depends on the severity of the depression and factors specific to the individual."

While the innuendo associated with the questions was not germane to the case at hand and was grossly out of proportion with the level of "depression" the wife was actually experiencing, the lawyer posing the questions had a threefold strategy: (1.) remind triers of fact of a fact in evidence (i.e., the wife had a diagnosis of depression), (2.) use the opposing expert to acknowledge, at least at a general level, the fact—although significantly aggrandized by the wife's lawyer—could have vocational implications, and (3.) test the manner in which the vocational expert handled the questions.

More discussion of the expert's response set is in order. If the expert, for instance, offered answers much beyond what was necessary to respond to the pending general questions—such as asserting the questions of the wife's lawyer implied a state of depression far in excess of what the wife was experiencing—the expert risked losing credibility and being perceived as an advocate of the husband, who was the expert's retention source. After all, the questions are general, hypothetical questions and even nonexperts including prospective jurors would likely be inclined to at least partially agree with the questioning lawyer. Much more than a partial concession embedded in an answer could connote to triers of fact that the expert was acting as an advocate, beholden to the retaining lawyer, rather than as an objective expert witness.

After the general questions are case-specific questions such as: "Wouldn't you agree that Ms. Smith's problems with depression pose a significant barrier to her returning to work—especially after her more-than-two-year absence from the work place?" "Isn't it true that Ms. Smith's depression will, more than likely, impair her ability to perform the types of complex tasks in which computer systems professionals regularly engage?" And, "Because of her mood-related problems, age, and trauma from her divorce, isn't it logical to conclude that Ms. Smith's ability to work on a day-to-day basis will be greatly impaired compared to her previous levels?"

Notice that all of the opposing lawyer's questions, both general and specific, are crafted to elicit yes/no answers and to control the expert by not inviting any elaboration. Often, when posed with questions of these types and when the deponent does not answer yes/no, the lawyer's retort when eliciting a response that is not helpful to his/her case is: "All I asked you is a yes/no question. Please just give me a simple answer to my question."

This patent lawyer statement has a threefold objective: (1.) cast the expert in the role of an advocate rather than objective expert, when the expert elaborates—especially when elaborating beyond the bounds of the question, (2.) regain control of cross-examination threatened, for example, when an expert artfully expounds with an answer to a question that damages opposing counsel's arguments, and (3.) refocus triers of fact on points the lawyer desires to make—points, regardless of their validity, that support the lawyer's arguments.

When appropriate, the expert should answer the questions as yes or no, explaining and elaborating when necessary. While the general questions posed above could be answered in a yes/no manner, although some limited elaboration is in order, proper responses to the case-specific questions require much more explanation including the expert's placement of the questions in proper perspective given opposing counsel's proclivity to embroider questions with innuendo that the wife's "depression" problems far exceed the evidence. These questions test experts' attentiveness, litigation savvy, and expertise and sophistication as vocational rehabilitation practitioners.

Examples of appropriate responses to the specific questions posed above include the following:

Q. Wouldn't you agree that Ms. Smith's problems with depression pose a significant barrier to her returning to work, especially after her more-than-three-year absence from the workplace?"

A. No. The records I reviewed do not include any contraindications to Ms. Smith returning to work. And, from my 30 years' experience as a vocational rehabilitation practitioner and knowledge of the professional literature, I have found that returning to work often has a positive affect on individuals' mental health. Ms. Smith tested well on intellectual measures I administered, and she has developed a skill set—through her education, training, work experiences, and transferable skills—that is high in demand in the area where she resides.

Q. Isn't it true that Ms. Smith's depression will, more than likely, impair her ability to perform the types of complex tasks regularly performed by computer systems professionals?

A. No. There isn't any evidence to support your statement in the records I reviewed or from my examination of Ms. Smith. Going back to her vocational testing from my exam, Ms. Smith demonstrated well-above-average intellect, and there was no indication that mood-related problems will interfere with her ability to pursue vocational rehabilitation.

Q. Because of her mood-related problems, age, and trauma from her divorce, isn't it logical to conclude that Ms. Smith's ability to work on a day-to-day basis will be greatly impaired compared to her previous levels?

A. Research in the vocational rehabilitation profession invariably cites two factors most predictive of one's wage-earning abilities: cognition—that is, intelligence and related things, such as a skill set developed via training and work experiences—and motivation. This latter factor deals with an individual's desire to work and earn employment income. Ms. Smith demonstrated well-above-average intelligence on testing administered during my exam, and she had an impressive record of educational, work, and earnings accomplishments before her separation from Mr. Smith. Within a reasonable degree of vocational rehabilitation probability, I am unaware of any reason why Ms. Smith would be unable to replicate her prior record of career development—including her earnings history—provided she becomes motivated to do so.

Awareness of lawyers' cross-examination objectives, along with insight into questions' motives and array of potential responses and implications of them, facilitates vocational rehabilitation experts' ability to anticipate and appropriately respond to questioning under oath. By extension, awareness and insight into opposing counsel's questions, along with the skills required to properly address these questions, allows experts to neutralize and deter questions intended to impeach their testimony.

A lawyer's strategy in attacking an opposing expert during a deposition or cross-examination at trial depends on many factors including:

- Success in gaining concessions from the expert
- Ability to use the expert as a conduit to restate points facilitative to the lawyer's position
- Attributions made about the receptivity an expert's testimony will have on triers of fact, and ability to neutralize, negate, or otherwise marginalize the expert.

When generating testimony not facilitative to their objectives, attorneys make real-time assessments of the risks/benefits associated with perpetuating the expert's testimony in front of triers of fact, including perceptions of positive/negative impressions the expert witness has and/or will make. This decision-making is often far less than objectively made and involves factors ranging from lawyers', jury consultants', adjusters', and others' perceptions of how evidence may or may not be admitted into evidence, and the affect of this evidence on triers of fact.

Chapter 11 presents more information about providing testimony. The components of trial testimony—direct examination, cross examination, and redirect examination—were discussed in Chapter 2.

3.4 Conclusion

Federal Rule 702 states the conditions under which expert evidence can be introduced. Vocational rehabilitation experts can apply several recognized methodologies to develop evidence central to their analyses of claims of loss of earning capacity. The evidence experts typically produce emanates from responses to interrogatory questions, affidavits, reports of vocational rehabilitation evaluations, and deposition and trial testimony. Documentary and testimonial evidence an expert provides is subject to intense, ongoing scrutiny and attack. Experienced experts are mindful of this and employ sound methodology to preserve their opinions' integrity. Additionally, they are adept at defending their opinions when questioned during hearings, depositions, and trials.

Appendix 3.1: Example of Expert Interrogatories

IN THE THIRTEENTH JUDICIAL CIRCIUT OF THE STATE OF FLORIDA
IN AND FOR HILLSBOROUGH COUNTY, FLORIDA
CIVIL DIVISION

OLIVIA R. THOMPSON,

Plaintiff,

vs.

JKL AUTOMOBILE INSURANCE
COMPANY; WALT WANDERLAY,
and PQL INSURANCE COMPANY,

Defendants,
______________________________/

PLAINTIFF'S BOECHER/SPRINGER REQUEST FOR PRODUCTION
TO DEFENDANT, JKL AUTOMOBILE INSURANCE COMPANY

Plaintiff, OLIVIA R. THOMPSON, by and through her undersigned counsel, hereby request Defendant, JKL INSURANCE COMPANY, pursuant to Rule 1.350, Florida rules of Civil Procedure, to produce a the office of counsel for the Plaintiff for inspection and copying, within the time period mandated by said rule, the documents and/or evidence requested below:

A. "PLAINTIFF" shall mean and refer to the Plaintiff's, his, her or their agents, attorneys, employees or representatives.
B. "YOU" and "YOURS" shall mean and refer to Defendant and all of your agents, attorneys, employees, insurance carriers or representatives, and claims adjusting agents.
C. "DEFENDANT" shall mean either one or all of the Defendants in the above-styled cause of action and include all of the Defendants, their legal representative insurance carriers and/or claims adjusting agents, the respective divisions, predecessors, subsidiaries or successors in interest, and any directors, employees, officers, agents, partners, attorneys, or representatives of any of them. When making reference to a specific Defendant, the specific Defendant to which you are referring should be clearly identified.
D. "DOCUMENT" OR "TANGIBLE ITEM" is intended to have the broadest possible meaning under the Florida Rules of Civil Procedure, and includes without limitation, and written, printed, electronic, recorded tape, graphic, or any matter of whatever nature or whatever form including all non-identical copies and drafts thereof and all copies bearing notations or marks not found on the original.
E. "EXPERT WITNESS" means the individual person or persons so identified in this case, their professional association or other related entities, or their employees.
F. "PERSON" or "ENTITY" unless otherwise specified, means a natural person, firm, partnership, trust, estate, association, corporation, proprietorship, governmental body, governmental agency or commissioner any other organization or entity.

G. "RELATE TO" or "RELATING TO" shall be construed to include "refer to", "summarizes", "constitutes", "contains", "studies", analyzes", "considers:, "explains", "mentions", "shows", "discusses", "describes", or "comments upon", and vice versa as it relates to said terms or phrases.

H. When names are requested, the address shall be the complete and current address naming the street and street number, together with the city, county and state for such address.

I. When addresses are requested, the address shall be the complete and current address naming the street and street number, together with the city, county and state for each such address.

J. Matters of Privilege. In the event you wish to asset "attorney/client privilege", "work product doctrine", or any other privileges to any documents or communication with sufficient identification to include: the nature of the document or communication, the instigator or sender of said communication or document, the recipient or all of the parties involved in the production of said document or communication, the date, the name of each person to whom the original or said document was sent or may have been present at the time of said communication, a brief summary of the document or communication or its subject matter with sufficient detail to permit the Court to reach a determination in the event a Motion to Compel is required, and an indication of the basis for the assertion of said privilege.

REQUEST TO PRODUCE REGARDING EACH OF YOUR EXPERTS

1. All documents or tangible items of whatsoever nature pertaining to the following:
   a. The scope of your employment of expert witnesses in this case and the compensation for such service.
   b. The general litigation experience of your expert witnesses in this case, including the percentage of work performed for plaintiffs and defendants.
   c. The identity of other insurance claims or legal actions in which each of your expert witnesses rendered opinions or evaluations for you during the last three years. (If you have identified a medical expert witness, you are not requested to identify instances where said expert witness provided an examination and evaluation of a claimant/party/plaintiff). The identity of other cases in which each of your expert witnesses in this case have testified by deposition or trial for you during the last three years (If any, see Request Number 3, below).
   d. Any approximation of the portion of the expert's involvement as an expert witness, which may be based on the number of hours, percentage of hours, or percentage.
2. Copies of any and all invoices, records, memoranda, check, check stubs, receipts, 1099's, tax records or any other form of financial information evidencing payment or compensation paid by Defendant (as defined herein) for services provided by your expert witnesses for the last three (3) years.
3. Copies of deposition and trial transcripts for testimony provided by your expert witnesses as identified in Request 1(d) above.
4. Your expert witnesses' most recent curriculum vitae or resumes.
5. All writings setting forth the opinions or observations of your expert witnesses in this case.

In support of this Request for Production, Plaintiff states that it is within the scope of rule 1.280 (b), Florida Rules of Civil Procedure; Plaintiff needs the opportunity to inspect these documents in preparation of this case; and that Plaintiff is unable, without undue hardship, to obtain the substantial equivalent by other means.

AUTHORITY. This discovery request is propounded pursue went to the legal authority of Allstate Insurance Company v. Boecher, 733 So. 2d 933 (Fla. 1999), approving Allstate Insurance Company v. Boecher, 705 So. 2d 106, (Fla. 4th DCA 1998); Springer v. West, 769 So. 2d 1068 (Fla. 5th DCA 2000); and/or Morgan, Colling & Gilbert, P. A. v. Pope, 798 So. 2d 1 (Fla. DCA 2001).

"We find no indication from either the language of rule 1.280(b)(4) or our opinion in Elkins that the rule was intended to shield a party from revealing the extent of its relationship with an expert witness." Boecher, 733 So. 2d at 999 (Fla. 1999). "It occurs to us that, in this pervasively computerized generation of doing business, any going concern would be sorely tried to establish burdensomeness in the mere retrieval of this kind of information. Surely, Allstate has the power to pluck the date from its own cyberspace. The burden placed on this party should be presumed to be no more difficult than selecting the correct keys on a board or icons on a screen. Allstate has nothing in this record to dispel such a presumption." Boecher, 705 So. 2d at 108 (Fla. 4th DCA 1998). "Where an insurer provides a defense for its insured and is acting as the insured's agent, the insurer's relationship to an expert is discoverable from the insured. To hold otherwise would render Boecher meaningless in all but a small class of cases. The information sought is relevant to the witness's bias and will enhance the truth-seeking function and fairness of the trial, as intended by Boecher." Springer v. West, 769 So. 2d at 1069 (Fla. 5th DCA 2000).

As for discoverability of similar information held by defense counsel, please see Morgan, Colling & Gilbert, P.A. v. Pope, 798 So. 2d 1 (Fla. 2d DCA 2001), which upheld a trial court's Order compelling discovery from the Plaintiff's counsel regarding any prior dealings of relationships between a law firm and the involved expert witness. "Recently, the Fifth District, in dicta, has suggested that 'a defendant may question the plaintiff about any relationship between his or her attorney and the plaintiff's expert.' Springer v. West, 769 So. 2d 1068, 1069 (Florida 5th DCA 2000). This conclusion is a natural and logical extension of the requirements that defendant insurance companies disclose their financial relationships with their chosen expert witnesses." Id, at 6.

CERTIFICATE OF SERVICE

I HEREBY CERTIFY that a true and correct copy of the foregoing document has been served by electronic mail pursuant to Florida Rule of Judicial Administration 2.516 to:

Appendix 3.2: Example of a Judge's Ruling on the Scope of a Vocational Expert's Test Administration

IN THE CIRCUIT COURT OF THE SIXTH JUDICIAL CIRCUIT
IN AND FOR PASCO COUNTY, FLORIDA

IN RE: THE MARRIAGE OF:
JOHN JACOB SMITH,

Petitioner/Husband,

v.
CASE NO: 12-2014-AP-1234-XY

DIVISION: "K"

JESSIE HUNTER SMITH,

Respondent/Wife
__________________________/

ORDER ON WIFE'S MOTION FOR PROTECTIVE ORDER TO PROHIBIT COMPELLING WIFE TO PRODUCE HER PSYCHOLOGICAL RECORDS AND TO PROHIBIT PSYCHOLOGICAL TESTING AS PART OF VOCATIONAL EVALUATION

THIS CAUSE came on to be heard on Monday, December 16, 2013, upon the Responded/Wife's Motion for Protective Order to Prohibit Compelling Wife to Produce her Psychological Records and to Prohibit Psychological Testing as Part of Vocational Evaluation. The Court having heard the sworn testimony of Michael Shahnasarian, Ph.D., the argument of the parties' counsel of record and being otherwise advised in the premises, it is therefore

ORDERED AND ADJUDGED as follows:

1. This Court has jurisdiction over the parties and the subject matter herein.
2. The Respondent/Wife's Motion for Protective Order to Prohibit Compelling Wife to Produce Her Psychological Records and to Prohibit Psychological Testing as Part of Vocational Rehabilitation is GRANTED in part and DENIED in part.
3. The Respondent/Wife shall not be required to produce any psychological records.
4. The Petitioner/Husband's expert, Dr. Michael Shahnasarian, shall be entitled to conduct, as part of his vocational evaluation, an MMPI-2 test of Respondent/Wife for the purpose of personality screening in regards to Wife's employment options.
5. The Court reserves ruling on the admissibility of Dr. Michael Shahnasarian's affidavit.
6. That this Court retains jurisdiction of this cause of action and of the parties hereto for the purpose of enforcing the executory provisions of this order, as well as for the entry of such other orders as might be deemed just or appropriate.
7. The Court reserves jurisdiction on the parties' request for attorney's fees and costs incurred herein.

DONE AND ORDERED in Chambers, Dade City, Florida, this ____ day of __________, 2014

____
Ronda Frank
Circuit Court Judge

COPIES FURNISHED TO:

Edward Astor, Esquire
Attorney for Petitioner/Husband

Dorothy Watkins, Esquire
Attorney for Respondent/Wife

Michael Shahnasarian, Ph.D.
Vocational Evaluator

John Jacob Smith
Petitioner/Husband

Jessie Hunter Smith
Respondent/Wife

Chapter 4

Processes Undergirding the Assessment of Earning Capacity

Synopsis

4.1 Introduction

The processes undertaken to conduct an assessment of earning capacity vary and depend on, among other things, claims made, evidence, referral questions, issues specific to the case, and the examinee's age, phase of career development, and cognitive status. Cases involving death, persons who have severe brain damage, children, and those with low levels of literacy, for example, require procedures different than those used to evaluate the claim of a college-educated, cognitively intact business executive who sustained orthopedic injuries and is pursuing a claim of loss of earning capacity.

At a general level, vocational evaluators implement similar procedures to formulate opinions. These include reviewing relevant records, performing an examination, conducting labor market research, and consulting with experts and collateral sources of information. This chapter describes procedures that vocational experts implement to frame their analyses and develop opinions.

4.2 Assessment of Earning Capacity

A. Records Review

Vocational experts must obtain a thorough and accurate understanding of examinees' backgrounds to identify relevant historical information; factors that could have relevance to past, present, and future work-related issues; and psychological factors germane to pending career development and vocational rehabilitation questions. Insight and theories about an examinee's reasons for underachievement or strong achievement, for example, may emerge from a prudent record analysis. In some cases, a careful analysis of records yields information that challenges an examinee's credibility. For instance, documentation of a claimant consistently providing misleading work history or education information while applying for a job may cause a vocational expert to be skeptical of the claimant's candor.

A Complaint and Responses to Interrogatories, when available, provide information about issues in contention. Generally, vocational experts review nonliability-related records. Helpful sources include:

- Employment records
- Academic records
- Earnings records
- Medical records
- Psychological records
- Job search records
- Military records
- Criminal records
- Tax returns
- Standardized test data
- Social Security Administration records
- Depositions of the plaintiff, family members, employers, and other experts (e.g., opposing counsel's experts including vocational expert)

Other potentially helpful records include surveillance and day-in-the-life video records. Additionally, vocational experts may benefit from reviewing records upon which their counterparts have relied—even if these are not records on which they would customarily rely. For example, because of a methodological preference (please reference Chapter 3), an expert may not ordinarily rely upon work-life expectancy tables; however, if her counterpart did, the expert may wish to review these records to ensure the counterpart's deductions were in concert with accepted methodologies.

Experts should review all available records related to disputed vocational issues. Cross-examination techniques often involve questioning the foundation of an expert's opinion with the insinuation that the expert has dispelled or is unfamiliar with important records. From subpoenas of records, record custodian depositions, and depositions of vocational experts, opposing counsel typically identifies records an expert possesses. The credibility of a vocational opinion may be undermined if pertinent records were not considered when an opinion was formulated. Occasionally, attorneys inquire about the relevance and importance of various records to an expert's opinion.

Ideally, experts should first review records before examining subjects. New records—such as depositions, expert reports, and information obtained through discovery—are typically generated as a case evolves, and records pertinent to a vocational expert's analysis must be reviewed in a timely manner. If updated records cause an expert to revise or amend earlier opinions, the vocational expert must make this known. Failure to do so could result in a ruling, if a new opinion is disclosed after the discovery phase has lapsed (please reference Chapter 2), that the expert has forfeited the opportunity to present any new or amended opinion. Additionally, as experts learn of new information that could have relevance, they should request to review documentation of the outstanding information.

Vocational experts typically review records about a subject to obtain the following information:

- Medical and psychological diagnoses
- Physical or psychological problems that may affect present or future career development
- Physician-advised restrictions
- Medical and/or psychological prognoses
- Prior medical history
- Need for adaptive aids or special accommodations
- Career-related information
- Demonstrated work and earnings history
- Types of jobs performed
- Transferable skills
- Employer performance appraisals and other information about vocational behavior (e.g., work attendance, eligibility for rehiring, relationships with supervisors and coworkers)
- Vocational capacity measured by scholastic achievement
- Cultural, familial, or social factors that may affect career development
- Workplace barriers
- Career development patterns (e.g., a record of job promotions or progressive advancement, stability of employment history)
- Personal motivation
- Work propensity (i.e., work participation including the tendency to pursue overtime, seasonal, or supplemental employment)
- Efforts to obtain employment and maximize vocational potential
- Potential disincentives that could inhibit career development, such as social and financial factors
- Indicators of secondary gain or malingering
- Motivation (i.e., the need for employment income or evidence of a strong work ethic)

While reviewing and compiling the types of information listed above, vocational experts often uncover details requiring further inquiry during their exams. Discovering before an examination that a claimant demonstrated a wide variance in earnings, for instance, will allow the expert to explore reasons for this history. Learning before meeting a claimant about such things as school difficulties after trauma to the head, employment difficulties after an assault, or problems in relationships with authority figures such as teachers, military personnel, law enforcement officers, or supervisors, likewise merits proper follow-up inquiry.

Vocational experts review records at two general levels: factual and analytical. The factual review involves obtaining pertinent examinee facts relating to vocational issues. For example, if the referral question is whether an experienced welder, suffering soft-tissue injuries to the cervical spine, has conducted a good-faith job search after being released to return to work, the vocational expert will likely review available job search and job application records, and tabulate information about numbers and types of efforts. This fact-gathering exercise will facilitate the expert's second level of analysis—a higher-order analytical assessment.

The second-phase *analytical* aspect of a vocational expert's review of records is more subtle and requires integrating, comparing, and synthesizing information from individual records, along with synthesizing other information such as knowledge about a specific industry and prevailing labor market conditions. Discovering evidence of invalid standardized test results, finding that a subject's presenting symptoms are not supported by medical records, or finding a subject noncompliant with recommended treatment, for example, can cause an expert to suspect secondary gain motivation. This suspicion can prepare an expert to test his theory during a subsequent exam. Experts' knowledge and experiences enable them to make deductions and formulate hypotheses from analyzing records and conducting research.

Intelligence gathered before a subject's examination, along with working theories related to a subject's vocational behavior, can greatly benefit an examiner in structuring a clinical interview and eliciting information during it. Examiners should avoid prejudging examinees based on information they review in records.

When testifying at trial or during a deposition, a vocational expert may be requested to refer to specific records, or may need to access a specific record in her possession. If the act of retrieving a record is not accomplished with a reasonable degree of aplomb, the expert risks being perceived as disorganized and/or careless.

Records can easily fall into disarray, especially if they are compiled over an extended period or if several individuals handle them (e.g., office staff during the regular evaluation process, attorneys during depositions, and copy services after depositions). Adopting an efficient method of organizing records to facilitate record-retrieval efforts on demand is strongly advised.

Experts are entitled to compensation for costs associated with copies of requested records. Requests for copies usually emanate from a subpoena of the expert's record custodian or at an expert's deposition. State statutes provide guidelines on allowable copying costs. Please see Appendix 4.1 for a sample letter explaining copying costs and associated logistics.

Vocational experts maintain records until a matter has been resolved. In most cases, experts purge records when the litigation ends, although attorneys occasionally request that records be returned.

B. Subject Examination

Whenever possible, vocational experts should examine those whom they are evaluating. Occasionally, an examination is impossible because the subject is unavailable, the court denies a request for an exam, or logistical problems make an examination untenable. A sample affidavit for a vocational rehabilitation evaluation appears in Figure 4.1; this affidavit includes a statement related to need for an exam.

An examination that addresses vocational questions typically consists of two parts: a clinical interview and administration of standardized tests. An exam's length depends on factors that include the complexity of a case, pending vocational questions, the pace at which an examinee works, the extent of testing administered, and the interference or cooperation a vocational expert encounters. Most examinations are completed at a vocational expert's office within six to eight hours. Sometimes, exams occur at locations such as a subject's home, a hotel conference room, or a court reporter's office within the jurisdiction where a lawsuit was filed.

Regardless of the location at which an exam is conducted, experts must instill proper examination protocol. This includes controlling extraneous variables that may threaten adherence to standardized test administration guidelines or otherwise corrupt the quality of information obtained, thereby compromising an exam's validity. Interference by an attorney or family member that disrupts an examination or threatens an exam's integrity, for instance, is reason to stop an examination, restate the requirements for exam conduct, and, if necessary, solicit outside assistance from the referring party or the court. In one case, a vocational expert retained by defense counsel terminated an examination because of an attorney's interference. The plaintiff's attorney accompanied his client at the exam. Despite the expert's request that the attorney refrain from participating in the clinical interview, the attorney intermittently preempted his client from answering questions with unsolicited exchanges that produced attorney-engineered responses. Because of the imminent threat this interference posed to the examination results, the expert decided to terminate the exam. The plaintiff attorney's behavior was subsequently brought to the attention of the presiding judge at a hearing. Although the judge ruled that the examination should be continued, he also ruled that the plaintiff's counsel had a right to be present with the stipulation that he was to remain a nonparticipating "fly on the wall."

At the beginning of an exam, vocational experts should provide an orientation of how the examination will be conducted. In some exams, subjects find it helpful to bring information that will aid their recall, such as a résumé, a medication list, and names of treating physicians. Before an examination, examinees or their counsel should alert vocational experts about any of their special needs such as an interpreter, literacy problems requiring a reader or recorder, seating accommodations because of orthopedic problems, or other special needs. In one case, a woman alleged acquiring chemical sensitivity problems secondary to exposure to a sick building, and she indicated that exposure to environmental irritants, such as colognes and perfumes, aggravated

AFFIDAVIT OF MICHAEL SHAHNASARIAN, PH.D.
AFFIDAVIT IN SUPPORT OF NEED FOR CONDUCTING
A REHABILITATION EXAMINATION

STATE OF FLORIDA

Before me, an officer duly authorized to take acknowledgments and administer oaths, personally appeared Michael Shahnasarian, Ph.D., who being over the age of eighteen and after being duly sworn, deposes and says:

1. I am Michael Shahnasarian, Ph.D., president of Career Consultants of America, Inc. In this capacity, I am engaged in the professional practice of vocational rehabilitation and life care planning.

2. I hold a doctorate in counseling psychology and human systems: I am certified as a rehabilitation counselor, certified as a vocational evaluator, licensed as both a psychologist and as a mental health counselor, and certified as a career counselor.

3. In addition to my professional training, I have been providing vocational rehabilitation and life care planning services professionally to individuals since 1981. I am experienced in providing these services to individuals with both physical and mental impairments.

4. To render as accurate of a rehabilitation opinion(s) as possible, my practice is to conduct a face-to-face examination with the individual I am evaluating. My typical examination process includes the following: a) interview of the individual and one guardian (typically from three to three and one-half hours; this interview focuses on physical problems, functional limitations and capabilities, activities of daily living, work history, mental health problems and concerns, and education and training), and b) administration of vocational tests (estimated to require four hours).

5. The face-to-face component of my examination is instrumental in helping me formulate independent opinions. It allows me to observe and assess the individual's physical functioning (e.g., problems with sitting, walking, writing, performing various tasks requested, etc.), mental functioning (e.g., concentration ability, remote/recent memory, interpersonal functioning, etc.), and general clinical presentation.

6. In addition to conducting a clinical interview, my examination protocol involves administering a battery of standardized tests that enable me to elicit vocationally relevant information. The tests that I administer provide objective measures of personality functioning, general mental functioning, and vocational interests. Results from testing allow me to more thoroughly assess an individual to arrive at an opinion within a reasonable degree of vocational rehabilitation probability.

7. At all times during my examination, the individual being assessed is at will to take breaks as required. The individual is also invited to alternate sitting and standing positions as needed. Every effort is made to make the individual as comfortable as possible, including offering various seating options and reading test items to the person, when needed. The individual is also given the option of having lunch brought in to him or her, or taking a one-hour or longer lunch break.

8. To accommodate the individual being evaluated, I will conduct my evaluation in a location as convenient to the individual as possible. I prefer to conduct the evaluation in my office. Unless the person is severely disabled, I prefer not to conduct my evaluation within the individual's home. If I do not conduct the evaluation within my office, I prefer to conduct it at a court reporter's office or another location where the examination will not be interrupted.9. I respect the individual's right to be de-

briefed after my examination. This debriefing will be scheduled upon the individual's request.

10. All examinations are conducted in a timely manner.

FURTHER AFFIANT SAYETH NAUGHT

____

Michael Shahnasarian, Ph.D.

The foregoing instrument was acknowledged before me the ______ day of ___________, by Michael Shahnasarian, Ph.D., who after being sworn deposes and says that the foregoing is true and correct to the best of his knowledge and who is personally known to me/has produced _____________ and who did/did not take an oath.

____

Notary Public—State of Florida
Commission: __________________
My Commission Expires:_________

Figure 4.1 *Sample affidavit*

her symptoms. Her advance request that staff at the vocational expert's office refrain from using these products was well received and provided her with a measure of comfort during the exam.

The following sections outline standard protocols vocational experts implement during their examinations.

1. Clinical interview

The quality of information vocational experts elicit during their clinical interviews, to a large degree, depends on their preparation and skill. Examinees represent all demographic and cultural groups, and present diverse academic and work backgrounds, along with a panoply of medical, cognitive, and psychological issues. Over the course of a week, one vocational expert examined a woman psychologically traumatized by a rape, a senior healthcare executive undergoing a divorce, and a non-English-speaking Cuban exile who arrived in the United States by raft and was subsequently injured while performing his job as a painter. In all cases, vocational experts must thoroughly identify and assess case-specific issues pertinent to assessing earning capacity. Underlying litigation, or the prospect of it, complicates this task. Secondary gain factors, general suspicion, and reaction to events inherent in the litigation process can complicate the task of obtaining accurate information.

Again, thoroughly reviewing available records before examining a subject facilitates the clinical interview and subsequent analyses vocational experts perform. This advance review enables vocational experts to focus the interview on subtle but important questions that may otherwise go unasked. For instance, an advance review of a subject's records may prompt an examiner to formulate questions about reasons for job terminations, gaps in employment, occupational changes and irregular earnings trends, side effects of prescribed medications, and the effects of various physical and psychological problems. Advance preparation through reviewing records could also prompt an examiner to research specific medical conditions or occupations unfamiliar to him. In some cases, consulting with treating professionals or other accessible experts before a clinical interview can be helpful. When retained by defense counsel in personal injury or medical malpractice cases, experts typically do not have opportunities to consult with treating professionals.

Again, vocational experts should remain objective when conducting an assessment of earning capacity. An expert's preparation for a clinical interview may uncover information such as inconsistent reporting of symptoms, noncompliance with treatment, concerns of malingering that treating professionals and/or others have expressed, and records documenting a criminal history and antisocial tendencies. While these types of information may affect preconceptions of an examinee, examiners should suspend their assessments until they have had the benefit of synthesizing all available information and, ultimately, culling pertinent information necessary to frame their independent opinions.

Of course, vocational experts should consider all available information and weigh it as merited with regard to pending questions. They should also avoid prejudging examinees. Objectivity and the application of science and practice standards hallmark credible, reliable vocational-expert opinions that are useful to those evaluating a claim's merit. Preconceived impressions about examinees can compromise a vocational expert's objectivity and, by extension, opinions.

When subjects of assessments of earning capacity arrive for their exams, they sometimes complete an intake form and other related documents such as a pain diagram and consent forms. To minimize spoilage and other external validity threats, examiners should require examinees to provide this information at the time of their exams—provided they are able to do so. Examiners should avoid transmitting, before an exam, documents an examinee is to complete.

Lawyers representing plaintiffs sometimes request that intake forms be provided before an examination. Compliance with a request of this sort invites involvement from parties other than the examinee and is generally contraindicated. Exceptions include occurrences when the examinee's competence is in question or an examinee's access to information necessary to respond is significantly compromised. Forms administered should elicit information necessary to address underlying referral questions. For example, subjects in personal injury cases often complete pain diagrams and symptom checklists at the onset of an exam. Intake forms are used to collect general information for cases that involve the assessment of physical and psychological problems in relation to career development. A sample Intake form is presented in Appendix 4.1 at the end of this chapter.

A Note about Intake Forms and Disputes over Administering Them

At times, counsel opposing an expert's retention source objects to intake forms an expert plans to administer. The objection could be made outright or contingent on opposing counsel's review and approval of documents before their administration. The bases of these objections tend to be grounded in arguments that an intake form may contain questions beyond a vocational expert's scope (e.g., how a motor vehicle accident occurred), and/or are too lengthy and unduly burdensome to complete because much of the requested information can be derived from extant records.

Quite often, lawyers' covert concerns in placing these objections pivot on the possibility their clients will (a.) disclose too much and potentially damaging information, and/or (b.) provide information inconsistent with previously documented information. In both cases, information memorialized on intake forms becomes documentary evidence that can undermine claims of loss of earning capacity—the bane of a lawyer pursuing this damage. Hence, these concerns spur lawyers' preemptory initiatives to quash this form of evidence from being developed.

Control permeates all lawyers' agendas. Any examination, especially when performed by an expert retained by opposing counsel, threatens a loss of control and the development of evidence countermanding damages claims sought.

Typically, when disputes about intake forms arise, the lawyer who retained an expert contacts him, presents opposing counsel's stated concerns, and solicits input in resolving the dispute. This input sometimes involves queries whether an expert will cede to opposing counsel's request to review an intake form before an exam—a concession strongly advised against (discussed in more detail below). When opposing lawyers cannot resolve an intake form dispute, they present their disagreements to the court. The court's decision binds an expert on examination procedures.

Experts who believe court-imposed restrictions compromise their ability to fully address referral questions should make this known in their reports. In a case in which a vocational expert's exam was limited to a clinical interview, for example, the expert provided in her report the following commentary: "It should be noted that the court restricted me from administering standardized tests to Mr. Williams. This type of assessment could be helpful if there is a suggestion of an occupational change for him."

Courts may impose limitations on an expert's use of an intake form, examination time, and planned testing protocol. Experts' recitations of how court-imposed exam restrictions potentially compromised their ability to address pending vocationally relevant issues can have significance in the following ways:

- Insulating the expert from unfounded cross-examination such as, "Why didn't you . . . ?"

- Identifying specific vocational areas of inquiry that were hampered due to court-imposed exam restrictions.
- Providing expert-based evidence that can be useful to counsel as grounds for appeal because of potential circuit court judge error in making a discovery ruling.

As noted above, an expert's disclosure of an intake form in advance of an examination is strongly discouraged. Needless to say, anticipation of a vocational rehabilitation evaluation will cue both an examinee and representing lawyer on to-be-posed questions. Further, publications—such as this that include sample intake forms—alert examinees and their counsel to questions likely to be posed during a clinical interview. Regardless, disclosing an intake form before an exam introduces the risk that a lawyer will collaborate with his client on how to complete it, thereby interjecting spoilage to the quality of information obtained.

An examinee's completion of an intake form, even when administered in an expert's office, requires monitoring. Vocational experts have reported instances of encountering examinees who ,left alone, were discovered to have been telephoning or texting their lawyers for guidance while completing intake forms and standardized tests.

In situations where the court has prohibited an intake form's administration, the vocational expert, of course, should conform with the ruling and proceed to orally elicit information the form otherwise would have generated. Experts should not include on intake forms or in their oral queries questions beyond the scope of referral questions they have been retained to address.

Beyond the obvious information examinees document on an intake form, a careful analysis of a completed intake form can provide much vocationally relevant information including an examinee's:

- Literacy, English language skills, and writing skills
- Attention to detail
- Efficiency
- Quality of information provided

In addition to evaluating information objectively, vocational experts must approach their clinical interviews consistently. Generally, clinical interviews focus on eliciting the following information:

- Vocational, personal, and social background information including allegations of impairment to pursue career development
- Chronology of vocational activity near an event in dispute
- Potential physical problems or psychological problems that may affect career development
- Activities of daily living
- Mental health
- Education and special training
- Career development

Throughout the clinical interview, vocational experts should assess examinees' overall presentation including nonverbal behavior, approach toward the examination, and apparent level of effort. Obsequiousness toward a vocational expert, superficial cooperation with the exam, pain behavior not supported by medical evidence, and tendencies toward overstatement or understatement should be noted. Information of this type can support hypotheses about a subject's candor or motivation, especially when integrated with other case-specific information and research. One case involved two married physicians who alleged various injuries from an automobile accident. During the videotaped portion of his wife's examination (videotaping was requested by the husband), the husband expressed his cooperation with the exam process, consoled his wife, made many unsolicited comments about her disabilities, insisted that she take breaks (which she indicated she did not need or want), and intermittently massaged his wife's neck. When videotaping was not in progress, however, the husband behaved boorishly toward the vocational expert, made threatening demands for records in the expert's possession, and behaved brusquely and indifferently toward his wife. These latter observations of the husband's behavior were consistent with those the wife's treating physicians presented, and raised questions about the degree of the husband's influence in his wife's symptom presentation and her claims of vocational disability.

At the end of this chapter, Appendix 4.3 presents an example of a clinical interview a vocational expert conducted in a personal injury case. More information about areas to investigate during a clinical interview is in the following sections.

Face-to-face examinations of subjects, while preferable, are not always possible. Logistical constraints, trial deadlines, and technicalities inherent in some cases—such as a judge imposing a limit on the number of compulsory exams a plaintiff is required to undergo—are among the reasons a vocational evaluator may be unable to examine a subject.

The excerpt below is from a deposition in which a vocational expert retained by defense counsel did not have an opportunity to examine the plaintiff, Ms. V. The plaintiff attorney insinuates that methodological limitations—in this case, lack of a clinical interview—have compromised the expert's ability to develop her opinions, and, consequently, less weight should be ascribed to them. The expert acknowledges limitations associated with her analysis, places the limitations in perspective, and requests on the record to examine the plaintiff—an important feature of this testimony. If the plaintiff attorney denies the expert's request and attempts to discredit the expert's methodology during cross-examination at trial, the expert can refer to her deposition testimony and apprise the jury of her request to examine the plaintiff, noting the plaintiff lawyer declined to grant this request. In this context, plaintiff's counsel risks the jury forming a perception of him as uncooperative with the discovery process or attempting to insulate his client from an examination in which information not helpful to the plaintiff's case could emerge, should he choose to attack the evaluator about the lack of an exam. When reading the excerpt, notice that plaintiff's counsel does not acknowledge on the record the expert's request for an examination. Generally, the expert can expect a request of this sort to be either ignored or dismissed through some oblique retort. The expert's testimony serves to blunt a potential attempt by plaintiff's counsel at trial to discredit her and erode the integrity of her opinions.

Q. Are you able to form your opinions on my client's work ability without meeting and speaking to her?

A. Ideally, I would like to examine her, and, if you would allow me that opportunity, I will be glad to do that. At this point, based upon the records I have reviewed, I feel confident in expressing the opinions based on the materials that are available to me. But I would like to have an opportunity to examine her, if that is possible.

Q. Well, you said that you have private patients yourself?

A. Yes.

Q. Do you give any of your private patients any advice, or any placement, or any help in their rehabilitation without first meeting them?

A. I occasionally have patients who call, and I provide guidance by phone.

Q. Okay, but that is not the preferred way; isn't that true?

A. If it is actually giving guidance, then it is not the preferred way. I was not asked to give Ms. V vocational guidance. I was asked to comment and provide a professional opinion about her career development and loss of earning capacity, so it is a different situation. It is not a comparable situation, because I'm not providing guidance to her. I'm offering an opinion.

Q. Okay, but all I'm saying is it would have been helpful to meet and speak with her and see her demeanor?

A. It possibly would have been helpful, but the medical records are very clear: She is at maximum medical improvement. Her restrictions are well defined, and I have good records and documentation from her employers about her preinjury and postinjury employment.

The preceding colloquy and explanation illustrate how experts must anticipate the consequences of their testimony. Sophisticated experts discern motives underlying superficially straightforward questions laced with innuendo, and fortify responses with necessary qualifications. More information about giving testimony is in Chapter 11.

a. Background information. Every case involving an assessment of earning capacity is unique. A subject's demographics (e.g., age, cultural background, significant relationships), family circumstances, residence, and plans for future residence, for example, may have unanticipated relevance in an evaluation of earning capacity.

In a family law case, a spouse's ability to resume her career development as a certified public accountant (CPA), her profession for eleven years before she left the workplace to raise two children, was at issue. While conducting his analysis, a vocational expert carefully considered one child's diagnosis of attention deficit disorder (ADD). The child exhibited severe behavioral problems and required significant supervision to complete homework and basic daily living activities. Because of the family's lack of financial resources to enlist outside support and the child's special needs, the expert concluded that the spouse retaining primary custody rights would be unable to aggressively develop a career or participate in more than part-time employment.

In another marriage dissolution case in which family background information was a particularly relevant consideration in a vocational expert's analysis, the court encountered a dilemma involving an only child, age thirteen, who both the petitioner and respondent agreed possessed the talent necessary to compete for an Olympic swimming medal. The child's world-caliber swimming coach, however, was more than a one-and-one-half-hour drive (one way) from the family's home, and both parents agreed their child should continue to train with his coach. Relocation closer to the coach's training facility was not a viable option. Further, no one other than a parent was available to transport the child. Although the ability of either spouse to earn wages was undisputed, at issue was the career-development opportunity cost presented to each parent in transporting their talented child to and from training sessions. This became the vocational expert's focus in his analyses of the parents' respective potential for career advancement and earnings.

Vocational experts must thoroughly understand and incorporate subject-specific circumstances into their analyses and earning-capacity opinions. While personal circumstances may not directly relate to a subject's earning capacity, as illustrated by the two examples above, the vocational expert risks conducting an inaccurate assessment and loss of credibility by not integrating pertinent personal factors into an analysis. For instance, skilled examiners carefully tend to details such as the subject's eye contact, speech patterns, demeanor, and inconsistent statements. Examiners are cautioned, however, not to over-extrapolate their inferences—a caution Sigmund Freud, an avid cigar smoker, notably voiced when a student asked whether his cigar smoking could be symbolic of unconscious phallic impulses. After carefully considering the question, Freud responded negatively and said, "Sometimes a cigar is just a cigar."

b. Chronology of vocational activity. A chronology of vocational activity provides perspective and a framework for an evaluator's investigation. It also helps to focus on issues central to the evaluation.

Helpful information in a vocational chronology includes facts about how the subject's career development evolved. An overview of the examinee's educational background, work history, and employment—at both the time of an issue in dispute (in cases involving disputes) and afterward—is standard. Also helpful is discerning the subject's perception of how her earning capacity has changed because of an event(s). In a case involving a high profile public administrator who alleged he was wrongfully terminated in retaliation for actions as a whistle-blower, for example, the claimant alleged that inflammatory media coverage and defamatory, unsolicited references from his prior employer made obtaining employment comparable to his prior employment unlikely. He detailed multiple futile job search efforts he initiated and suggested his career had been irreparably damaged.

In cases involving acquired disabling problems, it is helpful to discuss the onset of symptoms, how they affected the individual's ability to pursue vocational activity, effectiveness of treatment, and how career plans may have been altered. Efforts to mitigate career and earning capacity damages—such as attempting to implement accommodations, pursue retraining, or seek employment more compatible with residual capacities—are useful to cite when establishing a vocational chronology.

Excerpts from a vocational chronology in an evaluator's report follow. In this case, a plaintiff alleged to have sustained injuries resulting from a motor vehicle accident. He had been employed as a painting contractor, primarily performing supervisory tasks, and continued to perform this work with some modifications following the accident and through the time of the vocational rehabilitation evaluation. Plaintiff counsel's vocational expert opined that, because of accident-related injuries, the plaintiff's work-life expectancy has diminished. As can be seen in the evaluator's summary and impressions, which follow the chronology, the vocational expert, whom defense counsel retained, arrived at an alternate opinion.

Vocational Activity

Mr. Perry conveyed he completed his high school education in 1981 and earned an associate's degree in ornamental horticulture/landscaping in 1986. He informed me he developed scaffold-building and commercial-painting skills through on-the-job experiences.

In 1984 or 1985, Mr. Perry noted, his brother established Designer Painting in Largo, and he advised me he relocated from the Buffalo, New York, area in 1985 to join the business that year. Currently, he apprised me, his brother owns 70% of Designer, and he owns 30% of it. Mr. Perry reported Designer has been his sole employer since 1985.

Mr. Perry told me Designer specializes in commercial painting, including high-rise buildings and condominiums. He was not aware of the business' annual sales or number of employees at the time of his September 11, 2010, motor vehicle accident.

At the time of the September 2010 accident, Mr. Perry indicated, he worked from 60 to 70 hours per week and earned approximately $1,000 to $1,200 per week. Although he advised me the economic downturn adversely affected Designer, it did not affect his salary.

As a painting contractor with Designer, Mr. Perry conveyed, his job responsibilities at the time of the September 2010 accident included both "hands on" and supervisory tasks. He informed me he performed supervisory tasks 80% of his workday and hands-on tasks the remainder of his day.

Mr. Perry noted his supervisory tasks included:

- Staffing and coordinating projects in progress
- Inspecting work quality
- Coordinating work in progress with other skilled trades workers
- Turning in payroll records
- Maintaining daily reports

The hands-on tasks Mr. Perry performed, he apprised me, included:

- Demonstrating painting techniques
- Setting up rigging and carrying scaffold weights and related materials on rooftops
- Assisting with painting punch-outs
- Loading equipment and transporting it to job sites

Mr. Perry reported working on structures up to 32 stories high. He told me he performed his job at locations throughout southwestern Florida and that he drove from 16 to 18 hours per week, approximately 45,000 miles per year. He indicated he worked at heights and on uneven surfaces, and regularly assembled/climbed scaffolds and ladders. The projects on which Mr. Perry worked, he advised me, were up to $1.4 million.

While at project sites, Mr. Perry conveyed, he walked and stood extensively. He informed me he wore a hard hat, work boots, a harness that weighed 5 or 6 pounds, and occasionally a respirator. He also indicated he was exposed to various weather conditions.

Mr. Perry noted he performed bimanual tasks throughout his workday. The heaviest weight he handled, he apprised me, was from 75 to 100 pounds – sprayers, pressure washers, and block fillers. Further, Mr. Perry reported he performed the full range of body motions.

After his September 2010 accident, Mr. Perry recalled, his neck and left-shoulder symptoms onset immediately. He told me his lower-back problems began the next day. "When I woke up, I was having a real difficult time getting out of bed," he said.

Mr. Perry and I reviewed Dr. Watson's initial treatment notes. Dr. Watson did not recommend surgery; however, after multiple injections that did not relieve Mr. Perry's pain, the orthopedic surgeon referred him to pain management, Mr. Perry conveyed.

I inquired about his postaccident work participation, and Mr. Perry replied: "I struggled through. Sometimes I would just have to cut days short." He indicated he missed days of work when he was administered injections.

Mr. Perry advised me he abstained from tasks requiring lifting after his September 2010 accident. "I didn't do any more painting. It was just supervisory," he added, recalling intense lower back pain he experienced. He conveyed he continued working as a painting contractor, in a reduced capacity, until Dr. Young operated on his lumbar spine on December 14, 2011.

Several days after Mr. Perry's lumbar surgery, he informed me, he resumed his painting contractor job "in a supervisory role." He recalled he initially worked part time and increased his work participation to full time by mid-January 2012. Mr. Perry noted he has since continued to work full time.

Currently, Mr. Perry apprised me, he works from 60 to 70 hours per week. He reported his compensation is "still about the same" as it had been at the time of his September 2010 accident. "There's certain benefits that I've been cut back on. My medical insurance is covered through my wife," he said. Mr. Perry did not identify any other change in his postaccident employee benefits.

I asked Mr. Perry about the reason for the insurance change, and he responded, "Lower profits, company cutbacks." He expressed his belief that his compromised physical status contributed to Designer's lower profits. Mr. Perry estimated the value of his health insurance benefits, now paid by his wife's employer along with her contribution, is $800 to $900 per month. He reported all 18 of Designer's employees were affected by this cutback.

As for his current job responsibilities, Mr. Perry told me that, "for the most part," he continues to abstain from hands-on tasks. He indicated he purchased a crane (discussed in more detail later in this report) to help him move equipment and that he limits the length that he demonstrates painting techniques to short durations.

Additionally, Mr. Perry advised me he avoids climbing tall ladders, working on pitched surfaces, and walking on scaffolds. Essentially all of his work time is consumed with performing supervisory tasks, he conveyed.

I inquired whether the work tasks he currently performs are within his capacity, and Mr. Perry said: "Yeah, some of the large property walks [can be difficult]. I just cut my days short if I have to."

Mr. Perry denied that Dr. Young advised him to change occupations. He expressed his intent to continue his current employment, "as long as I can." I asked Mr. Perry whether his preaccident/postaccident career plans have changed, and he responded negatively.

Summary and Impressions

1. A 1981 high school graduate, Mr. Perry reported he earned an associate's degree in ornamental horticulture/landscaping in 1986 and developed scaffold-building and commercial-painting skills through on-the-job experiences. He advised me he joined Designer Painting in Largo, a business his brother founded, in 1985. Mr. Perry indicated he is a 30% owner of Designer and his brother owns the remainder of the business. At the time of his September 11, 2010, motor vehicle accident, he conveyed, his work as a painting contractor with Designer involved both "hands on" tasks (20% of his time) and supervisory tasks (80% of his time). Based on my understanding of Mr. Perry's job responsibilities, the painting contractor work he performed was semiskilled, his supervisory tasks required light exertion, and the hands-on work he performed required medium/heavy exertion. After his September 2010 accident, he recalled, his neck and left-shoulder symptoms onset immediately, and his lower-back problems began the following day. He described how symptoms and medical treatment he is associating with his 2010 accident adversely affected his work participation. Dr. Watson administered several epidural steroidal injections in Mr. Perry's lumbar spine before Dr. Young operated on Mr. Perry's back on December 14, 2011. Several days after the lumbar surgery, Mr. Perry related, he resumed his painting contractor job "in a supervisory role." He noted he eventually resumed full-time work by mid-January 2012 and he has since continued to work full time. He informed me he currently works from 60 to 70 hours per week, earns "still about the same" as he had been earning at the time of his September 2010 accident, and, "for the most part," continues to abstain from hands-on tasks. Mr. Perry discussed postaccident adaptations he has made, which include purchasing a crane to help him move equipment and limiting the length of time he demonstrates painting techniques to short durations. Additionally, he reported he avoids climbing tall ladders, working on pitched surfaces, and walking on scaffolds. He responded affirmatively when I inquired whether the tasks he currently performs are within his capacity. Mr. Perry denied that Dr. Young advised him to change occupations, and he told me he plans to continue his current employment "as long as I can." He did not cite any change in his career plans. In response to my query of whether he has assumed any higher-order supervising tasks since his ability to perform the full scope of hands-on work has diminished, Mr. Perry stated, "I help out a little bit more when bidding the new estimates for repaints." He acknowledged that Designer's business model includes developing protégés and striving to assume higher-level business administration tasks that enhance the business' profitability. Mr. Perry denied searching for a job since his 2010 accident, and he denied planning to do so. He indicated he is content with his current employment situation.
2. Mr. Perry's preaccident medical history and unrelated postaccident medical history is significant from a vocational rehabilitation perspective. Medical records document preaccident complaints of neck and back pain, and indicate he intermittently pursued chiropractic treatment. Mr. Perry apparently had longstanding preaccident problems with weight management. Preaccident records also include diagnoses of hypertension and sleep apnea. In October 2009, Mr. Perry underwent left-shoulder surgery. Records from Bay Area Orthopedic and Spine Medicine indicate he was in the midst of a physical therapy protocol when he sustained injuries from a February 3, 2010, motor vehicle accident; after this accident, he presented headache, neck, upper-back, and mid-back complaints. The last preaccident medical record I reviewed is a May 3, 2010, chiropractic note that includes recommendations for additional treatment (three times per

week) to Mr. Perry's cervical, thoracic, and lumbar spines. After his September 2010 accident, he was diagnosed with type 2 diabetes. Regardless of any additional disabling problems Mr. Perry may have acquired as a result of his September 11, 2010, motor vehicle accident, his preaccident and unrelated postaccident medical history likely would have cast limitations on his vocational functioning in the absence of his September 2010 accident.

3. Regarding problems he is associating with his September 11, 2010, motor vehicle accident, Mr. Perry said his neck pain has "pretty much resolved" and that he generally does not experience lumbar pain. Repetitive movements and/or bearing weight for more than 1.5 to 2 hours, he conveyed, are examples of exertional activities that cause his back to become symptomatic. He also discussed with me occasional problems of left foot drop and intermittent bilateral jaw pain. Imaging of Mr. Perry's cervical and lumbar spines detected evidence of degenerative disc disease. As noted above, he underwent several epidural steroidal injections before Dr. Young operated on his lumbar spine on December 14, 2011. In a February 8, 2012, office note, Dr. Young determined Mr. Perry sustained a permanent injury because of his September 2010 accident; the surgeon assigned a 6% permanent impairment rating. Dr. Dopler, a chiropractor, determined on March 14, 2012, that Mr. Perry had reached maximum medical improvement from a chiropractic perspective. Like Dr. Young, Dr. Dopler determined Mr. Perry sustained a permanent injury to his lumbar spine because of the September 2010 accident. Dr. Young documented restrictions for Mr. Perry on May 31, 2012, that included avoiding heavy lifting, and avoiding climbing and standing on high platforms or scaffolding. The most recent medical record I reviewed that addresses his functional capacities is a September 21, 2012, report by Dr. Smythe. This record includes the following statement: "The patient is currently able to do activities of daily living without limitations, able to work without limitations, and able to participate in sports without limitations." My prognosis for Mr. Perry's continued vocational rehabilitation is good. He should be capable of continuing to perform his job as he told me he has been since mid-January 2012. A suggestion that Mr. Perry's September 11, 2012, motor vehicle accident has diminished his work-life expectancy is speculative.

4. Mr. Perry displayed a normal gait while in my office and, apart from eyeglasses, did not use adaptive aids. He is cognitively intact. He denied having problems with driving. From a functional perspective, Mr. Perry estimated he is able to safely handle 30 to 35 pounds. No limitations with cervical spine or upper-extremity functioning were noted, although he indicated Dr. Young advised against overhead lifting. Mr. Perry estimated he is able to stand 30 minutes before overexerting himself or needing to rest, and he noted Dr. Young encouraged him to walk on a treadmill for 2 miles. He denied having problems with sitting. He does not take prescribed medications related to his 2010 motor vehicle accident. While meeting with me, Mr. Perry indicated he was not experiencing pain, and he said he has pain "only if I stay on my feet too long or overexert myself." From a mental health perspective, he assessed he is well adjusted. I found Mr. Perry pleasant and likable. Along with his education, training, on-the-job experiences, and transferable skills, these factors are assets to him in his vocational rehabilitation. The evidence I reviewed does not support a claim of loss of earning capacity attributable to Mr. Perry's September 11, 2010, motor vehicle accident.

5. I have requested to review several records including tax returns and documentation of Mr. Perry's earnings; employment and business records; updated medical records, both preaccident and postaccident, along with any compulsory medical evaluation reports; Mr. Perry's deposition and interrogatory responses; and school records. If additional information I review causes a change in my opinions, I will make this known.

6. It should be noted that the court restricted me from administering standardized tests to Mr. Perry. This type of assessment could be helpful if there is a suggestion of an occupational change for him.

c. Potential physical or psychological problems that may affect career development. An occupation can require myriad demands—physical and/or mental—to perform, and, likewise, individuals possess the gamut of physical and mental capacities. The better the person/occupation match, the more likely a successful vocational outcome will yield. This premise is fundamental to vocational rehabilitation, and maintaining it as the touchstone of a vocational rehabilitation evaluation is paramount. Vocational experts evaluate the interface between the requirements necessary to perform an occupation and an examinee's capacities to meet the requirements, ultimately translating matches between the two to earning capacity.

While unskilled, physically demanding occupations may require employees to lift and carry heavy objects and to perform the full range of body motions, unskilled, sedentary office-based or precision-handwork occupations typically require much different physical and mental demands. These requirements may include repetitive fine motor movements requiring hand-eye coordination, sitting for extended periods, and performing work within precise limits or standards. The job responsibilities and environmental conditions associated with performing an occupation dictate the essential physical and mental capabilities an incumbent must possess. A construction superintendent, for example, may have nominal lifting responsibilities. Her job, however, may require extended walking on uneven surfaces at construction sites, climbing ladders to inspect roofs, and exposure to harsh weather conditions—all of which may be problematic for a person with a lower-extremity, vestibular, or vision impairment.

A vocational expert cannot assess a subject's ability to perform an occupation without (a.) a thorough understanding of an occupation's demands, and (b.) a valid appraisal of an examinee's physical and mental capabilities. Besides assessing an individual's ability to perform a job in question, this analysis facilitates responding to questions about, for example, the need for and possibility of job accommodations, alternate vocational options if the examinee cannot return to past relevant work because of a physical and/or mental impairment, and retraining options.

To determine potential physical, cognitive, and psychological impairments that could affect a subject's career development, vocational experts should elicit the following information during their clinical interviews:

- The examinee's assessment of all physical, cognitive, and psychological problems, along with functional limitations and activities/conditions that aggravate symptoms.
- If an examinee presents acquired disabilities as a result of circumstances such as personal injury, medical malpractice, negligence, work-related injury, or another event, establish whether the examinee sustained trauma to the head or a loss of consciousness. When pertinent, identify the area of the head experiencing trauma and length of loss of consciousness.
- The examinee's primary disabling problem(s).
- The examinee's understanding of medical and/or psychological diagnoses.
- A complete medical history. With an acquired disability, the vocational expert should also inquire about any unrelated physical and/or psychological problem the examinee has since experienced.
- Future medical treatment scheduled or contemplated.
- Names of treating professionals and records of medical treatment the examinee has had.
- Use of adaptive aids or equipment (e.g., support braces, cane, wheelchair).
- Medications and any side effects.
- The examinee's functional capabilities related to lifting, carrying, walking, standing, sitting, bending at the waist, performing upper- and lower-extremity motions, operating a motor vehicle, and so forth.
- Potential exacerbation of problems secondary to exposure to various environmental conditions such as cold and hot temperatures, dampness or high humidity, and environmental irritants.
- Specific physician-advised restrictions.
- The examinee's assessment of the stability of his condition (e.g., does the examinee believe his condition is stable, improving, or worsening?).

d. Activities of daily living. Understanding problems an examinee may have with basic daily living activities—such as sleeping, hygiene and self-care, performing household and yard maintenance chores, and pursuing avocational interests—may provide insight about her ability to perform vocationally. An examinee's needs for assistance or compromised ability to perform various daily living tasks could reveal difficulties the person may encounter in the workplace. Information of this sort is especially helpful when an assessment of earning capacity involves a person with an acquired disability.

Often, when evaluating the vocational capacities of someone with acquired disabilities, qualified vocational experts are also asked to address an examinee's need for related rehabilitation services; this request is more likely to be made if the vocational expert is also a Certified Life Care Planner . For instance, to function at maximum capacity, an examinee may benefit from private tutoring, job coaching, or attendant care services. In this context, an understanding of an examinee's activities of daily living is especially important.

Asking how an examinee spends an average day can also prove insightful. For example, a vocational expert may conclude that an examinee allegedly injured through medical malpractice is capable of some work activity, albeit diminished compared to preincident levels. If evidence from the clinical interview suggests a significant portion of the examinee's activities of daily living are idle, nonproductive, and lacking in pursuit of vocational rehabilitation, however, questions about motivation, secondary gain, assumption of a disability mentality, and/or need for professional rehabilitation guidance may arise. This information can help the expert confirm opinions about an examinee's work capacity and to prescribe interventions, as appropriate and necessary, to facilitate vocational rehabilitation.

e. Mental health. A background in counseling or psychology is necessary to assess how sequelae associated with welcome/unwelcome lifestyle changes, career transitions, and acquired physical, cognitive, and psychological problems affect an examinee. Mental health problems can be quite complex and profound in how they impact a person's ability to function vocationally. A skilled vocational evaluator will carefully consider an examinee's psychological profile when generating vocational opinions.

Vocational experts should not only be conversant with the implications of disorders described in the Diagnostic and Statistical Manual of Mental Disorders—Fifth Edition (DSM-5), they should also be alert to general mental health problems that confront the subject of an earning capacity assessment. Problems with adjusting to disability, changes in body image and diminished self-concept because of disfigurement or loss of a limb, or changes associated with the ending of a long-term relationship in which one member has been significantly dependent upon the other member, are examples of cases in which an individual may not exhibit psychological symptoms sufficient to support a clinical diagnosis, yet involve situations in which the examinee is exhibiting symptoms necessary to consider in a vocational assessment.

A combination of mental health concerns can adversely affect one's psyche and, correspondingly, career development. In cases such as these, a major contributor to career underachievement can be lack of self-esteem, which leads to inhibition and diminished ability to take risks. In turn, these problems stifle career progression and advancement. The self-fulfilling prophecy phenomenon is sometimes inherent in this cycle.

An examinee's mental health problems can manifest through various behaviors ranging from self-isolation to aggressiveness. The evaluator must distinguish examinee-specific character traits from behaviors attributable to the examinee's presenting situation. For instance, an examinee's feelings of humiliation, considering his need to request assistance with basic self-care because of an acquired disability, are quite understandable. Of course, some personality characteristics are innate and independent of any trauma or life situation the person has experienced. For example, an introverted examinee's infrequent socialization and absorption in self-directed activities, such as reading or extensive computer use, may be longstanding characterological traits, independent of expressed shame associated with a wrongful termination. On the other hand, psychological distress with its accompanying behaviors sometimes emanates from an issue in dispute. A salesperson who was the victim of an assault, for instance, may become less outgoing and friendly, and even develop psychological symptoms that suppress future career progression; feelings of vulnerability and problems with self-motivation can arise from this type of experience. Vocational experts should be alert to acquired psychological problems that could suppress an examinee's work performance and career development, thereby affecting earning capacity.

In personal injury cases involving traumatic brain injury, vocational experts may witness certain unusual behaviors during their clinical interviews. Observations of mental processing difficulties—such as problems with expressive (spoken) or receptive (heard or read) language (exhibited, for example, via word retrieval problems and tangential discourse), and evidence of amnesia or a thought disorder—should be carefully considered.

Subjects with head injuries often behave in a ways that belie the symptoms associated with the injury to the region of the brain that has been traumatized. A subject who experienced a frontal lobe brain injury, for example, may exhibit disinhibition during a clinical interview. An example of this behavior is a subject who ignores generally accepted interpersonal boundaries and closely inspects documents on an examiner's desk during a clinical interview. In cases in which a head injury is suspected, a neuropsychologist can inform the vocational expert of the likely cognitive deficits that can affect vocational functioning. Experts should be cognizant when a referral to a neuropsychologist or other specialist is in order.

While conducting a mental health assessment, examiners should obtain a history of a subject's psychological treatment, including reasons and types of treatments, and inpatient psychiatric admissions. If an examinee is currently undergoing mental health treatment, the vocational expert should identify treatment issues, knowledge the examinee may have of diagnoses, and the examinee's understanding of work-related implications associated with current psychological conditions. Additionally, it is important to understand the examinee's perception of her mental health status, along with specific mental health concerns such as problems with anger and stress management, depression, relationship problems, financial difficulties, and suicidal ideation. Issues related to substance abuse, past legal history, and antisocial behavior may also be relevant.

Through their clinical interactions with examinees, vocational experts should also assess:

- Ability to recall remote and recent information
- Interpersonal skills
- Degree of compliance with examination protocol
- Affect (demeanor)
- Nonverbal behavior
- Impression the examinee would likely make as a job candidate

Standardized testing, detailed later in this chapter, helps to obtain behavioral information that may be difficult to gather during a clinical interview, and to supplement, confirm, or cause a vocational expert to revise impressions formulated during a clinical interview.

f. Education and special training. Obtaining information about an examinee's education and training is fundamental to every vocational evaluation. The vocational expert should inquire about:

- Formal education and training including any associated special circumstances
- Special commendations or items of note related to educational experiences
- Reasons for not completing basic levels of education or reasons for documented school problems such as truancy or school suspensions
- Performance on standardized admission and achievement tests
- Military education and training
- Employer-sponsored training
- Remedial education experiences or prior learning problems
- Work-related specialty credentials, active and ¬inactive
- Continuing education
- On-the-job training
- Special skills or talents (e.g., second language, musical, martial arts)

Understanding an examinee's educational background, training experiences, specialized knowledge, and skills acquired from work experiences enables a vocational expert to identify viable occupations and developmental experiences for the examinee. When a vocational expert concludes that a person cannot return to past work for reasons that may include limitations caused by disabilities, noncompetition stipulations, or industry-related factors, a transferable skills analysis facilitates an evaluation of alternate work opportunities that remain viable.

The concept of transferability of skills assumes individuals develop a generic set of skills through education, training, and work experiences. Once identified, these skills have the potential to be applied in other occupations or vocational venues. Field and Dunn (2014) discussed the historical foundations and development of transferability of skill assessment.

After performing a vocational evaluation of a truck driver who experienced traumatically induced glaucoma with residual visual deficits, for example, an examiner concluded that the examinee's disabling problems precluded a return to work in his premorbid occupation. Via a transferability-of-skills analysis, the examiner identified several skills remaining within the examinee's capacity and then identified alternate occupations to which the skills could be applied. Although the vocational expert concluded the examinee sustained a loss of earning capacity because of the work-related accident, he identified various occupations that remained accessible to the examinee, making use of his transferrable skills. Additionally, the expert offered a vocational rehabilitation plan that involved augmenting the examinee's residual skill set through retraining; this helped reduce the examinee's earning capacity loss. Dispatching, warehouse inventory control, and fleet maintenance occupations were among those within the examinee's residual capacity, and the vocational expert determined the examinee possessed transferable skills sufficient to transition into these occupations with nominal retraining.

g. Career development. A thorough work history obtained by a vocational evaluator includes a chronology of an examinee's job titles, names of employers, dates of employment, and earnings. Gathering information about specific job responsibilities associated with recent occupations an examinee performed is especially important and, when an examinee's ability to return to prior employment in view of acquired disabilities is an issue, becomes an important basis of expert opinion. Also potentially important in these circumstances is information concerning whether reasonable accommodations could allow an examinee to resume prior employment and, if not possible, transferable skills the examinee possesses to facilitate vocational rehabilitation.

Vocational evaluators should inquire about the following career development information:

- Career and job satisfaction
- Present employment status and changes in work schedules or compensation
- Work attendance
- Need for work accommodations, along with employer accommodations that might have already been extended
- Reasons for leaving jobs, and eligibility for rehiring with prior employers
- Perceptions about employer performance appraisals and job performance
- Job security
- Sources of income and expenses

Assessing examinees' efforts to mitigate loss of earning capacity is often relevant while conducting a vocational rehabilitation evaluation. Mitigation efforts are particularly pertinent, for example, in employment law cases involving allegations of wrongful termination. To assess mitigation efforts, the vocational expert should ask about the extent of an examinee's job search, methods used, and initiatives to enhance potential job placement. Analyzing documentation of these efforts is always recommended.

Further, a vocational expert must assess how events in dispute may have affected an examinee's career plans. This determination is especially important when subjects are in the exploration or establishment phases of their career development, or when substantial evidence suggests a person would have likely realized a major advancement in earning capacity if not for an event she encountered. For example, in a case involving the extremely premature birth of quadruplets (twenty-three-week gestational period), the parents experienced overwhelming psychological distress and intensive demands on their time for an extended period after their babies' births. Eventually, three of the babies died, and the surviving child had multiple disabilities requiring significant parental attention. Throughout the ordeal, both parents developed severe psychological problems. The father of the quadruplets, a thirty-four-year-old owner of a computer hardware exporting business he founded four years earlier, was essentially absent from his previously profitable and growing business. His business dissolved within two years after his babies' births, and he attributed the demise of his business to his diminished involvement in it. After analyzing industry trends and reviewing a business plan the father developed before the quadruplets' births, the vocational expert concluded that the father's future earnings would have greatly exceeded his demonstrated earnings history if not for the events he experienced after the birth of his children. Besides relying upon an examinee's demonstrated earnings history as a benchmark of earning capacity, experts should assess unrealized earning capacity to arrive at a comprehensive assessment of a claim of loss of earning capacity.

Earning capacity assessments involving allegations of disability or restricted work ability typically include a determination of an examinee's ability to resume past employment, especially most recent occupations. Information related to residual capacities and job demands, transferable skills, potential employer accommodations, and job reengineering may be relevant. To aid in this assessment, vocational experts should analyze examinees' perceptions of their abilities to return to prior employment, and abilities to engage in work activities involving various physical and cognitive demand levels. Typically, this can be accomplished through a series of questions, beginning with recent employment and continuing with work involving progressively less exerting and/or less cognitively complex employment.

Reasons an examinee presents for an inability or compromised ability to return to past relevant work activity should be explored. Further, vocational experts should clinically correlate and evaluate subjective reports with respect to medical and other pertinent evidence—such as surveillance—and information the vocational expert obtains from other sources, including job descriptions and information about occupational demands.

Information about an examinee's intentions and views on pursuing career development may bolster theories an expert formulates. For instance, an expert may determine prospective employment for an unemployed examinee is a financial disincentive. In a case where a bank executive ceased working after acquiring soft-tissue injuries in a slip-and-fall incident, a vocational expert learned the claimant realized a higher income than what she had been earning while working; this income was derived from several sources including a private disability policy and workers' compensation benefits. She was also pursuing a significant loss of earning capacity claim in which the party she sued admitted liability. During the clinical interview, the examinee elaborated about how returning to work could alter a jury's perception about the extent of her career development damages, thereby potentially diminishing the size of a verdict for lost wages. The examinee also conceded that she could likely return to office-based employment. Obviously, this information raised the expert's suspicion about the examinee's motivation to return to work. Vocational experts should routinely assess motivation associated with financial needs and potential for financial gain, along with other secondary gain motives, while conducting their analyses.

An excerpt from a clinical interview demonstrating how a vocational expert elicited information from a forty-five-year-old service technician employed by an electric utility company follows. In this case, the examinee underwent two cervical fusion surgeries. The vocational expert assessed effects on the plaintiff's career development and earning capacity the second surgery caused. Based on her interview and other information amassed during the evaluation, the vocational expert concluded that, although the examinee was unable to return to his prior work, he was capable of pursuing sedentary and light-duty work with restrictions including avoiding repetitive head movements. The expert's opinion about residual earning capacity, in part, involved reliance upon labor market research. Additionally, the vocational expert presented a retraining scenario that identified specific training programs, costs for training, duration of training, and earnings ranges after a specified retraining period.

Q. You left school in the 10th grade?
A. Eleventh.
Q. Why did you not complete your high school education?
A. I started working, just started doing other things, didn't think it mattered at the time. And, actually, it probably wouldn't have mattered at all had I been able to continue being employed at XYZ Electric Company. I wouldn't have needed that at all.
Q. Have you ever taken the GED exam?
A. Yes.
Q. How many times?
A. Once.
Q. Were you successful?
A. I was.
Q. When was that?
A. That would have been just before '78, because in order to hire on at XYZ Electric, you have to have a GED.
Q. And you've had training, on-the-job training, at XYZ—
A. Yes.
Q. —by your employer? What kind of training have you had?
A. Well, you start off as a laborer and move up to a ground man and then to an apprentice, up to about—I went to about a six-step apprentice and then became a lineman, and then they train you each step of those ways as a training process. And then CPR, full-type rescue.
Q. You completed a lineworker apprenticeship?
A. It took me about three and half years to become a lineman.
Q. What other training have you had specific to your work as a lineworker or your job as a service technician at XYZ?
A. None that I can think of. I mean, we always have safety meetings, and auto safety, and first aid and all. But as far as any specific training other than what you did on the job, I think I had to—went to something like a day and a half course to—they had to accept other people or something to make sure that you got along good with other employees, that the whole company went through, that type of stuff. You know, anything that a major company would put people through.
Q. Did you have special licenses, for instance, to operate the service vehicles?
A. A commercial driver's license, Class A.
Q. Do you still hold that?
A. Yes.
Q. When did you first obtain your CDL?
A. When they required—whatever year it was that you're required that—it started off as chauffeur's license, you know, back in the '70s. And then somewhere in the '90s, they decided they'd go to the CDL situation.
Q. So you're experienced in operating things like bucket trucks?
A. Yes.
Q. What other vehicles? Utility vehicles?
A. I haven't done it in a long time, a line truck, which is a miniature crane. Well, it's really not a miniature crane. Crane operation is different than a line truck. It's the same principal, but different. You have to be—in order to operate a crane at XYZ Company, you have to be trained explicitly to be an equipment operator to operate a crane. But to operate a line truck, you can just be a lineman, operating the booms for setting poles and all.
Q. You can operate booms?
A. Yes.
Q. And you had experience in setting—
A. Poles and anything out of a bucket truck, or climbing poles.
Q. And your other skills, you have knowledge of residential and commercial electrical wiring?
A. No. They consider a lineman to be unskilled labor according to classifications that—it's countrywide, it's considered unskilled labor. And in order to be—to wire, like, an inside house, they don't consider a

lineman to be skilled to wire electrically inside the house. Now, we can run the lines outside and everything, but it's slightly different, and I'm sure more codes are involved.

Q. You have knowledge of electrical code?

A. No.

Q. What other skills did you have other than what we've already discussed, repairing streetlights, the line work, operating the different vehicles that we've already discussed, including booms, setting electrical poles? What other skills would you—

A. That's it. That's what I've done since I was twenty years old until I was forty.

Q. Do you have knowledge of inspecting the electrical equipment, such as capacitors?

A. Yes. That's—anything to do with being a lineman at XYZ Electric, I was extremely efficient at it.

Q. And then repairing, you did some maintenance and repair work?

A. Yes, streetlights and line services and being able to spot any particular problem or potential problem on a line, quite frankly, is a skill that is acquired through years of experience. And that's why they had picked me if they had a problem circuit, to go find it, because I could spot minute problems that might create major problems. You know, anybody can spot a major problem, go out there, a wire is laying on the ground, obvious it broke down. You know, or a car hit a pole.

Q. Apart from the Class A, CDL, do you have any other work-related credential?

A. No.

Q. Do you have any other special skills such as musical instrument skills, martial arts, second language skills?

A. No.

Q. Do you have a computer in your home?

A. Yes.

Q. What do you use it for?

A. Solitaire.

Q. Do you have knowledge of Windows applications or other software programs?

A. No. I can't type, and any—my wife does all of that. Any printing of documents or anything, she does that.

Q. So that's all you use it for is games?

A. Yes.

Q. You've had no supervisory experience?

A. No.

Q. And you were a union employee with XYZ, correct?

A. At some point in time during my history at XYZ, I was in the union, but most of the time I was not.

Q. Were you when you left XYZ?

A. No.

Q. Do you think you could go back and do your old job as a service technician at XYZ?

A. No.

Q. What would prevent you from doing that?

A. Every single thing that you do at the electric company is looking up or, like, especially that extendo-thing drawing on capacitor banks. You have to get directly underneath the switch and run a thirty-five-foot pole up there, bend halfway over backwards and get a little tiny bar into a ring about that big (indicating). I would think that would be impossible. And working on streetlights, you have to—once you set up the bucket truck and get up there, you have to directly get under the streetlight and then look straight up into it. So, I mean, everything is not just looking up a little bit. I mean, you've got to look way up. And they even the line patrol, normally—like, for example, if I had to patrol this line going down Elm Street, you ride on the inside lane of traffic with your rotating light on, and pull over off the side of the road, use a pair of binoculars, and you've got to bend yourself up under the windshield to look up on that pole. And then, when you drive by the pole, depending on what type of equipment is on the pole, you've got to twist around in the seat, go over sideways and look out the back window. There's just no way on earth that I could do that.

Q. Can you think of any accommodation that could be made for you to go back to your old job?

A. Could you think of any accommodations? How do you not look up? You know, I mean, if you're in the bucket and you come and here's the streetlight and you've got to drop the lid, and then you've got to actually—all the guts are inside of it. You know, it's not just changing a bulb. That actually reminds me of repairing streetlights. They would have trouble then. They would go by in their spare time and would try a bulb. If the bulb worked, they would consider it complete. If it didn't work, they would write a memo to me to go fix the light. There's capacitors, starting aids, photocell sockets and different connections in there that you've really got to bend and twist and really look up in there to try to spot what is the problem with it. And then, you know try to change the capacitor in something that's—I mean, you've got to bend your neck.

Q. Before your employment ended and before the surgery—

A. Uh-huh.

Q. —you had been a long-term employee with XYZ?

A. Yes.

Q. How were your performance appraisals?

A. Excellent. Well, you know, back when I was an apprentice or something, not wearing gloves, you know. But as far as the department that I was last in for the last ten years, all performance—my efficiency ratings were the highest among the four people who did the job that I did.

Q. What were your plans for your career before the surgery in 2008?
A. I planned on staying doing exactly what I was doing until hopefully, around fifty-eight, they were going to offer me a package to retire early, and I would leave. And I would have plenty of money saved up. And I thoroughly enjoyed the job that I had. It's considered one of the best in the line department jobs that you could have. And only four of us had it out of the whole company.
Q. What about now, what are your plans for your career?
A. I'm thinking about the school board. That's about the only thing I've been able to come up with. And I'm really not—I believe that I'll be able to do that. Now, will I get it, I don't have any idea.
Q. Are you actually going to run as a county—
A. Yes, I think. I'm considering it.
Q. When is the election?
A. It would be November 4th of this year.
Q. Year 2014, right?
A. Yes.
Q. Do you know what that job pays?
A. I have a ballpark idea that it might pay $28,000. But I'm not a hundred percent positive. It might only be $22,000. I really don't know.
Q. $22,000, $28,000, somewhere in there?
A. Yes. Somewhere in there is what I believe it pays.
Q. And that's not a full-time job, is it?
A. I don't think so, right.
Q. Tell me why you believe you're qualified as a serious candidate who could actually get—
A. I put three kids through our public school—private school in the beginning and through our public school system, and I know what I can't stand about our public school system, and I know—I believe I would be able to make a difference socially in that type of job.
Q. Do you have the support of the Republican Party?
A. There are three different people that are—that I've talked to about it, and they said that they would back me in that, but that's three people. I think I would need more than their votes, but they are people on the executive committee. I feel confident I can get at least three votes, mine and my wife's and my son's.
Q. Good start. You would be in trouble if you didn't have those, right?
A. Yeah.
Q. If you were to be elected, do you believe you would be able to perform the job duties?
A. I'm not a hundred percent positive what the job duties are, but I've seen the type of chairs that they sit in, and they're extremely comfortable chairs.
Q. So you believe you could perform the job?
A. Yes. They're better than I've seen in your office, and you've got some nice-looking chairs.
Q. They're high-back.
A. Yeah. They've got the big—actually, some ladies that sit there, the chairs probably come about a foot over their heads.
Q. Well, let me ask you a question in that regard. If you were provided an ergonomically correct chair that fit you—
A. What did you call it?
Q. Ergonomics is the—
A. Supportive chair.
Q. —supportive chair that would give you the support that you believe you need—
A. Uh-huh.
Q. —for your head and your neck. Do you believe you would be capable of performing an office-based job?
A. Yes.
Q. On a regular, ongoing basis?
A. It depends, you know, you can't just sit back and have a reclining chair there all day. I'm sure there's got to be something involved. Like with the school board scenario, that's not eight hours a day in the chair, you know. It depends on what you're doing in the chair. Do you know what I mean?
Q. Like with telephone work, typical office jobs.
A. You know, I've always had a problem with that because I've worked outside all my life. And one of the guys that used to work with me went to an inside job. And we start kidding him, "How in the world can you sit there all day?" You know, "How do you sit in this office all day?" And we make fun of him like that. I really have a hard time comprehending what somebody does in a chair for eight hours a day. I know you're doing something. You're doing an office job.
Q. This is pretty much how I spend much of my day—talking to people, writing, reviewing documents, using a computer, talking on the phone.
A. I think I could do that.
Q. So you do believe you could perform a sit-down job if you had a correct chair?
A. Yeah, more than likely, I think so.
Q. What do you believe your earning capacity is right now if you were to go out and look for a job? You obviously think $22,000 to $28,000 is at least within your reach.
A. Well, no, that's what I would like to be able to get. Actually, a little running joke from some phrase I read somewhere—I can read, write, and make change—is my capabilities. So I don't know what you can do when you read, write, and make change. Work at a convenience store? I don't know. But my son actually works at a convenience store, and he gets paid $8 an hour. But I don't know that I could do that for

a straight eight hours, you know, standing there or sitting on a stool and doing the type of stuff that you have to do.

Q. Have you applied for any job since—

A. No.

Q. Do you intend to look for a job?

A. Yes.

Q. When?

A. Shoot for the—I'm seriously considering shooting for the school board.

Q. Is there any reason that you haven't applied for any jobs since your second neck surgery?

A. I don't know how—I don't have any idea of what I can do. Somebody—you know, if I could find a job that I could go there when I felt good and only do what didn't bother me, I will certainly try one. That's why I'm thinking about the school board. I think that's something that meets—I don't know if I'm qualified enough to do it, but from what I've seen so far, I feel that I could physically do that job. That's the job that I've seen that I believe that I could do. And that's what I'm shooting for. Because I can work in pain if I know: Okay, I've got to go off and I've got to do this this evening, go to a meeting or I've got to do this for this day. But if I've got to do this this day and then do it the next day and the next and the next and the next, I would just as soon not, as try to do something that I'm locked into rigidly on a repetitive basis, like a normal-type job that you have to show up nine to five, or whatever, every single day. I feel like I would be calling in sick and not be able to, you know, do it. And I'd hate to be fired, and I don't like rejection.

Q. You have questions about your ability to maintain sustained employment?

A. Exactly.

Q. Would you be amenable to retraining?

A. Yes.

Q. Have you approached any organization or agency like the Division of Vocational Rehabilitation for help in your career?

A. I don't know who they are, so, no, I have not.

2. Administration of standardized tests

Standardized tests vocational experts administer generally relate to three broad categories: mental functioning abilities (these include tests popularly known as IQ or aptitude tests), personality, and occupational interest. Table 4.1 identifies tests frequently used in vocational evaluations.

The battery of tests examiners prescribe varies. In some cases, an expert's familiarity with a test and expertise in interpreting its results influences test selection. In other cases, accessibility to standardized tests may determine tests used. Test publishers restrict access to standardized tests, and the measures require varied qualifications to purchase and administer. Regulatory and credentialing organizations specify minimum requirements those who purchase the instruments must possess. Inappropriately using tests, misinterpreting test results, and reckless or misleading use of standardized test data can have deleterious consequences for all parties relying on an evaluation's findings.

Restrictions on test procurement vary and depend on conditions such as constructs a test measures and the degree of skill and training necessary to administer and interpret its results. Generally, measures of intelligence and personality have more restrictions on procurement than other measures.

Test results can provide objective information on many subtle personality factors. Constructs ranging from addiction proneness to potential for creative initiative, for example, can be assessed when valid personality test data is obtained and accurately interpreted. Some standardized tests—such as the Minnesota Multiphasic Personality Inventory-2 (MMPI-2)—include validity measures that examine a subject's behavioral tendencies including symptom magnification, denial, and over virtuous presentation. Shahnasarian, Lassiter, and Kaiser-Ulrey (2006) discussed the use of the MMPI-2 in ¬vocational rehabilitation evaluations. Aptitude and ability tests can measure constructs ranging from general intelligence to distinct areas of aptitude and ability, such as manual speed and dexterity, and visual analysis capabilities. Interest inventories help discern a subject's vocational preferences and aid in career decision-making and planning.

In all cases, test batteries vocational experts prescribe should be made considering referral questions, prevailing facts, and examinee background characteristics. A carefully selected test battery that is appropriately administered, accurately interpreted, and skillfully integrated with other assessment data helps provide a strong foundation for an expert's opinions and allows the expert to make valid inferences about pending vocational questions. Experts must weigh information obtained through standardized testing with all other evidence that emerges during a vocational rehabilitation evaluation.

Obtaining valid test data requires examiners' compliance with test administration, scoring, and interpretation protocols. Accordingly, examiners must comply with standards published in test manuals and promulgated by professional associations. Of course, examiners should interpret and rely only upon test data that can be competently used.

Any departure from standard testing protocol should be noted and considered when interpreting test results. Unusual

Table 4.1
Frequently Administered Tests in Vocational Evaluations

Test Category	Examples of Frequently Administered Tests
Mental Functioning	Career Ability Placement Survey Multidimensional Aptitude Battery - II Shipley Institute of Living Scale Slosson Full-Range Intelligence Test Stanford Binet Intelligence Scales - Fifth Edition Wechsler Adult Intelligence Scale - Third Edition Wechsler Intelligence Scale for Children - Fourth Edition Wechsler Memory Scale - Third Edition Wide Range Achievement Test - 3 Wonderlic Personnel Test
Personality	Beck Depression Inventory - Second Edition California Personality Inventory Children's Depression Inventory Culture-Free Self-Esteem Inventory Millon Clinical Multiaxial Inventory - III Minnesota Multiphasic Personality Inventory - 2 Revised NEO Personality Inventory 16 Personality Factor Test
Occupational Interests	Campbell Interest and Skill Survey Kuder Occupational Interest Scales Self-Directed Search Strong Interest Inventory

circumstances may include extending accommodations to subjects, such as providing a functionally illiterate subject with a reader during testing or providing a translator for a non-English-speaking subject. Observing a subject's behavior during testing can also be insightful. Excessive breaks during testing, for example, may underlie an examinee's trouble maintaining attention or performing under stress. Further, analyzing an examinee's performance on an intelligence test may reveal tendencies to expend inconsistent or suppressed levels of effort. Extraneous factors that could inhibit performance, such as an examinee's long fingernails on a task requiring hand-eye coordination, should also be noted.

When prescribing a test battery, examiners should ascertain whether the examinee has recently taken the test(s) planned for administration. An examinee's familiarity with a test could lead to spurious results. Cultural issues must also be considered when selecting standardized tests and interpreting results.

Vocational experts often receive requests for an examinee's test data through subpoenas or depositions. Experts should comply with administrative codes that govern the safekeeping and transmittal of standardized test records within her jurisdiction and respond accordingly. Absent a court order requiring the release of test data, administrative codes in most jurisdictions require experts to release restricted test data only to appropriately qualified professionals.

More information about psychometric assessment in forensic vocational rehabilitation appears in Robinson and Drew (2014).

C. Labor Market and Associated Research

Vocational experts typically conduct labor market research to address questions spawned from an analysis of clinical interview and standardized test information. Labor market and associated research frequently relates to:

- Skill level and functional requirements associated with occupations in question
- General availability of jobs and current job openings
- Retraining programs including specific programs, duration and cost of training, and earnings ranges of graduates
- Prevailing wages associated with occupations in question
- Projections about demand for incumbents employed in various occupations
- Industry trends
- Availability of adaptive aids

Sources of the information cited above include U.S. Department of Labor publications, state departments of labor and other organizations that gather and distribute occupational information, education and training institutions, professional and trade associations, employment agencies, job advertisements, wage surveys, vendors of adaptive equipment, the World Wide Web, and people resources including employers, placement specialists, and human resources personnel. An examiner's knowledge, resourcefulness, and creativity contributes to the quality and type of information obtained. Barros-Bailey and Heitzman (2014) outlined methods to conduct labor market research, and Barros-Bailey and Karman (2014) discussed types of occupational and labor market information of interest to forensic vocational consultants, along with sources to obtain the information.

A vocational expert's research of adaptive aids in a case that involved a young cardiologist who sustained a hearing loss proved particularly helpful. Because the cardiologist regularly used stethoscopes to detect potential problems such as heart murmurs, intact hearing was essential. Indeed, with impaired hearing, his continued practice of medicine raised questions of whether he was meeting an acceptable standard of care. Because of his concerns, the cardiologist ceased practicing. After obtaining records detailing the cardiologist's hearing deficits, the vocational expert contacted several stethoscope manufacturers. One manufacturer collaborated with the cardiologist's audiologist to develop a customized stethoscope with an amplification device; this initiative salvaged the cardiologist's career development within his specialty and preempted a potentially large claim of loss of earning capacity.

D. Consultations and Collateral Sources of Information

In addition to information obtained from an examinee, available records, and independent research, vocational experts occasionally seek information from collateral sources when assessing earning capacity. Experts pursue this data because of questions that arise during a clinical interview or from information gathered while analyzing a case's facts. Occasionally, examinees, such as persons with brain injuries or children, cannot provide the requested information. In other cases, examinees may be noncompliant or less than fully cooperative.

The following are the most common sources of collateral information:

- Family members, significant others, and caregivers
- Employers
- Case managers
- Other experts

A summary of the type of information that may be helpful from each of these sources follows.

1. Family members, significant others, and caregivers

Family members, significant others, and caregivers sometimes corroborate or contradict an examinee's report, as well as provide information when an examinee is uncertain or lacking information. Additionally, they can clarify an examinee's statements, provide a different perspective, and/or provide supplemental information that allows an examiner to more fully assess information elicited from an examinee. Examiners typically solicit information from family members or significant others under the following conditions:

- An examinee's mentation is an issue (e.g., head injury, condition requiring a guardian, psychological problems).
- An examinee's credibility is questionable.
- An individual may have a low level of mental functioning (e.g., limited intellect, academic underachievement).
- Cultural differences prevail.
- The examinee depends upon others for significant care activities (e.g., basic self-care, managing household finances, and limited ability to participate in activities of daily living, such as performing household chores and engaging in childcare activities).
- The spouse of a plaintiff may be pursuing a consortium claim that merits a vocational rehabilitation expert's attention.

Consider, for example, the case of a twenty-eight-year-old male who had a slip-and-fall accident in a supermarket. His background included a ninth-grade education, learning disabilities, and preinjury employment limited to unskilled, heavy work. The plaintiff's wife had been the family's primary wage earner. Because of the accident, the plaintiff developed orthopedic and chronic pain problems that precluded him from returning to work. Further, he alleged his limited intellect rendered him dependent on his wife to manage their finances and most activities required to maintain their home. He contended his acquired disabilities rendered him unable to provide his daughter consistent and complete childcare services. Consequently, his wife's family responsibilities and obligations increased, and she was unable to pursue her career development as aggressively as she had before her husband's accident. A jury awarded her compensation for damages to her career development and for the lost value of her husband's services. After her husband's accident, the plaintiff's wife pursued less-demanding employment—so she could care for her husband and daughter—at a lower rate of pay than what she had been earning before her husband became injured. This case illustrates the importance of conducting a comprehensive vocational rehabilitation assessment that considers the earning capacity of the examinee as well as those who have also been affected by issues in dispute.

In all cases, vocational experts who desire to consult with a collateral source should make this interest known to their retaining party before initiating it, and they should attain approval/authority before proceeding. In most cases, experts retained by counsel opposing a plaintiff are prohibited from contacting any party who has a relationship with the plaintiff, such as healthcare providers, family members, and employers.

2. Employers

A subject's most recent employer, as well as past employers, may provide insight about an examinee's job responsibilities, performance compensation, and work habits, which can refine opinions about earning capacity. Employers may also be able to address questions in disability cases about the viability of job accommodations and the possibility of placing an examinee in an alternate position. In all cases, examiners should obtain permission before contacting an examinee's recent or past employers. Paquette and Heitzman (2014) discussed job analysis techniques.

3. Case managers

Occasionally, the subject of an earning capacity evaluation will have received vocational rehabilitation services from a case manager. Case managers—whose jobs are to facilitate injured workers' disability adjustment and return-to-work initiatives—often participate in workers' compensation cases. They sometimes coordinate treatment and provide guidance on retraining, job placement, and job coaching.

A vocational expert's consultation with a case manager employed by a large manufacturing company proved especially helpful in a case involving an injured machine operator. The case manager and vocational expert pooled their knowledge of the subject and collaborated on how his residual abilities could be harnessed and applied in a new position. Management at the company was amenable to the proposal of developing a new position for the subject, enabling him to resume work in a challenging position at his preinjury rate of pay.

4. Other experts

For purposes of assessing earning capacity, information documented in records that a vocational expert reviews may be incomplete, in need of clarification, or dated. In cases such as these, consultation with other experts may be in order. For instance, questions a vocational expert may develop about special workplace requirements, restrictions, and prognoses can be addressed during a consultation with a physiatrist—a doctor specializing in physical medicine and rehabilitation—who is familiar with an examinee.

Vocational experts should be aware that other experts may seek their input, including those treating the subject and those solely involved in litigation the subject is pursuing. For example, physicians consult with qualified rehabilitation professionals for guidance on how to facilitate their patients' return to work after treatment. This occurs most often when the examiner also possesses expertise in areas such as psychology and case management. Physicians may solicit information to help with decisions ranging from prescribing medication to prescribing skilled care. Economists and accountants often rely on vocational experts' opinions in their computation of damages associated with wage loss claims, and will occasionally inquire about details of an expert's vocational opinion.

4.3 Conclusion

Situations arise in which adhering to the procedures for conducting an assessment of earning capacity as specified in this chapter is neither possible nor practical. A subject in a wrongful death case, for instance, obviously cannot be examined by a vocational expert. Time constraints, a subject's impaired status, or unavailability of a subject may also require deviations from generally accepted methods. Any departure from standard methods as well as unusual occurrences that arise during the evaluation process should be noted.

Appendix 4.1: Sample Letter Addressing Copying Costs and Associated Logistics

Via Facsimile

Date: ____________________

Client Name: ______________________________

Career Consultants of America/Dr. Michael Shahnasarian has been issued a subpoena/request to provide copies of the materials we have in our file relative to the above-named individual.

To expedite this request, we ask that you provide a purchase order or an authorized signature by return fax. Until we have received one or the other of these, we cannot begin the copying process. Because there are large quantities of copies, you may be requested to forward a prepayment.

Copy charges are in accordance with Florida Statute 64BS-10.03 Costs of Reproducing Medical Records

(2a.) For the first 25 pages, the cost shall be $1.00 per page

(2b.) For each page in excess of 25, the cost shall be $0.25.

(3.) For other entities, the reasonable costs of reproducing copies of written or typed documents or reports shall not be more than $1.00 per page.

Additionally, for shipping we will charge whatever amount we are charged, based on the courier or delivery service used, either FedEx or Choice (for local deliveries). The rate charged for our personnel to spend time preparing files for copying, such as sorting, and shipping is $50.00 per hour.

Thank you for your cooperation. Please note that all charges are approximate.

Estimated cost for approximately 300 copies, records custodian fee, and shipping is :

25 pages @ $1 per page -	**$ 25.00**
275 pages @ $0.25 per page -	**$ 68.75**
Shipping (Choice)	**$ 25.00**
Records Custodian fee (1 hour)	**$ 50.00**
TOTAL CHARGES	**$168.75**

Name of Firm______________________________ Date____________

Purchase Order No. ___________________________

Authorized Signature _________________________

Please return to Attn: Margaret Meade, Records Custodian

Appendix 4.2: Client Intake Form

Please complete this form in detail. If needed, ask for assistance. Not all questions will apply; write *N/A* (not applicable) if questions do not apply, and use the back of pages, if necessary.

BACKGROUND INFORMATION (please print)

First Name:	Middle:	Last:
Address:		
City:	State:	Zip:

Home Phone: ______________________ Mobile Phone: __________________

Date of Birth: ______________________ Age: ___________________________

How did you get to the exam? ____

Please respond to the following:	Yes	No	Comment
Do you have a valid driver's license?	☐	☐	____________________
Do you have doctor-advised driving restrictions?	☐	☐	____________________
Do you have problems with driving?	☐	☐	____________________

Date of Accident/Incident _________________

Please generally describe accident/incident. ____

____

Did you strike your head? ☐ Yes ☐ No ☐ Don't Know

Did you lose consciousness? ☐ Yes ☐ No ☐ Don't Know If so, for how long? ____________________

List each problem you have as a result of the accident/incident. Continue on the back if necessary. Be specific.

1) ____
2) ____
3) ____
4) ____
5) ____
6) ____
7) ____

What problems listed above, if any, did you have **before** the accident/incident?

____

Check problems with mental functioning you have had **since** the accident/incident.
☐ No Problems
☐ Memory Problems
☐ Concentration Problems
☐ Mental Alertness Problems
☐ Speech Problems
☐ Attention Span Problems
☐ Other

Please provide examples of any problems you checked:

____

____

Race: ____________________ Are you: ☐ Right-handed ☐ Left-handed ☐ Both

Birthplace: _________ Citizenship:____________ First Language (if not English): ____________

Height: __________ **Current** Weight: __________ Weight **Before** Injury/Incident: ___________

What caused your weight change? ____

____

Describe your efforts to control your weight: _______________________________________

Marital Status ___________ Date Married _____________ Number of times married? __________

Spouse/Partner's Name (first and last) _____________Spouse/Partner's Date of Birth ____________

Spouse/Partner's Job Title and Place of Employment ___________________________________

Names, ages and gender of your children: ____

____

Describe any disabling problems or special needs your spouse/partner or children have:__________

____

Describe your home (*Example: 2,000 sq. ft. 2-story house, 800 sq. ft. apartment, 1,500 sq. ft. mobile home, etc.*):

____

What is the size of property your home is located on?______________________

How long have you lived at your present home? __________________________

Do you: ☐ rent your home or ☐ own your home?

If you lived somewhere other than your current home at the time of the accident or incident, explain your reasons for relocation: ____

____

Do you plan to leave your home? Explain if necessary:_________________________________

Describe any changes you have made to your home due to disabilities (*Example: installed ramp, installed handrails, etc.)*: ____________________

Is access within your home limited? If so, how? ____________________

Do you have any pets or farm animals? If so, please describe:____________________

How many people live with you and how are they related? (*Example: John Smith, Uncle, 72 years old)*____________________

At the time of your injury/incident, what was your job title? ____________________

Employer ____________________ Rate of pay ____________________

Present employment status: ☐ Employed ☐ Unemployed ☐ Disability

Present job title: ____________________

Present employer: ____________________

Present rate of pay: ____________________

PHYSICAL CONDITION AND MEDICAL INFORMATION

What is your understanding of diagnoses physicians have rendered?

____

____

List each surgery you had **before** the accident/incident.

Type of Surgery	***Year or Age***	***Surgeon***

Please describe below any significant medical problems you had prior to the accident/incident.

____

____

Of the problems you acquired as a result of the accident/incident, what is your primary problem(s)? Please explain. ____________________

____

____

If you are having problems with pain, please identify the affected body parts and provide information about your pain using a 0-to-10 scale (zero indicates no pain and 10 represents the worst pain possible):

Body Part in Pain	**Pain Intensity on 0-10 scale**	**Activities/conditions that worsen pain**	**Comments**

List your doctors treating for problems associated with the accident/incident in question:

Doctor's Name	***Specialty***	***Last Appointment***

List the doctor, examination date, and reason for your last doctor's visit.

____

____

List scheduled appointments you have with medical professionals and note the reason.

____

____

List each surgery you had **after** the accident/incident.

Type of Surgery	***Year or Age***	***Surgeon***

Are you scheduled for other surgery? If so, list the surgeries and dates. Also, list recommended/anticipated surgeries.

Type of Surgery	***Date of Surgery***	***Surgeon***

Since the accident/incident, have you had any unrelated medical problems? If so, please explain.

____

____

____

Check each type of treatment you have had **since** the incident/injury:

- ☐ Physical Therapy
- ☐ Occupational Therapy
- ☐ Speech Therapy
- ☐ Massage Therapy
- ☐ Aquatic Therapy
- ☐ Psychotherapy/Counseling
- ☐ Group Therapy
- ☐ Biofeedback
- ☐ Other: ____________________
- ☐ Cognitive Rehabilitation
- ☐ Acupuncture
- ☐ Chiropractic Treatment
- ☐ Prescribed Home Exercise
- ☐ Pain Management
- ☐ Specify any injections you have had:

____

____

____

List **current** treatment/therapy. ______________________________

List all adaptive aids you use (*Example: cane, TENS unit, lumbar support pillow, traction device, cervical collar, etc.*). ______________________________

____

List your medications. Continue on back of this page if necessary, or provide a medication list, if available.

Medication	***Purpose***	***Dosage/Frequency***

Which medications listed above were you taking **before** the accident/incident?

____

Describe side effects caused by medication: ______________________________

____

Have you taken medication within the last 24 hours? If so, describe.

____

____

PHYSICAL CAPACITIES

How much weight can you safely lift and carry? ______________________

Has any physician advised a lifting restriction? If so, explain.

____

What problems, if any, do you have when lifting?______________________

Check all problems below that you have. Describe your problems in the space provided.

☐ Turning head to right ______________________

☐ Turning head to left ______________________

☐ Bending head forward ______________________

☐ Leaning head back ______________________

☐ Use of right hand or arm ______________________

☐ Use of left hand or arm ______________________

☐ Use of right foot or leg ______________________

☐ Use of left foot or leg ______________________

OTHER PROBLEMS:

____

____

____

Using the definitions below, rate your **current** ability to perform the following physical activities during an 8-hour work day, even if you are not employed at present (assume regularly scheduled breaks).

1 – Never	Cannot do for any amount of time	
2 – Occasionally	Up to 33% of the time	(0–2.3 hrs/day)
3 – Frequently	From 34% to 66% of the time	(2.3–5.5 hrs/day)
4 – Constantly	More than 67% of the time	(5.5+ hrs/day)

	Circle One				*Explanation*
Walking	1	2	3	4	______________
Standing	1	2	3	4	______________
Sitting	1	2	3	4	______________
Bending at waist	1	2	3	4	______________
Squatting	1	2	3	4	______________
Kneeling or getting on hands/knees	1	2	3	4	______________
Climbing stairs	1	2	3	4	______________
Pushing/pulling	1	2	3	4	______________
Reaching with right hand	1	2	3	4	______________
Reaching with left hand	1	2	3	4	______________
Handling	1	2	3	4	______________
Gripping right hand	1	2	3	4	______________
Gripping left hand	1	2	3	4	______________
Right-arm extension overhead	1	2	3	4	______________
Left-arm extension overhead	1	2	3	4	______________
Right-arm extension horizontal	1	2	3	4	______________
Left-arm extension horizontal	1	2	3	4	______________
Driving	1	2	3	4	______________

In general, how many minutes/hours are you able to do the following without resting or overexerting yourself?

Walk ______________ Stand ______________ Sit ______________ Drive ______________

What type of transmission does the vehicle you drive have? ☐ automatic ☐ manual

Have changes been made to it? ______________ How often do you drive? ______________

Do you have a disabled person parking placard? ______________

Describe any problems you have with driving: ______________________________

____

Do you have trouble with the following? If so, explain.

Balance***	N	Y	______________
Hearing	N	Y	______________
Vision	N	Y	______________

Smell N Y ____________________

Taste N Y ____________________

Breathing N Y ____________________

Bowel/bladder N Y ____________________

Dental Health N Y ____________________

Fatigue N Y ____________________

***Have you fallen since the accident/incident? Describe any subsequent falls.

____

*** Have you had medical care or additional problems because of subsequent falls? Please explain.

____

Check all conditions that worsen your problems, and explain your difficulty.

☐ Outdoors ____________________

☐ Cold Temperatures ____________________

☐ Hot Temperatures ____________________

☐ Dampness/High Humidity ____________________

☐ Noise ____________________

☐ Vibration ____________________

☐ Fumes, dusts, gases ____________________

List all restrictions your physicians have advised.

Physician	***Restrictions***

ACTIVITIES OF DAILY LIVING

Do you have problems sleeping? ______ If so, what is the cause?

____

____

____

How many hours do you sleep per night? ____________________

What time do you usually go to sleep? ____________________

What time do you usually wake up? ____________________

Do you nap? If so, explain. ____________________

List all sleep aid medications you take.

____

Do you have problems with nightmares? If so, describe any repeated themes.

____

Do you have problems with grooming or self-care? If so, describe.

____

If any people assist you in your daily care, please note who helps you and the type of assistance provided. ____

Are there household chores you did **before** the injury/incident that you cannot do now? If so, list them here.

____

____

Please identify below any service(s) you employ because of the accident/incident.

Services	Cost	Comment
Housekeeping	________	______________________________
Yard Maintenance	________	______________________________
Pool Maintenance	________	______________________________
Personal Care	________	______________________________

Other/Explanation: ____

____

____

Please describe your current leisure activities, and provide an explanation, if applicable, for any change **since** the accident/incident in question.

____

____

____

____

Please describe in detail how you spend a typical day.

____

____

____

____

____

____

MENTAL HEALTH

Please indicate if you have experienced any of the following, and provide an explanation for items you checked yes:

Yes	No		Explanation
☐	☐	Mental health treatment before the subject incident	______________________
☐	☐	Family history of mental illness	______________________
☐	☐	Prescriptions of antidepressants or other psychotropic drugs before the subject incident	______________________
☐	☐	Loss of consciousness before the subject incident	______________________
☐	☐	Do you believe you currently need mental health treatment?	______________________

Have you ever had any mental health treatment **before** the incident in question? If so, please describe.
____
____

Please describe all mental health treatment you had **after** the incident in question.
____
____

Use the following scale (1–4) to indicate the extent that the mental health problems listed concern you:

(1) Not at all (2) Somewhat (3) Moderately (4) Very much

____ Anger
____ Anxiety/Stress Management
____ Change in Eating Pattern
____ Child Management Problems
____ Conflict with Family Members
____ Concern about Physical Health
____ Feeling Depressed
____ Marital or Significant Other Relationship
____ Financial Problems
____ Legal Problems
____ Loneliness
____ Use of Alcohol or Drugs
____ Sexual Problems
____ Thoughts of Suicide
____ Feeling Guilty

Please explain your primary mental health concerns: ______________________
____
____

EDUCATION AND SPECIAL TRAINING

	Name	Major/Degree	Dates Attended	Graduation Date
High School				
Vocational Training				
College				
College				
Graduate School				
Employer-Sponsored Training				
Employer-Sponsored Training				
Employer-Sponsored Training				
Continuing Education				
Other Training				

How did you perform in school? ______________________________

____

If you were tested in the following, note your score.

SAT ____________ ACT ____________ Other ____________

☐ I do not recall scores from prior standardized testing.

Did you ever repeat a grade in K-12? If so, what grades and why? ______________________________

____

While in school, what kind of classes were you in:

☐ Regular classes ☐ Honors classes

☐ Accelerated classes ☐ Remedial classes

☐ Special education ☐ Emotionally handicapped

☐ Other special programming: ______________________________

Please explain: ______________________________

____

List any special skills you have (*Example: computer, foreign languages, musical, athletic, artistic, etc.*).

____

____

List all the work-related credentials you hold or have held (*Example: licenses, certifications, registrations, etc.*).

____

____

Describe on-the-job training you have had. ______________________________

____

Do you have access to a computer? ☐ Yes ☐ No Describe your computer skills (*Example: software you are able to use, programming skills, etc.*):______________________________

____

List skills that you have developed through training and work experience. Please be specific.

____

____

____

____

____

Have you considered retraining? ☐ Yes ☐ No If so, describe. ______________________________

____

WORK EXPERIENCE

List each job you have held. Start with your most recent job and continue in reverse order. **It is important to fully complete this information.**

JOB TITLE	EMPLOYER	DATES	WAGES	REASON FOR LEAVING

CAREER DEVELOPMENT

Which job do you consider your most skilled or challenging? ________________________________

____

Were you ever terminated from a job? ☐ Yes ☐ No If so, from what job(s) and why? ______________

____

Have you ever made a claim for workers' compensation benefits? ☐ Yes ☐ No If so, explain.

____

How many hours per week did you work at the time of the injury/incident? ____________________

Describe employment benefits associated with the job you held at the time of the injury/incident.

____

____

Describe the job responsibilities you had at the time of the injury/incident. ____________________

____

____

____

What was the heaviest amount of weight you lifted/carried in your job?

____

List your job's physical requirements (*Example: extended sitting or standing, climbing ladders, exposure to extreme temperatures, etc.*). ____

____

____

Did you take time off work **after** the injury/incident? If so, how long? ______________________

____

Describe any military experience you have had. Include branch of service, dates, discharge rank, military occupation, and type of discharge. ____

____

List volunteer work experience you have had during the past 5 years.

____

List other organizations in which you participate (*Example: church, social clubs, community organizations, etc.*).

____

____

What were your employment earnings during the year **before** the injury/incident? ________________

____

What were your highest earnings during your work career? Please list the amount and year. ____________________

____

Estimate your average monthly expenses. ____

Describe your financial situation. ____

____

List all sources and amounts of your present income.

Source	***Amount per Month***

Have you applied to the Social Security Administration for disability benefits? ____________________

If so, what was the disposition on your application? ______________________________________

____

I certify that I have completed the information requested accurately and to the best of my ability.

______________________________ ______________________________

Signature **Date**

Copyright 2014. Career Consultants of America, Inc. All rights reserved.

Appendix 4.3: Sample Clinical Interview

IN THE CIRCUIT COURT OF THE TWELFTH JUDICIAL CIRCUIT
IN AND FOR MANATEE COUNTY, FLORIDA
CIVIL ACTION

CASE NO: 2014 CA 01234

NATALIE I. COOPER

Plaintiff,

vs.

LUCY A. CROSS AND A1A
AUTOMOBILE INSURANCE
COMPANY,

Defendants.
________________________________/

VIDEOTAPED COMPULSORY VOCATIONAL EXAMINATION OF

NATALIE COOPER

EXAMINED BY: Michael Shahnasarian, Ph.D.

DATE: June 28, 2012

TIME: 8:01 a.m. to 12:27 p.m.

PLACE: Bradenton Hotel
Beach Drive West
Bradenton, Florida

REPORTED BY: AnneMarie Rogers, Court Reporter
Notary Public
State of Florida at Large

VIDEOGRAPHER: Joanna Miller, Videographer

COMPULSORY VOCATIONAL EXAMINATION

Q. Okay. Good morning again, Ms. Cooper.
A. Good morning.
Q. I introduced myself while we were waiting for the court reporter. I'm Dr. Michael Shahnasarian. And what I have been asked to do is to conduct a vocational rehabilitation evaluation today. That's what I'm going to be doing. They're going to be two parts to the exam. One part is going to be the interview, which I'm going to do first. And during the inter-

view, I'm going to be asking you questions about your injuries. I have a fair amount of information from records I've reviewed, so I am familiar with your case. We're here specifically about your February 26, 2007, auto accident.

A. Right.

Q. And what I'm going to be asking you are questions about injuries that you sustained as a result of the accident, how they affect you, what limitations you may have, what restrictions you have. I'll ask you more about your job. I know you were a bank teller.

A. Yeah.

Q. Okay. And I'll ask you about that and how your injuries affect or don't affect your ability to do your job that you still are doing and so forth—

A. Okay.

Q. —okay?

A. Yep.

Q. And I will ask you other types of questions generally about your injuries because I'm also going to be considering future needs that you have, rehabilitation needs specifically.

A. Okay.

Q. We're obviously being recorded today, and your lawyer, Mr. Marx, had requested that this be video recorded. You're aware of that, obviously, there's a lot of equipment right in front you.

A. Yes.

Q. Okay. And of course, there's a court reporter who's sitting at your right-hand side. You're aware of that as well?

A. Yes.

Q. Okay. And do I have your permission to proceed with this examination being recorded?

A. Yes.

Q. Okay. If there's something you don't understand that I say at any time today, please let me know, either that I say or something that's in writing, let me know. Otherwise, if you respond, I will assume that you understood what I'm asking you.

A. Okay.

Q. And if you need a break, let me know as well. We'll be very informal. This is not a medical exam. I'm not going to be doing any type of physical examination of you. It's going to be basically, as I said, two parts: questions that I'm going to ask you during the interview, and then the second part is going to be the testing. And when we get to that part, I will explain it to you. But it's basically paper and pencil testing. Some of it's going to be aptitude, some of it's going to be interests, and some of it's going to be personality.

A. Okay.

Q. So I expect our interview will go about three hours more or less. We'll take breaks about every hour and ten minutes. The video recorder informed me that she has tapes that need to be changed about that interval—

A. Okay.

Q. —so that's a natural time to take a break. But if you want to take a break, you know, at any time before then, let me know—

A. Okay.

Q. —okay? I will be very sensitive to that.

A. Okay.

Q. Also, if there's anything else I can do to make you as comfortable as possible, let me know. You're also aware that I'm not going to be treating you.

A. Correct.

Q. I'm just here today for the evaluation—

A. Right.

Q. —and as part of the litigation that you're pursuing.

A. Right.

Q. So part of what that means is that we're not going to have a traditional doctor to patient relationship.

A. Right.

Q. If you were to come to see me privately, things you would tell me would be confidential, they'd be privileged.

A. Right.

Q. But because of the nature of my involvement in your case, other parties are going to have access to data that comes from today.

A. Yes.

Q. You understand that?

A. Yes.
Q. Okay. And do I have your consent and permission to proceed with that understanding?
A. Yes.
Q. Okay. I'm going to apologize in advance because this is going to be a little bit painstaking. I'm going to go through a very structured interview so that I collect the information that I need to collect in an organized way. So if you can be patient with me. As I said, I'm going to apologize because it is a little bit painstaking. But I brought some records with me. I'm going to be referring to them, I'm going to be taking a lot of notes, and if you can just bear with my interview structure, that would be very helpful.
A. Yeah. Sure.
Q. How did you get here today, Ms. Cooper?
A. I drove.
Q. Okay. You live in Bradenton?
A. Yes.
Q. And you came in what type of vehicle, an automobile, SUV?
A. My car.
Q. Okay. And is it automatic transmission?
A. Yes.
Q. How long was your commute?
A. Ten minutes.
Q. And you have a valid driver's license I take it?
A. Yes.
Q. I have a date of birth of 3-15-68. Is that right?
A. Yes.
Q. Do you have any doctor-advised driving restrictions?
A. No.
Q. Okay. So you're 44 years old?
A. Yes.
Q. Any problems with driving?
A. No. I do have a problem where I try to be careful for my neck, sometimes with bending, but other than that, no.
Q. Generally no problems, but you have some problems when you move your neck side to side or up or down?
A. Right.
Q. Okay.
A. So I try to be extra careful pulling out.
Q. Do you wear contact lenses or eyeglasses?
A. No.
Q. How is your vision?
A. I'm supposed to have 20/20. I had LASIK done a number of years back.
Q. Did you have it on both eyes?
A. Yes.
Q. What year was that when you had that done?
A. I think that was—I think it was January.
Q. And just watching you walk today, it looks like you walk normally. It doesn't look like you limp or favor either side.
A. No, I don't think so.
Q. Are you using any type of adaptive aids right now? For example, you don't have a neck brace obviously.
A. Yeah.
Q. Are you using any type of adaptive aids?
A. I'm not sure what that means. I do have a—the TENS unit I use at home.
Q. Okay.
A. That's—
Q. That's an example of one. Are you using any adaptive aids today as you are sitting here talking to me?
A. No.
Q. Now, I understand from reading the records and specifically your interrogatories that you have problems with pain?
A. Yes.
Q. And it's ongoing pain?
A. Yes.

Q. I'm going to give you a diagram. It's a pain diagram. I will give you this in pencil in case you want to make any changes to it. If you don't mind putting your name and today's date at the top.
A. Is today the 28th, today?
Q. Yes.
A. All right. Thank you.
Q. You'll see there are two drawings of a body, one on your left is labeled front, which represents the front of your body, and the one on the right is labeled back.
A. Uh-huh.
Q. And then you'll see it's also labeled right side, left side.
A. Uh-huh.
Q. And at the top of the page, there are different symbols that correspond to different types of pain: burning, aching, stabbing, pins and needles, and so forth. So what I would like you to do is assume that the two drawings represent your body from the back, left and right. And I would like you to go ahead and use those symbols or any other notation you want to make to help me understand when you have pain, what part of your body is affected and what type of pain you experience.
A. Okay. That's it.
Q. All right. Thank you.
A. I think that's all of them.
Q. Okay. I'll come back to that in a second. At the time of the accident, I understand that you were employed as a teller/manager by Landmark Bank?
A. Correct.
Q. And what is your current employment status now?
A. I'm a—I'm employed with National Bank. I'm a teller.
Q. Okay. And I had your —I think in your deposition you stated your rate of pay preinjury or at the time of the accident was $30,000 approximately?
A. Yes.
Q. And your current rate of pay I believe you testified—is it $26,500?
A. Yeah. I don't remember even what—yes, it sounds about right.
Q. Okay.
A. Yeah.
Q. Are you working forty hours a week now?
A. Yes.
Q. In the accident, did you hit your head?
A. No.
Q. Any loss of consciousness?
A. No.
Q. Now, going back to the pain diagram that you just completed, you marked your neck, your left shoulder area all the way down into your left arm.
A. Right.
Q. And then you indicated numbness, I believe—
A. Yes.
Q. —right stabbing, pins and needles in your left-hand fingers?
A. Yes.
Q. And you indicated here mid-back pain and lower back pain?
A. Right.
Q. Okay. Do you have ongoing pain in all the areas that you documented?
A. Yes. The lower back wasn't too much of a problem, but within the last six months to a year, it's just getting worse and worse, the low back. I also have pain down my right leg, but it's not all the time, so I didn't know if I should put that down there or not. It's kind of --
Q. However you want. I want you to be complete. I want to give you every opportunity to explain all of your symptoms to me.
A. Yeah.
Q. So if you want to supplement that, feel free to do so.
A. Yeah. It's—it's like on the inside. It's not—it's not on the front or the back, it's on the inside, so I don't know how to—
Q. Take your time.

A. Yeah. That is not right. Okay.
Q. So, again, just to make sure we got it complete, you have ongoing pain in your neck, left arm, mid-back and lower back?
A. Right.
Q. And you have intermittent pain in your—you've marked now your right leg?
A. Correct.
Q. Entire right leg?
A. Right.
Q. Did you erase something here?
A. Yeah. I accidentally put on the wrong—the wrong leg, because it's only the right leg.
Q. Okay. Just to make sure—so it's just the right leg, not the left leg?
A. Correct.
Q. You erased the left leg?
A. Yes.
Q. Now, the pain distribution—does your neck pain radiate into your left arm?
A. It's always there so it's—I don't feel like it's—I don't know if it's radiating or not because that's constant. I constant have pain with my neck and my shoulder and my arm.
Q. Okay. Where's the most severe pain that you have?
A. My neck.
Q. Do you have any problems with headaches?
A. Yes, every day.
Q. Do you have any headache triggers?
A. Headache triggers. I'm not sure, something—not that I know of, I don't.
Q. What is the duration of a typical headache?
A. All day.
Q. Do you have a headache now?
A. No.
Q. Do your headaches respond to medication?
A. Yes and no.
Q. Can you explain that?
A. They gave me pills at a doctor's office for headaches, and they weren't working, and I asked the doctor about it. And he said, well, if you take too many of them, they will give you headaches too so—
Q. So are you taking any medication for your headache pain now?
A. No.
Q. Okay.
A. Well, I have, yes. I have medication. I did not take it today—
Q. Right.
A. —yet.
Q. When you have a headache, generally you take it?
A. Yes. That or Tylenol. I try to switch off.
Q. And do your headaches respond to medication?
A. Sometime it does, sometimes no.
Q. Now, this right leg pain, that's a fairly recent onset?
A. Yes.
Q. Do you have any idea what causes of that?
A. I—probably from my lower back, I imagine.
Q. Okay. You think it's a product of lower back pain?
A. Sure.
Q. Does your—
A. Yes.
Q. Does the pain from your low back radiate into the right leg?
A. Yes.
Q. Have we discussed all of the problems you're currently experiencing as a result of the accident?
A. Yes.
Q. Okay. Do you have any type of mental functioning problems: memory, concentration, mental alertness?

A. Well, I mentioned to the doctor yesterday, within the last six months, a year, I am starting to, like, forget things and dates. I don't know if it's from the medication. But they did switch it in February. So I don't know if that's the cause, but, yeah.
Q. Okay. You have problems with recall—
A. es.
Q. —that began to manifest six to twelve months ago?
A. Yes.
Q. And you presented this problem to the doctor yesterday?
A. Yes.
Q. Who was it?
A. His name is Dr. Firestone.
Q. Firestone?
A. I think it is.
Q. Okay.
A. I mentioned it before to Dr. Goodman. That's my real doctor.
Q. Okay. Dr. Firestone—He's treating you, Dr. Firestone?
A. No, no. That was—he did the exam for—for my case. My real doctor, Dr. Goodman, I mentioned to them, the nurse practitioner.
Q. Allen Goodman?
A. Yes.
Q. Is Dr. Firestone a neurologist?
A. He's not my doctor so I don't even know.
Q. Okay.
A. He just sent me to an evaluation yesterday.
Q. You previously discussed it with Dr. Goodman?
A. Right. Well, the nurse practitioner—
Q. Okay.
A. —that helps.
Q. Did any healthcare professional discuss with you what they believe is causing these memory difficulties?
A. No. We didn't—we didn't get into a conversation really about it.
Q. So it's Dr. Goodman's physician assistant?
A. Yes.
Q. It was your assessment that it could be a product of medication side effects?
A. Right.
Q. Any other type of mental functioning difficulties you're experiencing?
A. No.
Q. Okay. Let's go back to the pain that you have now. You described it using symbols. Let's see, aching—aching pain in your neck, and aching and stabbing in your left shoulder and left arm; is that right?
A. Also stabbing was in the neck, too—
Q. Okay.
A. —yes.
Q. And the same in your back, your low—your mid- and low back use the same symbols?
A. Yes.
Q. And the same in the right leg?
A. Yeah. The right leg, though, is more like a shooting pain going down. There's no symbol for shooting pain.
Q. Okay. Well, I appreciate you qualifying that.
A. Lower back has got a lot of back spasms lately in my lower back.
Q. How often do you have the spasms in your lower back?
A. Oh, lately I've been having them every day. It's on and off.
Q. Now, you've had one surgery since this accident happened, right?
A. Yes.
Q. And that was a one-level cervical fusion?
A. Yes.
Q. That was—let me see here. That was by Dr. Farmer on October 6th, 2011?
A. Yes.

Q. Do you know what your diagnoses are at this time other than having had that surgery on your neck, what doctors are saying is causing these other symptoms that you're experiencing?
A. From my accident.
Q. Okay. Do you know if they are saying that is the cause specifically?
A. No, I don't know.
Q. You're not aware of any pending diagnoses?
A. No.
Q. Let me just get a little more background information. You're right- handed, right?
A. Yes.
Q. And I have a height of 5 feet 3 inches; is that correct?
A. 5′4 actually.
Q. And your weight currently is?
A. 155.
Q. Do you recall what it was at the time of the accident in 2007?
A. Probably the same.
Q. Okay.
A. Close to it.
Q. Your weight's been stable?
A. Yeah.
Q. I understand you had a gastric bypass. That was in 2004?
A. Correct.
Q. And since that time, you've been able to maintain a stable weight?
A. Yes.
Q. And I know you've had one marriage, right?
A. Yes.
Q. Currently divorced?
A. Correct.
Q. Single, divorced?
A. Yes.
Q. And when did that marriage end?
A. We divorced in July 2009.
Q. Was the dissolution of your marriage in any way related to the accident?
A. No.
Q. And you have, I understand, three children?
A. Yes.
Q. Eric is how old?
A. Eighteen.
Q. And Sean?
A. Fifteen.
Q. Okay. And then you have a daughter Jessica?
A. Yes.
Q. Age?
A. Thirteen.
Q. Thirteen. The children, are they healthy? Any disabling problems?
A. No.
Q. And the place that you live in Bradenton, is it a house, apartment?
A. It's—I rent a condo.
Q. Okay. How many bedrooms, bathrooms?
A. Two bedroom, two bath.
Q. So it's like in a complex?
A. Yes.
Q. Condominium complex?
A. Yes.
Q. Multilevel?
A. Two—two-story.

Q. Two level. How long have you lived there?
A. Since September of 2007.
Q. So you moved there after your accident?
A. Yes.
Q. At the time of your accident, where were you living?
A. In my house.
Q. You lived in the marital home?
A. Correct.
Q. Did your relocation have anything to do with the accident?
A. No.
Q. Have any made any disability modifications to your condominium in which you currently live?
A. No. I'm on the first floors.
Q. Okay.
A. And I rent so—
Q. Do you have any problems with accessibility in your home?
A. No.
Q. And you have a shared custody agreement is what I understand?
A. Yes.
Q. And your kids live with you 50 percent of the time?
A. Yes.
Q. The three of them? All three?
A. Yes.
Q. Okay. And that's the same situation—I think that was the situation at your deposition. That's the same situation now?
A. Yes.
Q. Okay. Let me get a little bit more information about your medical history. We talked already about two procedures that you had: the gastric bypass in June of 2004 are the records.
A. Yes.
Q. And then the bilateral LASIK procedures were in January of 2007?
A. Right.
Q. Did you had any other surgeries before the accident?
A. No.
Q. At the time of—let's say near the time of the accident, like an hour before, a day before the accident, what was your physical condition like at that time?
A. Well, before the accident, I used to go to the gym, and after the gastric bypass, I went to the gym, I worked out.
Q. You regularly exercised—
A. Yeah.
Q. —before your accident?
A. I would be in the gym four days—four times a week for an hour or two each time. I was probably in the best shape ever in my life. I was on no medication, nothing.
Q. Did you have any medical problems or restrictions of any sort near the time before your accident?
A. No.
Q. Now, the body parts that we've been discussing earlier that you indicated that you have problems with, had you ever sustained injury to any of those body parts before?
A. No.
Q. And never had any symptoms in these body parts either?
A. No.
Q. Other than what we've discussed, the gastric bypass surgery, the LASIK surgeries—
A. Uh-huh.
Q. —is there anything else remarkable in your medical history before the accident?
A. No.
Q. Since the accident occurred in February of 2007, have you had any related medical problems going forward from the date of the accident?
A. Well, I am anemic, so I did have to get—I did have to get blood. And I have gone for iron IV treatments.
Q. You've had IV treatments for problems with anemia?
A. Right.

Q. When was your most recent treatment for anemia?
A. Last month.
Q. What was done?
A. I was finishing one of the iron IV treatments.
Q. Okay. So that was in May of 2012?
A. Yes.
Q. How many IV treatments have you had let's say in the past twelve months?
A. Five. It was one each week.
Q. We're talking about the last twelve months, so this would go back to June of 2011.
A. Right. It was before that.
Q. Okay.
A. The one before that. The time before.
Q. During the last twelve months, you've had five IV treatments for anemia?
A. Correct.
Q. And who is treating you for that problem?
A. It's by Dr. C, and it's at the Cancer Center.
Q. Dr. C?
A. Yeah. Cis—it's a long name.
Q. Okay. C-i-s-s-e-r-n-o-s-t-o-n-i-a?
A. Yep. Yes. Dr. C.
Q. You haven't been diagnosed with cancer?
A. No.
Q. But you said a cancer center.
A. That's where they perform it.
Q. Okay. When were you diagnosed with anemia?
A. I don't—I don't know.
Q. Was it before or after the accident?
A. It was before the accident, but it wasn't really a problem before until last year. I did iron pills and I was fine.
Q. Did your anemia problems cause you to miss any work in the last—well, let's say—
A. Yes.
Q. —during the year?
A. Yes.
Q. Okay. How many days have you missed because of anemia problems?
A. Well, I've actually used sick time to go to my appointments, so I haven't taken entire days. Three hours every week or so.
Q. So these are unrelated problems, the anemia?
A. Correct.
Q. And what is your best estimate of the total number of hours or days that you've missed during 2012? We're almost done with half of this year. Today is June 28th.
A. So you figure for two hours a day, about ten hours.
Q. And that's for treatment?
A. Correct.
Q. Do you have any restrictions that are a product of your anemia?
A. No.
Q. Do you have any scheduled anemia-related treatment?
A. No.
Q. Is that the only unrelated problem that you have?
A. Yes.
Q. Have we discussed your entire medical history now?
A. Yes.
Q. Everything that's significant?
A. Yes.
Q. No other hospitalizations, fracture injuries, nothing of that nature that you can think of?
A. No.
Q. What is your major problem or problems that you have now because of the accident?

A. I am in pain 24/7.
Q. And it's the areas that we discussed earlier?
A. Correct.
Q. Okay. Let's talk about the pain intensity levels that you experience. Let me look at your pain diagram to kind of guide us through this. Let me start with the top of what you marked there. Your neck, if you had to rate that on a zero-to-ten scale, zero's no pain at all, one's a minor distraction, all the way up to a ten, ten is the high—the upper limit, one step away from going to an emergency room, intolerable pain, what would you rate your pain in your neck?
A. An eight.
Q. You can give me a range if there's a variable.
A. Seven or eight.
Q. What types of activities or conditions worsen your pain?
A. I'm sure standing all day at work. If it's colder outside, if it's damp or wet, it's seems to be worse. I'm sure stress.
Q. And then you have your left shoulder. Can you rate the pain in that area?
A. I would say same, seven, eight. It's been not—but all of them has been higher, and they've all been maybe as low as maybe—we can probably say six.
Q. But on average, it's been—
A. Seven, eight.
Q. Okay. And the same things worsen it?
A. I'm sorry?
Q. The same things contribute it to—
A. Yes.
Q. —worsening it?
A. Yes.
Q. Okay. And then into your left arm, how would you rate the pain in that part of your body?
A. The same thing, seven, eight.
Q. Okay. Then we're going into your mid back.
A. Same.
Q. Same thing—
A. Yeah.
Q. —seven or eight? And then your low back, which you mentioned is—I think you said that's getting worse recently?
A. Yeah. I would say eight or nine.
Q. Okay. And then also your right leg. You mentioned you don't always have symptoms there, but when you do have symptoms there?
A. Probably a seven, seven or eight.
Q. Okay. We discussed all the body parts you have your pain in?
A. Right.
Q. And it's the same thing that makes these symptoms worse?
A. Yes.
Q. Now, you mentioned your doctors who are treating you. Dr. Goodman is still treating you?
A. Yes.
Q. Do you know what Dr. Goodman's specialty is?
A. No.
Q. And the surgeon, Dr. Farmer, did Dr. Farmer release you?
A. Yes.
Q. Do you remember when you last saw him?
A. I believe it was December of last year.
Q. Okay. When did you last see Dr. Goodman?
A. I see him every single month so May.
Q. You see Dr. Goodman every month?
A. Yeah, once a month. So it was in May.
Q. Is Dr. Goodman a pain management specialist?
A. I believe so.
Q. You believe so?
A. I believe so.
Q. Does Dr. Goodman prescribe you meds?

A. Yes.
Q. All of them?
A. Yes. I'm sorry, the appointment, I guess the last one was June because I have my next one already for—July 11th is my next appointment, so it was around there, June.
Q. Other than Dr. Goodman, is anyone else treating you?
A. No.
Q. So he's the only person you're seeing at this time for accident-related problems?
A. Correct.
Q. What about the doctor who was treating you for anemia?
A. That was Dr. C.
Q. When did you last see Dr. C?
A. That was in May.
Q. May of 2012?
A. I'm trying to think of when my—
Q. Do you have any—
A. It was early June. I'm sorry.
Q. June. Okay. Do you have any appointments scheduled to see Dr. C again?
A. No, not yet. I will make a follow-up with him, but it won't be for months.
Q. You saw him in June, I'm sorry, Dr. C last—
A. Yes.
Q. —June?
A. Yeah.
Q. So how are your current problems with anemia?
A. I'm okay right now.
Q. Okay.
A. It's a little bit low, but I've done the treatments, and I have to go back to him to be rechecked in a couple of months.
Q. So sometime this summer?
A. Yes.
Q. Later—in late summer?
A. Right. Yes.
Q. When you say you're a little low, what do you mean by that?
A. Iron level.
Q. Iron level?
A. (Nonverbal response)
Q. Okay. Do you get tired near the end of the day? Tell me how that manifests—
A. When it's—
Q —the anemia issues.
A. Right now, no. Before I went for these treatments, yes, I was getting tired real easy.
Q. Before the IV treatments then?
A. Correct.
Q. You were tired when? Just throughout the day or as the day progressed?
A. As the day progressed.
Q. Do you tire pretty easily? Do you get very tired? Do you need to nap or do you just feel like weak?
A. Yeah, just a little bit—just a little tired.
Q. Now, I know in addition to the surgery that Dr. Farmer performed, you had a number of injections—
A. Yeah.
Q. —primarily by Dr. Goodman.
A. Yes.
Q. But I know you initially had some trigger points by Dr. Wahlberg?
A. Yes.
Q. And then you had a number of cervical facet injections prior to the surgery?
A. Yes.
Q. And then after the surgery, I believe you had two rhizotomies that Dr. Goodman performed, right?
A. Yes. I guess that's the name. I'm—I'm not aware of the name of the procedure.
Q. The last one I had was from March 22nd, 2012.

A. Yes.
Q. Have you had any since then? Any injections or any type of procedure since then?
A. No. It's just two. We did one month and then went back and they did the other one. We did the left side first and then we went back and they did the right side.
Q. Okay.
A. It's a radiofrequency.
Q. Are any more surgeries scheduled or recommended for you?
A. I'm not sure.
Q. Has anyone discussed any more procedures?
A. Dr. Goodman mentioned that I may need another surgery.
Q. Did he say what that would be?
A. No.
Q. Are you doing okay? Do you need a break?
A. Yeah. Can we take a break?
Q. Yes. If you need a break at any time, you tell me. But I'll prompt you. But you certainly feel free to initiate it.

(Whereupon a break was taken.)
THE VIDEOGRAPHER: We're rolling.

Q. Okay. We were talking about treatment that you had before the accident.
A. Yes.
Q. And I know you've also had physical therapy?
A. Yes.
Q. Chiropractic treatment?
A. No chiropractic.
Q. No? None?
A. No.
Q. Okay. Pain management?
A. Yes.
Q. Okay. And of course the injections?
A. Yes.
Q. Have you had any other treatment or therapy?
A. No.
Q. Are you in any kind of treatment or therapy currently?
A. No.
Q. And you mentioned that you have a TENS unit.
A. Yes.
Q. Do you have any other adaptive aids?
A. No.
Q. How often do you use your TENS unit?
A. A lot. Sometimes—sometimes every single day when I get home from work. I may skip a day here and there, but many days.
Q. And your medications, tell me what medications you're taking.
A. I have a Fentanyl patch.
Q. How often do you change that?
A. Every thirty days.
Q. Okay. Any other medications?
A. Yes, Dilaudid.
Q. Do you know your—and that's for pain I take it?
A. Yes.
Q. As is the Fentanyl patch, right?
A. Yes.
Q. Do you know your dosage of the Dilaudid?
A. It's eight milligrams, and I take it four times a day.
Q. Any other meds?

A. Yes. I have a muscle relaxer. It's—I can't remember the name. It's Cyclobenza-something.
Q. Do you have a medication—
A. Yes.
Q. —list?
A. Yeah, I do.
Q. Go ahead and refer to that.
A. Okay. It's—yeah, Cyclobenzapar. Let's see. And it's ten milligrams.
Q. Do you take that once a day?
A. No, three times a day.
Q. And can you spell it for me?
A. It's C-y-c-l-o-b-e-n-z-a-p-a-r.
Q. Okay.
A. And then there's another one I just started with. It's another muscle relaxant I take one time at night before bed.
Q. What is the other one?
A. It's Hydropor—
Q. Go ahead and spell it.
A. I'll spell it.
Q. Yeah.
A. H-y-d-r-o-p-o-r-p-h-o-n-e.
Q. And you take that once a day?
A. Once at night.
Q. And what is—
A. I'm sorry. That's the—that's the—that's the wrong one. Sorry.
Q. Okay.
A. That's the—that's the Dilaudid.
Q. Dilaudid you take—
A. Sorry.
Q —four times a day or once a day?
A. I'm sorry?
Q. How often do you take the Dilaudid?
A. Four times a day.
Q. Okay.
A. And that's eight milligrams.
Q. Okay.
A. I'm sorry. The other one, the other muscle relaxers is—it's spelled C-a-r—
Q. Okay. Well, let's go back. You had the Cyclobenzapar.
A. Right.
Q. You told me you take that. That's ten milligrams, three a day. That's a muscle relaxer, right?
A. Correct.
Q. Excuse me. And then you had another muscle relaxer.
A. Right.
Q. And what is the name of that one?
A. It's C-a-r-i-s-o-p-r-o-d-o-l.
Q. Okay.
A. 350 milligrams.
Q. 350 milligrams?
A. Yes.
Q. And you take that once a day?
A. Once at night. Once before bed.
Q. Okay. Any others?
A. No. We've got—you've got the Fentanyl patch and—no.
Q. So four different meds?
A. Yes.
Q. Okay. And you mentioned earlier, you weren't taking any medication near the time before the accident?
A. No, no medicine.

Q. Do you have any side effects from your medications?
A. One of them, I believe it's the one—I get dry mouth—
Q. Okay.
A. —something horrible. And the one at nighttime, it makes me—it knocks me out, very sleepy with. Other than that, no.
Q. Have you taken your regular medications in the last twenty-four hours?
A. Yes.
Q. Let me ask you now what you can and can't do. What's within your capacity and what limitations do you have. Starting with lifting and carrying. How much are you able to safely handle?
A. I try not to lift anything.
Q. Okay.
A. I get my kids to do it for grocery shopping, and I have people at work that help me with lifting stuff. I'll carry bread in, but I try not to—I try not to lift anything.
Q. Well, what do you feel you can handle? How much are you able to safely handle?
A. I have never been tested. Five pounds.
Q. Okay. Have doctors actually imposed a lifting restriction?
A. I —I know they've mentioned before when I had the surgery nothing over ten pounds.
Q. Do you know—are you aware of any current lifting restrictions?
A. No.
Q. But what— what type of problems do you have with lifting and carrying weights?
A. I hurts my neck and my back.
Q. Do you have any—well, you mentioned earlier—are you limited in moving your neck side to side? Do you have range of motion restrictions? Is it reduced?
A. It hurts.
Q. Moving it side to side?
A. Right.
Q. How about up and down, flexing—
A. Yes.
Q. —and extending your neck?
A. Yeah.
Q. Okay. So all neck movements cause you to have additional pain?
A. Correct.
Q. Now, you are right-handed, right?
A. Correct.
Q. And do you have any problems with your right hand or arm?
A. Sometimes it's very rare, but like these fingers have been numb (indicating). I've had pains down some, but it's—
Q. Your fourth and fifth digits?
A. Yeah. And it's in the right arm. But it's not anything—it's here and there and it's not constant. It's the left arm that's the problem.
Q. And you don't have to do this, but you can just tell me. Are you able to extend your arms out horizontally?
A. Yes.
Q. Are you able to turn your palms over, both?
A. Yes.
Q. Can you touch your fingers to your thumbs?
A. Yes.
Q. Can you make a fist with both hands?
A. Yes.
Q. Are you able to extend your arms overhead?
A. Yes.
Q. Okay. Do you have any problems with your fine motor coordination? That would be things like buttoning buttons, picking up little objects like small coins, things like that?
A. Yeah.
Q. Okay.
A. I mean, I was tested in West Palm. I—those things that they tested me with—
Q. Okay.

A. —and I had problems with my—with my left hand.
Q. Your right hand is intact?
A. Yeah.
Q. But your left hand is less proficient?
A. Yes.
Q. And that's because of the accident?
A. Yes.
Q. Now, you mentioned the right leg. You have problems with that in terms of pain?
A. With my right leg.
Q. Right leg. Intermittently?
A. Yes.
Q. Not all the time?
A. Right.
Q. Do you have any loss of function in your right leg?
A. No.
Q. And I take it walking and standing like today, for brief durations, that's within your tolerance? Not a problem for a brief duration?
A. Not for brief, yeah. No, it's no problem with brief.
Q. Now, what do you feel is within your tolerance walking-wise before you overdo it or overexert yourself? How long are you able to walk?
A. I have never timed myself.
Q. Let's say you were to go shopping at a mall or you would take a walk in your neighborhood or whatever, what would be within your tolerance before you overdo it?
A. Probably an hour maybe.
Q. How about standing? Again, not at attention, but as you do in your job as a teller, where you're moving, displacing your weight, what's within your tolerance?
A. The same thing probably. An hour, max.
Q. And sitting, again, with repositioning normally, what would be within your tolerance?
A. Same thing. About that.
Q. An hour?
A. An hour, yeah.
Q. How about driving?
A. Yeah, same thing.
Q. Okay. An hour again?
A. An hour, yes.
Q. Now, you've mentioned you have automatic transmission vehicle. Have you made any disability modifications to it?
A. No.
Q. Do you have a parking placard or sticker for persons with disabilities?
A. No.
Q. Any problems with bending?
A. Yes, my back, lower back.
Q. You avoid doing that because of your back issues?
A. Yes.
Q. How about lower extremity movements such as kneeling, squatting, climbing stairs?
A. As far as?
Q. Limitations, restrictions, problems, worsening your symptoms, anything like that?
A. Not for kneeling really. I try to avoid as much stuff as possible so it doesn't aggravate. Steps, yes. Steps, I don't really have steps to go up and down anywhere.
Q. Do you think you're getting better, worse, staying the same? What would you say about your condition?
A. Worse, definitely.
Q. What's getting worse? I think you said your low back is getting worse?
A. Yeah.
Q. Anything else?
A. Yeah, my neck and my back and the pain and, you know, it used to be a little bit better, now it just seems to be getting worse and worse.

Q. Have you had any problems with your balance?
A. No.
Q. All right. How about your other senses? For example, we talked about vision already. Sense of hearing?
A. No.
Q. Taste, smell?
A. No.
Q. Any problems with breathing?
A. No.
Q. Any bowel or bladder problems?
A. No.
Q. Did you injure any teeth in the accident?
A. No.
Q. And I know you're having problems with fatigue related to your anemia.
A. Yes.
Q. Any other problems with fatigue?
A. No.
Q. Have you had any falls since the accident occurred?
A. No.
Q. Okay. And you did mention the environmental conditions that worsen your symptoms. I believe you said dampness and humidity?
A. Yes.
Q. And also the cold I think you mentioned?
A. Yes.
Q. Anything else?
A. Probably stress.
Q. Okay. That's more of a—
A. Yeah.
Q. Not really environmental, but I appreciate that. I made a note of that.
A. I mean, as the days go by, you know, being at work all day—
Q. Right.
A. —so it starts to hurt more.
Q. Okay. Tell me—you mentioned there isn't a current lifting restriction that you have that you're aware of.
A. Right.
Q. Do you have any physician restrictions?
A. No.
Q. None that you're aware of?
A. None, no. Correct, none that I'm aware of.
Q. Do you have any problems with your sleep?
A. Yes.
Q. I think you mentioned the medication you take knocks you out?
A. Yeah.
Q. So—
A. I still wake up. I mean, when I take it, it knocks me out, but I still wake up in the—during the night.
Q. And what causes you to wake up?
A. I can't get into a position that I'm not in pain.
Q. You have interrupted sleep?
A. Yes.
Q. How many times a night is your sleep interrupted?
A. It could be from two or three times to ten times.
Q. Okay. So two to ten times a night?
A. Easily, yes.
Q. And that's secondary to positional discomfort?
A. Yes.
Q. Position, that's what causes you—
A. Yes.

Q. Okay. And then tell me your sleep pattern. You go to bed at what time?
A. 10:30 or so.
Q. 10:30 p.m. And then you get up around what time?
A. Like 6:00, 6:30.
Q. Do you nap during the day?
A. No. I actually lay down in my car at lunchtime, and I try to take my hour lunchtime and—
Q. You have a one-hour lunch break?
A. Yes. And I'm in my car every day.
Q. Now, do you take any medication to help you sleep?
A. No.
Q. How about nightmares, any problems with that?
A. No.
Q. Are you able to do all your grooming, self-care?
A. Yes.
Q. You're independent now?
A. Yes.
Q. Any problems with that?
A. I just—I'm a little bit slower. It still hurts to lift, you know, my arm. I try to do everything with my right arm.
Q. What about housework, do you perform the same housekeeping chores you did before the accident?
A. No. I get my kids to do everything.
Q. What type of housework do you—do you actually do, for example, launder clothes, prepare meals, any type of cleaning?
A. I make dinner.
Q. You prepare the family's dinner meal?
A. Yeah, usually. See, I get help with everything. Like for clothes, my kids will carry to the machine. I mean, I start the machine up, put the soap in, but they bring me the clothes. They put the clothes in the machine.
Q. Do you make your own bed?
A. Yes, lots of times with help with my daughter.
Q. Who does the grocery shopping?
A. I grocery shop and my kids bring everything in. Sometimes one or two of the kids may come with me. They usually bring all the bags in and put stuff away. I'll carry bread or eggs in, something light.
Q. Do you have a housekeeper?
A. Excuse me. No.
Q. Do you employ anybody to provide services to you for accident related—
A. No.
Q. —reasons? And you live in a condo, so there's no yard to maintain?
A. Correct, no yard.
Q. Tell me about your fitness. It sounds like fitness was your major leisure pursuit prior to the accident; would that be accurate?
A. Yeah.
Q. What other recreational activities did you pursue?
A. Before?
Q. Yes.
A. Go to the movies, go to the mall, go to the beach, bowling, miniature golf, go out to eat, go to the comedy club. I don't know what else. Many things.
Q. Do you still pursue those activities?
A. No, not all of them.
Q. What about fitness, are you still active?
A. No.
Q. No. You no longer go to a fitness center?
A. No.
Q. When is the last time that you went to a fitness center?
A. Before the surgery. I mean the accident. Excuse me.
Q. Okay.
A. Before the accident.

Q. Back in February of 2007?
A. Yes.
Q. Have you discussed that with your doctors whether there is some type of prescribed exercise they might recommend for you?
A. No.
Q. What do you do now in terms of your recreational pursuits?
A. I've been to movies, out to eat. I've taken walks. I've been to the mall. I don't—I don't do them as long as like what I did before. I could have gone to the mall all day. Now I will go for half an hour, forty-five minutes and I want to get out of there.
Q. Okay. Those are your typical recreational pursuits?
A. Yeah.
Q. Now, you perform your job at National Bank in Bradenton?
A. Sarasota.
Q. Sarasota. And what days of the week do you work?
A. Monday through Friday and occasional Saturday.
Q. On weekdays, what are your work hours?
A. Usually it could be from 7:45 to 4:15, or 8:15 to 5:15.
Q. So, I'm sorry, they're either 7:00—
A. 7:45 to 4:15, 4:30 to 8:15, or 8:30 to 5:15.
Q. So the second shift—I'm sorry, 8:15 to—
A. 8:15 or 8:30 to 5:15. It varies day to day.
Q. Do you have your schedule made out in advance?
A. Not right now. We're shorthanded—
Q. Okay.
A. —so it's day by day.
Q. And when you work on Saturdays, what is your weekend schedule?
A. 9:00 to 12:00. When we work on Saturday, we would do cut hours during the week.
Q. When you work on Saturdays, your hours are cut during the week?
A. Correct.
Q. Okay. So you mentioned you get up I think you said 6:15-ish—
A. Uh-huh.
Q. —more or less? Drive to work? It's close by?
A. In Sarasota. Downtown Sarasota. So I'm like ten, twelve miles to work.
Q. How long does it take you?
A. Fifteen, twenty minutes.
Q. What do you do at the end of your workday? Do you usually come home, or what's your schedule like after that?
A. Yeah, I usually come home or in fact if it's my days with the kids, I have to pick up my kids, and they're on the way.
Q. So on days you have custody of your children, you pick them up on your way home?
A. Correct, unless it's school time, they just walk to my house.
Q. Okay. And how do you spend the rest of the evening? What's your routine?
A. Figure out what's for dinner. I try to sit down, relax, get changed, then see about something for dinner, what do I make for the kids. Getting them ready for tomorrow.
Q. Okay.
A. They do their own—their own stuff. I just basically tell them.
Q. Spend the evening preparing your dinner meal and spending time with your family?
A. Yes.
Q. How about weekends, anything you do in particular? Clubs, organizations, church services, anything like that?
A. No.
Q. Are you active in any of your kids' school activities or extracurricular activities?
A. No.
Q. So that's what you told me is generally your activities of daily living?
A. Yes.
Q. Do you socialize at all?
A. Not really, no. I do have a boyfriend, but he comes over for dinner or I might go to his house. We go out sometimes for dinner, take a ride maybe.

Q. Okay. Let's go into another category then. Mental health issues. Have you ever had any mental health treatment?
A. No.
Q. Either before or after the accident?
A. No.
Q. Any mental illness in your family?
A. No.
Q. Have you ever been prescribed any medication for mental health related reasons?
A. No.
Q. Antidepressant?
A. No.
Q. Anti-anxiety?
A. No.
Q. Ever have a loss of consciousness or a trauma to your head before the accident?
A. No.
Q. Do you feel you need mental health treatment now?
A. No.
Q. I think you had an evaluation with Dr. Wallace before the gastric bypass. I think I saw a record of that.
A. I'm not sure—
Q. You don't remember it?
A. Oh, that—
Q. That was just for—that's a standard of practice when they do something like that.
A. Oh, for the gastric bypass—
Q. Yes.
A. —yes. You know, just do it and—I did a test before the gastric bypass.
Q. Okay. How would you describe your psychological status at this time, overall?
A. Good, I guess. For the most part maybe, sometimes with my back and neck, sometimes I would say probably a little depressed, but nothing of—that I need medicine or anything. Discouraged I guess is more like the word.
Q. But in terms of your ability to work, would I be correct in surmising that your emotional issues that you just discussed with me would not interfere with your ability to work?
A. That's correct. I can't—I have to work. I have kids.
Q. But they don't interfere with your—
A. No.
Q. They don't compromise your ability to work?
A. No. No.
Q. Are you having any difficulties with depression?
A. No.
Q. Anxiety?
A. No.
Q. No suicidal thoughts, anything of that nature?
A. No.
Q. Any financial difficulties?
A. No.
Q. Okay. Are there any mental health concerns or problems that would be significant or that you would feel I need to know about or you would like to discuss with me?
A. No.
Q. You're not experiencing any mental health concerns or problems?
A. No.
Q. Now let me ask you some questions about your schooling. And I think I saw you graduated from Manatee High School in 1986?
A. Yes.
Q. Okay. Okay. Do you have any other formal education or training?
A. No.
Q. Did you have any instruction through the employers that you had in any type of money management, cash handling, customer service, anything like that?
A. No.

Q. No? Okay.
A. No.
Q. So you developed your skills as a teller from on-the-job experience?
A. Yes.
Q. Do you recall how you did in school, your scholastic performance?
A. Probably was As and Cs I got in school.
Q. Do you remember taking any standardized tests that the students take like the FCAT or—
A. Yeah.
Q. —SAT?
A. I know I took them. I don't know what I got on them.
Q. Have you ever repeated a grade in school?
A. No.
Q. What type of classes were you in? Were you in regular classes, accelerated? Any remedial classes?
A. Regular.
Q. Just regular.
A. Regular classes.
Q. Any second language skills?
A. No.
Q. Any special type of skills that you possess such as music, writing, art, martial arts—
A. No.
Q. —anything of that nature? And any type of work-related credentials that you either hold or held in the past?
A. No.
Q. Any kind of licenses, certifications—
A. No.
Q. —registrations?
A. No.
Q. Okay. And the other job training you've had has been, I would presume, in cash handling?
A. Yeah, cash handling, their computer systems.
Q. What type of computer systems?
A. I don't know what—it's just a—
Q. It's a proprietary system?
A. I—I really don't know. I didn't—
Q. What kind of things do they do, the systems?
A. Well, just for our basic daily work of cashing checks and deposits and anything we need to do banking related like that.
Q. For bank related recordkeeping?
A. Correct.
Q. And you've had on-the-job training in customer service?
A. Yeah.
Q. You deal with the public daily?
A. Yes.
Q. And I know you were a supervisor at one time, right?
A. Yes. Not at National.
Q. Yes, Landmark.
A. Yeah.
Q. And so you've had on-the-job training in that, supervision?
A. Yes.
Q. Has that primarily been the on-the-job training that you've had?
A. Yes.
Q. Okay. Do you have a computer at home?
A. Yes.
Q. And how are your computer use skills?
A. I really don't use my computer that much, but basic, I would say.
Q. You're able to get on the Internet?
A. Yes.

Q. Generate e-mail?
A. Yes.
Q. Are you familiar with Microsoft applications—
A. So for—
Q. Like Word, Excel, PowerPoint?
A. I —I use them but not that—I'm not good at that at all. I'm not that good.
Q. Is there any other software that you're able to use?
A. I—not that I'm aware of, no.
Q. Do you do your banking online?
A. Yes.
Q. Have you taken any courses through the American Banking Association?
A. No.
Q. So the major skills that you—well, let me go back and tell you what I have for your work history. I tried to reconstruct it as best as I could from the records. I know you started with National Bank in 2008.
A. Yes.
Q. And then you've been a teller the whole time?
A. Yes.
Q. And then before that, you were with Countywide, which became Landmark?
A. Yes.
Q. And a teller/manager from 1998 through 2008?
A. Yes.
Q. And then prior to that, you were with Southeast Bank and Countywide as a teller?
A. Yes.
Q. That was from 1993 through '98?
A. It was just Southeast, it wasn't—
Q. Southeast?
A. It wasn't Countywide.
Q. It became Countywide later?
A. No. Southeast Bank got bought out, and I left Southeast and I went to Countywide.
Q. Okay. Who did you work with before Southeast Bank?
A. BIG Rental Car.
Q. What was your job title?
A. A customer service rep.
Q. And do you remember your dates of employment?
A. I think I started there in '88 —
Q. 1988.
A. —to—1988 that I started up—I had moved back to New York, so I started there in '88, and we moved back down in 1992. I got transferred from one location to another, and then I worked until I had my son, so until '93.
Q. And that's why you left because of the birth of your son?
A. Correct.
Q. And Southeast Bank you said you left—was there a reduction in force when they were bought out?
A. Yes. They were—they had let people—I wasn't let go, I just decided—they were bought out by Great Big Bank, and I didn't want to work with Great Big, so I went to Countywide along with almost all the other employees.
Q. And then you were affected in a reduction in force with Landmark?
A. Correct.
Q. Do you like your job currently?
A. Yes.
Q. You enjoy being a teller?
A. Sure. Yes.
Q. What is it that you enjoy about it?
A. We're down for employees so—it used to be the employees and the customers and seeing different people or seeing the same people. You just get talking to customers and you find out—
Q. You enjoy the relationships—
A. Yeah.
Q. —that you've established—

A. Yes.
Q. —with coworkers and customers?
A. Yes.
Q. So going back to the kind of skills that you've been able to develop through your work, what would you say are the primary skills that you develop? For example, do you use a cash register?
A. No—
Q. No.
A. —a computer.
Q. You use a computer.
A. Right.
Q. So use of a computer to process—do you do commercial or what type of bank teller work do you do?
A. We do both. We do personal, commercial, cashing checks, make deposits, make payments.
Q. Okay. So you use a computer to process banking transactions?
A. Yes.
Q. What other types of skills has your work allowed you to develop?
A. That's about it.
Q. Do you have to count the money at the end of the day? Are you responsible—
A. My drawer.
Q —for deposits?
A. No. Well, for my drawer. I'm responsible for the money in my drawer.
Q. Okay. And so tell me what's involved with doing that.
A. Just we count money, plug it into our computer and tell us whether or not you balance.
Q. You have to reconcile—
A. Yes.
Q. —at the end of the day—
A. Right.
Q. —cash that you handle?
A. Correct.
Q. How much cash do you handle on a daily basis?
A. 10, $20,000.
Q. Up to $20,000 a day?
A. It varies. It could be a couple of thousand, it could be—it depends what comes in.
Q. Sure. What other things do you do? Do you make out money orders? Do you—
A. Well, we don't have money orders. We have cashier's checks. It's basically the same thing.
Q. Prepare cashier's checks?
A. Yeah. It's still all on a computer.
Q. You don't have any supervisory responsibility currently?
A. No.
Q. But previously you have?
A. Yes.
Q. And how many tellers did you supervise?
A. At Countywide or Landmark, one, two—four.
Q. Are you a Notary?
A. No.
Q. You have never been one?
A. No.
Q. Okay. Do you have anything to do with safety deposit boxes?
A. No.
Q. Have you in the past?
A. No.
Q. What other type of specialty skills has your job enabled you to develop?
A. I've—I've ran—I had control of the vault, which basically is buying and selling money back and forth into the vault. Tellers—teller. My other teller would sell the cash to me I would put into the vault and have to balance it at the end of the day, same like my drawer.
Q. So you were managing monies transferred into a vault?

A. Correct. Also for the ATM also. I'm being trained on the ATM to balance it, and we've put cash in, handle the deposits that are in the ATM.
Q. Do you do anything with the security people who come and take the money away, like the Brink's people or those types of people?
A. I have. I have in the past when I have the vault. I don't have it—
Q. What do you do—
A. —presently.
Q —in the past that was with a—what would you do? You would oversee transfer of monies to—
A. To the armor car to—yeah, so it would be two of us.
Q. Oversee transfers of money to armed security guards?
A. Correct.
Q. What about cross-selling other banking products or services; is that a skill that you developed?
A. Yes.
Q. What type of banking products or services would you cross-sell?
A. Checking accounts, savings accounts, loans.
Q. What about them?
A. We basically get them over to our customer—we—I don't get involved in the checking or savings accounts or loans at all.
Q. Would you refer them?
A. Yeah, I would refer it over to my customer service.
Q. What about investment products?
A. Yes.
Q. So if you felt that was a need, you would detect by your interaction of a customer, then you would say, we have these other things and these people can help you?
A. Yeah. We don't talk about insurance products. I just say, I can get you in touch with my rep.
Q. And did you get a commission of a sale if it was consummated?
A. We—we do if—if we—if the overall office meets a—a score, and I also have so many sales. But I don't get paid individually for each sale, no.
Q. It's by the team?
A. Correct.
Q. So the skills that we've been discussing and have been identified, I know you've had a fair amount of—well, probably a lot of—you have been a teller for many, many years—
A. Yes.
Q. —so you've had a lot of on-the-job experience, cash handling, use of computers for bank-related recordkeeping, customer service, you do that daily, supervision of bank tellers, you developed skills from that in the past.
A. Yes.
Q. You've used computers to process banking transactions, you've reconciled cash handled on a daily basis, up to $20,000 you estimated on average—
A. Yes.
Q. —a variance there.
A. Yes.
Q. Prepare cashier checks, managing monies transferred into a vault, an ATM.
A. Yes.
Q. Overseeing transfers of money to armed security guards.
A. Yes.
Q. Cross-selling bank services and products. And we talked about what those are.
A. Yes.
Q. Checking accounts, bank accounts, loans, investment products.
A. Yes.
Q. Are those the primary skills that you developed through your experience and on-the-job training?
A. Yes.
Q. Any other significant ones that you can think of that I haven't identified?
A. No.
Q. Have you thought of other retraining that you might want to pursue?
A. No.

Q. Okay. And you like your job, from—
A. Yeah.
Q. —what you told me. So looking at the work history, all of your work experience since 1993 has been as a teller—
A. Yes.
Q. —working in banks?
A. Yes.
Q. Okay. Do you want to take a break now?
A. Yes.
Q. Good. Why don't we do that.

THE VIDEOGRAPHER: Yes.

A. Yeah.

(Whereupon a break was taken.)

THE VIDEOGRAPHER: Okay, sir. I'm rolling.

Q. So we're talking about your skills and just start now talking a little bit more about your work history. And so, again, at the time of your accident, you were employed by Landmark as a teller/manager? We're going back to 2007 now.
A. Yes.
Q. Were you also doing teller functions as well as managing people?
A. Yes.
Q. Okay. Was there a breakdown or were you pretty much doing them simultaneously?
A. Simultaneously. I was also training for assistant manager.
Q. And you worked how many hours a week at that time?
A. Forty.
Q. Was it a retail bank?
A. Yes.
Q. Was that in Sarasota?
A. Bradenton. I worked at downtown Sarasota also, but I've been at a few different branches.
Q. And you—
A. But I ended up in Bradenton.
Q. And you were earning about $30,000 annually?
A. Right.
Q. And you performed your teller/manager job—would you be sitting, standing? What would you be doing?
A. Everything.
Q. Both, stood. What percent of the time were you standing and/or walking?
A. Fifty. 50/50.
Q. Fifty percent of your time involved sitting and fifty percent of your time was standing?
A. Standing and walking.
Q. What was the amount of weight that you were required to handle on that job?
A. How much, I'm sorry?
Q. How much weight did you have to handle? What would be the heaviest thing generally that you would handle? What was required of you to handle?
A. I was—the only thing of weight would be coin, boxes—boxes of coin. Nothing else. Really, everything was paperwork, everything else.
Q. And what would be the weight of the boxes of coins that you would handle?
A. I —I don't know how much they weigh.
Q. Pardon me?
A. I don't know how much they weigh.
Q. Less than ten pounds?
A. Probably, yeah.
Q. Okay. Now, then, I take it you didn't have to do that that often, handle boxes of coins?
A. Probably—no. On a daily basis.
Q. Okay. You could break it down and take maybe half of the contents out and do it that way if you had to?
A. No. No.
Q. You had to take the whole box?

A. Whole box, yeah.
Q. Okay.
A. We have that now at my job now, but I don't handle that. I have the other employees lift everything.
Q. Okay. So it's basically like you said, 50 percent of sitting, 50 percent of standing; when you'd have to handle something, it would be up to 10 pounds?
A. Right.
Q. And anything else significant in terms of physical demands of your teller/manager job?
A. Well, at that time, for our safe box, we weren't—we helped customers. Sometimes for the elderly, if they were standing right next to us, we would carry their boxes to the—to the viewing room. And that's it as far as lifting.
Q. You would help elderly customers with handling their safety deposit boxes?
A. Correct. Excuse me.
Q. Now, you also mentioned that you were training for an assistant manager job?
A. Yes.
Q. And can you help me understand that more?
A. Well, that involved basically everything I did, plus then we had reports, and I'd be working more with the manager.
Q. Okay. You lost your job I guess for a reduction in force; is that correct?
A. Right. Right.
Q. Did the demise of your job have anything to do with the accident?
A. No.
Q. So after the accident, were you away from work for a period of time?
A. When the accident first happened, I was out of work for four—four days or so, four or five days. And then I started physical therapy. So I was leaving early, coming in late any time I was doing physical therapy, three times a week.
Q. So that treatment interrupted your work participation?
A. Oh, yeah. They were looking to—to fire me. They never said that but I was getting attitude.
Q. You had the surgery—let me look back here. You had the surgery after your employment with Landmark ended, because the surgery was in 2011?
A. Yes.
Q. But you had other things that you had treatment, the physical therapy primarily?
A. Right.
Q. Okay. Over time, I take it, your neck symptoms worsened?
A. Yes.
Q. And you—when did you go back to full-time work; after your therapy was done and so forth?
A. I went to physical therapy for three months—
Q. Okay.
A. —and I was full time.
Q. So the accident didn't cause you to lose your job?
A. No.
Q. And then you were fortunate to get your current job with National Bank in September 2008?
A. Yes.
Q. How long were you out of work then?
A. Just from July, mid-July to—July, August, and I started with them early—beginning of September.
Q. Did you get severance benefits with that?
A. No.
Q. So two months after your employment with Landmark you secured your current job with National?
A. Yeah. It was like a month and a half.
Q. Okay. That's very good.
A. Yeah.
Q. It was a bad economy at that time. And your job title is teller?
A. Yes.
Q. And you work in another retail environment?
A. Yes.
Q. Similar to the one you had at Landmark?
A. Yes.
Q. Do you—now, do they have a drive-through or are you inside the bank?
A. Inside, but we do have a drive-through. It's attached.

Q. You do the inside part, right?
A. Yes. Well, I do both.
Q. You do both?
A. Yeah.
Q. So since your employment with National began, you had to have surgery?
A. Yes.
Q. When did you start with them, in September of 2008?
A. Beginning September—
Q. September of '08?
A. Yes, September of '08.
Q. How long were you out of work after that surgery?
A. October, November and December, and I went back the beginning—I ran out of time. I couldn't take any more time.
Q. So when did you go back to work, December?
A. Beginning of January.
Q. January of 2012?
A. Yes.
Q. And have you been —have you continued to perform your teller job full time to date?
A. Yes. I have the other employees though, whoever, to help me. And I don't lift anything. They—they lift everything for me.
Q. Now, are your job responsibilities similar to those that you had while you were a teller and teller/manager at Landmark?
A. No. There's less stuff that I have now than what I had with Landmark.
Q. Okay. You worked both at a—what percent of the time would you say you work as a drive through teller?
A. It's—they're—it's attached. The counter for the lobby is here (indicating). You turn around—
Q. Okay.
A. —and there's the drive up. So we do—
Q. I see.
A. —we go back, both.
Q. Right.
A. So it's—
Q. One station?
A. Yeah.
Q. You work at a work—your workstation enables you to perform both—provide banking services inside the bank as well as at a drive-through?
A. Yes.
Q. You perform the same type of tasks that you did before—
A. Yes.
Q. —in terms of, you know, interacting with the public, using a computer, processing transactions, reconciling your—
A. Yes.
Q. —your transactions during the day? All of those things?
A. Yes.
Q. So your job responsibilities are similar to what you did before?
A. Yes.
Q. And when I say "before," I mean before the accident.
A. Oh, no. Well, then I did a lot more stuff at Landmark—
Q. Okay.
A. —and Countywide.
Q. The scope of your job responsibilities was larger at Landmark?
A. Yes. I don't do half as much as I did there. I did reports. I don't do any of that stuff.
Q. You had more administrative responsibilities—
A. Yeah.
Q. —because you were manager—
A. Correct.
Q. —and in that training position?
A. Right. Correct.

Q. The physical demands of what you do now are comparable to what you did at Landmark would you say or are they different?
A. No, they're less. We're not as busy a—
Q. Okay.
A. —Landmark was. They were a lot busier. We're not even half the business.
Q. So the volume, the customer volume is lower?
A. Yeah.
Q. Now, you do about half of your job sitting, half standing still?
A. No. We stand. I cannot—I can't sit at my job.
Q. How about when you're in a drive-through?
A. No.
Q. No?
A. No. When there's no customers, I try to sit down here and there, but, no, we—
Q. You perform your job standing the entire shift?
A. Yes.
Q. Standing or walking I guess?
A. Yes. I try to sit down but—that's if there's no customers.
Q. What's the heaviest weight you handle now?
A. I —I don't. I don't lift anything. Paper.
Q. You rely on coworkers to do anything that requires lifting?
A. Yes.
Q. What's the most physically demanding work task you perform?
A. I'm not sure exactly—
Q. Well, what's to you—what's the most physical job responsibility or task that you're required to do?
A. I —I really don't do anything physical lifting. I mean, for—probably placing the canisters to send out to the drive-up maybe. That's probably the—
Q. You would have to place canisters in—
A. In the little holder and press a button and it gets sent out.
Q. Where is it? Is it overhead?
A. Yeah, it's overhead. It's like, you know—
Q. You exchange canisters with customers just to process transactions?
A. You know, well, I just place it up there, we hit a button and it gets sent out so—
Q. You place it where?
A. It's in the—the tube system. It's like—where it drops, it's like a base, so we just put it back in the base and hit the little button and it sends it out to them.
Q. Okay. Are your job responsibilities within your capacity, what's required of you at this time?
A. Not really because I'm—I'm asking all the other employees to lift things where I should be doing it. I have the ATM, but I can't— don't lift the canisters for them, so I have to get someone else to help me with that.
Q. What are the canisters?
A. They're the canisters that actually go into the ATM that hold the money for the machine.
Q. Okay. You rely on employees or your coworkers?
A. Yes, to carry them. They have to—money has to be added once a week. It has to be balanced every day or once a week now.
Q. You rely on coworkers for—give me some examples of things you ask them to do.
A. Take the canisters out and carry them into another area. I put the money in the canisters, close them. They carry the canisters and put them back in.
Q. So with carrying and transferring canisters—
A. Right.
Q. —that's one thing you're asking them for help with?
A. Correct.
Q. What else?
A. The worst I can—the ATM. That's—that's pretty much on the ATM. For my job, I have them carry coins out when we need it. We have a daily box where we put all of our work—paperwork in. I have someone carry that. And we lock it up each night. Our vault doors—we have timers. We have—I have half the timer, the other—combo—excuse me, and the other person has the other half. After I put mine in, I have—they open it. They actually physically open the door.

Same with the night drop, from the night before, I put in my combo, they put in theirs, and they open it up, the vault door open it up and get the night-drop stuff out. I let them bend. I let them get it. I let them lock it back up.

Q. Are there any accommodations that are extended to you?
A. They—they tried to in my station. I have a—I raise my computer up to be at like eye level. I have a—a wrist pad for the entire length of my keyboard.
Q. Do other employees have that wrist pad?
A. No. I have a special mouse.
Q. Let me go back.
A. Oh, sorry.
Q. You raise your computer to avoid the need to flex and extend your neck?
A. Correct.
Q. That's why you did that?
A. Yes. Well, we had a lady that came out and did an evaluation on my station, what I did. And these are things that she suggested.
Q. Okay. So someone from who, from what, from the bank?
A. No. No, outside of the bank. It was Dr.—Dr. Goodman I believe did a—asked for an evaluation of my station.
Q. So they called that an ergonomic?
A. Yes. Yes.
Q. And that Dr. Goodman—the change to your workstation was done pursuant to Dr. Goodman's ordering of this ergonomic—
A. Correct.
Q. —evaluation?
A. Yes.
Q. So you have—we're talking about other accommodations. One is the computer. You had this ergonomic evaluation. Somebody recommended that the angle be changed so that you would avoid flexing and extending your neck?
A. Yes.
Q. And then you told me you were provided with a wristband.
A. Right. It's the length of my keyboard.
Q. For your computer keyboard.
A. Right.
Q. Anything else?
A. Yes. There's—on my phone, I have a—I don't know what they call it. It's a—like a pad on the phone where—so it rests so I'm not—
Q. Okay.
A. —leaning my head.
Q. So it's some type of a, let's say—
A. A rubber—I don't know what it's called though. It goes on the head—
Q. This is to place on your neck and your—oh, it's to place on your shoulder?
A. On my shoulder, right (indicating). It's to place on my shoulder so I'm not bending.
Q. Okay. Anything else?
A. And the mouse. I have a mouse that's—I think it's like a Trackball I think it's called. You don't move it, you move the ball instead. Like the ball's on top.
Q. So it's a special computer mouse?
A. Yes.
Q. And how does that help you?
A. It—I guess for—for after a while, so I don't have pains that go into my neck. And it's just—you don't have to move the mouse. Your hand just stays there.
Q. I see. The ball is on top of the mouse?
A. Yes.
Q. So you use the mouse with your right hand or your left hand?
A. My right hand.
Q. Your right hand?
A. Yeah. So it's—it's not—I'm not moving around. I can set my hand straight and I just move the ball and it's got the buttons on either side.
Q. So it minimizes your need to move your—your right arm?

A. Right.
Q. Are your coworkers supportive of you?
A. Yes.
Q. And your supervisors are supportive of you?
A. Yes. They get a little frustrated making them lift everything on a daily basis, but they still do it. And, you know, they are still supportive.
Q. Has any—well, currently—let me go back—you are working you said forty hours a week?
A. Yes.
Q. Are you salaried or hourly?
A. Hourly.
Q. And your compensation is what an hour, $12 an hour?
A. Yeah. I'm not—12 and change I think it is an hour. I'm not even sure.
Q. Approximately $12 an hour?
A. Yes. I think it's 12 and a little bit over. 12.20.
Q. Approximately 12.20?
A. Yeah, something like that. That's bad. I don't know how much I make.
Q. Has any doctor recommended an occupational change for you?
A. No.
Q. Do you feel that you would be earning more money if not for the accident at this point in time, or do you feel things probably would be the same since you had that reduction in force and you had to get a new job, which you did in two and a half—or less than two months?
A. I probably—I think I would probably—I think I would probably be making—I'd be making more because I was training for assistant manager at Landmark. I probably would have been trained for—cross-trained for the other side. And they get paid commissions, incentives, and whatnot.
Q. So the reason you believe you would be earning more money is because you were training for a higher-level position?
A. Correct.
Q. Is there a reason you haven't been able to pursue that kind of career path since the accident?
A. Probably because I'm missing so many days of work. I miss a day here, a day there. I'm surprised they haven't fired me yet. I'm missing so much work.
Q. And that's for accident-related reasons that you're missing so much work?
A. Yes.
Q. How have your performance appraisals been during—well, when was your last performance appraisal?
A. It was February—February I believe of this year.
Q. Okay. And how was it?
A. Very good. Actually good. I got meet and exceeds on almost all of the categories.
Q. How about your work attendance since your return to work in January of 2011?
A. Um—
Q. I'm sorry, 2012. You had the surgery in 2011.
A. Right.
Q. And then you were out until January 2012. Since you returned to work in January of 2012, how has your work attendance been?
A. I still have appointments, doctors' appointments.
Q. Okay. Can you give me some idea of how many days you've missed at work since January 2012 and went back to work? Now, I know you've had some time away for anemia.
A. Right.
Q. So apart from anemia—
A. Yeah.
Q. —due to accident related. And part of it I know is commingled because you have litigation stuff like today.
A. Right.
Q. I'm not really treating you.
A. Right.
Q. But it's not really a medical appointment.
A. Right. It—
Q. But for— for medical reasons.

A. It varies because sometimes I would try to work a longer day other days and I would just leave early for the doctors' appointments so—or like these days, I'm using sick days or I take an hour or two less in my pay and just didn't get paid for.
Q. Okay.
A. It's kind of hard to—
Q. Let me try to be specific with the question.
A. Right.
Q. For accident-related medical problems—
A. Right.
Q. This is an accident-related litigation problem today—
A. Right. Right.
Q. —not medical but—and not anemia problems—
A. Right.
Q. —solely for accident-related medical problems, what would—
A. All right. Well, Dr. Goodman I see every month, so this is no—well, I haven't gotten to the—
Q. However you want to put it. Either hours or days or whatever.
A. Yeah, I'm trying to think.
Q. The best way you could do it.
A. All right. So let me see. It's got to be probably about ten days for just—ten, twelve days.
Q. Okay. Ten to twelve days for accident-related medical problems?
A. Yeah. That's not counting days that I just left early. I'm just actual days that—yeah.
Q. Is your employment secure with National Bank?
A. Well, they're not saying they're firing me yet, but I'm getting a lot of attitude again because of appointments. But they've never said, you're—we're going to fire you. They've never come out and said that, but it's like, oh, you have another appointment. And it's like with an attitude they are saying.
Q. This is your supervisor?
A. Yes. They sent me an e-mail the other day when I told them that I needed a day off for doctors, and, like, you need to give us more time. We'll approve it this time, but next time you need to give us a lot more time notice.
Q. This has to do with your work absences?
A. Right.
Q. At this point, do you believe your job is secure?
A. I—I can't say that. I don't—I don't know.
Q. You don't know one way or the other?
A. Right.
Q. You're able to perform the essential functions of your job I take it? You have help with some of the things that are—
A. Right.
Q. —marginal, but the essential functions of your job with the accommodations that are extended to you?
A. Yes. Definitely doing it with pain though. And I do take my pills all day every day. And they probably would fire me if they were to ask me if I'm taking them. They would probably fire me over it.
Q. Are you looking for a job at this time?
A. No.
Q. Have you made any job applications since you secured your current employment with—
A. No.
Q. —National?
A. No.
Q. Do you have any plans to begin a job search?
A. No.
Q. Has any doctor suggested to you that you're not going to be able to continue to work into the future?
A. No, just Dr. Goodman said I would have problems with my neck even after the surgery.
Q. You mean the future surgery?
A. I'm sorry?
Q. You mean future surgery or the one you already had?
A. The one I already had. He mentioned that I would probably—might need another surgery.
Q. Right. That's the one we talked about before?
A. Right.

Q. So he said—you had the surgery in 2011, and he said that even then you're still going to have problems with your neck—
A. Uh-huh.
Q. —but he didn't suggest that it would threaten or diminish your work life going forward?
A. No. He just said I—I would have problems. He didn't—
Q. Okay.
A. —specifically say "job."
Q. I'm getting close to finishing with my interview. I appreciate your patience with me. Your income currently, is it solely your employment income?
A. And I do get child support.
Q. And how much do you get in child support?
A. Well, it's going to be changing now that my son is 18, but as of the last, I was getting $400 a month for the three kids, total.
Q. 400 total for three kids?
A. Yeah. So a third of that will be coming off I think this month.
Q. Have you applied for Social Security Disability?
A. No.
Q. Do you have any intention or plans to do that?
A. No.
Q. Before you became injured, what were your career plans?
A. Current plans as?
Q. Career plans.
A. I'm sorry?
Q. Career.
A. Oh, career plans. I'm sorry. Like—like I said, I was looking to advance in the company. I was looking—
Q. Advance within the Landmark—
A. Correct.
Q. —organization?
A. Right. I was training for assistant manager and I was looking just to be the branch manager, have my own branch.
Q. What about your current career plans?
A. I don't have any. Keep my job, I guess.
Q. That's your current career plans?
A. Yeah, keep my job and not get fired, preferably.
Q. So in terms of your assessment of how the accident affected your earning capacity, if I understand correctly—
A. Uh-huh.
Q. —you feel that you—well, the Landmark employment ended and that's not related to the accident?
A. Correct.
Q. Okay. It's the reduction in force and so forth?
A. Right.
Q. But you feel that you would be at a higher earnings level because you were in this situation where you were advancing to an assistant manager?
A. Right.
Q. And since then, you've gotten your teller job?
A. Right.
Q. Okay. Am I correct in understanding that?
A. Yes.
Q. Are there any other effects that you feel the accident has had on your earning capacity other than what you just mentioned to me about not being able to progress as you had planned preinjury?
A. Yeah, that's right.
Q. Is there anything that I have not asked you or that you want to discuss in more detail that you feel would be helpful to me in evaluating your claim of loss of earning capacity?
A. No. No. I think you covered it all.
Q. Okay, Ms. Cooper. Well, thank you. That will conclude the interview portion of the exam, so we're at another good spot for a break.
A. Okay. Yes.

Q. And when we come back, we'll have just the testing left.
A. Okay.

(Whereupon a break was taken.)

(Whereupon the proceedings concluded at 12:27 p.m.)

REPORTER'S DEPOSITION CERTIFICATE WITH ACKNOWLEDGMENT

STATE OF FLORIDA)
COUNTY OF MANATEE)

I, ANNEMARIE ROGERS, COURT REPORTER, Certified Shorthand Reporter, certify that I was authorized to and did stenographically report the foregoing proceedings; and that the transcript is a true record of the proceedings.

I FURTHER CERTIFY that I am not a relative, employee, attorney, or counsel of any of the parties, nor am I a relative or employee of the parties' attorneys or counsel connected with the action, nor am I financially interested in the action.

DATED this 9th day of July, 2012.

____

ANNEMARIE ROGERS, COURT REPORTER

Chapter 5

Earning Capacity and Loss of Earning Capacity

5.1 Introduction

Judges and others charged with officiating over judicial proceedings admit into evidence vocational experts' and others' opinion testimonies to help triers of fact understand and evaluate technical information beyond the comprehension lay people ordinarily possess. Experts should not advocate for either opposing party. Rather, they serve as educators and facilitators, lending their skills, knowledge, and expertise to help triers of fact process and integrate vocational information with other information under deliberation.

Given the outwardly benign, helpful role ascribed to a vocational expert—theoretically, a well-educated, credentialed, experienced, and disinterested party in a dispute, framing analyses and opinions on scientific methods in a well-established discipline—one would expect a high degree of confluence among expert opinions. Those familiar with litigation, however, know that vocational opinions can be quite disparate. Although two well-qualified vocational experts may employ similar methods of inquiry, analyze identical records and other information, and interpret the same test data, one expert may conclude that a subject has sustained no vocational damages resulting from an event in question, while another expert may find catastrophic, multimillion-dollar damages.

Who is the jury, arbitration panel, judge, or other trier of fact to believe? The absence of credible information on which to rely invites triers of fact to rely on subjective factors to guide decision-making—the antithesis of our justice system's aim.

Vocational expert opinions vary widely for many reasons. Some reasons, such as an expert overvaluing or undervaluing a claim of loss of earning capacity because he is financially beholden to a retention source, are less noble than others. Lack of experience or knowledge in appreciating vocational damages can also contribute to variances in expert opinions. Despite the causes of varying assessments, they disadvantage triers of fact in finding the truth. After all, the raison d'etre of a vocational expert is to assist triers of fact to appreciate and process technical information beyond their understanding (Shahnasarian, 2012).

Shahnasarian and Lassiter (2002) found lawyers do not have confidence that vocational evaluators' findings are either consistent or objective. Their study provided support for the need to develop more universal and comprehensive methods to assess vocational capacity.

Myriad nuances inherent in a given case can complicate vocational experts' work. A claimant's personal attributes, geographic considerations, and industry trends are but a few case-specific factors that may necessitate special consideration.

Unlike the relatively mechanical processes medical doctors employ to deduce impairment ratings with the *AMA Guides to the Evaluation of Permanent Impairment* (2009) or that psychologists employ when consulting the *Diagnostic and Statistical Manual of Mental Disorders* (DSM-V) (2013) to diagnose mental disorders, the vocational evaluator's task of assessing earning capacity defies these types of analyses.

Guidelines to identify and evaluate the impact of fourteen key factors associated with loss of earning capacity follow. The factors cited herein were derived from a comprehensive literature review, and the proposed guidelines for evaluating the impact of these factors, initially presented in the first edition of *Assessment of Earning Capacity* (Shahnasarian, 2001), have since been empirically tested and proven effective in reducing variances among evaluators' assessments of earning capacity loss (Shahnasarian, 2004; 2010).

Shahnasarian (2004a) used the fourteen factors delineated in this chapter's latter sections as a basis to develop the Earning Capacity Assessment Form (ECAF), revised and published in a second edition, the Earning Capacity Assessment Form–2 (ECAF-2), in 2010 (Shahnasarian, 2010b; 2010c). The ECAF-2, along with research supporting its use, is also described later in this chapter, and postulates undergirding the ECAF-2 follow. These postulates aid in understanding the instrument's intended uses, potential, and limitations.

Reviews of the ECAF-2 appear in Field (2012) and Gibbs and Crtalic (2013). Athanasou (2013) presented research on the ECAF-2 in Australia, and Shahnasarian and Hill (2014) provided a review of the instrument's use worldwide.

5.2 Postulates Undergirding the ECAF-2

Shahnasarian and Leitten (2008) and Shahnasarian (2010) identified ten postulates undergirding the ECAF and ECAF-2:

> **Postulate #1:** When evaluating loss of earning capacity claims, there are premorbid and postincident factors that could be facilitative (drivers) as well as detrimental (inhibitors) to a claimant's vocational rehabilitation. These factors merit analysis.
>
> **Postulate #2**: ECAF factors that are drivers include low scores on measures of the following:

- Stability of Career Development
- Work Propensity
- Demonstrated Earnings History
- Career Motivation
- Cognition

Postulate #3: ECAF factors that are inhibitors include high scores on measures of the following:

- Phase of Career Development
- Subject Specific Issues
- Ability to Apply Prior Skills
- Future Career Development Prospects
- Prognosis
- Need and Capacity for Retraining
- Preexisting Vocational Handicaps
- Acquired Vocational Handicaps
- Vocational Adjustment Issues

Postulate #4: Drivers and inhibitors can be quantitatively and qualitatively evaluated by qualified vocational rehabilitation evaluators.

Postulate #5: Drivers and inhibitors have an interactive effect on vocational rehabilitation potential, assuming an individual is motivated to pursue vocational rehabilitation.

Postulate #6: Positive drivers can help mitigate earning capacity damages, assuming an individual is motivated for this.

Postulate #7: The ECAF can be used to generate a quantitative index of drivers.

Postulate #8: The ECAF can be used to generate a quantitative index of inhibitors.

Postulate #9: Driver and inhibitor indices can be used to assess claims of loss of earning capacity, with corresponding degrees of loss.

Postulate #10: At times, Drivers can take on Inhibitor qualities and Inhibitors can take on Driver qualities.

5.3 Factors Affecting Career Development and Earning Capacity

Shahnasarian (2001) reviewed literature specific to career development, vocational rehabilitation, psychology, and economics, and identified fourteen factors generally associated with capacity to pursue career development and earn wages—topics vocational evaluators frequently address. Further research and analysis led Shahnasarian and Leitten (2008), and Shahnasarian (2010) to categorize these fourteen factors into

Table 5.1
The Fourteen Earning Capacity Assessment Form-2 (ECAF-2) Factors, Specified by Category

Inhibitors	
	Phase of Career Development
	Subject Specific Issues
	Ability to Apply Prior Skills
	Future Career Development Prospects
	Prognosis
	Need and Capacity for Retraining
	Preexisting Vocational Handicaps
	Acquired Vocational Handicaps
	Vocational Adjustment Issues
Drivers	
	Stability of Career Development
	Work Propensity
	Demonstrated Earnings History
	Career Motivation
	Cognition

two groups: Inhibitors (factors that could suppress one's vocational rehabilitation) and Drivers (factors that could facilitate an individual's vocational rehabilitation). Shahnasarian (2001) developed a hierarchical rating scheme using the fourteen factors in the development of the Earning Capacity Assessment Form and the Earning Capacity Assessment Form-2 (ECAF-2) (Shahnasarian, 2010). More information about the factors, their rating criteria, and interpretations of examinee profiles are in the *Professional Manual for the Earning Capacity Assessment Form-2* (Shahnasarian, 2010).

Table 5.1 identifies the fourteen ECAF-2 factors by category. More information about the factors follows.

Shahnasarian and Leitten (2006) conducted an exploratory factor analysis of the ECAF factors and found they are also related in other ways. Highlights from ECAF research appear later in this chapter. Readers interested in the instrument's validation should reference the *Professional Manual for the Earning Capacity Assessment Form-2* (Shahnasarian, 2010).

A. Inhibitors

1. Inhibitor 1: Phase of career development

Besides evaluating pertinent historical circumstances while preparing future vocational behavior projections, vocational evaluators should assess relevant present and future factors likely to affect an individual's career development and earning capacity. Career development professionals acknowledge five phases of career development through which most individuals pass: growth, exploration, establishment, maintenance, and withdrawal (Super, 1957). The growth phase is characterized by the development of attitudes, interests, needs, and aptitudes associated with self-concept; initial vocational preferences are developed during this phase. During the exploration phase, occupational choices are narrowed to general career directions. The establishment phase is characterized by work experience and settling down within a field of work that uses one's talents and demonstrates the appropriateness of previous career decisions. During the maintenance phase, individuals continually adjust to improve and maintain their career positions. Finally, during the withdrawal phase, reduced work output and eventual retirement typically occur.

Age, level of career maturity, and vocational accomplishments to date are considerations when assessing an individual's phase of career development. Evaluators should thoroughly analyze reasons that may cause an individual to experience a regression, premature plateau, or interruption of progression through successive phases of career development.

The relevance of an individual's phase of career development arose in a claim for future wage loss involving a twenty-nine-year-old individual with a bachelor's degree in liberal arts. At the time of his motor vehicle accident, which caused him permanent orthopedic injuries and chronic pain, the plaintiff was completing prerequisite science and mathematics courses for admission to medical school. He had already taken the Medical College Admission Test and attained a competitive score. The vocational evaluator retained by plaintiff's counsel determined that, in the context of the plaintiff's career development, his ability to progress to higher phases and realize a correspondingly higher earning capacity had been interrupted. In essence, his injuries prohibited him from attaining his latent earning capacity that had yet to be fully realized and converted. The following excerpt appeared in the vocational expert's report:

> Before the 2012 accident, Mr. Peterson completed a bachelor's degree and additional training that enabled him to become licensed as a massage therapist. He indicated he intended to pursue admission to medical school; to this end, Mr. Peterson was completing requisite science and mathematics courses. He has taken the Medical College Admission Test, and his performance is within competitive limits. Mr. Peterson was in the exploration/establishment phase of his career development at the time of the 2012 accident. I am unaware of any reason why he would have been unable to proceed with his stated preaccident career plans if not for his

> acquired injuries and associated functional limitations. Because of his acquired disabling problems, he will be fortunate to maintain his current employment as a teacher, and it is improbable that he will be able to proceed with his preaccident career plans of becoming a physician.

2. Inhibitor 2: Subject-specific issues

All people confront life circumstances that can affect their ability to pursue work-related activities. These circumstances affect individuals uniquely and should be evaluated in each earning capacity assessment.

There is no generally accepted standard to quantify the influence of individuals' circumstances and their ability to work and earn wages. A reasonable measure of clinical judgment is in order when assessing how subject-specific issues affect and will affect earning capacity. Field, Choppa, and Weed (2009) provided guidelines on how practitioners can apply clinical judgment in their analyses. Transportation problems, lack of support from significant others, special family needs, financial difficulties, or lack of other resources necessary to pursue career objectives are examples of circumstances subjects may encounter as they pursue their career development.

One cannot overstate the importance of a thorough clinical interview to identify and assess personal factors that can affect an individual's career development. A myriad of subject-specific circumstances—too numerous to list in this text—can potentially affect individuals' abilities to pursue their career development and maximize latent earning capacity. While assessing subject-specific issues that relate to career development, vocational evaluators should also consider how potential barriers could be mitigated.

Additionally, personal circumstances can affect work stability. For instance, in a dual-career marriage in which one spouse's job requires periodic relocation, the other spouse may leave jobs to accompany his spouse more frequently than would otherwise be the case. In a situation like this, the partners may have an agreement that one spouse's career development will take priority over the other's, which could lead to suboptimization of one spouse's career achievement. Analyzing personal circumstances that could affect work stability is essential to gain insight about how and why a subject's work history has evolved in the manner known to the evaluator.

3. Inhibitor 3: Ability to apply prior skills

An acquired disability may limit or exempt one from work she previously performed. If individuals cannot pursue past work and they possess few or no transferable skills to apply to future work activities, they will be handicapped in pursuing career development and will likely realize a loss of earning capacity.

Transferability of skills refers to an individual's ability to apply previously developed work skills and specialized knowledge to meet the requirements of jobs or occupations other than what the person has performed. Regulations promulgated by the Social Security Administration consider transferability of skills to be most probable between occupations or jobs when (1) the same or lesser degree of skill is required, (2) the same or similar tools and machines are used, and (3) the same or similar raw materials, products, processes, or services are involved. The vocational evaluator must consider degrees of transferability when performing a transferability of skills assessment.

A transferability of skills analysis typically begins with examining an individual's work history and identifying demonstrated competencies. The following sources can facilitate this analysis:

- Job descriptions that provide a breakdown of requisite skills, knowledge, and work behaviors
- Descriptive statements made by those knowledgeable about the work in question
- Interviews of job incumbents or supervisors
- Observation of the work being performed
- Research through print materials, software, and other employment-related resources that provide authoritative information about job responsibilities and requirements. Many publications of the U.S. Department of Labor, trade and professional associations, and specialized software applications provide detailed analyses of jobs and the skills required to perform them.

Once transferable skills have been ascertained, the vocational evaluator should assess how the examinee's established skill set comports with skills required to perform alternate occupations. In some cases, previously developed skills might have diminished in value because of lack of recent use, changes in technology since the skill was last applied, or acquired disabilities that restrict use of the skill. While performing a transferability of skills analysis, vocational evaluators should also consider the degree to which retraining may be required—along with associated training modalities, costs, and duration—to restore previously developed skills to competitive levels.

In the context of an assessment of earning capacity, a transferability of skills analysis culminates in facilitating a determination of whether a subject's inability or compromised ability to pursue prior employment—which may rely on transferable skills to maximize earning capacity—has caused the subject to experience a loss of earning capacity. Differences between a subject's preincident and postincident earning capabilities that cannot be offset by a subject's transferrable skills or retraining help measure lost earning capacity. Vocational adjustment issues (discussed below), physical and cognitive capacity for retraining, and resources available to a subject should also be considered when analyzing transferability of skills.

As an example, consider the case of a paramedic who sustained a lower-back injury requiring him to undergo a laminectomy and discectomy. He filed a complaint alleging that his injuries prohibited him from securing and maintaining employment and compensation commensurate with his preinjury levels. The plaintiff resigned from his job after the injury; his rate of pay had been $11.21 per hour. After reviewing medical records, a vocational expert concluded that the injured worker was, indeed, unable to return to his prior employment. While recreating the plaintiff's work history, however, the expert identified many transferable skills the plaintiff had developed through his work as a paramedic and through other employment as a hospital unit clerk, emergency room technician, and patient care technician. For instance, the expert learned that the plaintiff had experience entering doctors' orders into a computer, operating a switchboard to answer and route telephone calls, performing triage of patients, starting IVs and drawing blood, changing wound dressings, and assisting nursing staff with light-duty tasks. The plaintiff testified in his deposition that as a patient care technician, "I was more the [emergency room] department's choreographer, if you will, which required more clerical skills, computer skills, phone skills." The expert concluded that many of the skills the plaintiff developed remained within his postinjury exertion capabilities. Summarized below are the expert's opinions.

Based on my assessment of Mr. Franklin's prior work as a paramedic and his postinjury restrictions, I do not believe he is capable of returning to his preinjury work as a paramedic. Mr. Franklin is a younger individual (thirty-seven years old) who has completed an associate's degree. He has work experience and skills as noted. While Mr. Franklin has acquired impairments that prohibit him from returning to his prior employment as a paramedic, I am unaware of a reason he would be unable to apply his transferable skills to sedentary and light-duty occupations. He remains capable of performing, for example, the following occupations: pediatric home healthcare attendant, medical services dispatcher, patient admission coordinator, and medical laboratory technician. My preliminary assessment of Mr. Franklin's background indicates that his earning capacity in these types of occupations ranges between $10.00 and $12.00 per hour.

4. Inhibitor 4: Future career development prospects

Industry trends, marketplace vicissitudes, economic downturns, and changes in management philosophy can profoundly affect a person's career development. Additionally, technological advances—such as automated financial transactions offered through the Internet and electronic commerce—have affected millions employed in financial services and related industries worldwide. Regional events, like the 2014 events in Ukraine and Crimea, also affect workers worldwide.

Anticipating future events that may affect an individual's capacity to earn wages is not always possible. When formulating an earning capacity opinion, however, vocational evaluators should have a general awareness of contemporary trends and developments that could affect a subject's employability. Additional research is sometimes necessary.

In a family law case involving a former husband's request for a reduction in alimony four years after the dissolution of a marriage, the former husband—a fifty-one-year-old physical therapist—alleged he could not earn wages commensurate with his earnings at the time the judge imputed the alimony. Specifically, the former husband cited industry changes brought by managed care and changes in physical therapy service delivery; he represented to the court that these changes resulted in a reduction of his earning capacity. After researching labor market projections and changes within the healthcare industry, the vocational expert found support for the former husband's representations and concurred that his earning capacity had indeed diminished. The expert's evidence persuaded the court to realign the former husband's alimony payments with the expert's estimate of the former husband's reassessed earning capacity.

While reviewing a plaintiff's preaccident work history as a small bank branch manager, a vocational expert noted changes within the banking industry that, in his opinion, were material in formulating preaccident earning capacity projections. The following statement appeared in the expert's report:

> It should be noted that the banking industry has undergone significant changes during recent years. For instance, Ms. Jones' former employer (City Bank) merged with another financial institution (County Bank), which in turn has been acquired by yet another financial institution (State Bank). These changes have occurred since the 2013 motor vehicle accident. Concomitant with changes in the banking industry have been significant restructuring of positions, consolidation of jobs, downsiz-

ings, and closings of numerous bank offices and branches. I believe that changes within the banking industry, including changes that have occurred with Ms. Jones' former employer (City Bank), are important to consider in developing projections of Ms. Jones' earning capacity before the 2013 accident.

5. Inhibitor 5: Prognosis

Although an individual may be able to pursue work activities at the time a vocational assessment is conducted, the vocational expert should anticipate how disabilities and vocational handicaps will affect the person over the remainder of his work life. For instance, a projected diminution in functional capacities could limit future work force participation and truncate work life expectancy. The National Institute of Public Health is among the organizations that compile longitudinal data examining the relationship between various disabilities and career development outcomes.

Because assessments of earning capacity include valuing a subject's future earning capacity, evaluators should fully assess how a subject's disabilities and prognosis, within a reasonable degree of vocational rehabilitation probability, will likely influence future career development. A background in medical aspects of rehabilitation along with good input on an individual's current and projected physical and/or cognitive status is necessary to perform this type of analysis. Degenerative problems associated with a lower-back injury, for instance, may prohibit a truck driver from pursuing this occupation in ten to twelve years. If a vocational expert does not possess the expertise to assess the interaction between physical problems and vocational activities over time, a referral to a qualified rehabilitation professional will be needed to formulate an opinion about future earning capacity.

In some cases, continuing in an occupation may exacerbate an individual's physical problems, and a vocational evaluator may determine that a career change is in order. This recommendation arose in a case of a truck driver who underwent a lumbar fusion and had residual problems with lower-back pain secondary to extended sitting. In the evaluator's opinion, continued employment as a truck driver was contraindicated from a vocational perspective. Although the subject was capable of driving a truck, with difficulty, and had been employed in this capacity at the time of the assessment, the vocational evaluator further concluded it was improbable that the examinee could continue his occupation over the remainder of his work life. Accordingly, this assessment was factored into the evaluator's projection about the subject's future earning capacity.

Some disabilities are progressive and degenerative. Others, like scarring from a burn accident, are stable and may not cause an individual to experience any functional limitation, restriction, or problem with pain; however, the social stigma associated with severe disfigurement can significantly affect career development. Considerations of this sort are important in assessing future earning capacity. Examples of how a vocational evaluator can incorporate a subject's prognosis and ability to pursue future career development into an earning capacity opinion are presented later in this chapter.

6. Inhibitor 6: Need and capacity for retraining

Inhibitor 3, Ability to Apply Prior Skills, described above, addressed the notion of transferability of skills as a key factor related to an assessment of earning capacity. If the subject of an earning capacity assessment has experienced a diminution of skills, or possesses few or no substantive transferable skills, the examiner becomes tasked with evaluating the subject's need and capacity for retraining.

Need for retraining can arise when individuals acquire disabling problems that prohibit them from resuming prior employment and applying previously developed skills in alternate occupations. Sometimes individuals are in the process of developing skills necessary to establish themselves in an occupation when they develop impairments that prohibit them from pursuing their career objectives. This situation occurred when a young person in the midst of completing a dental hygiene training program developed incomplete quadriplegia because of a trip-and-fall accident. Although a candidate for vocational rehabilitation, pursuing her career development as a dental hygienist no longer remained a postinjury option, and retraining was required to mitigate vocational damages. In other cases, an absence from the workplace, or lack of use of previously established skills, knowledge, and abilities can necessitate retraining.

Capacity for retraining relates to ability to participate in and benefit from learning experiences that advance employability and earning capacity prospects. It is often a function of physical, cognitive, and psychological subject-specific variables.

The following sources can facilitate an evaluator's assessment of a subject's need and capacity for retraining:

- Scholastic records
- Restrictions that treating professionals and qualified examiners specify in records and articulate during depositions, consultations, and other communications
- Subjective limitations examinees present

- Postinjury physical and cognitive assessments
- Comparisons of preincident and postincident vocational activity
- Results of functional capacity assessments

A vocational expert's analysis of an examinee's need and capacity for retraining in a marriage dissolution case follows. The assessment begins with an overview of prior education, training, and work experience, noting the examinee's absence from the workplace and the implications of this from a skill-set perspective. Then, the expert evaluates how functional capacities—both physical and mental—interface with past and present job responsibilities. Also integrated in the assessment of need and capacity for retraining are special considerations—in this case, childcare needs an autistic child requires. After distilling this information and supplementing it with labor market research, the expert's assessment concludes with recommendations for retraining, along with associated costs, timeframes, and specifications of posttraining earning capacity and future career development prospects.

1. Ms. Jackson informed me she earned a bachelor's degree in nursing in May 1999, and passed the registered nurse (RN) licensing exam in July 1999. The work experience she reported, which was from 1999 through 2007, involved hospital-based, clinical nursing jobs. Ms. Jackson noted she specialized in labor and delivery nursing. She apprised me she voluntarily resigned from her last position—RN in a labor and delivery unit at Regional Medical Center—in March 2007, one month before her first of two children were born. Regarding her compensation, Ms. Jackson recalled her terminal rate of pay was $32 per hour, and the highest earnings she reported was in 2006—approximately $50,000. She has not had employment since March 2007. Although she identified some physical limitations associated with her lower back, Ms. Jackson assessed that her prior RN labor and delivery job remains within her capacity. She cited her absence from the workplace since March 2007, noting this likely is diminishing her competitiveness for positions comparable to those she previously performed. Ms. Jackson added, however, "I'm sure I would be [competitive] if I had a little bit of training and got back up to speed." While discussing her career plans, she indicated she prefers to secure another labor and delivery nurse job, and she also identified home-based nursing as an attractive vocational venue. Ms. Jackson impressed me as motivated to resume her career development.
2. Ms. Jackson identified lumbar and right-knee problems that affect her functional capacities. Based on her representations, I recommend that Ms. Jackson restrict her vocational activity to tasks requiring sedentary and light exertion. She should be capable of performing the essential functions associated with the type of labor and delivery nursing work she previously performed.
3. Ms. Jackson discussed with me special needs her daughter has secondary to autism; however, she noted her child is "on track to be in a mainstream school. She has a good prognosis to lose the autism diagnosis." I appreciate that Ms. Jackson may need some assistance with childcare issues as she resumes her career development.
4. Although Ms. Jackson indicated her RN license remains active, she cited a 3-year absence from the workplace. I recommend that she participate in a nursing refresher course, and I have identified a course of this type, offered by Hillsborough Community College. This 280-hour course costs $1,799, and is designed for nurses who are reentering the workplace or transitioning back into a clinical setting. It is presented as a combination of webinars, lectures, hands-on interactive labs, and clinical rotation. There is also a 4-week clinical component at a local hospital. A course of this type will enhance Ms. Jackson's competitiveness for nursing positions.
5. Labor market research I conducted successfully identified several nurse positions I believe are appropriate for Ms. Jackson to pursue. Again, a nurse refresher course will enhance her competitiveness. According to a 2008 wage survey published by the Bureau of Labor Statistics and specific to the Bradenton-Sarasota-Venice metropolitan statistical area, median annual wages for registered nurses were $27.01 per hour. This wage rate, in my opinion, represents Ms. Jackson's earning capacity.
6. Based on her vocational profile, it is my opinion that, if she were to so chose, Ms. Jackson could successfully transition into healthcare administration occupations offering higher rates of pay. She has the capacity to earn a master's degree in an area allied to healthcare administration. After obtaining a graduate degree, Ms. Jackson would likely be competitive for positions offering compensation of approximately $70,000, annually.

7. Inhibitor 7: Preexisting vocational handicaps

A person with a disability who acquires additional disabling problems can experience compounding effects from vocational handicaps caused by the interaction of new and old disabilities and associated problems. For example, an individual with paraplegia may have mobility impairments and problems with incontinence. If this individual were to then acquire handicaps from a cerebrovascular accident that include mild-to-moderate hemiparesis on the dominant side, the limiting effects of the preexisting mobility and incontinence problems would likely be magnified. Activities such as self-catheterizing, propelling a wheelchair, and using hand controls would quite likely be more difficult, if not untenable.

Newly acquired disabilities, unrelated to preexisting disabilities, can synergize with those to which an individual has learned to adapt and yield a compounded outcome, adversely affecting functional capacities. An individual with a disability, for example, may be able to implement workplace adaptations that allow for generally unimpaired career development. Acquiring an additional disability, however, may cause previously unmanifested vocational problems to emerge, as well as introduce new vocational handicaps caused by both the new disability and the interaction of the new disability with preexisting disabilities. In effect, one (disability and set of associated vocational handicaps) plus one (disability and associated disabling problems) may equal more than two (disabilities that independently coexist).

A thorough understanding of a subject's preincident medical and psychological history, level of functioning, and presence of vocational handicaps is essential to evaluate how new disabilities affect present and future earning capacity. This challenge occurred in a case of a young adult with a congenital hearing impairment who later experienced a severe injury to his dominant upper extremity. The injury was significant not only because of his impaired arm and hand functional deficits, but also because the impairments severely compromised his ability to engage in sign language—his primary preincident communication mode. The preinjury communication deficits to which he had adapted since birth were magnified after his upper extremity and hand injuries. A portion of the vocational evaluator's analysis of how the disabling problems affected the individual and his postaccident career development opportunities follows.

> Mr. Adams, age nineteen, was a community college student when he sustained injury to his right, dominant upper extremity. As a result, Mr. Adams continues to experience residual problems including ongoing pain, significant reduction in range of motion in the digits, hand and entire extremity difficulties, and diminished tactile sensitivity. His results from the Purdue Pegboard test administered during my evaluation indicate his fine motor coordination, and manual speed and dexterity is poor. Mr. Adams' level of mental functioning was in the low-average range. In addition to right upper extremity functional limitations, his injuries have compromised his ability to use sign language—his primary means of communication. While assessing vocational damages Mr. Adams has and will sustain, it is important to note his preinjury problems with deafness posed a significant vocational handicap. Most likely, because of his communication difficulties, he would have pursued hands-on, manual work if not for the accident. Because of the injury to his right upper extremity and his residual functional problems, however, his career development opportunities have been seriously damaged and compromised. Besides losing access to preinjury career options, Mr. Adams' opportunities for career advancement and promotion, once established in his career development, have been damaged. Additionally, he will likely experience longer search times and periods of unemployment between jobs throughout his work life. Mr. Adams' preexisting hearing-impairment problems and the vocational handicaps he acquired as a result of the injuries to his right upper extremity will compound, introducing new vocational handicaps. In my opinion, the injuries that Mr. Adams sustained to his right upper extremity will restrict him to work in the unskilled and possibly semiskilled ranges. He will have difficulty with work requiring computer use or any work involving fine motor coordination. Despite his preaccident hearing deficits, I am unaware of any reason he would have been unable to pursue skilled precision-handwork occupations before the accident.

8. Inhibitor 8: Acquired vocational handicaps

In addition to functional deficits mental or physical impairments invoke, vocational handicaps can further compromise career development and earning capacity. In some cases, vocational handicaps are latent or infrequently manifest; however, in other cases, vocational handicaps secondary to a disabling problem(s) may be foreboding and obviate work participation.

The following vocational handicaps stem from acquired disabling problems:

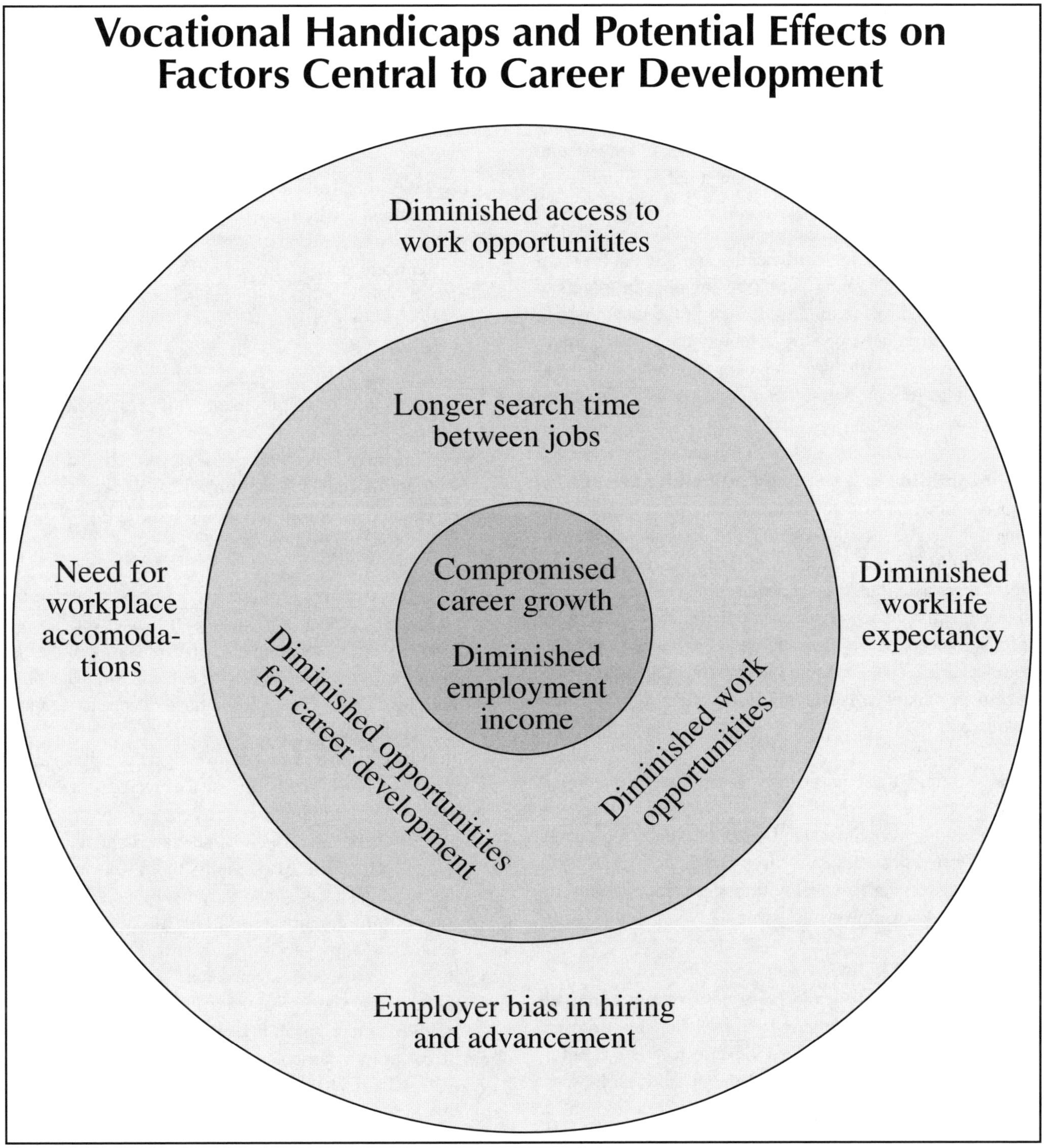

Figure 5.1 *Vocational handicaps and potential effects on factors central to career development*

- Diminished access to work opportunities
- Need for workplace accommodations
- Employer bias in hiring and advancement
- Diminished work-life expectancy

These vocational handicaps can affect earning capacity in myriad ways, for example, by causing an individual to experience longer search time between jobs and, correspondingly, longer periods of unemployment between jobs, diminished work opportunities, and diminished opportunities for career development. In terms of affect on earning capacity, the outcomes can include compromised career growth and diminished employment income. Figure 5.1 identifies vocational handicaps that sometimes emanate from a mental or physical impairment and adversely affect earning capacity.

Psychological problems individuals encounter secondary to a disability, such as poor self-image and lack of self-esteem, can develop into tendencies to discount abilities, inhibit risk-taking, and spawn a self-fulfilling prophecy that reinforces underachievement. Again, the vocational evaluator should be aware of these psychological dynamics and account for them in an assessment of earning capacity. Mitigating the effects of vocational handicaps is discussed often in the rehabilitation literature; accordingly, positive disability adjustment should also be assessed. More discussion about how acquired vocational handicaps can diminish earning capacity is presented later in this chapter.

9. Inhibitor 9: Vocational adjustment issues

Vocational adjustment relates to anticipated difficulties in making a career transition because of personal, vocational, and disability-related factors. Similar to the compounding effects preexisting and newly acquired disabilities can cast, subject-specific characteristics can either inhibit or facilitate a positive vocational adjustment. The following are examples of idiosyncratic characteristics that can affect an individual's success in making a career transition after acquiring new disabilities:

- Being of advanced age as compared to being a younger individual
- Having cognitive limitations or, alternately, being gifted in cognitive ability
- Possessing personality traits that are relatively resilient or, conversely, particularly vulnerable to setbacks

Individuals' capacities to make positive vocational adjustments relate to their abilities to recover from setbacks that newly acquired disabilities pose. Several factors can influence this, including the severity of the disabilities, how established the individual had been in her career development, transferability of skills, and resources available to facilitate career change (e.g., money, supportive family members, and services to promote vocational rehabilitation).

As in all considerations in an assessment of earning capacity, an analysis of an individual's ability to make a positive adjustment after incurring a disability that affects career development includes a thorough examination of subject-specific information along with a degree of clinical judgment. Multiple factors can affect an individual's capacity to make a positive vocational adjustment, thereby negating or minimizing loss of earning capacity. Personality profiling can facilitate this assessment.

B. Drivers

1. Driver 1: Stability of career development

An often-cited axiom in the behavioral sciences—the best predictor of future behavior is past behavior—is particularly relevant in assessing earning capacity. Vocational evaluators can analyze the following to assess the stability of a subject's career development:

- Changes in career focus
- Longevity of employment with previous employers
- Consistency between jobs performed and industries within which the subject has worked
- Eligibility for rehiring with prior employers
- Continuity of employment

Generally, a stable work history presages favorable future career development. An analysis that uncovers an unstable, erratic work history can lead an evaluator to infer that the subject's future career development will simulate prior employment patterns, unless substantial evidence to supplant this notion emerges.

Vocational evaluators should investigate potential causes of a less-than-stable work history, such as reasons inherent in a subject's occupation or industry and personal circumstances. Subcontractors in the construction trades and contractors who work in high-tech industries exemplify those who sometimes earn wages at higher rates than they likely would realize if they were full-time employees of an organization. Occasionally, a contractor's or a subcontractor's work history may, at first glimpse, appear unstable. Subsequent analysis and understanding, however, may reveal that, what may overtly appear as a pattern of career instability may actually be an artifact of employment in a particular occupation or industry. Some individuals work intensive hours on a seasonal or project basis; however, once the project or season concludes, they may have an extended absence from the workplace. This type of employment lends to developing a work history with multiple employers and possible periods of unemployment of varying intervals. Placing an examinee's career development record in proper perspective is essential to assessing its stability.

In a litigated personal injury case, a twenty-four-year-old subject with a tenth-grade education and an unskilled work history sustained a lower extremity injury that restricted lifting/carrying to fifty pounds, and also limited standing and walking. The plaintiff's vocational expert concluded that the subject lost access to potentially high-paying manual labor jobs. This loss of access, reasoned the plaintiff's expert, reduced the plaintiff's earning capacity because he was no longer able to pursue the universe of work opportunities he could have pursued before the injury. After investigating the plaintiff's academic and work histories, however, the vocational expert defense counsel retained concluded that no compelling evidence justified a loss of earning capacity claim. This opinion was based primarily on the defense expert's assessment of the plaintiff's unstable preinjury academic and work histories. The defense's vocational expert—who concluded the plaintiff's unstable preaccident work history likely would have persisted regardless of any injury the subject sustained—cited the following features of the plaintiff's vocational profile as a basis for her opinion:

- Multiple school suspensions
- History of antisocial behavior
- Indicators of developmental delay as early as age five with subsequent placement in exceptional student education
- Early diagnosis as a student who had emotional disabilities
- School evaluations that indicated a borderline intelligence
- Terminations from all three preinjury entry-level jobs held

The defense's vocational expert concluded that the plaintiff likely would have continued his unstable employment pattern in minimum wage jobs. Because the plaintiff continued to possess sedentary, light-, and medium-exertion work capacities, and remained cognitively intact, the expert determined that no loss of earning capacity attributable to the dispute in question was merited. An excerpt from the defense expert's deposition testimony follows:

Q. Did you see a pattern evolving with Mr. Smith regarding his working versus not working?
A. Yes.
Q. Okay. What did you see?
A. I saw this man having several unskilled jobs that were brief in tenure. He had difficulty holding a job, not necessarily becoming employed. He did secure several jobs. But he had difficulty either meeting his employer's expectations or performing the job because of factors such as his personality, his temperament, compliance with attendance—things of that nature.
Q. Do you think that's likely to continue?
A. I'm hoping he'll mature. He's still a young man. And I want to be optimistic for him.
Q. Do you think that Mr. Smith, based on your evaluation of him, has always tried to keep employment?
A. Are you asking me about his motivation to be employed?
Q. Yes sir.
A. He did not impress me as a highly motivated individual.
Q. When he lost a particular job, did he attempt to get another job?
A. He was a very poor historian. I had difficulty eliciting information from him.
Q. But you had his employment records, correct?
A. I don't believe I had all of his employment records, but I had some. There were periods in which he was unable to account for his vocational activity. And he attributed that to memory difficulties.
Q. Did you do any job assessment or employability studies for Mr. Smith?
A. Yes.
Q. What did you do?
A. I examined his vocational background, the types of skills that he developed during his career, which I assessed to be unskilled. Really nothing of any substance in terms of aiding him, in terms of a transferability of skills perspective. He does have limitations in his intellectual ability that likely will not enable him to move past the unskilled strata in his future career development.
Q. Okay.
A. I examined the medical records, including deposition testimony by physicians who essentially said this man should be capable of performing sedentary, light, or medium exertion work, which requires lifting of up to fifty pounds.
Q. Okay.
A. And my assessment is that this man should be capable of performing unskilled work that falls within those exertion parameters.
Q. Do you believe that Mr. Smith has experienced any loss of earning capacity due to the injury to his leg?
A. My assessment is that, regardless of the incident in which he injured his leg, he likely would have pursued unskilled, entry-level jobs in the future, regardless of any problems he acquired that reduced his functional capabilities. He had been a low-achieving, troubled youth. And my assessment is that it's unlikely that he would have advanced much beyond the minimum wage rate—again, regardless of anything that happened as a result of the incident—and he quite likely would have had difficulty maintaining sustained employment. I believe Mr. Smith is capable of performing work that allows him to earn wages comparable to what he would have been capable of earning prior to the incident, and that there is no basis, within a reasonable degree of vocational reha-

bilitation probability, to suggest that the incident will cause him any future loss of earning capacity.

Q. Are you of the opinion that people with a background of antisocial behavior, or the use of alcohol or drugs can never achieve more than minimum wage?

A. Not necessarily. Every case is different, and Mr. Smith needs to be evaluated in terms of his entire background.

Q. And you're of the opinion, when you evaluate his entire background, that this gentleman would never be capable of earning more than minimum wage?

A. Or thereabouts, regardless of what happened as a result of the incident; that's my opinion.

2. Driver 2: Work propensity

Work propensity represents an individual's historical level of work participation. Vocational evaluators can assess this by examining how actively involved in work activities an individual has been during his career. In the absence of some intervening variable, a person who has demonstrated a high propensity to pursue work activities can generally be expected to maintain prior levels. Conversely, those who have demonstrated a low propensity to pursue work activities can likewise be expected to maintain this pattern.

Absence from the workplace to provide services to an ill family member is an example of an intervening variable that could impact work participation. When analyzing a subject's work propensity, her proclivity for pursuing overtime work and supplemental employment (i.e., moonlighting) should be assessed. In some cases, lack of financial need, family commitments, or personal preferences may explain an individual's decision to pursue less than full-time, ongoing employment. Some individuals, for instance, choose to pursue temporary work because of the flexibility it offers.

Assessing a plaintiff's work propensity proved especially important in litigation involving a work-related accident in which an unskilled worker acquired multiple injuries that he alleged rendered him unemployable. Approximately three months before the accident, the plaintiff secured his relatively high-paying manual labor job, which involved cleaning clogged sewer lines at commercial buildings and private residences. The plaintiff's vocational expert asserted the plaintiff's rate of pay at the time of the accident represented his earning capacity, and that this amount was an appropriate benchmark on which to base projections of future earning capacity loss. The defense expert, however, reconstructed the plaintiff's work history from employment records and found that, during the eighteen-year period predating the industrial accident, the plaintiff's work propensity was less than fifty percent. Further, investigation of the plaintiff's occupation at the time of the accident revealed that prior job incumbents demonstrated high turnover rates. This information led the defense-retained vocational expert to conclude that, regardless of the accident, the plaintiff probably would not have maintained the employment he had been performing at the time of the accident beyond a six-to-twelve-month period, and that the plaintiff's future work propensity—in the absence of the accident—would have likely simulated his preaccident work propensity.

3. Driver 3: Demonstrated earnings history

Establishing a baseline index of an individual's earning capacity is a primary task for vocational evaluators. In many cases, this analysis includes reliance on a subject's demonstrated earnings; among the best sources of information for this are FICA earnings history reports from the Social Security Administration, W-2 wage and tax statements, copies of tax returns, and payroll records from prior employers. In some cases—for instance, when a subject has been self-employed or has been a contract employee—assessing actual compensation can be complex.

The relevance of a subject's demonstrated earnings history will vary; for example, it would likely be given significant weight in a wrongful termination case involving a salesperson with a twenty-year work history. In a case involving an injured, traditional-age college student with minimal work history, on the other hand, past earnings would probably be given little weight as an index of earning capacity. When analyzing past earnings, vocational evaluators should question whether demonstrated earnings reasonably reflect the subject's past earning capacity and can be reasonably relied upon to gauge future earning capacity. To aid this analysis, a subject's age, education, training, work experience, and the prevailing labor market should be considered. Generally, earnings realized during years proximate to an evaluation are given more weight than remote years as indexes of a subject's demonstrated earning capacity.

While evaluating demonstrated earnings histories, vocational evaluators should keep in mind that subjects do not always convert their true earning capacities. Consequently, an earnings history analysis should involve determination of whether the subject's record reflects the capacity to generate compensation.

Instances of unrealized earning capacities arise frequently in divorce cases involving high-income families in which both spouses are well educated and have demonstrated a capacity to earn wages at a rate commensurate with their education and experience at some time during their careers. When financial need is not an issue, the spouse with the lesser earning capacity may withdraw from the work force; although the spouse may not be working and earning wages, he nevertheless possesses an earning capacity—albeit latent—that should be thoroughly assessed.

A vocational evaluator assessing the earning capacity of a pathologist's wife learned of her background as a registered nurse. Although she had not worked in this capacity during the nine years preceding her evaluation, she maintained her nurse license through continuing education. The evaluator identified a nurse refresher course offered at a local community college, and the soon-to-be ex-wife pursued this retraining to sharpen previously developed skills that had gone unused. With this remedial training, she quickly became reemployed as a nurse and realized earnings consistent with her prior earnings record.

4. Driver 4: Career motivation

Arguably, the most important element in earning capacity assessment is a person's motivation to convert latent career development potential. Motivation, as a personality trait affecting work tendencies and productivity, has been studied by behavioral scientists for more than 100 years. Early theorists, like Frederick Taylor, related motivation in the workplace to incentives. Isaac Maslow and Frederick Herzberg later proposed theories of motivation based on individual needs—ranging from need for security to need for self-actualization—as the key to understanding how individuals approach work activities. Industrial psychologists generally agree that factors affecting motivation are quite complex, difficult to distinctly categorize, and vary across persons.

Like subject-specific issues that may affect earning capacity, a thorough understanding of a subject's frame of reference is required to assess the relationship between level of motivation and career development progression. This analysis may also provide insight about circumstances underlying a subject's tendencies toward underachievement and overachievement.

There are incredible stories in rehabilitation circles about people like Stephen Hawking, an astrophysicist disabled by a neuromuscular disease who, despite the severity of his disability and vocational handicaps, has become one of today's most renowned scientists. A pilot program the Social Security Administration sponsored during the 1990s—Project Network—offered individuals who had been receiving long-term benefits for multisystem disabilities an opportunity to receive professional assistance in attempting to return to work; participants did not risk losing their disability benefits. With the aid of vocational rehabilitation services, a surprisingly high number of program participants returned to gainful employment. Questions about why some individuals are motivated to overcome challenging circumstances and pursue productive careers while others become virtually incapacitated by far lesser circumstances will undoubtedly persist.

Motivation alone is not always sufficient to enable an individual to thwart all career development obstacles encountered. An evaluation of a subject's motivation to maximize career development potential, however, is central to assessing earning capacity. An individual's career motivation can include the following indicators:

- Record of career accomplishments
- Record of work participation, including work attendance and pursuit of overtime work or supplemental employment
- Initiatives to enhance existing skills
- Reasonableness of job search efforts
- Attempts to return to work after acquiring a disability or encountering a personal setback
- Efforts to pursue rehabilitative services to help overcome work-related obstacles
- Use of discretionary time to further career development
- Volunteer work activity

An underlying question in many earning capacity assessments is whether there is evidence of secondary gain or malingering. To render opinions within a reasonable degree of probability about a subject's vocational behavior and motivation, an efficient vocational evaluator thoroughly reviews all available information. This analysis includes a review of potential disincentives that may inhibit an individual from initiating career development efforts, such as financial disincentives, desire to avoid work and personal responsibilities, and fear of loss of attention from family members, friends, or medical professionals.

Substance abuse and psychological problems acquired after a traumatic event can also affect motivation. In a lawsuit filed after she was assaulted in a public building, a plaintiff was criticized by defense counsel for not pursuing her career development as aggressively as she did before the assault. Allegations of secondary gain emerged. The vocational expert that plaintiff's counsel retained, however, concluded the plaintiff exhibited symptoms consistent with posttraumatic stress disorder. The expert also opined that the sequelae of the plaintiff's psychological problems, rather than an attempt to magnify symptom presentation for sake of secondary gain, triggered the plaintiff's postaccident behavior. Higher-order analyses of these types are important to consider when evaluating apparent changes in a subject's level of career motivation.

5. Driver 5: Cognition

An individual's mental abilities and/or deficits have significant implications when evaluating work viable for the subject of an earning capacity assessment to pursue. Cognitive deficits can greatly influence access to work opportunities.

Problems with cognition may be congenital or stem from events such as a head injury secondary to trauma, cerebrovascular accident, dementia, or mental disorder. Medications can also affect cognition. In pediatric cases, developmental delay can have a wide-ranging effect on future career development and earning capacity.

Like many cases involving disabling problems, each case in which a subject's cognition is an issue in the assessment of earning capacity is unique. Some deficits in cognition are mild, difficult to detect, or inconsequential to an individual's ability to realize his career development potential. On the other hand, cognitive deficits can be profound and entirely obviate future vocational activity. Problems with short- or long-term memory, concentration, organization, ability to execute multistep tasks, and mental dulling are examples of mental processing difficulties that can restrict one's employability. Cognitive deficits can also affect a wide range of functional capabilities beyond mentation, such as speech, vision, and gross and fine motor coordination. Vocational evaluators must appreciate the intricacies of how cognitive deficits can affect a person's ability to perform the range of tasks associated with a vocational activity. A thorough neuropsychological evaluation can help identify the extent of a subject's cognitive impairments and the potential for remediating deficits.

When evaluating how cognitive disabilities will affect an individual's earning capacity, social perception is another aspect to consider. An individual who appears mentally confused or who displays an inappropriate affect, for example, may be socially stigmatized and handicapped in her career development efforts, even though, in reality, the individual may be quite able to perform the work tasks in question.

5.4 Assessing Affect on Earning Capacity

The preceding discussion addressed factors from the Earning Capacity Assessment Form-2 (ECAF-2) affecting earning capacity, perhaps one of the most complex of all human constructs to measure. The prominence of the fourteen factors described above in a pending evaluation will vary by case; some may or may not relate. Further, personal characteristics, such as intellectual abilities, motivation, and resources available to a subject—such as money and access to influential people—in some cases may more than compensate for any vocational handicap that threatens an individual's career development. President Franklin Delano Roosevelt exemplifies a rare individual who possessed both extraordinary personal resources (e.g., intellect, motivation, charisma) and capital resources (e.g., money, influence, family legacy) that enabled him to overcome physical barriers caused by polio and achieve greatness in his career development.

Vocational evaluators should assess both the degree to which the fourteen ECAF-2 factors are operating at the time an earning capacity assessment is conducted, as well as anticipated future impact. Discerning the degree these factors affect and will affect the subject of an earning capacity assessment is critical to conducting a comprehensive and accurate assessment.

A. The Earning Capacity Assessment Form-2 (ECAF-2)

The ECAF-2 facilitates vocational evaluators' assessments of the fourteen factors associated with earning capacity; the factors are arranged categorically (Inhibitors and Drivers). Four statements, presented in a graduated arrangement and reflecting increasing levels of impairment relative to the factor in question, follow each factor. The presentation of descriptors in a hierarchical format reinforces the premise that the degree of potential impairment a respective factor poses is relative, and evaluators' ratings must be considered in toto.

After evaluators complete the individual factor ratings, the ECAF-2 directs them to construct a factor ratings profile. The Professional Manual for the Earning Capacity Assessment Form-2 (Shahnasarian, 2010) provides information on developing factor ratings and interpreting profiles, which are ultimately keyed to an impairment to earning capacity scale. This scale (see Figure 5.2) enables evaluators to quantify assessments of claims involving loss of earning capacity.

Opinions about loss of present and future earning capacity range from no loss to complete and catastrophic loss. Within these parameters, the vocational evaluator may determine that a subject sustained some degree of loss of present and/or future earning capacity.

Shahnasarian and Leitten (2009) did not discern a statistical basis to establish cutoff scores for driver or inhibitor items relating to specific outcomes on the Impairment to Earning Capacity Rating Scale shown in Figure 5.2 The researchers concluded their findings likely reflect the complex interrelatedness of medical, psychological, vocational, and economic variables that can affect an evaluation of a claim of loss of earning capacity.

Again, vocational evaluators must apply sage clinical judgment when rating the degree to which the ECAF-2 factors will likely affect the subject of an earning capacity assessment. Individual differences, resources available to the subject, and labor market conditions are a few considerations vocational evaluators should integrate in their analyses. The degree to which the factors are affecting a subject—as well as those likely to affect a subject in the future—should be framed within the context of all information known about the subject. Of course, the vocational evaluator should also consider the degree to which factors that threaten earning capacity could be mitigated.

1. Overview of Earning Capacity Assessment Form Validity Studies

Two pilot studies involving the ECAF presaged subsequent validation studies. The first pilot test included a group of twelve gubernatorial appointees to a state vocational rehabilitation agency; the second study involved a group of thirty-five professional counselors at a conference titled "Career Counselors as Vocational Experts." These pilot tests helped refine ECAF use.

The ECAF's initial validation study (Shahnasarian, 2004c) involved seventy-eight vocational rehabilitation counselors the Florida Division of Vocational Rehabilitation Services employed. Subjects were randomly assigned either to a control group or to one of two experimental groups in which they used the ECAF to evaluate claims of loss of earning capacity presented in three fact patterns. In all cases, variances within experimental group assessments were significantly less than variances among control group subjects. Further, subjects' use of the ECAF reduced within-group variances in estimates of loss of earning capacity.

In a study examining the relevance of the ECAF's fourteen factors, practicing vocational rehabilitation experts used the ECAF to assess seventy pending claims of lost earning capacity (Shahnasarian and Leitten, 2008). In 74.5 percent of the cases, the experts agreed or strongly agreed that the ECAF facilitated efforts to discern a loss of earning capacity, and the factors of motivation and cognition were most often identified as material in identifying potential loss of earning capacity. Not surprising, the highest correlation (.848) was between demonstrated earnings history and work propensity. A factor analysis yielded three clusters with Eigen values ranging from 1.02 to 4.98. The investigators discerned commonalities as follows:

- Cluster I, composed of five ECAF factors (stability of career development, work propensity, demonstrated earnings history, career motivation, and need and capacity for retraining) represent global factors affecting career development.
- Cluster II, likewise, composed of five ECAF factors (phase of career development, future career development prospects, prognosis, acquired vocational handicaps, and vocational adjustment issues) represent disability-related factors.
- Cluster III included a sole ECAF factor: ability to apply prior skills, which, accordingly, the investigators termed ability to apply prior skills.

Also of note in the ex post facto analysis study was the frequency of factors found particularly relevant in a pending analysis. Cognition was cited as pertinent in 69.6 percent of the cases, and career motivation was cited in 66.7 percent of the cases.

Shahnasarian and Leitten (2008) reported a longitudinal study in which positive work attitudes were highly predictive of return to work and minimal loss of earnings, especially when accompanied by higher levels of intelligence; this finding supported the investigators' 2006 factor analysis results. The study incorporated both demographic variables and stan-

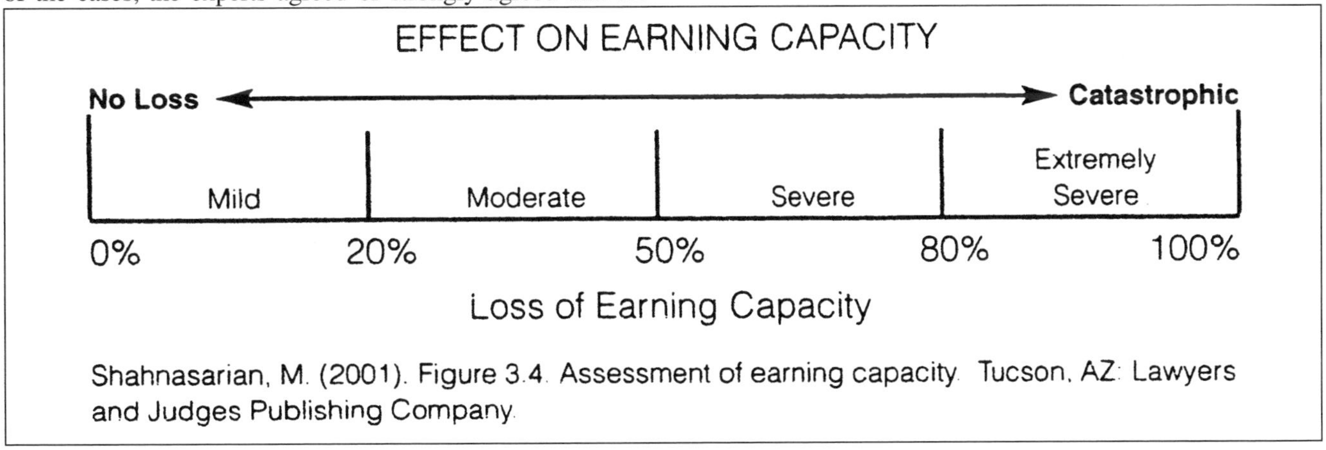

Figure 5.2 *The impairment to earning capacity rating scale*

dardized test data to analyze ECAF factors and to configure models predictive of return to work. Subjects participated in a telephone interview from five to seven years after undergoing a vocational rehabilitation evaluation in conjunction with a pending claim of loss of earning capacity. Fifty-four percent of the subjects reported postevaluation employment and 45.8 percent reported being employed at the time of their interviews. Significant positive correlations were found during the five-to-seven-year measurement interval between return to work and the following variables: Education, Verbal IQ, and Full Scale IQ. Further, a significant inverse correlation between return to work and scores on the MMPI-2 L-scale emerged. A stepwise discriminant function analysis found that use of two variables, Full Scale IQ and Work Interference scale scores from the MMPI-2, resulted in an 83.3 percent correct return-to-work classification rate.

2. Overview of Earning Capacity Assessment Form Reliability Studies

Shahnasarian and Leitten (2008) evaluated the reliability of the ECAF, using a test-retest design over a two-week interval. Twenty-five subjects applied the ECAF to three case studies, and test-retest reliability coefficients measuring subjects' assessments of loss of earning capacity ranged from .85 to .97 ($p < .01$), with an overall correlation coefficient of .98 ($p < .01$). As subjects gained experience using the ECAF, they reported its utility increased.

Test-retest correlation coefficients for the fourteen ECAF factors were also computed by case. Thirteen of the fourteen correlation coefficients (92.9 percent) were significant at either the .05 or the .01 levels; Acquired Vocational Handicaps was the lone ECAF factor not to rise to the level of statistical significance. This finding lends credence to the ECAF postulates related to the categorization of ECAF measures into drivers and inhibitors, as well as to overall ability to apply the ECAF to measure loss of earning capacity.

Shahnasarian (2009a) conducted a study to investigate how the ECAF could mitigate the effects of examiner bias, which Shahnasarian and Leitten (2008) surmised poses perhaps the greatest threat to inter-rater reliability. The investigator used a single-blind, random assignment experimental design to compare vocational experts' assessment of damages in two case studies. Thirty-two practicing vocational experts used a prototype of the ECAF-2 to facilitate their analyses. Group assignment—perceived retention by a plaintiff lawyer or by a defense lawyer—served as the study's independent variable, and subjects' responses to three referral questions served as dependent variables. No significant differences between group ratings of the dependent variables emerged, supporting the investigator's hypothesis that the ECAF-2 can help mitigate between group rater differences.

An exploratory study of the ECAF-2's inter-rater reliability (Shahnasarian, Leitten & Tremp, 2010) included fours raters' assessments of 20 claims of loss of earning capacity. Correlation coefficients at the .01 levels emerged in analyses of all 14 ECAF-2 factors, and ranged from .71 to .90. Analyses of ECAF-2 Drivers and Inhibitors, and raters' estimates of loss of earning capacity yielded the following correlation coefficients: ECAF-2 Inhibitors, .91; ECAF-2 Drivers, .93; and loss of earning capacity assessments, .94. Subjects agreed or strongly agreed the ECAF-2 facilitated their evaluations 78.6% of the time.

B. Guidelines for Assessing Present and Future Loss of Earning Capacity

Vocational evaluators assess both present earning capacity and potential loss of future earning capacity. Frequently, questions concerning future loss of earning capacity arise in wage claims involving acquired disabilities and employment law.

The ECAF-2 can assist in analyzing factors that may affect present and future earning capacity. Once these factors have been identified and assessed, the vocational evaluator is better able to quantify present earning capacity, and then develop an opinion, within reasonable vocational rehabilitation probability, about future loss of earning capacity.

The ECAF-2 can be particularly useful when the assessment of latent or future loss of earning capacity is evident, but difficult to quantify. Examples of these cases include:

- Pediatric patients who have permanent injuries
- Individuals early in their careers who have yet to demonstrate an adequate baseline of career achievement sufficient to extrapolate assumptions of future achievement
- Individuals who have not realized their full earning potential because their career development was interrupted (e.g., a college-educated individual who was actively raising children and not employed outside the home at the time of an injury)
- Individuals who anticipate experiencing degenerative problems and/or other vocational handicaps
- Self-employed individuals who become impaired in their ability to develop their careers but continue to pursue entrepreneurial activities
- Individuals who lack a demonstrated earnings record

C. Factor Analysis Approach to Assessment of Earning Capacity: Three Examples

Summaries of three cases illustrating how a vocational evaluator assessed changes in present and future earning capacity caused by acquired disabilities follow. Although some facts presented in the cases may be similar to those in other cases that lawyers and vocational evaluators encounter, each case has unique facts and nuances that necessitate independent consideration and assessment.

1. Example one: Head injury to a previously college-bound seventeen-year-old

At age seventeen, a high school honor student sustained a moderate closed-head injury because of a motor vehicle accident. The daughter of an emergency room physician, her parents reported her preaccident vocational aspirations included pursuing undergraduate studies as an English major followed by law school. Medical records were unequivocal about the degree of cognitive and interpersonal impairments the subject sustained, and a neuropsychologist that defense counsel retained opined that she would require supervision to live independently. She did not pursue postaccident employment through the time of her vocational rehabilitation evaluation. Regarding her postaccident vocational activity, the subject completed high school and then attended part-time, remedial courses at a community college; her scholastic performance was well below high-school-level standards.

A vocational evaluator examined the subject when she was twenty-one years old, four years after the accident, and after the period during which she had likely reached her residual capacity to make cognitive gains. Even with many accommodations extended to her, the vocational evaluator noted, pursuing her education after the accident had been difficult. The evaluator deduced from his analysis of both the subject's family background and her premorbid scholastic performance that her stated preaccident career plans would have been viable if not for her acquired disabilities. In addition to identifying anticipated care needs via a life care plan and recommending vocational rehabilitation services, the evaluator provided the following assessment of vocational damages.

> The injuries Ms. Yoder sustained occurred during her senior year of high school. She had been in the exploration phase of her career development. Her disabling problems will likely preclude her from advancing beyond unskilled employment. Within a reasonable degree of vocational rehabilitation probability, Ms. Yoder will be fortunate to secure and maintain employment offering compensation between minimum wage and $10.00 per hour (present value) during her work life. This represents a best-case vocational rehabilitation outcome. Further, because of her acquired vocational handicaps, Ms. Yoder—assuming this best-case scenario—will sustain a future loss of earning capacity that will range between 10 percent and 40 percent over the remainder of her work life.

2. Example two: Construction worker with orthopedic injuries from industrial accident

The subject, Mr. Miller, survived a seven-story fall from a scaffold at a construction site where he had been performing his job as a working construction supervisor. He sustained multiple orthopedic injuries. His coworker, who had also fallen from the scaffold, died at the accident scene. Although the subject responded well to postaccident rehabilitation treatment, his physicians restricted him to light-duty work after he reached maximum medical improvement. Posttraumatic stress disorder was also diagnosed. The subject returned to work with his former employer, who accommodated him in a supervisory position. After his return to work and reassignment to a higher-level, supervisory position, the subject's rate of pay increased.

The subject disclosed job performance difficulties when a vocational evaluator examined him, two years after his industrial accident. Mr. Miller had left school in the eleventh grade, had no general equivalency diploma (GED), and had a measured IQ in the low-average range. He returned to work with his preaccident employer approximately six months before the examination. Throughout his career, he worked as a construction laborer—a job to which he was clearly unable to return. The evaluator offered the following opinions about how the industrial accident affected the injured worker's earning capacity:

> The work history Mr. Miller presented included work requiring heavy exertion within the construction industry. Of his various skills, Mr. Miller considered himself most adept in the demolition of concrete walkways, ceilings, and walls. At the time of the accident, All-American Builders employed him as a working supervisor. Based on my understanding of Mr. Miller's prior work responsibilities, he had been performing semiskilled work requiring heavy exertion. The medical records I reviewed document an extended period before his physicians released him to return to work requiring less exertion. Since his return to work, he has

been working fewer hours than he had been at the time of the accident. He cited fatigue as a reason for his lessened postaccident work participation. My analysis of Mr. Miller's current job responsibilities as a construction supervisor indicates he is required to perform different, more skilled tasks than were previously required of him. He reported his postincident job "was more or less made available to me." While discussing his current job performance and his postaccident position, Mr. Miller expressed doubts about his ability to competently perform his job; he referenced both lack of training and skill as reasons for concern. Based on his representations of his current job responsibilities and my analysis of his job description, Mr. Miller is performing skilled work requiring light exertion. The job responsibilities associated with his current employment do not appear commensurate with his level of intellect, training, or work experience. Although his present job responsibilities appear to be within his physical capabilities, Mr. Miller seems lacking in background necessary to perform his job effectively. Besides his physical problems and residual functional limitations, records indicate he has experienced psychiatric problems as a result of the accident. On one hand, he is fortunate to have his current job. Based on my review of employment records and statements he made to me about his current job responsibilities, along with information gathered while examining Mr. Miller, he does not appear qualified to perform his job responsibilities. I do not believe he is capable—outside his current place of employment—of securing and maintaining the type of employment currently extended to him. If Mr. Miller's job with All-American Builders were to end and he was required to pursue employment commensurate with his earning capacity, within a reasonable degree of vocational probability, his earnings would be reduced to between $7.00 and $9.00 per hour. Concerning his future earning capacity, Mr. Miller has acquired several vocational handicaps that merit consideration. Besides loss of access to work opportunities previously available to him, he is vulnerable to vocational handicaps that include longer search time between jobs, potential employer bias in hiring and advancement, potential need for workplace accommodations, diminished opportunities to pursue overtime work, and reduced potential for advancement. Cumulatively, the vocational handicaps Mr. Miller has acquired because of his work-related accident will exert a mild/moderate affect on his vocational functioning, further reducing his future earning capacity by 20 to 50 percent over the remainder of his work life.

3. Example three: Psychological injury to midlife professional

While on the premises of a hotel parking lot, a forty-nine-year-old woman, Ms. Bontrager, was assaulted and robbed. She was on a business trip when the incident occurred. Her employment as a computer show manager involved overseeing the operations of large computer shows at convention centers throughout the Northeast. Although she did not sustain any permanent physical impairment because of the incident, psychologists retained by both defense and plaintiff's counsel agreed that the subject was experiencing active symptoms of posttraumatic stress disorder. The psychologists, however, disagreed about her degree of impairment. Among the subject's most severe presenting problems were depression, sleep difficulties, headaches, poor self-image and loss of self-confidence, fear of leaving home (especially after dark), word retrieval difficulties, and problems with becoming easily startled. She returned to work after the incident; however, she traveled to computer shows less frequently and indicated that she chose not to pursue business-development tasks after work hours—an important part of her job—as she had done previously. The subject's manager provided deposition testimony that the subject performed her job less effectively after the incident.

Ms. Bontrager underwent a vocational rehabilitation evaluation approximately one year after the assault. The vocational evaluator cited postaccident evidence indicating the scope of her work activities constricted and she performed her job less effectively than she did before the incident. Problems with initiation, low self-esteem and self-confidence, and inhibition were determined especially problematic in view of the subject's job responsibilities. During her clinical interview, Ms. Bontrager, who had been participating in psychotherapy since the incident, disclosed feelings of vulnerability and was quite emotional. The evaluator concluded that Ms. Bontrager's continued employment as a computer show manager was exacerbating her psychological distress and elaborated as follows:

> Obviously, Ms. Bontrager no longer derives the level of job satisfaction she reported having before the incident, and she is associating the assault with her job as a computer show manager. At this time, I

do not believe that Ms. Bontrager's continued participation in her job is in her best interest; indeed, it may be counterproductive to her psychological rehabilitation. I recommend that she take a six-to-twelve-month leave of absence from her employment with AAA Computer Shows. Her condition should be reassessed at the end of this period to determine whether returning to her job as a computer show manager is indicated. If not, I recommend that Ms. Bontrager seek alternate employment. If this option is determined not to be in her best interest, she will likely realize a reduction in her compensation of approximately 20 percent. Restoring Ms. Bontrager to her preassault level of work functioning—in any job she pursues—within six to twelve months will be a formidable challenge. My prognosis for Ms. Bontrager's vocational rehabilitation is guarded. Without adequate psychological treatment and resolution of her presenting psychological problems, she will be at risk of a significantly shortened work life and underachievement. Ms. Bontrager is a fifty-year-old individual who, in addition to having psychological and career-related problems, is also experiencing significant marital problems. Her sources of support are scarce and she has limited resources to aid her.

The defense attorney tested the evaluator's analysis and opinions by questioning employer accommodations, loss of earnings to date, transferability of skills to employment offering compensation commensurate with employment as a computer show manager, and the psychological affect of taking a leave of absence as recommended. The following discussion is an excerpt from the deposition:

Q. Let me just recap my understanding of what we have here. Ms. Bontrager is continuing to work for her present employer, correct?
A. Yes.
Q. And her employer is accommodating her, correct?
A. They are extending accommodations to her.
Q. With regard to her earnings, is there any evidence that she has had an actual loss of earnings—not earning capacity—as a result of the incident at my client's hotel?
A. I know there have been shows in which she has not participated that she would likely have participated in if not for the assault. So I do know there have been lost opportunities for her to earn money as she would likely have. I'm assuming she had more opportunities to increase her earnings beyond what is reflected on her last tax return.
Q. Back to her employer and this issue of accommodations. Are you aware if her employer has taken any negative personnel action against her because of the inability to participate in the computer shows you identified?
A. I'm not aware of any negative action that's been taken.
Q. If she chose to, could she work in a job that does not require her to travel, such as her past job as a human resources manager?
A. She hasn't worked as a human resources manager in five years.
Q. Do you believe that she still possesses the skills to do so?
A. She probably possesses some skills; however, she is at a competitive disadvantage having been out of the position for five years. And of course, the psychological problems that she's acquired as a result of the incident—
Q. Would not allow her to do that?
A. There are many human resources functions I would not recommend for this woman based upon the problems she's acquired. For instance, doing stand-up training in a corporation, I don't believe, would be indicated for her. I certainly would not recommend it for her.
Q. Do you believe Ms. Bontrager could enhance her earnings by returning to a job as a human resources manager, as she performed in the past?
A. If I were to assume that she could ably perform that type of job, she would likely have earnings comparable to what she earned as a computer show manager; however, I don't believe that's an appropriate placement for her.
Q. In your discussion with Ms. Bontrager, did you recommend to her that going back to work in an office might benefit her by taking her out of the work environment she's in now, since it might cue the incident that she experienced last year?
A. At the point I examined her, I did not have my opinions finalized, and I don't recall if I made a specific recommendation of that type. But we did discuss how her continued performance of her job is exacerbating her stress.
Q. Would it be reasonable to make that kind of a recommendation for someone who is suffering from post-traumatic stress disorder?
A. Generally?
Q. Yes.
A. At a general level, I don't think it's an unreasonable recommendation. But I think every case needs to be looked at specifically. And I think what is reasonable for this woman is to have the benefit of the type of intensive treatment that her psychologist has recommended. And I believe taking a leave of absence and

reassessing her situation is clearly in order for her.

Q. Are you not concerned that removing her from a work setting would reduce her self-esteem and reinforce the concept of dysfunction rather than the concept of function during the six-to-twelve-month period you are recommending?

A. I think Ms. Bontrager is having a very difficult time functioning right now. And she needs some professional help and some guidance, and she needs to refocus. I believe the path she's going down is one that's not in her best interests, and I can't possibly endorse it as a vocational rehabilitation professional. What I'm recommending is a type of sabbatical during which she participates in intensive therapy as recommended by her psychologist, and removes herself from an environment that she associates with the assault and is interfering with her ability to recover from the trauma she experienced. Her situation is very tenuous at this point—personally, psychologically, and career-wise.

D. Unconventional and Questionable Approaches to Assessment of Earning Capacity: Three Examples

Generally, the precision of a vocational expert's assessment depends on how thoroughly factors associated with earning capacity have been examined and evaluated with respect to pertinent labor market and other germane information. Precision can be compromised when vocational evaluators fail to thoroughly assess factors known to correlate with earning capacity.

Earning capacity assessments can lose integrity when evaluators make abstract inferences and stray from subject-specific information. The more remote the data is from the subject, the greater the risk that the data may distort facts. An example is the use of computers with databases of occupations that allow vocational evaluators to configure vocational profiles (typically limited to mental and physical capabilities) intended to simulate basic subject characteristics. The occupations composing the database usually include basic, generic information. Once an evaluator develops a cursory vocational profile, a search process is typically initiated by cross-referencing the profile with the database of occupations, coded by characteristics, either to include or to exclude occupations that theoretically should be considered in an earning capacity assessment. This process is laden with problems that threaten the precision of the assessment, including a) overextrapolating from batch-processed or statistical data, b) assuming that the database used is valid for the subject—including assumptions that the data is current and exhaustive—making broad and sometimes speculative assumptions about an individual's career development, and c) ignoring or understating significant career development factors. Examinations that involve nominal consideration of subject-specific factors are sometimes substituted for legitimate examinations because vocational evaluators lack the acumen to analyze the fourteen factors previously outlined.

Beware of assessments performed by experts who have marginal credentials, use incomplete records, deviate from accepted examination protocol, or employ questionable evaluation methods. For sake of illustration, three examples of unconventional and questionable earning capacity assessments/methodologies follow.

1. Example one: Failure to develop a full vocational profile

A thirty-four-year-old high school graduate was unemployed at the time of a motor vehicle accident that occurred four years earlier, and she had six years' experience as a server in a restaurant. She stated that she left the workplace before the accident to have a child. Interestingly, medical records predating the accident indicate the subject sought treatment for essentially the same problems as those she complained of after the accident. Additionally, postaccident medical records included suspicions of somatization and symptom embellishment. Treatment after the accident included a microsurgical cervical discectomy and a microsurgical cervical fusion. The subject was released to return to work with sedentary work restrictions. Citing government statistics, a vocational evaluator the subject's attorney retained opined the subject sustained an earning capacity loss from 22 percent to 100 percent. She provided the following statement during her deposition about how she arrived at her assessment:

If I look, on average, to what happens to somebody with her particular profile, meaning her age, education, sex, according to the U.S. Department of Commerce, that on average there's going to be a disparity in earning capacity, between $15,291 and $19,688, annually. My opinion is that, if she continues with medical treatment so she can get better and go back to work, she will have a loss of earning capacity of 22 percent. But if she is not able to go back to work, her loss of earning capacity will be 100 percent. A person with her profile who develops a work disability on average earns $15,291, versus $19,688 for somebody with her profile who has no work disability. So, if you divide the $15,291 into the $19,688, you get 78, or a 22 percent loss of earning capacity.

Statistical information can provide helpful input to a vocational evaluation; however, as noted repeatedly in this book, questions about earning capacity must be considered within the context of the specific facts at hand and characteristics of the subject. In the preceding case, the vocational evaluator's almost exclusive reference to aggregate statistical data for her opinion on loss of earning capacity was simplistic and certainly does not require the analysis of an "expert." Among the factors notably disregarded in her analysis were the subject's preinjury medical history and work history, motivational factors, and assets to vocational rehabilitation. The evaluator acknowledged in her deposition that she did not have any documentation related to the subject's earning history.

2. Example two: Computing earning capacity loss on the basis of theoretical loss of job accessibility

An elementary school teacher filed a complaint alleging that while she was a customer in a supermarket, an employee, "in a negligent manner, pushed a cart through swinging doors with excessive force. Defendant failed to warn plaintiff of the dangerous condition. As a direct and proximate result of negligent acts and omissions of the defendant, plaintiff was hit by the door, suffered physical injuries, medical expenses, loss of income, loss of capacity to earn income, pain and suffering, mental anguish and loss of enjoyment of life, all of which will continue into the foreseeable future." After the incident, the plaintiff returned to her job with complaints of neck and right-shoulder pain; she underwent conservative treatment. No medical doctor restricted her from returning to work; indeed, three years elapsed before she was examined by a vocational evaluator. Medical records were somewhat contradictory: a physician retained by the subject's attorney diagnosed "myofascial pain syndrome and myosotis." A physician retained by the defense attorney, however, indicated that the subject had no physical problems. In either case, there were no physician-advised restrictions. The vocational evaluator plaintiff's counsel retained computed the number of preincident jobs he determined accessible to the plaintiff and compared this to the number of postincident jobs he found her capable of performing. According to his analysis, the "injuries" the subject acquired exempted her from 73 percent of the occupations available to her before the incident. Further, compared to the median wage of preincident occupations accessible to the claimant, the evaluator concluded that the median wage of occupations accessible to her after the incident were approximately 10 percent less. Therefore, the vocational evaluator opined, the plaintiff was entitled to a loss of earning capacity award of approximately 10 percent of her preinjury capacity for the remainder of her work life.

The vocational evaluator's position was weak because no physician advised restrictions for the subject, and she continued to perform her preincident job without any performance difficulties, accommodations, or attendance problems. Subjective complaints, alone, undergirded the evaluator's rationale in determining postincident jobs purportedly no longer within the subject's capacity. Besides using insufficient evidence to support his rationale for diminishing postincident occupational accessibility, the evaluator rendered opinions about functional limitations and restrictions that appear beyond his scope of expertise. Further, no evidence supported the evaluator's speculation that the subject aspired to any employment other than her employment as a teacher. She had achieved tenured status, her employment was secure, and she indicated that her work was gratifying. Other problems in this loss of earning capacity analysis relate to the evaluator's methods in determining appropriate preincident and postincident occupations. Although this case was not tried, the evaluator would have likely encountered difficulty with suggesting damages in a case in which the plaintiff has secure employment in her chosen profession, is fulfilled and earning the same or higher compensation, and has not been medically advised to change occupations. Requesting compensation for a theoretical loss of access to jobs—and a corresponding theoretical diminution in earning capacity—that the plaintiff has not contemplated pursuing in the past or in the present is a tenuous position, at best.

3. Example three: Overreliance on selected statistical data of little value

Counsel representing an individual who filed a claim under the Americans with Disabilities Act hired a vocational evaluator to quantify limitations the plaintiff's disabilities caused. The plaintiff was employed as a customer service clerk by a regional bank. Because of her impairments, reasoned the evaluator, the plaintiff was precluded from a significant class of jobs and from performing the full range of an even larger number of jobs, as compared to the average person having comparable training, skills, and abilities. The vocational evaluator provided the following conclusion:

> In her preinjury condition, Ms. Bass, by virtue of her education, training, and background, would have been capable of performing approximately 927 occupations. In her postinjury condition, however, she is capable of performing approximately 138 occupations. Further, because of geographic restrictions, Ms. Bass would be limited to less than the 138 occupations she could perform in her current medical condition.

Defense counsel filed a motion to strike the declaration of the plaintiff's vocational evaluator; this motion was granted. In arriving at her decision, the judge commented that the evaluator offered nothing but legal conclusions and unsupported—and likely unsupportable—conclusions about the number of jobs for which the plaintiff qualified before and after her injury. The judge noted that neither the evaluator's background nor the facts on which she relied were set forth in any substantial way. The evaluator's opinion was further determined to have no probative value, and the judge commented, "An expert who supplies nothing but a bottom line supplies nothing of value to the judicial process."

5.5 Conclusion

Earning capacity assessments too often rely on nonsystematic processes and subjective criteria that lead to wide variances in opinions between opposing vocational experts who have ostensibly based their analyses on the same or similar set of facts. The methods presented in this chapter promote the conduct of comprehensive vocational evaluations that focus precisely on factors affecting earning capacity.

Part II

Conducting Vocational Assessments

Chapter 6

Assessment of Earning Capacity in Cases of Acquired Disabilities

6.1 Introduction

Careers and career plans, in many respects, can be likened to structures such as houses or buildings. Some are but a concept—thoughts and intentions that, for various reasons, do not come to fruition. Others evolve to blueprints, and yet others become partially or fully constructed at various rates, shapes, sizes, costs, and degrees of perfection. Some structures are strong; some are weak. The quality of materials and labor used in construction may be superior or inferior, varying in resilience to internal and external stressors. Some structures incorporate a bold or stately veneer; others appear unstable and project poor craftsmanship. Interest and demand for a structure's design and function tend to change over time, as does its use and configuration.

Similar to structures constructed of brick, mortar, and other materials, individuals' careers and career plans vary widely on factors that include the phase and level of development, demand for skills and talents, and foundational factors including education and specialized training, skills, and work experiences. Chapter 5 detailed fourteen factors that can affect one's career development and earning capacity.

Just as inclement weather, fire, or other external forces can damage a structure, acquired disabilities that reduce an individual's physical or mental capabilities can damage career development and earning capacity. In the same way that some structures withstand hurricane-force winds and others unexpectedly crumble without any apparent outside force, some individuals develop their careers despite major disabilities they have acquired, while others capitulate their career development after incurring seemingly minor or insignificant trauma.

In some ways, methods vocational evaluators employ to assess earning capacity approximate those a building inspector employs to assess prospective damage a fire, tornado, flood, or other calamity caused to a structure. An inspector assesses imminent damages as well as damages that may later manifest. Occasionally, the full effect of damages is not apparent. Loose shingles on a roof, for instance, may not need immediate replacement; however, a building inspector may project a replacement schedule two to three years earlier than might otherwise be the case. Similarly, a vocational evaluator may conclude that physical injury may truncate an individual's work life.

Present and future damages to career development and earning capacity must be comprehensively and accurately assessed to articulate damages an acquired disability causes. Robinson and Drew (2014) also addressed providing consultation in civil injury litigation. Every vocational assessment is unique and must be based on information, findings, and case-specific information that emerge from a pending vocational evaluation.

Vocational evaluators assess how acquired disabilities affect an individual's employability and earning capacity. They most often address issues related to the interaction of acquired disabilities and vocational capacity in the following forums:

- Medical malpractice
- Personal injury
- Workers' compensation
- Private disability insurance policies
- The Social Security Administration
- Product liability

The standards governing vocational damage claims may vary widely between legal forums and jurisdictions. For instance, in workers' compensation cases in Florida, an individual presenting a claim of permanent total disability must prove there are no occupations she can perform. This standard differs from the Social Security Administration's standard. In this latter forum, an administrative law judge considers age, transferable skills, residual capabilities, and vocational adjustment to determine whether a substantial number of work opportunities exist that a claimant can perform on a sustained basis. Many private insurance disability policies have other standards, which typically relate to whether the policyholder is capable of performing her prior occupation. For instance, a trial attorney with depression symptoms may assert that the severity of his problems prevents him from pursuing his previous occupation, and he is therefore entitled to disability benefits as specified in a privately held insurance disability policy. In this case, even though the policyholder may be able to perform other occupations, he may qualify for disability benefits his policy specifies if he can prove his mental health problems render him incapable of performing his prior occupation. Claims related to long-term disability insurance are discussed in Chapter 10.

In medical malpractice and personal injury cases, plaintiffs can pursue compensation for vocational damages—assuming they prevail in liability disputes—by demonstrating a causal relationship between an event in question and their earning capacity. If an event—such as an automobile accident that permanently impairs an individual, or a physician's failure to diagnose a medical condition that ultimately diminishes an individual's cognitive capabilities—is judged within a reasonable degree of probability to compromise a plaintiff's career development or earning capacity, the plaintiff can pursue compensatory damages to recover the alleged earning capacity loss. Loss of earning capacity and opportunities to mitigate vocational damages are often prominent questions in these cases.

6.2 Central Vocational Questions

The following issues often arise during an assessment of earning capacity related to acquired disabilities:

- Preincident (injury) earning capacity and skills
- Residual functional capabilities and limitations
- Transferable skills, and need and capacity for retraining
- Costs of retraining, if applicable
- Presence of acquired vocational handicaps
- Postincident (injury) earning capacity
- Loss of earning capacity
- Mitigation efforts
- Future rehabilitative needs

Interest in the preceding areas corresponds to specific vocational issues in dispute. Depending on the facts and other case-specific details, some areas may be highly relevant and disputed while others are irrelevant. A discussion of each area follows.

A. Preincident (Injury) Earning Capacity and Skills

Establishing a benchmark of an individual's premorbid earning capacity is a prerequisite to analyzing potential comparative postincident earning capacity changes. Trends in earnings history, projections about the demand for skills, and a professional analysis of a person's preincident career development prospects facilitate the formulation of preincident earning capacity estimates.

B. Residual Functional Capabilities and Limitations

To determine a subject's most promising career options, vocational evaluators should consider acquired restrictions and disabling problems while developing a vocational profile and assessing prevailing labor market conditions. This assessment has particular relevance when analyzing a subject's capability to return to prior work, examining activities that remain within a subject's capabilities, and evaluating viable future work activities.

C. Transferable Skills, and Need and Capacity for Retraining

If the subject of an earning capacity assessment is deemed unable to return to prior work or pursue previously identified, viable career objectives because of acquired disabilities, the vocational consultant then analyzes the subject's transferable skills, along with need and capacity for retraining. This analysis prognosticates the feasibility of alternate employment and long-term career development prospects. The difference between premorbid earning capacity and earning capacity associated with occupations that remain within the subject's capability are typically foremost considerations.

D. Costs of Retraining

A vocational evaluator may conclude an individual who acquired disabling problems can best preserve her career development and earning capacity via retraining. When vocational evaluators propose retraining scenarios, the following factors merit attention: length and costs of retraining, reasonable levels of compensation after retraining, and comparison of earnings levels and opportunities for career development following retraining with comparable preincident measures.

An example of a retraining plan, with responses to questions that allow for comparative analyses of preincident earning capacity and earning capacity after proposed retraining, is presented below. This case involved a twenty-six-year-old warehouse receiver who sustained a severe left-femur fracture; his rate of pay had been $12.00 per hour. As a result of his injuries, physicians advised him to avoid squatting, climbing stairs, prolonged standing and walking, and lifting more than twenty pounds. Based on these restrictions, a vocational evaluator determined the individual was unable to return to his preinjury employment; however, the evaluator noted the individual had many assets for vocational rehabilitation and provided a retraining plan to facilitate this. Excerpts from the evaluator's report follow:

> Based on my analysis, Mr. Travis cannot return to his employment as a warehouse receiver. He possesses few transferable skills to aid his vocational rehabilitation. His current earning capacity without retraining is in the minimum wage range. Fortunately, he is an appropriate candidate for retraining, and I support these efforts. Mr. Travis is a younger individual, age twenty-six, who is independent in transportation and does not use adaptive aids other than eyeglasses. He denied having problems related to his cervical spine functioning, use of either upper extremity, or fine motor functioning. He repositioned normally while seated. Results from testing administered during my examination indicate that Mr. Travis' level of mental functioning is in the average range. He appears cognitively intact. He demonstrated excellent interpersonal skills. These factors are assets to Mr. Travis' vocational rehabilitation.
>
> Mr. Travis expressed interest in pursuing training related to computer-assisted drafting at All-American Vocational Technical School. His stated career aspirations are viable from a vocational rehabilitation perspective. According to information provided by All-American Vocational Technical School, the next computer-aided drafting program will begin June 4, 2015. The duration of the program is nineteen months, five days per week (8:00 A.M. to 2:00 P.M.). The cost of the program is $5,630, including tuition, books, supplies, and an activity fee. According to a wage survey conducted by All-American Vocational Technical School, beginning salaries for graduates of their computer-assisted drafting program is $15.00 per hour. A 2014 wage and benefits survey published by the Suncoast Human Resource Management Association and Suncoast Compensation & Benefits Association, Inc., reported that the average hiring compensation rate for drafters in the Tampa/St. Petersburg area is $34,500, annually. A 2014 occupational wage report based on data from the U.S. Bureau of Labor Statistics indicated that median hourly wage rates for drafters in the Tampa/St. Petersburg area were $19.34 per hour. Within a reasonable degree of vocational rehabilitation probability, Mr. Travis would be capable of attaining this median wage rate within five years.

E. Presence of Acquired Vocational Handicaps

An earning capacity assessment is incomplete if it does not consider permanent vocational handicaps secondary to a disability and take into account how acquired vocational handicaps may affect a person's future career development and earning capacity. A discussion of vocational handicaps appears in Chapter 5.

F. Postincident (Injury) Earning Capacity

In cases that involve an individual with an established work history, vocational evaluators should assess how acquired disabilities have and will affect the person's ability to pursue career options available before an incident in question. This analysis sometimes requires consideration of how an individual's career path likely would have evolved absent the acquisition of disabling problems. Even when an individual can resume preincident employment, vocational evaluators should determine whether acquired disabilities and/or vocational handicaps threaten present/future earning capacity. If the subject can pursue prior employment but has limitations in work participation, diminished capacity to earn income from commissions or other incentives, or diminished promotion and career advancement opportunities, for example, both present and future earning capacity may diminish. Similarly, assuming the subject cannot return to preincident employment, the vocational evaluator must determine a reasonable postincident earnings standard based on an earning capacity assessment as outlined in Chapter 4.

G. Loss of Earning Capacity

The question most frequently posed to a vocational consultant regarding a person with acquired disabilities is whether the individual has sustained a loss of earning capacity. Addressing this question involves assessing whether the acquired disability exempts or limits the subject from returning to preincident employment and career development opportunities with no adverse effects. If there are no changes and none are anticipated, it is generally presumed that no loss of earning capacity has occurred or will occur. A loss of earning capacity, however, is generally deduced when a vocational evaluator concludes the following:

- The individual's ability to pursue preinjury career development is impaired
- There are no opportunities to fully mitigate the effect acquired disabilities pose

Generally, vocational evaluators conclude a loss of earning capacity results when a) individuals' abilities to access preincident occupations and/or career opportunities diminish, and b) the residual career opportunities are less remunerative. Assessing loss of earning capacity can become more complicated in cases of acquired disabilities that involve a child, a person who had yet to realize her earning capacity, cases involving owners of startup businesses, or other circumstances in which evidence suggests an individual's preincident earnings history does not represent current or future earning capacity. If a vocational evaluator concludes a subject has sustained a loss of earning capacity, the evaluator must then quantify the earning capacity loss; this analysis should incorporate an assessment of opportunities to mitigate career-related damages.

H. Mitigation

Mitigation involves reasonable activities subjects can undertake to ameliorate or remedy career development and associated earning capacity damages. Assuming an individual with an acquired disability can pursue his career development, vocational evaluators may form opinions about whether the individual has exhibited good faith mitigation efforts. For example, a house painter, after injuring his dominant hand, demonstrated evidence of good faith mitigation by undergoing retraining to pursue a career as an interior designer; he realized postinjury earnings greater than he generated before becoming injured. It should be noted that instances of a subject earning more money after experiencing a disabling event that causes him to change occupations is more often the exception than the rule.

Assessing efforts to mitigate vocational damages includes evaluating the intensity, consistency, and quality of a subject's postincident vocational rehabilitation efforts. Questions about malingering, secondary gain, and suboptimization of efforts sometimes emerge when a vocational evaluator suspects that a person has not made concerted efforts to mitigate vocational damages after acquiring a disability.

I. Future Rehabilitative Needs

Qualified rehabilitation professionals occasionally develop a life care plan—a document that identifies care needs anticipated for an individual because of acquired disabilities—to address questions about future medical and associated damages. Life care plans typically identify projected needs such as diagnostic tests, treatment and therapies, nursing and related care, medications, and adaptive equipment. In some cases, recommendations for vocational rehabilitation are also included. Examples of recommendations to promote vocational rehabilitation include vocational guidance services to aid in career planning and job placement, participation in a work hardening program, tutorial assistance, and retraining programs. These recommendations typically appear in a life care plan or a vocational expert's report.

Life care planning is a specialty consulting service, and not all vocational rehabilitation experts possess the qualifications and expertise necessary to develop a life care plan—especially in a sensitive, technical, high-stakes case. Pomeranz, Yu, and Robinson (2014) provided a recent summary on life care planning.

Appendix 6.1, at the end of this chapter, includes a life care plan prepared for an individual who sustained multisystem impairments—including spinal cord injury and traumatic brain damage, both with diffuse sequelae—because of an airboat accident. The evaluator determined the claimant was not a candidate for vocational rehabilitation; hence, the life care plan does not include recommendations for this. Footnotes specify sources of cost information—as much as possible, actual costs charged by the claimant's healthcare providers. Notice that the life care plan incorporates anticipated increased need for rehabilitation services, secondary to acquired disabling problems, as the claimant ages.

6.3 Noteworthy Considerations

Two situations often place extra scrutiny on vocational experts when they assess claims of loss of earning capacity that plaintiffs with acquired disabling problems assert. One is when records contain divergent or disparate information, such as medical opinions about an individual's physical capabilities and restrictions. Another is when an expert forecasts a future loss of earning capacity—even though an individual is actively employed and earning wages commensurate with preincident levels. More discussion about these situations follows.

A. Divergent or Disparate Medical Opinions

Occasionally, sources of information upon which vocational experts rely present disparate or mixed assessments. For instance, a physician retained by plaintiff's counsel may develop restrictions and a prognosis for a plaintiff that are greatly at odds with an assessment developed by a physician retained by defense counsel. Since vocational experts typically are not medical experts, they must restrict their opinions to areas within their expertise. Reconciling differences in medical opinions can be challenging.

What should a vocational expert do when medical opinions on which she relies (e.g., diagnoses, restrictions, prognoses) are mixed or divergent? Experts risk losing credibility if they unabashedly assign greater weight to an opinion of a physician retained by the same attorney who retained her while ignoring or minimizing contrary medical opinions opposing experts express—unless a good reason can be provided for this decision. Certain circumstances, however, may justify a vocational evaluator's decision to adopt a particular physician's view as a basis for developing vocational opinions. For example, an expert may give greater weight to the opinions of one physician over another under the following circumstances:

- Surveillance videotape shows an individual performing activities that contradict a physician's assessment of the subject's functional capacities.
- Test data generated during a vocational evaluation provides a rationale for adopting a certain position.
- Medical information from one source is more current.
- The vocational evaluator detects inconsistencies in the subject's behavior that provide a basis to challenge physician opinions about capabilities and limitations.

When disparate medical opinions of consequence to a vocational expert emerge and there is no basis to apportion more weight to one set of opinions over another, experts should develop independent scenarios around each medical opinion. In some cases, the expert may have bases—derived, for example, vis-a-vis surveillance showing a claimant engaging in activities requiring greater exertion than what a physician reckoned the claimant capable of performing, and/or a set of physician assessments that is more current than other assessments—that enable a vocational expert to ascribe more weight to one of the disparate opinions. Appendix 6.2 presents a sample report of a vocational rehabilitation evaluation.

B. Current Employment and Projections of Future Earning Capacity Loss

Opinions concerning future loss of earning capacity often encounter intense challenge, especially when the subject is employed at the time of an earning capacity assessment and is earning compensation proximate to preincident levels. Anticipated degenerative problems and acquired vocational handicaps are particularly important considerations in projecting future earnings. Chapter 5 discusses factors necessary to consider when formulating opinions about present and future earning capacity.

In a case involving a police officer injured in an off-duty collision, a vocational expert concluded that a loss of earning capacity resulted—even though her employment with her preaccident employer continued, and her compensation was not adjusted after her postaccident reassignment to a civilian administrative position. This opinion was largely based on the subject's acquired disabilities and change in work status from a certified police officer to a civilian employee. The loss could be measured by comparing her preaccident level of compensation, which continued to be her postaccident rate of pay despite reassignment to a new job, with the fair market value of the new civilian position to which she was assigned. Further, the vocational expert concluded that the former police officer would likely sustain additional future earning capacity damages. The following opinions appeared in the expert's vocational rehabilitation report:

> At the time of the December 18, 2013, motor vehicle accident, Ms. Seminole was employed as a detective. Among other things, her job exposed her to threat of physical altercations and personal harm. After the accident, Ms. Seminole was reassigned to an investigator administrative position. Her reported job satisfaction has diminished. Although Ms. Seminole indicated her employer has been accommodating and supportive, she expressed concern about her job security. The records I reviewed included a pay matrix for the City of Neptune; this document indicates that individuals at Ms. Seminole's pay grade (Police Master Officer, Step 11) earn $24.33 per hour. Ms. Seminole, however, no

longer performs the job responsibilities associated with this position; she is performing administrative job tasks that do not require the job incumbent to be a certified police officer. Based upon my understanding of her present job responsibilities and rates of pay at the City of Neptune, a reasonable estimate of an annual pay range commensurate with her postaccident job is between $22,500 and $37,000. Ms. Seminole's present job responsibilities appear within her capacity; her compensation has yet to be adjusted to reflect the value ascribed to the work she currently performs. She will probably not be able to return to her preinjury job. Over time, the likelihood that Ms. Seminole's compensation will be adjusted to reflect the pay associated with her job responsibilities, or that she will be released or replaced by another individual who is a candidate for her present job and seeks compensation commensurate with its pay range will increase. Potential future management changes, economic pressures, and other factors beyond her control also make her more vulnerable to external sources that bear on her career development opportunities.

Regarding her future earning capacity, Ms. Seminole's preinjury job as a detective offered career development and advancement opportunities that are no longer available to her. Among the vocational handicaps she has acquired as a result of the 2013 accident are diminished access to preinjury work activities, need for workplace accommodations, and diminished opportunities for career development. Likelihood of a truncated work life is another significant vocational handicap that, within a reasonable degree of vocational rehabilitation probability, will adversely affect Ms. Seminole's future earning capacity. Conservatively, these vocational handicaps will further reduce her residual earning capacity by 15 percent over the remainder of her work life. If she were to lose her job at the City of Neptune, Ms. Seminole would be vulnerable to additional vocational handicaps such as employer bias in hiring and advancement opportunities, likelihood of extended search time between jobs, and diminished work opportunities.

Portions from the vocational expert's deposition in which he addressed questions related to the opinions presented above follow. During this dialogue, the expert explains his rationale for assigning a 15-percent loss in residual future earning capacity; Chapter 5 includes a discussion of the types of vocational handicaps the expert references.

Q. Can you explain to me your opinions regarding why you believe Ms. Seminole is going to have a truncated work life and additional future earning capacity loss?

A. I am rendering an opinion that Ms. Seminole is going to have an additional earning capacity loss over the remainder of her work life, and my opinion is based on a number of vocational handicaps that I believe she's acquired; I've listed some of those in my report. For instance, need for workplace accommodations, diminished opportunities for career development. That has to do with things like lessened opportunities for promotion, overtime work, advancement opportunities not being as plentiful as they otherwise would have been if she had been in a different career path, and a truncated work life. And my opinion is that, collectively, these vocational handicaps will erode her residual earning capacity by an additional 15% over the remainder of her work life. I'm basing that on my understanding of Ms. Seminole's acquired disabling problems, my understanding of the types of career needs and surgery that physicians have recommended she undergo in the future, the fact that as people get older—and Ms. Seminole is a younger individual in the prime of her career—people often have problems with degenerative changes, exacerbations, flare-ups. I'm also familiar with literature published by the National Institute of Health that attests to a relationship between the types of disabling problems Ms. Seminole has and a shortened work life. Of course, her problems with chronic pain and depression also need to be considered. Cumulatively, looking at her over the remainder of her work life—not just a snapshot that we have now—it's my opinion that her vocational handicaps will further erode her future earning capacity by approximately 15%.

Q. And how do you come up with the opinion of 15%?

A. Basically, I'm looking at her future loss of earning capacity on a continuum of 0% to 100%—zero being no future loss of earning capacity and 100% being catastrophic or total loss of future earning capacity. I further consider gradations on this scale in terms of future loss of earning capacity being mild, moderate, severe, or extremely severe—just short of catastrophic. My assessment is that Ms. Seminole's acquired vocational handicaps will have a mild affect on her future earning capacity. Applying this scale and my assessment of her vocational handicaps that result from her injuries, I estimate that Ms. Seminole's vocational handicaps will further reduce her future earning capacity by 15% over the remainder of her work life.

Q. If I understand what your opinions are—and these are just rough numbers—she's making around $50,000 a year now. You believe in the future she's only going to be able to make somewhere between $22,500 and $37,000, and so you would say that she has somewhere around a $20,000-a-year wage loss plus an additional 15% wage loss because of this truncated work-life expectancy?

A. No. That's not completely accurate.

Q. Okay. Help me out there.

A. What I'm saying is that a realistic assessment of her current earning capacity is in the range of $22,500 to $37,000. That is an assessment of her fair market value earning capacity at this time.

Q. Okay.

A. And what I'm saying is that if you look at her over the remainder of her work life—which is what we have a responsibility to do, not just her earning capacity today—she is going to have additional future erosion of her earning capacity of approximately 15%. That's not solely because of the truncated work life; it's cumulatively, as a result of all of these vocational handicaps I've identified that she's acquired because of the 2013 accident.

6.4 Conclusion

Vocational evaluators who assess the earning capacity of persons with acquired disabling problems should have a sound background in assessment, medical and psychosocial aspects of rehabilitation, and knowledge of rehabilitation counseling. This background facilitates evaluators' abilities to evaluate and integrate the relevance of prospective disabling problems, and understand how they relate to complex vocational questions.

Appendix 6.1: Sample Life Care Plan

LIFE CARE PLAN

Prepared for

Aaron Allen Rogers

Michael Shahnasarian, Ph.D.
March 31, 2014

Life Care Plan for Aaron Allen Rogers

TABLE OF CONTENTS

Life Care Plan for Aaron Allen Rogers

CONTRIBUTORS TO LIFE CARE PLAN

The individuals listed below provided recommendations for this Life Care Plan

Contributor	Specialty	Consultation Date	Telephone
Dr. Michael Shahnasarian	Rehabilitation Psychologist	03/13/14 03/10/14	(813) 265-9262
Dr. James Lowden	Neurosurgeon	03/17/14 No recommendations	(865) 305-5555
Dr. Bruce Yago	Urologist	03/17/14	(865) 305-5555
Dr. Gary Henri	Ophthalmologist	03/17/14	(865) 521-5555
Dr. Otis Saunders, DO	Pulmonologist	03/17/14	(615) 322-5555
Dr. Patrick Harper	Neuropsychologist	03/25/14	(407) 644-5555
Dr. Andrew Ingles	Optometrist	03/25/14	(423) 562-5555
Dr. Marc Thompson	Neurologist	03/28/14 02/03/14 Report	(407) 644-5555
Dr. Sharon Huxtable	Physiatrist	*	(865) 541-5555
Dr. Brian Icona	Orthopedic Surgeon	*	(865) 558-5555
Dr. David Goodman	Otorhinolaryngologist	*	(615) 343-5555

*Note: Treatment recommendations from Dr. Sharon Huxtable (Physiatrist), Dr. Brian Icona (Orthopedic Surgeon), and Dr. David Goodman (Otorhinolaryngologist) have yet to be fully specified.

Life Care Plan for Aaron Allen Rogers

BACKGROUND INFORMATION

NAME:	Aaron Allen Rogers
DATE OF BIRTH:	November 03, 1951
ONSET OF DISABLING PROBLEM:	February 07, 2012, work-related airboat accident
RACE:	White
DOMINANT HAND:	Right
HEIGHT:	5 feet 7 inches
CURRENT WEIGHT:	190 pounds
PREACCIDENT WEIGHT:	190 pounds
MARITAL STATUS:	Married, Cheryl Rogers, born February 21, 1951
NAMES AND AGES OF CHILDREN:	Aaron Allen, 35 AnneMarie Elizabeth, 30
RESIDENCE:	Speedwell, Tennessee
PRESENTING PROBLEMS:	Traumatic brain injury, spinal cord injury Double vision Aching base/back of head Right shoulder weakness and limited range of motion Bowel and bladder incontinence/urgency Memory difficulties Trachea damage resulting in breathing issues Balance trouble Fatigue "Overly sensitive nerves" Erectile dysfunction Left calf numbness/aching Difficulty speaking due to paralyzed right vocal cord Throat problems causing choking on food/drinks/saliva several times per day

Life Care Plan for Aaron Allen Rogers

EVALUATIONS

Item	Duration	Frequency	Estimated Cost	Recommended By
PSYCHIATRIC EVALUATION	Year 1	One Time*	$175 - $190	Dr. Harper Dr. Shahnasarian Dr. Thompson
Note: Additional recommendations will follow. *Dr. Thompson's report, dated 2/03/14, stated "Patient referred to - Psychiatry."*				
Per Brenda at the Behavioral Medicine Group, P.C., office of Dr. John Simon, psychiatrist, 865-264-5555 (Knoxville, TN): Psychiatric evaluation, $190. *Per the Center for Psychiatry, P.C., office of Dr. Kelley Yoder, psychiatrist, 865-691-5555 (Knoxville, TN): Psychiatric evaluation, $175.*				
NEUROPSYCHOLOGICAL EVALUATION*	Year 1 - 10	One Time	$1,500 - $1,520	Dr. Harper Dr. Shahnasarian Dr. Thompson
**Note: Dr. Thompson's report, dated 2/03/14, stated "Patient referred to - Neuropsychology."*				
Per Brenda at the Behavioral Medicine Group, P.C., office of Dr. Jacob Mendenhall, 865-264-5555 (Knoxville, TN): Neuropsychological evaluation and assessment, $1,520. *Per Dr. Malcolm Toole, neuropsychologist at Toole Psychology Clinic, 865-531-55555 (Knoxville, TN): Neuropsychological evaluation, $1,500.*				
PAIN MANAGEMENT EVALUATION*	Year 1	One Time	$250	Dr. Thompson
**Note: Dr. Thompson's report, dated 2/03/14, stated "Patient referred to - Pain Management."*				
Per Courtney at Pain Consultants, office of Dr. James Doore , 865-579-5555 (Knoxville, TN): Pain management evaluation $250.				
ENDOCRINOLOGY EVALUATION*	Year 1	One Time	$185 - $225	Dr. Thompson
**Note: Dr. Thompson's report, dated 2/03/14, stated "Patient referred to - Endocrine"*				
Per Lori at Endocrinology Consultants, office of Dr. Daniel Nemoy , 865-637-5555 (Knoxville, TN): Endocrinologist evaluation, $185 to $225.				
NEUROSURGEON EVALUATION*	To Be Determined	To Be Determined	$175	Dr. Thompson
**Note: Dr. Thompson's report, dated 2/03/14, stated "Patient referred to - Neurosurgeon."*				
Per Mr. Rogers' medical record, dated 5/02/13, from Stellar Neurosurgery , P.C., office of Dr. James Lowden, neurosurgeon, 865-305-5555 (Knoxville, TN): Neurosurgeon evaluation, $175.				

Life Care Plan for Aaron Allen Rogers

EVALUATIONS

Item	Duration	Frequency	Estimated Cost	Recommended By
UPDATE LIFE CARE PLAN	Year 10	One Time*	$8,000	Dr. Shahnasarian Dr. Harper Dr. Thompson
**Note: Dr. Thompson's report, dated 2/03/14, stated "Patient referred to – life care planner, he is at increased risk of dementia and seizures."*				
Per Dr. Michael Shahnasarian: Update Life Care Plan, $8,000.				

Life Care Plan for Aaron Allen Rogers

THERAPEUTIC NEEDS

Item	Duration	Frequency	Estimated Cost	Recommended By
PSYCHOLOGICAL COUNSELING	Year 1	1 Session Per Week For 10 - 20 Weeks, Then 1 Session Every Other Week For 10 - 20 Weeks	$190 Per Session	Dr. Harper Dr. Shahnasarian
**Note: Per Dr. Shahnasarian, results from March 2014 testing indicate Mr. Rogers is experiencing severe depression; however, he responded negatively when asked if he believes he is in need of mental health treatment. Per Dr. Harper, psychotherapy, year 1, 1 session per week for 10 to 20 weeks, then every other week for 10 to 20 weeks. Reassess potential to benefit from additional treatment at the end of this protocol.*				
Per Brenda at the Behavioral Medicine Group, P.C., office of Dr. Jacob Mendenhall, 865-264-5555 (Knoxville, TN): Psychological counseling, $190 per session.				

FAMILY COUNSELING	Year 1	5 - 10 Sessions*	$190 Per Session	Dr. Harper Dr. Shahnasarian
**Note: Assess potential to benefit from additional family therapy at the end of this protocol.*				
Per Brenda at the Behavioral Medicine Group, P.C., office of Dr. Jacob Mendenhall, 865-264-5555 (Knoxville, TN): Family counseling, $190 per session.				

COGNITIVE REHABILITATION	Year 1	2 - 3 Sessions Per Week For 3 - 6 Months*	$180 Per 15-Minute Session	Dr. Harper Dr. Thompson
**Note: Per Dr. Harper, reassess potential to benefit from additional treatment at the end of this period. Dr. Thompson's report, dated 2/03/14, stated "Therapy Ordered - Cognitive Behavioral Therapy." Additional recommendations will follow.*				
Per Mr. Rogers' medical record, dated 2/26/13, from Regional Medical Center , 865-374-5555 (Knoxville, TN): Cognitive rehabilitation, $180 per 15-minute session.				

BRAIN/HEAD INJURY SUPPORT GROUP	Year 1 - Life	Monthly	No Charge	Dr. Harper
Per The Rehabilitation Center , www.rehabcntr.org, 865-541-5555 (Knoxville, TN) and Regional Medical Center Brain Injury Services Coordination (Knoxville, TN): The Brain Injury Support Group (BISG) meets on the first Monday of each month at 7 p.m. The location is at Rehabilitation Center at Regional Medical Center. Contact person is Patty Dagwood , telephone number 865-541-5555.				

Life Care Plan for Aaron Allen Rogers

THERAPEUTIC NEEDS

Item	Duration	Frequency	Estimated Cost	Recommended By
PHYSICAL THERAPY *	Year 1 – Life	*	$180 Per Session	Dr. Thompson
**Note: Dr. Thompson's report, dated 2/03/14, stated "Therapy Ordered - Physical Therapy."*				
Per Mr. Rogers' medical record, dated 2/05/13, from Regional Medical Center, 865-374-5555 (Knoxville, TN): Physical therapy, $180 per session.				
UROLOGIST FOLLOW-UP	Year 1 - Life	2 Visits Per Year	$73 Per Visit	Dr. Yago Dr. Thompson
**Note: Dr. Thompson's report, dated 2/03/14, stated "Patient to continue care with ENT, Primary Care, and urology."*				
Per Mr. Rogers' medical records, dated 7/12/13, from Yago Urology , P.C., office of Dr. Bruce Yago, 865-305-5555 (Knoxville, TN): Urologist follow-up, $73 per visit.				
INTERVENTIONAL PULMONOLOGIST FOLLOW-UP*	Year 1 - Life	To Be Determined	$247	Dr. Saunders
**Note: If problems with stridor or shortness of breath develop.*				
Per Mr. Rogers' medical record, dated 4/02/13, from Tennessee Medical Group , 615-936-5555 (Nashville, TN): Pulmonologist office visit, $247 (this includes return office visit, $160, plus max breathing capacity, $24, plus bronchospasm evaluation, $63).				
ENT/OTORHINOLARYNGOLOGIST FOLLOW-UP	Year 1 - Life	2 Visits Per Year	$237 Per Visit	Dr. Saunders Dr. Thompson
**Note: Dr. Thompson's report, dated 2/03/14, stated "Patient to continue care with ENT, Primary Care, and urology."*				
Per Mr. Rogers' medical record, dated 9/06/12, from the Tennessee Medical Group , office of Dr. David Goodman, 615-343-5555 (Nashville, TN): ENT follow-up, $237.				
OPTOMETRIST FOLLOW-UP	Year 1 - Life	2 Visits Per Year	$90 Per Visit	Dr. Ingles
Per the Tennessee Eye Clinic, office of Dr. Andrew Ingles, 423-562-5555 (LaFollette, TN): Optometrist follow-up, $90 per visit.				
OPHTHALMOLOGIST FOLLOW-UP	Year 1 - 4 Or 5 Year 4 Or 5 - Life	Every 1 - 2 Years Every 2 Years	$80 Per Visit	Dr. Henri Dr. Thompson
**Note: Dr. Thompson's report, dated 2/03/14, stated "Patient referred to – Neuro-ophthalmology."*				
Per Mr. Rogers' medical record, dated 5/06/13, from Southern Ophthalmology, office of Dr. Gary Henri , 865-521-5555 (Knoxville, TN): Ophthalmology follow-up, $80 per visit.				

Life Care Plan for Aaron Allen Rogers

THERAPEUTIC NEEDS

Item	Duration	Frequency	Estimated Cost	Recommended By
PHYSIATRIST FOLLOW-UP	Year 1 – Life	2 Visits Per Year Or As Needed	$270 Per Visit	Dr. Thompson
**Note: Dr. Thompson's report, dated 2/03/14, stated "Patient referred to - Physiatry = PM&R."*				
Per Mr. Rogers' medical record, dated 10/25/12, from W & W Associates, PLLC, office of Dr. Sharon Huxtable, 865-541-5555 (Knoxville, TN): "Physiatrist office visit EP comprehensive, $270."				
NEUROLOGIST FOLLOW-UP	Year 1 - Life	1 Visit Every 2 Months	$160 Per Visit	Dr. Thompson
Per Neurology Associates, office of Dr. Bruce Matthews, 865-693-5555 (Knoxville, TN): Neurologist evaluation, $200; Neurologist follow-up, $160 per visit.				
NEUROPSYCHOLOGIST FOLLOW-UP	To Be Determined	To Be Determined	$200 Per Visit	Dr. Thompson
Per Dr. Malcolm Toole, neuropsychologist at Toole Psychology Clinic, 865-531-5555 (Knoxville, TN): Neuropsychological follow-up, $200 per visit.				
PRIMARY CARE FOLLOW-UP	Year 1 – Life	2 Visits Per Year Or As Needed	$195 Per Visit	Dr. Thompson
**Note: Dr. Thompson's report, dated 2/03/14, stated "Patient continue care with ENT, Primary Care, and urology."*				
Per Mr. Rogers' medical record, dated 2/14/13 from the office of Dr. Greg Langston, internal medicine physician, 865-522-5555 (Speedwell, TN): Primary care follow-up, $195 per visit.				
PSYCHIATRIC FOLLOW-UP	To Be Determined	To Be Determined	$120 - $150 Per Visit	Dr. Thompson
Per Brenda at the Behavioral Medicine Group, P.C., office of Dr. John Simon, psychiatrist, 865-264-5555 (Knoxville, TN): Psychiatric follow-up, $150 per visit. *Per the Center for Psychiatry, P.C., office of Dr. Kelley Yoder, psychiatrist, 865-691-5555 (Knoxville, TN): Psychiatric follow-up, $120 per visit.*				
OCCIPITAL NERVE BLOCK*	Year 1	Series Of 3; Then 1 Injection Every 4 Months	$253 - $350 Per Injection	Dr. Thompson
**Note: Dr. Thompson's report, dated 2/03/14, stated "Potential Greater occipital nerve block."*				
Per the 2014 Physicians' Fee Reference: Greater occipital nerve block, $253 to $350 per injection.				

Life Care Plan for Aaron Allen Rogers

THERAPEUTIC NEEDS

Item	Duration	Frequency	Estimated Cost	Recommended By
PELVIC MUSCLE FLOOR THERAPY*	Year 1	6 Sessions	$277 - $1,561 Per Session	Dr. Shahnasarian

**Note: Mr. Rogers was in the process of completing a 6-session protocol of pelvic muscle therapy in March 2014.*
Per the American Urological Association, Inc., www.auanet.org, Health Policy Brief: Coding Corner. Volume XXI, Number 3, published 03/05/2013: "Pelvic Floor Muscle Rehabilitation (PFMR) consists of biofeedback procedures and physical therapy procedures. The American Urological Association (AUA) and the American Physical Therapy Association (APTA) recommend using the following (CPT) codes for the PFMR". (CPT code) 51784 for Electromyogram (EMG) - charged first and last visit only; The following can be billed for each session: 90901 - biofeedback training any modality, 90911 - biofeedback muscle training, 97032 - electrical stimulation application. Recommended protocol, six sessions.

Per the 2014 Physicians' Fee Reference: Pelvic muscle floor therapy, $427 to $1,136 per session.
- *This includes CPT code 51784 (electromyogram, first and last session only), $437 to $569.*
- *The following CPT codes are per session for 6 sessions each protocol: CPT code 90901 (biofeedback training any modality), $95 to $100, plus CPT code 90911 (biofeedback perineal muscle training), $180 to $259, plus CPT code 97032 (constant attendance, manual electrical stimulation), $152 to $208.*

Per the 2014 National fee analyzer: Pelvic muscle floor therapy, $277 to $1,561 per session
- *Electromyogram, CPT code 51784, $789 to $1,134 (first and last session only)*
- *Biofeedback, any modality, CPT code 90901, $77 to $123, plus Biofeedback, perineal muscle training, CPT code 90911, $132 to $212, plus manual electrical stimulation constant attendance, $68 to $92.*

Life Care Plan for Aaron Allen Rogers

DIAGNOSTIC TESTS

Item	Duration	Frequency	Estimated Cost	Recommended By
SWALLOW STUDY	Year 1	One Time*	$247	Dr. Saunders
**Note: Additional recommendations will follow.*				
Per Mr. Rogers' medical record, dated 2/05/13, from Regional Medical Center , 865-374-5555 (Knoxville, TN): Swallow function, $247.				

Item	Duration	Frequency	Estimated Cost	Recommended By
BLOODWORK	Year 1 - Life	2 Times Per Year	$101 Each Time	Dr. Yago
Per the Laboratory Group, 813-289-5227: Blood Analysis, $101 (this includes CBC, $40; Comprehensive Metabolic Panel, $46, and drawing fee, $15).				

Item	Duration	Frequency	Estimated Cost	Recommended By
TRANSRECTAL ULTRASOUND	Year 1 - 2	One Time*	$407 - $723	Dr. Yago
Per the 2014 Physicians' Fee Reference: Transrectal ultrasound, $407 to $546. *Per the 2014 National Fee Analyzer: Transrectal ultrasound, CPT code 76872, $542 to $723 each time.*				

Item	Duration	Frequency	Estimated Cost	Recommended By
MRI BRAIN WITH DTI AND SWI*	Year 1	One Time*	$1,815	Dr. Thompson
**Note: Dr. Thompson's report, dated 2/03/14, stated "MR brain with and without contrast with diffusion tensor imaging (DTI) with susceptibility weighted imaging (SWI) to rule out trauma that can be missed by test done to date."* *Additional recommendations will follow.*				
Per Elvira at the Diagnostic Center, 865-684-5555 (Knoxville, TN): MRI brain with and without contrast, with DTI (diffusion tensor imaging), and with SWI (susceptibility weighted imaging), $1,815.				

Item	Duration	Frequency	Estimated Cost	Recommended By
MRI CERVICAL/THORACIC/LUMBAR SPINE*	Year 1	One Time*	$2,031 - $2,472	Dr. Thompson
**Note: Dr. Thompson's report, dated 2/03/14, stated "MR cervical/thoracic/lumbar spine on 3 Tesla unit."* *Additional recommendations will follow.*				
Per Elvira at the Diagnostic Center, 865-684-5555 (Knoxville, TN): MRI cervical/thoracic/lumbar spine in 3 Tesla, without contrast, $2,031; with contrast, $2,472.				

Item	Duration	Frequency	Estimated Cost	Recommended By
BONE SCAN	Year 1	One Time*	$200	Dr. Thompson
**Note: Dr. Thompson's report, dated 2/03/14, stated "bone scan."* *Additional recommendations will follow.*				
Per Elvira at the Diagnostic Center, 865-684-5555 (Knoxville, TN): Bone density scan, $200.				

Life Care Plan for Aaron Allen Rogers

DIAGNOSTIC TESTS

Item	Duration	Frequency	Estimated Cost	Recommended By
ELECTROENCEPHALOGRAM*	Year 1	One Time	$666 - $1,213	Dr. Thompson
**Note: Dr. Thompson's report, dated 2/03/14, stated "Electroencephalogram." Additional recommendations will follow.*				
Per the 2014 Physicians' Fee Reference: Electroencephalogram (EEG), CPT code 95812, 1 hour, $666 to $820; EEG greater than 1 hour, CPT code 95813, $762 to $923. *Per the 2014 National Fee Analyzer: Electroencephalogram (EEG), 1 hour, $832 to $1,117 for CPT code 95812; EEG greater than 1 hour, CPT code 95813, $903 to $1,213.*				
ELECTROMYOGRAM (EMG)/NERVE CONDUCTION VELOCITY (NCV) *	Year 1	One Time	$892 - $1,804 For 2 Extremities	Dr. Thompson
**Note: Dr. Thompson's report, dated 2/03/14, stated "EMG/NCV right upper/right lower extremity." Additional recommendations will follow.*				
Per the 2014 Physicians' Fee Reference: EMG/NCV of right upper and right lower extremity is $892 to $1,240 (this includes Electromyogram (EMG), CPT code 95861, two extremities, $472 to $610, plus Nerve Conduction Velocity (NCV), 2 extremities, 1 to 2 studies each extremity, CPT code 95907, $420 to $630). *Per the 2014 National Fee Analyzer, the estimated cost of EMG/NCV of right upper and right lower extremity is $1,141 to $1,804 (this includes Electromyogram (EMG), CPT code 95861, two extremities, $669 to $1,060, plus Nerve Conduction Velocity (NCV), 2 extremities, 1 to 2 studies each extremity, CPT code 95907, $472 to $744).*				
EVOKED POTENTIALS*	Year 1	One Time	$498 - $1,035	Dr. Thompson
**Note: Dr. Thompson's report, dated 2/03/14, stated "lower extremity evoked potentials."*				
Per the 2014 Physicians' Fee Reference: Evoked potential, lower limbs, $498 to $696. *Per the 2014 National Fee Analyzer, the estimated cost of evoked potentials in lower extremities, CPT code 95926, $653 to $1,035.*				
SLEEP STUDY	Year 1	One Time	$669 - $2,493	Dr. Thompson
**Note: Dr. Thompson's report, dated 2/03/14, stated "sleep study."*				
Per the 2014 Physicians' Fee Reference: Sleep study attended by a technologist, CPT code 95807, $669 to $1,250. *Per the 2014 National Fee Analyzer, the estimated cost of sleep study, CPT code 95808, attended by a technologist, $1,750 to $2,493.*				
KIDNEY FUNCTION TEST	Year 1 – Life	Annually	$47 - $97	Dr. Thompson
**Note: Dr. Thompson's report, dated 2/03/14, stated "Medications: I discussed manufacturer recommends liver, kidney, cardiac function. They will ensure safety of medications with their primary care physician."*				
Per the 2014 Physicians' Fee Reference: Renal function panel, $47 to $64. *Per the 2014 National Fee Analyzer, the estimated cost of a renal (kidney) function test, CPT code 80069, is $66 to $97.*				

Life Care Plan for Aaron Allen Rogers

DIAGNOSTIC TESTS

Item	Duration	Frequency	Estimated Cost	Recommended By
LIVER FUNCTION TEST	Year 1 – Life	Annually	$44 - $81	Dr. Thompson

**Note: Dr. Thompson's report, dated 2/03/14, stated "Medications: I discussed manufacturer recommends liver, kidney, cardiac function. They will ensure safety of medications with their primary care physician."*

Per the 2014 Physicians' Fee Reference: Liver function test, $44 to $58.
Per the 2014 National Fee Analyzer, the estimated cost of a hepatic (liver) function test, CPT code 80076, is $55 to $81.

Item	Duration	Frequency	Estimated Cost	Recommended By
CARDIAC FUNCTION TESTS	Year 1 – Life	Annually	$481 - $742	Dr. Thompson

**Note: Dr. Thompson's report, dated 2/03/14, stated "Medications: I discussed manufacturer recommends liver, kidney, cardiac function. They will ensure safety of medications with their primary care physician."*
Per the American Heart Association, www.heart.org, blood testing may include the following: Cardiac enzymes, c-reactive protein, fibrinogen, homocysteine, lipids, triglycerides, BNP (b-natriuretic peptide), and prothrombin.

Per the 2014 Physicians' Fee Reference: Cardiac function tests, $543 to $742 (this includes $62 to $83 for cardiac enzymes; plus $56 to $68 for c-reactive protein; $42 to $58 for fibrinogen; plus $113 to $185 for homocysteine; $78 to $99 for lipid panel, plus $24 to $37 for triglycerides, plus $146 to $180 for B-type natriuretic peptide; plus $22 to $32 for prothrombin time.
Per the 2014 National Fee Analyzer, the estimated cost of a cardiac function test is $481 to $638 (this includes cardiac enzymes, CPT code 82552, $66 to $100; C-reactive protein, CPT code 86140, $48 to $67; Fibrinogen, CPT code 85384, $59 to $73; Homocysteine, CPT code 83090, $94 to $100; Lipid profile, CPT code 80061, $71 to $103; Tryglycerides, CPT code 84478, $29 to $36; B-type natriuretic peptides, CPT code 83880, $86 to $124; and Prothrombin, CPT code 85610, $28 to $35.

Item	Duration	Frequency	Estimated Cost	Recommended By
PITUITARY LAB WORK	Year 1	One Time	$576 - $838	Dr. Thompson

**Note: Dr. Thompson's report, dated 2/03/14, stated "pituitary lab work."*
Per the Medline Plus, U.S. National Library of Medicine, National Institutes of Health (NIH), Pituitary Disorders, www.nlm.nih.gov/medlineplus/pituitarydisorders.html: Diagnostic tests for pituitary disorders are ACTH (adrenocorticotropic hormone); FSH (follicle stimulating hormone); Somatotropin; IGF-1 (insulin-like growth factor 1); LH (luteinizing hormone).

Per the 2014 National Fee Analyzer, the estimated cost of pituitary lab work is $576 to $788 (this includes ACTH, CPT code 82024, $155 to $208; FSH, CPT code 83001, $93 to $125; Somatotropin, CPT code 83003, $89 to $121; AGH-1, CPT code 84305, $146 to $209; and LH, CPT code 83002, $93 to $125).
Per the 2014 Physicians' Fee Reference: Pituitary lab work, $664 to $838 (this includes $179 to $235 for ACTH; plus $107 to $125 for FSH; plus $96 to $117 for somatotropin; plus $178 to $236 for AGH-1; plus $104 to $125 for LH).

Life Care Plan for Aaron Allen Rogers

AIDS FOR INDEPENDENT LIVING

Item	Duration	Frequency	Estimated Cost	Recommended By
PRISM EYEGLASSES*	Year 1 - Life	Replace Every 2 - 3 Years	$116 - $340 Per Pair Of Prism Lenses Or Eyeglasses	Dr. Shahnasarian Dr. Henri Dr. Ingles
**Note: Mr. Rogers presently uses prism eyeglasses.*				
Per Mr. Rogers' medical record, dated 5/06/13, from Southern Ophthalmology, office of Dr. Gary Henri , 865-521-5555 (Knoxville, TN): Prism, $116 (this includes Freshell Prism only, $36, plus office visit, $80). *Per Mr. Rogers' medical record, dated 8/02/13, from Tennessee Eye Clinic, office of Dr. Andrew Ingles, 423-562-5555 (LaFollette, TN): Prism eyeglasses, $340 (this includes Bifocal sphere cylinder, $140, plus Prism 1 to 5 diopters, $30, plus Polarized bifocal, $80, plus Lab supplied PAL Essilor Natural, $90).*				

COMMUNICATION PENDANT	Year 1 - Life	Monthly	$29.95 Per Month	Dr. Shahnasarian
Per Medical Alert, http://emergency.medicalalert.com: Emergency medical communication pendant, $29.95 per month. The waterproof alert buttons come in 2 discreet options, either a pendant or wrist band style. The medical alert system includes: medical alert base unit, rechargeable battery back-up, 24-hour monitoring service, lifetime system warranty, and plug-in power supply and phone cord.				

Life Care Plan for Aaron Allen Rogers

DRUG AND SUPPLY NEEDS

Item	Duration	Frequency	Estimated Cost	Recommended By
ABSORBENT UNDERGARMENTS*	Year 1 - Life	10 - 12 Undergarments Per Month	$60 Per Pack Of 80	Dr. Shahnasarian
**Note: Mr. Rogers estimated he uses 10 to 12 absorbent undergarments per month.*				
Per Walgreens Pharmacy, www.walgreens.com: Dignity ultrashield disposable absorbent undergarments, $60 per pack of 80; Attend maximum protection absorbent undergarment, $60 per pack of 80.				

Item	Duration	Frequency	Estimated Cost	Recommended By
NITROFURANTOIN 100 mg*	Year 1 - Life	1 Capsule Per Day	$56.40 - $83.10 Per 30 Capsules	Dr. Yago
**Note: Per Dr. Yago, antibiotic for cystitis. Mr. Rogers' medication list, dated 1/24/14, stated "Nitrofurantion/Mono/Mac 100 mg (8/19/13) 1 per day."*				
Per Walgreen's Pharmacy, www.walgreens.com, 877-250-5555 per Customer Service: Nitrofurantoin 100 mg, $83.10 per 30 capsules. Per pharmacy staff at CVS Pharmacy, 813-264-5555, www.cvs.com: Nitrofurantoin 100 mg, $56.40 per 30 capsules.				

Item	Duration	Frequency	Estimated Cost	Recommended By
OXYCODONE ACETAMINOPHEN 5/325 mg*	Year 1 - Life	1 - 2 Tablets At Night	$61.11 - $82.27 Per 60 Tablets	*
**Note: Mr. Rogers' medication list, dated 1/24/14, stated "Oxycodone/Acetaminophen 5-325 mg 1 - 2 tablets at night."*				
Per Walgreen's Pharmacy, www.walgreens.com, 877-250-5555 per Customer Service: Oxycodone Acetaminophen 5/325 mg, $61.11 per 60 tablets. Per pharmacy staff at CVS Pharmacy, 813-264-5555, www.cvs.com: Oxycodone Acetaminophen 5/325 mg, $82.27 per 60 tablets.				

Item	Duration	Frequency	Estimated Cost	Recommended By
AMOXICILLIN-CLAVULANATE	Year 1 – Life As Needed	1 Tablet 2 Times Per Day For 12 Days	$52.37 - $87.93 Per 24 Tablets	*
*Note: Mr. Rogers' medication list, dated 1/24/14, stated "Amox-Clav 875 mg 1 tablet twice a day for 12 days."				
Per Walgreen's Pharmacy, www.walgreens.com, 877-250-5555 per Customer Service: Amoxicillin Clavulanate, $87.93 per 24 tablets. Per pharmacy staff at CVS Pharmacy, 813-264-5555, www.cvs.com: Amoxicillin Clavulanate, $52.37 per 24 tablets.				

Item	Duration	Frequency	Estimated Cost	Recommended By
FLOVENT HFA 220 mcg, 12 gm	Year 1 - Life	2 Puffs Two Times Per Day	$312.95 - $313.20 Each	*
**Note: Mr. Rogers' medication list, dated 1/24/14, stated "Flovent HFA 220 mcg Inhaler 12 gm 2 puffs twice a day."*				
Per Walgreen's Pharmacy, www.walgreens.com, 877-250-5555 per Customer Service: Flovent HFA 220 mcg, 12 gm, $313.20 each. Per pharmacy staff at CVS Pharmacy, 813-264-5555, www.cvs.com: Flovent HFA 220 mcg, 12 gm, $312.95 each.				

Life Care Plan for Mark Wayne Byers

DRUG AND SUPPLY NEEDS

Item	Duration	Frequency	Estimated Cost	Recommended By
RAPAFLO 8 mg*	Year 1 - Life	1 Tablet Per Day	$128.48 Per 30 Tablets	Dr. Yago
**Note: Per Dr. Yago, for neurogenic bladder problems. Mr. Rogers' medication list, dated 1/24/14, stated "RapaFlo 8 mg Once a day."*				
Per Walgreen's Pharmacy, www.walgreens.com, 877-250-5555 per Customer Service: Rapaflo 8 mg, $128.48 per 30 tablets.				
ASPIRIN 81 mg	Year 1 - Life	1 Tablet Per Day	$11.99 Per 200 Tablets.	*
**Note: Mr. Rogers' medication list, dated 1/24/14, stated "Baby Aspirin 81 mg."*				
Per Walgreen's Pharmacy, www.walgreens.com, 877-250-5555 per Customer Service: Bayer aspirin 81 mg, $11.99 per 200 tablets.				
COENZYME Q10	Year 1 - Life	1 Softgel Per Day	$36.99 Per 60 Softgels	*
**Note: Mr. Rogers' medication list, dated 1/24/14, stated "CoQ-10, 1 per day."*				
Per Walgreen's Pharmacy, www.walgreens.com, 877-250-5555 per Customer Service: Nature's Bounty CoQ10, $36.99 per 60 softgels.				
CRANBERRY 4200	Year 1 - Life	1 Softgel 3 Times Per Day	$19.49 Per 250 Softgels	*
**Note: Mr. Rogers' medication list, dated 1/24/14, stated "Cranberry 4200 plus C 3 times a day."*				
Per Walgreen's Pharmacy, www.walgreens.com, 877-250-5555 per Customer Service: Nature's Bounty Cranberry 4200 plus C, $19.49 per 250 softgels.				
VITAMIN C	Year 1 - Life	1 Softgel 3 Times Per Day	$8.99 Per 100 Softgels	*
**Note: Mr. Rogers' medication list, dated 1/24/14, stated "Vitamin C 500 mg 3 times a day."*				
Per Walgreen's Pharmacy, www.walgreens.com, 877-250-5555 per Customer Service: Nature's Bounty Vitamin C 500 mg, $8.99 per 100 softgels.				
ALIGN PROBIOTIC	Year 1 - Life	1 Capsule Per Day	$40.99 Per 42 Capsules	*
**Note: Mr. Rogers' medication list, dated 1/24/14, stated "Align Probiotic once a day."*				
Per Walgreen's Pharmacy, www.walgreens.com, 877-250-5555 per Customer Service: Align probiotic, $40.99 per 42 capsules.				

Life Care Plan for Mark Wayne Byers

DRUG AND SUPPLY NEEDS

Item	Duration	Frequency	Estimated Cost	Recommended By
MOBIC	Year 1 - Life	1 Tablet Per Day Or As Prescribed	$193.85 Per 30 Tablets	Dr. Thompson
**Note: Per Dr. Thompson, anti-inflammatories - Mobic*				
Per Walgreen's Pharmacy, www.walgreens.com, 877-250-5555 per Customer Service: Mobic, 7.5 mg, $193.85 per 30 tablets.				
ROBAXIN	Year 1 - Life	1 Tablet Per Day Or As Prescribed	$52.27 Per 30 Tablets	Dr. Thompson
**Note: Per Dr. Thompson, muscle relaxer - Robaxin*				
Per Walgreen's Pharmacy, www.walgreens.com, 877-250-5555 per Customer Service: Robaxin 500 mg, $52.27 per 30 tablets.				
VIVACTIL	Year 1 - Life	1 Tablet Per Day	$117.13 Per 30 Tablets	Dr. Thompson
**Note: Per Dr. Thompson, antidepressant - Divactil*				
Per Walgreen's Pharmacy, www.walgreens.com, 877-250-5555 per Customer Service: Vivactil 5 mg, $117.13 per 30 tablets.				
DEPAKOTE	Year 1 - Life	1 Tablet Per Day or As Prescribed	$49.10 Per 30 Tablets	Dr. Thompson
**Note: Per Dr. Thompson, anticonvulsant - Depakote*				
Per Walgreen's Pharmacy, www.walgreens.com, 877-250-5555 per Customer Service: Depakote 125 mg, $49.10 per 30 tablets.				

Life Care Plan for Aaron Allen Rogers

HOME/FACILITY CARE

Item	Duration	Frequency	Estimated Cost	Recommended By
CASE MANAGER	Year 1 - Life	1 Hour Per Week	$75 - $90 Per Hour	Dr. Shahnasarian
**Note: Ms. Rogers has been providing this service.*				
Per Dr. Shahnasarian: Case management services, $75 to $90 per hour.				

Item	Duration	Frequency	Estimated Cost	Recommended By
PERSONAL CARE ATTENDANT	Year 1 - 10 Year 10 - Life	4 Hours Per Day 6 Hours Per Day	$10 - $25 Per Hour	Dr. Shahnasarian Dr. Harper
**Note: Per Dr. Shahnasarian, Mr. Rogers' wife (Cheryl Rogers, born February 21, 1951) has been providing these services, which include general assistance with self-care as needed; monitoring medication intake; scheduling medical appointments; running household errands; transportation; housekeeping; and general oversight. Ms. Rogers was diagnosed with non-Hodgkin lymphoma, and she undergoes intermittent protocols of chemotherapy (her next protocol will be in April 2014). Per Dr. Harper, Year 1 to life, 20 to 30 hours per week, to include transportation services and assistance with farm chores. Mr. Rogers' wife has been providing this service.*				
Per the U.S. Department of Labor, Bureau of Labor Statistics, www.bls.gov., Occupational Outlook Handbook 2013-2014 Edition, Nursing Aides, Orderlies, and Attendants, http://www.bls.gov/ooh/healthcare/nursing-assistants.htm: Personal care attendant services, $10 to $12 per hour. Per Linda at Home Health Agency, Inc., 423-562-5555 (LaFollette, TN): Personal care attendant, $25 per hour.				

Life Care Plan for Aaron Allen Rogers

TRANSPORTATION NEEDS

Item	Duration	Frequency	Estimated Cost	Recommended By
SPINNER KNOB FOR STEERING WHEEL*	Year 1 - Life	Replace Every 3 - 5 Years	$895 Each Time	Dr. Shahnasarian
**Note: Mr. Rogers currently uses this device.*				
Per Transportation Systems, 813-246-5555 (Tampa, FL): Hand control equipment, knob on steering wheel, $895; Installation is free of charge if the equipment is purchased at Transportation Systems.				

Item	Duration	Frequency	Estimated Cost	Recommended By
DRIVER EVALUATION	Year 1 - Life	1 Time In Year 1, And Then Every 3 Years*	$350 Each Time	Dr. Shahnasarian Dr. Harper
**Note: Per Dr. Shahnasarian, additional recommendations will follow. Per Dr. Harper, if Mr. Rogers does not pass the evaluation, he will require an attendant to provide him transportation services. Dr. Harper does not believe it is safe for Mr. Rogers to drive at this time. Recurrent driver evaluations may be in order.*				
Per Kelly at Rehabilitation Center , 865-541-5555 (Knoxville, TN): Comprehensive driving program, $350 for a 2 to 3 hour evaluation. The evaluation is a two-part evaluation: a clinical assessment and an on-the-road test.				

Item	Duration	Frequency	Estimated Cost	Recommended By
DISABLED PERSON PARKING PERMIT	Year 1 - Life	Renew Every 2 Years	No Charge	Dr. Shahnasarian
Per the Tennessee Department of Revenue, Vehicle Services Division, www.tn.gov/revenue: Disabled person parking placard, no charge. Expires 2 years after issuance.				

Life Care Plan for Aaron Allen Rogers

PERSONAL FITNESS

Item	Duration	Frequency	Estimated Cost	Recommended By
THERABANDS (2)	Year 1 – Life	Replace Every 6 – 12 Months	$17.49 Per Pack of 4 Therabands	Dr. Shahnasarian
Per Performance Health, www.shop.performancehealth.com: Theraband multi-tube pack, $17.49 per pack of 4.				

Life Care Plan for Aaron Allen Rogers

ARCHITECTURAL RENOVATIONS

Item	Duration	Frequency	Estimated Cost	Recommended By
HOME ENVIRONMENTAL ANALYSIS	To Be Determined	To Be Determined	$475	Dr. Shahnasarian
**Note: Mr. Rogers currently lives in a rural area in Speedwell, Tennessee. He desires to relocate to Florida, and he has been attempting to sell his property. Some disability modifications have been made to Mr. Rogers' Tennessee residence (an approximately 1,700-square-foot, single-story house on 25 acres, with various farm animals; Mr. Rogers indicated his property has become difficult for him to maintain since his February 7, 2012, accident).*				
Per Brandy at Home Solutions, 877-317-5555 (Hendersonville, TN): Home modification assessment, $475. The assessment is waived if they are hired to do the home modification/renovation.				

Life Care Plan for Aaron Allen Rogers

POTENTIAL COMPLICATIONS

Per Dr. Thompson's report, dated February 3, 2014:

- He is at increased risk of dementia and seizures.
- Potential tertiary care clinic.
- Potential nervous system medications.

Appendix 6.2: Sample Report of a Vocational Rehabilitation Evaluation in a Case of Alleged Acquired Disabilities Prepared for Anderson Matisse By Michael Shahnasarian, Ph.D., February 24, 2014

A 28-year-old claimant pursued a loss of earning capacity claim after a motor vehicle accident. To place the claim in proper perspective, the vocational evaluator considered several facts including the claimant's:

- Unimpressive scholastic and work history
- Criminal history
- Significant preaccident medical history including injuries similar to those he associated with his motor vehicle accident
- Postaccident use of illicit drugs
- Optimistic prognoses by treating physicians along with absence of restrictions
- Test results that suggest symptom exaggeration

Additionally, the evaluator determined the claimant displayed poor motivation to pursue vocational rehabilitation, partially evidenced by his considerable time spent in nonproductive activities, and opined that the claimant's focus on litigation was inhibiting his motivation. The evaluator found the claimant's allegations of loss of earning capacity unmerited. Documentation (including preaccident and postaccident medical records, scholastic records, employment records, and criminal records), clinical interview information, and standardized test data provided the grist for the evaluator's analysis.

Overview

Anderson Matisse was referred to me for a vocational rehabilitation evaluation. A Complaint outlines allegations of injuries he sustained as a result of a motor vehicle accident on September 26, 2011. According to November 25, 2013, Answers to Interrogatories, Deluxe Car Interiors employed Mr. Matisse as a driver at the time of his accident.

On February 24, 2014, I conducted a vocational rehabilitation evaluation of Mr. Matisse at my office in Tampa. My examination consisted of a clinical interview, which required 3 hours and 30 minutes, and the administration of a battery of tests that required an additional 3 hours and 30 minutes for him to complete. Aaron Hill from my office assisted with the testing portion of my exam. Before my exam, I was told a videographer and Mr. Matisse's lawyer, Marcus Lewis, would attend; however, no third party attended my exam. Soon after I began my exam, Mr. Matisse offered a lengthy colloquy about biases among defense examiners.

Mr. Matisse arrived alone and 1 hour and 10 minutes late. About his tardy arrival, he indicated he thought the exam time was 1 hour later than its scheduled time. Ten minutes after I began my exam, Mr. Matisse announced that he received "a call from my detective" on his mobile phone, and he left my office to complete his call. "I do some work with law enforcement," he offered upon his return. Throughout my clinical interview, Mr. Matisse intermittently texted messages on his mobile phone while conversing with me.

From his home in Plant City, Mr. Matisse indicated, he drove an automatic transmission auto to my office. He conveyed his commute required from 45 to 50 minutes. He advised me he holds a valid driver's license and does not have physician-advised driving restrictions. Mr. Matisse noted the vehicle he operates "has a massager that helps me out a little." He added that, while driving, he adjusts his seating to accommodate for lower back discomfort.

Concerning the September 2011 motor vehicle accident, Mr. Matisse apprised me he struck his head; he denied losing consciousness. During his December 13, 2013, deposition, when asked to describe each injury for which he is claiming damages in this case, Mr. Matisse reported:

- Lower back pain
- Jaw pain
- Right leg pain
- Left shoulder pain
- Headaches/migraines

Mr. Matisse told me he experiences jaw pain "once in a while. I catch myself grinding my teeth a lot." As for his left shoulder pain, he stated: "It comes and goes, and my [left] arm gets weak. I have a throbbing sensation [in my left shoulder]," and he indicated this occurs four or five times per month.

I inquired about headaches and migraines, and Mr. Matisse said: "I get the migraines a lot. I take Excedrin to try to keep them away."

When asked whether he ever experienced any of the preceding problems before his September 2011 accident, Mr. Matisse initially responded negatively and then referenced a 2008 motor vehicle accident that caused him to experience "a bulge in my neck and in my [lower] back." He went on to reference chiropractic treatment he underwent, and he reported he fully recovered from injuries he experienced in 2008.

Mr. Matisse recollected his last treatment with a physician for injuries related to his 2008 accident was in 2009 or 2010. He denied injuring the other aforementioned body parts before September 26, 2011.

Regarding mental functioning, Mr. Matisse cited problems with concentration. "I don't know if that's caused from the accident. It just started recently. Other people have pointed it out to me," he said. As an example, he cited tendencies to engage in disjointed conversations.

Vocational Activity

According to his 2013 deposition testimony, Mr. Matisse completed the eighth grade. He reported he attempted to obtain a GED but did not complete the necessary courses. Mr. Matisse testified that he abandoned the GED program when he obtained employment with Burger King, about which he stated, "I worked at Burger King for 2 days, and then I quit." His next employment, according to Answers to Interrogatories, was with Little Cesar's Pizza, beginning in 2005.

In his Answers to Interrogatories, Mr. Matisse indicated he was employed by American Furniture, earning $9 per hour, from 2005 to 2006; and Best Furniture from 2005 to 2006, earning $12 per hour. He indicated he was employed from 2008 to 2009 with Westside Parking, earning $16 per hour, and from 2009 to 2011 with Pools Only, earning $12 per hour as a pool technician.

Mr. Matisse provided information about his education and work history similar to information in his deposition and interrogatory responses. He advised me his employment with Deluxe Car Interiors, a business specializing in customizing automobile interiors, began in March 2011 and continued through the time of his September 26, 2011, motor vehicle accident. As a driver, Mr. Matisse conveyed, his job responsibilities included transporting vehicles to his place of employment and dealerships, inspecting vehicles, and marketing his employer's services while picking up and dropping off vehicles.

At the time of his September 2011 accident, Mr. Matisse informed me, he worked from 40 to 60 hours per week and earned $12 per hour. "I also made commission depending on how many cars I'd bring from dealers," he added. He noted his earnings ranged from $500 to $2,500 per week.

As for the physical demands associated with his former driver job, Mr. Matisse stated, "I'd lift a clipboard and my pen, just for notes and signing stuff." He estimated he drove 200 miles per day to destinations throughout the Tampa area "just to get more business for our company." He did not identify any other noteworthy physical demands.

Mr. Matisse recalled his lower-back symptoms onset the day after his September 26, 2011, accident. He volunteered that he and his attorney, Todd Smerconish, discussed treating with Dr. David, a chiropractor – the first physician with whom he treated after his accident.

After his 2011 accident, Mr. Matisse recollected, he had "a few days" of work absences. "They were understanding at first," he said, apprising me his supervisor at Deluxe became less tolerant of his need to miss work to attend physician appointments. "They started cutting my hours. I took that as a hint," Mr. Matisse said and went on to add: "So I called my lawyer. It wasn't that I couldn't perform. I felt I was on the verge of losing my job. I wasn't moving as fast. My lawyer had a file clerk job, and I took it."

Mr. Matisse reported a law firm, Smerconish & Mustard, P.A., hired him as a file clerk. "I worked for him before that, like 4 or 5 years ago [as an asset recovery worker]," he stated. Mr. Matisse told me his employment with Smerconish & Mustard began in July 2012.

As a file clerk, Mr. Matisse indicated, his job responsibilities included general filing, processing mail, and storing boxes of legal records. He advised me he handled boxes weighing from 5 to 10 pounds. Mr. Matisse conveyed his job required extended walking and standing, which became incompatible with his accident-related injuries. "I couldn't do that," he stated.

Because of Mr. Matisse's job performance difficulties, he informed me, his work hours were reduced from 37.5 to 25 per week, which is his current work participation. At least 9 months ago, he apprised me, his job with a Smerconish & Mustard was changed from file clerk to asset recovery worker. "I couldn't stand full time for filing, and they needed someone full time for filing. They worked with me and put me in another position," Mr. Matisse said about why his job changed. He reported he has continued to perform his asset recovery job to date.

Currently, Mr. Matisse told me, he works 25 hours per week and earns $10 per hour. "I like what I'm doing right now," he stated. He indicated he performs his job in a cubicle, and extensively uses a computer and telephone. Mr. Matisse engages in sedentary tasks, he advised me.

Concerning his current job responsibilities, Mr. Matisse said: "I have to produce at least 15 letters per day. It is something I do want to make a career out of." He advised me he researches databases to identify potential beneficiaries whom his firm then recruits in attempts to cultivate clients.

Mr. Matisse responded affirmatively when I asked whether his job responsibilities are within his capacity; however, he expressed his belief he is unable to increase his work participation beyond his current level. "I wouldn't be able to sit there 8, 9 hours a day. I wouldn't be able to stand 8, 9 hours a day," he stated.

I asked Mr. Matisse whether any physician is restricting his work participation. Although he did not identify any, he told me Dr. Perez advised "light duty."

Records Reviewed

Records from the following sources were reviewed with this evaluation:

- Florida Traffic Crash Report
- Complaint
- Answers to Interrogatories, November 25, 2013
- Deposition of Anderson Matisse, December 13, 2013
- Diagnostic Group, includes billing
- Florida MRI
- Jackson Dentistry, P.A., includes billing
- Tampa Pain Management, includes billing
- Injury Solutions, includes billing
- Rogers & Associates
- Disc Institute, includes billing
- Kirk Enterprise McCoy Hospital
- Hillsborough Medical, includes billing
- SNL Pharmacy, includes billing
- Bock Radiology, includes billing
- Pinellas MRI, includes billing
- Orthopedic Center
- Back Pain Management Group, billing only
- Spine Specialists, includes billing

- Suncoast Orthopedic & Pain, includes billing
- Wellness Group, includes billing
- Bay Orthopedics, includes billing
- Samuel Jackson, DMD
- Scott Berringer, MD
- Lori Boston, DO, includes billing
- Robert M. Dunning, MD
- Mark O. Evergreen, DC
- Bill R. Rogers, MS
- Francisco Gatwick, MD
- Brian Garcone, DC
- Richard Hunter, Ph.D., includes billing
- Robert Perez, MD, includes billing
- Gary Morris, MD
- Brenda Moscato, MBA
- Joseph Simpson, MD
- Richard E. Standish, DC
- John M. Swift, MD
- Fred Troy, MD
- Mike White, MD
- Michael G. Zelner, MD

Assessment Measures

The following assessment measures were used in this evaluation:

- Clinical Interview
- Patient Pain Diagram
- Wahler Physical Symptoms Inventory
- Multidimensional Aptitude Battery-II
- Wide Range Achievement Test – Revision 4
- Grooved Pegboard Test
- Beck Depression Inventory-II
- Self-Directed Search Form R
- MMPI-2

Background Information

The following background information was obtained from records and my clinical interview:

FULL NAME:	Anderson Matisse
DATE OF BIRTH:	June 19, 1986
ONSET OF DISABLING PROBLEMS:	September 26, 2011, motor vehicle accident
DOMINANT HAND:	Right

HEIGHT:	5 feet 11 inches
CURRENT WEIGHT:	185 pounds
PREACCIDENT WEIGHT:	170 to 175 pounds
MARITAL STATUS:	Single/never married
CHILDREN:	None
RESIDENCE:	Plant City, Florida
PRESENTING PROBLEMS:	Leg pain Jaw pain Right leg pain Left shoulder pain Headaches/migraines
SURGERY SINCE ACCIDENT:	Lumbar epidural steroid injection under fluoroscopy, Mike White, MD, June 7, 2012 Lumbar transforaminal epidural steroid, fluoroscopy, radiological examination and interpretation of lumbar epidurogram, Mike White, MD, July 19, 2012 Right L4-5 selective nerve root block, Lori Boston, DO, January 11, 2013 Right L4-L5 therapeutic transforaminal epidural steroid injection, right L5-S1 therapeutic transforaminal epidural steroid injection, Lori Boston, DO, February 17, 2013 Right side L4-L5 laminotomy and discectomy, John Swift, MD, March 12, 2013
TREATMENT SINCE ACCIDENT:	Chiropractic treatment Pain management
PRESENT TREATMENT:	None
TREATING DOCTORS:	Dr. Gatwick, pain management
MEDICATIONS:	Oxycodone, pain Naproxen sodium, inflammation Excedrin, headaches
EDUCATION:	Completed eighth grade No GED
EMPLOYER AT TIME OF ACCIDENT:	Deluxe Car Interiors
JOB TITLE AT TIME OF ACCIDENT:	Driver
RATE OF PAY AT TIME OF ACCIDENT:	$12 per hour, 40 to 60 hours per week

PRESENT WORK STATUS: Part-time Asset Recovery Worker, Smerconish & Mustard, P.A., $10 per hour, 25 hours per week

Clinical Interview

Introduction

Anderson Matisse presented as an unshaven, brown-eyed male who had hair on his lip and chin. He appeared his stated age of 27, and he wore a T-shirt and blue jeans. Mr. Matisse informed me he does not wear corrective lenses, and he said his vision is "good. I would say 20/20."

At the onset of my clinical interview, I presented Mr. Matisse a pain diagram to complete, and he stated: "It sucks. I got to do it again." He went on to complain about the duration of his lawsuit and added, "Jason [defense attorney] is really going out of his way," referencing his experiences with litigation he is pursuing.

Although he affirmed my observation his gait appeared normal, Mr. Matisse noted he occasionally experiences pain radiating from his lower back into his right lower extremity that affects his gait. He did not use adaptive aids during my exam.

Mr. Matisse reported he is right hand dominant, 5 feet 10 inches tall, and weighs 185 pounds. He told me he weighed between 170 and 175 pounds at the time of his September 26, 2011, motor vehicle accident. He attributed his weight gain to diminished activity and said, "I'm more of a homebody now." Mr. Matisse indicated he is single/never married and that he does not have children. During his 2013 deposition, he stated, "I'm Indian, but from Trinidad and Tobago." Mr. Matisse went on to testify that he became a U.S. citizen in 1999.

When asked about his home, Mr. Matisse advised me he lives with his mother (born in 1955) and father (born in 1946) in a two-story, 3,700-square-foot house with five bedrooms and four bathrooms his parents own in a residential area. He conveyed he has lived in his home 13 or 14 years.

I asked Mr. Matisse whether he plans to relocate, and he responded affirmatively, "whenever I can start working full-time again." He went on to cite financial constraints due to diminished postaccident employment income. "I went from working 40 hours a week to 25 [hours per week]," Mr. Matisse said. He denied that his home has been modified for disabilities, and he cited no accessibility limitations within it.

Physical Condition and Medical Information

Mr. Matisse informed me he had no medical problems or restrictions near the time before his September 26, 2011, motor vehicle accident. "I was fine," he said, noting he was asymptomatic before his 2011 accident and regularly "worked out."

Regarding his preaccident medical history, Mr. Matisse cited an appendectomy at age 22 or 23. He also apprised me a cyst on the top of his head was removed in 2009 or 2010; otherwise, he reported his preaccident medical history was unremarkable. No significant postaccident medical problems were identified.

On March 12, 2013, Mr. Matisse indicated, he underwent lower back surgery performed by Dr. Swift. Mr. Matisse was not aware of any current diagnosis, although he offered that Dr. Gatwick "wants me to get an X-ray on my lower back. I'm experiencing a lot of [lower back] pain." He advised me an MRI he underwent detected numerous abnormalities in his lower back. The primary problem Mr. Matisse associates with his 2011 motor vehicle accident, he conveyed, is his lower-back pain with intermittent right-lower-extremity radiculopathy.

Mr. Matisse informed me he experiences ongoing lower back pain that occasionally radiates "all the way down" his right lower extremity. He noted he also sometimes has mid-back pain, which he assessed may be caused by "slouching" and postural changes he makes in response to his lower-back pain.

As for how his lower-back pain manifests, Mr. Matisse cited burning and pins-and-needles sensations. I inquired about activities and conditions that exacerbate his lower-back symptoms, and he responded: "I don't play any sports anymore. I used to go to the beach a lot. I don't do that anymore." He went on to reference difficulties with dressing. "It's not that I can't do it. It's more or less that I don't want to hurt myself any worse," Mr. Matisse said.

While conversing with me at 9:40 a.m., Mr. Matisse noted his only symptomatic body part was his lower back. He estimated he experiences radicular symptoms into his right lower extremity "three times a week, maybe."

After his lower back and right lower extremity, Mr. Matisse apprised me, his most symptomatic body part is "my jaw. I'm constantly grinding [my teeth]." He reported Dr. Jackson prescribed him a mouth guard; however, Mr. Matisse said: "I quit using it. It got annoying. I wear it if the pain is bad, bad."

I inquired about headache triggers, and Mr. Matisse replied, "I don't know what causes the headaches." He said his headaches occur "a couple times a week" and typically last "4 to 6 hours, depending on how fast the Excedrin [works to alleviate it]." Mr. Matisse offered that his brother is a pharmacist and recommended that he take Excedrin.

Using a 0-to-10 scale, with a zero indicating no pain and a 10 representing the worst pain possible, Mr. Matisse rated his pain intensities in the following body parts:

- Lower back – 7
- Right lower extremity – "When it's actually hurting me, about an 8 or 9. I'll get to a point where I can't even walk."
- Bilateral jaw, when present – "maybe like a 7, 8"
- Left-shoulder, when present – "maybe like a 6 or 7"

The only physician currently treating Mr. Matisse, he advised me, is Dr. Gatwick, a pain management specialist whom he last saw 2 weeks before my exam. He conveyed he sees Dr. Gatwick for medication monitoring every 28 days.

Mr. Matisse noted Dr. Swift discharged him approximately 5 weeks after his March 2013 operation and that he has not since seen him. I referenced the orthopedic surgeon's March 27, 2013, postoperative note, and Mr. Matisse indicated "that could've been" the last contact he had with Dr. Swift. He apprised me he saw Dr. Perez once, on the recommendation of Dr. Gatwick.

Apart from his L4-L5 laminotomy and discectomy, performed by Dr. Swift on March 12, 2013, records indicate Mr. Matisse underwent lumbar epidural steroid injections (administered by Dr. Prescott in June and July 2012), an L4-5 nerve root block (Dr. Boston, January 2013) and L4-L5/L5-S1 transforaminal epidural steroid injections (Dr. Boston, February 2013). Please see the Review of Medical Records, Operations/ Procedures section of this report for a detailed list of Mr. Matisse's postaccident procedures. Regarding future surgery, he recounted, "Dr. Gatwick thinks I may need to get another surgery done [on my lower back]."

Concerning treatment and therapy since his 2011 accident, Mr. Matisse reported chiropractic treatment and pain management including injections. He denied having pain management injections since his March 2013 surgery. No current treatment or therapy was identified. As for adaptive aids, Mr. Matisse told me he intermittently uses a mouth guard – most recently "a couple of weeks ago."

When asked about medications, Mr. Matisse indicated he takes oxycodone, naproxen sodium, and Excedrin. He advised me he takes Excedrin "only when I get the headaches." Mr. Matisse denied taking any medication near the time before his September 2011 accident. No current medication side effects were identified.

During the 24 hours before my exam, Mr. Matisse conveyed, he had taken oxycodone and naproxen sodium. He responded affirmatively when I inquired whether he has complied with taking his medications. "If I don't take them, I'm in so much pain I can't do anything," he offered.

A medical record dated July 17, 2013, reports Mr. Matisse's random urine drug test was positive for marijuana and negative for Percocet, which he had been prescribed by Dr. Gatwick. Dr. Gatwick then apparently issued him a warning. This occurred again on October 8, 2013, when Mr. Matisse tested negative for any drugs. On November 17, 2013, Mr. Matisse was administered a urine drug screen, and he again tested positive for THC and marijuana.

I referenced documentation in Dr. Gatwick's notes about Mr. Matisse's use of marijuana and prescribed medications. Mr. Matisse stated: "I don't understand how that happened," referencing his lab results. He went on to offer: "I'm on probation. I can't smoke [marijuana]," and he denied any consumption of it.

Regarding physical capacities, Mr. Matisse informed me he is able to safely lift and carry no more than 10 pounds. The only physician-advised lifting restriction he cited was recommended by Dr. Swift during his postoperative course. Mr. Matisse complained that lifting exacerbates his lower-back pain.

Mr. Matisse noted no restrictions with any cervical spine movements. He said about using his hands and arms, "I move them fine." During my clinical interview, Mr. Matisse demonstrated he could touch each finger to his thumb on either hand, make a fist with either hand, and extend his arms horizontally without problems. Although he apprised me he can extend his arms overhead, he reported these movements exacerbate his lower-back symptoms. Mr. Matisse told me his fine motor functioning is intact in both hands.

As for physical, everyday activities, Mr. Matisse indicated he has no problems walking or standing for short durations. While seated for periods of more than 60 consecutive minutes, he repositioned normally; he often displaced his weight on his right side. Mr. Matisse advised me he avoids bending his waist and lower extremity movements.

Generally, Mr. Matisse conveyed, he can drive from 15 to 20 minutes, sit from 60 to 90 minutes, and stand approximately 10 minutes before overexerting himself or needing to rest. "I don't walk much at all. I'm probably one of the laziest persons in the world. Walking more than 5 minutes is out of the question," he stated.

Mr. Matisse informed me he operates an automatic transmission vehicle, daily. He denied modifying his vehicle or having a parking placard for persons with disabilities. "I should have one [parking placard], but I don't know how to get a hold of one," Mr. Matisse added.

The following additional physical problems were identified by Mr. Matisse:

- Breathing – "I don't know if it's from the accident or not. I have a problem with breathing heavy. It definitely started happening after [the September 2011 accident].
- Exposure to cold temperatures – exacerbates his lower-back pain

I asked Mr. Matisse whether his teeth-grinding proclivity has caused him dental problems. He replied, "Not that I'm aware of."

Concerning physician-advised restrictions, Mr. Matisse noted he continues to observe Dr. Swift's previously referenced restrictions. Mr. Matisse opined that his condition is worsening, and he referenced his lower back.

Activities of Daily Living

Mr. Matisse cited difficulty sleeping and said: "I barely sleep. My body gets tired, but I barely sleep." He elaborated about positional discomfort that interrupts his sleep. Mr. Matisse responded negatively when I inquired about problems sleeping before his September 26, 2011, motor vehicle accident.

Usually, Mr. Matisse apprised me, he goes to sleep between 2:00 and 4:00 a.m., and awakens at 8:30 a.m. He denied napping, taking sleep aid medication, or having problems with nightmares.

When asked about grooming and self-care, Mr. Matisse reported he is independent. "If I need help, I'll ask for it," he added.

I asked Mr. Matisse about his participation in household chores. He responded: "My mom does everything for me: cooking, laundry. [I am] not asking [for her help]. She just does it. She knows it will be easier [for me]." He told me his mother performs the full range of housekeeping chores for him. "I could do it. It would just put more restrictions on me," Mr. Matisse said.

Mr. Matisse acknowledged he could prepare himself light meals. "Cooking a four-course meal, it would involve constantly standing," he said, indicating this would exacerbate his lower-back symptoms. Mr. Matisse also acknowledged he could launder his clothes. "I just stay in my room and play video games all day. I got my bed and my living room in my room, so there's no reason to leave," he stated. Mr. Matisse denied that a housekeeper or other outside services are employed for accident-related reasons.

Regarding yard maintenance, Mr. Matisse advised me his mother maintains their yard. "She gets out there and pushes the lawnmower. It's crazy. I asked her if she needs help, and she says, 'No, I've got it,'" Mr. Matisse said. Before his 2011 accident, he conveyed: "I did the mowing, the weed eating. I actually did it for exercise."

During his 2013 deposition, when asked about activities in which he is no longer able to participate, Mr. Matisse testified:

> *Sports. Working out. I've tried to walk a little bit on a treadmill, but that didn't really work out too much. I don't walk up the stairs because it puts too much strain on my back. I don't really go out anymore, because if I stand for a long period of time, like right now if I stand up straight because I'm having problems with my back, it's causing like a pain in my side in my leg.*

Mr. Matisse elaborated about how much he enjoyed playing sports, especially basketball, before his 2011 accident. He informed me he no longer participates in sports. "I haven't tried. It sucks. I play video games, one game and one game only," Mr. Matisse stated, referencing Call of Duty, a "first-person shooting game."

As for his work schedule as an asset recovery worker, Mr. Matisse noted working Monday through Friday, from 10:00 a.m. to 3:00 p.m., with a 15-minute break at 1:00 p.m. He apprised me he awakens between 8:00 and 8:30 a.m., showers, dresses, and leaves his home between 9:00 and 9:15 a.m. to drive to the office of Smerconish & Mustard in South Tampa.

After work, Mr. Matisse reported: "I go straight home, and that's it. I have a pretty strict routine." When he returns home, he told me, he plays video games for 5 hours. "Yesterday, I played all day: from 9:00 a.m. until 12:00 or 1:00 in the morning," he said.

I inquired about other activities of daily living, and Mr. Matisse responded: "I hang out with my friends once in awhile. We don't really do much, just hang out."

Mental Health

Mr. Matisse denied participating in mental health treatment before his September 26, 2011, motor vehicle accident or ever being prescribed antidepressants or other psychotropic medications. He also denied having a family history of mental illness. Mr. Matisse opined that he currently needs mental health treatment, and he said, "I get a lot of anxiety."

I referenced documentation of a psychological evaluation he underwent with Dr. Hunter in January 2012. Mr. Matisse responded: "I was just in so much pain, I wouldn't do anything, go anywhere. I don't know if my mom said something [that precipitated the evaluation]." He denied participating in any postaccident mental health treatment.

In 2013, Mr. Matisse testified that he had been arrested five times:

- Aggravated assault, firearm discharge, age 19
- Delivery of cocaine, possession of cocaine, and possession of cocaine with intent to sell, age 21, resulting in two felony convictions
- Stalking
- Trafficking oxycodone
- Violation of probation based on testing positive for cocaine

We reviewed Mr. Matisse's criminal record, as he presented during his 2013 deposition. He noted he successfully completed his last probation on January 25, 2014.

Concerning his overall psychological status, Mr. Matisse suggested his demeanor and temperament have significantly changed. He apprised me how he lacks the desire to pursue many activities he enjoyed before his 2011 accident. "There's certain things I do want to do, I just can't physically do them," he stated. Mr. Matisse reported he enjoyed an active social life before his accident.

The primary mental health concerns Mr. Matisse identified related to anxiety, depression, and finances. He attributed his anxiety to his compromised functional capacities. "It drives me nuts all the things I can't do," Mr. Matisse said. As for financial worries, he said, "I went from making a lot of money to just being able to pay my bills."

Mr. Matisse attributed his depression to his compromised functional capacities and unwelcome lifestyle changes. As an example, he stated: "I'd spend $2,000 a night at a bar. That's the type of life I was living before. I was leading a lot of street life. I was affiliated with a lot of girls in strip clubs. That's the kind of life I was living." Mr. Matisse went on to offer he drives a Mercedes CLS.

No current problems with sexual activity were identified by Mr. Matisse. I inquired about thoughts of suicide, and he said, "It's went through my head." Mr. Matisse indicated he does not consider himself at risk of self-harm.

Mr. Matisse informed me he is the youngest of four children born in his family. He noted he has a brother who is a pharmacist, a sister who holds a doctorate degree in physical therapy and practices as a physical therapist, and a brother who is a supervisor with Verizon in Plant City. Mr. Matisse apprised me his mother is a machine operator in a warehouse. "My dad is in hospitality. I don't know what he does. We don't communicate too much. We're not on the best speaking terms, but we're civilized toward each other," he said.

During my clinical interview, Mr. Matisse was pleasant and likable, and he projected a normal affect. He was interpersonally skilled, and he impressed me as confident and outgoing. His cognition was intact, and his memory and concentration were good/fair. Mr. Matisse spoke clearly and coherently. He did not exhibit a thought disorder.

Education and Special Training

Mr. Matisse reported he left school during the ninth grade. "My grades were OK until I started skipping school," he said about his scholastic performance. I inquired about his scores from prior standardized testing, and Mr. Matisse told me that, during the eighth grade, his scores were in the top 10 in his school. He indicated he repeated the eighth grade due to attendance problems.

Through Armwood High School, Mr. Matisse advised me, he pursued a GED course but did not complete it. "I was too busy working. I was a knucklehead when I was growing up. I made a lot of wrong decisions," he stated. No other formal education or training was identified. "I'm a very quick learner as far as my job. They love me at work," Mr. Matisse offered.

No work-related credentials or second-language skills were identified. Mr. Matisse cited on-the-job training in customer service, computer systems use, and sales. He said about his computer use skills, "I'm very good on computers," and he informed me he is able to use Microsoft programs. "I use Word every day to write letters to our clients and potential clients," Mr. Matisse said, conveying he is also able to use PowerPoint and Excel.

Through training and work experience, Mr. Matisse noted, he has developed the following skills:

- Use of databases such as Florida Treasure Hunt to identify potential beneficiaries
- Customer service and client relations
- Swimming pool maintenance
- Use of hand and power tools
- Delivery driving including delivering automobiles
- Sales
- Typing from 85 to 90 words per minute

I asked Mr. Matisse whether he has considered retraining, and he responded affirmatively. He did not identify any specific training objectives, although he said: "I'm a very quick learner. I just want all this accident stuff to finish up before I pursue something else." He apprised me he has three additional compulsory medical evaluations, in addition to a mediation in April. "My employer is my lawyer, so they know I got to do all of these visits. If it was anyone else, I'd be fired by now," Mr. Matisse stated, referencing the flexibility his present employer extends to him.

Career Development

The following work history was obtained from records and my clinical interview:

Job Title	*Name of Organization*	*Dates*
Part-time Asset Recovery Worker	Smerconish & Mustard, P.A.	2012 – present
Driver	Deluxe Car Interiors	2011 – 2012
Swimming Pool Service Technician	Pools Only Pool Supply	2009 – 2011
Parking Attendant	Westside Parking	2008 – 2009
Customer Service Representative	Best Furniture	2005 – 2006
Customer Service Representative	American Furniture	2005 – 2006
Pizza Deliverer	Little Cesar's Pizza	2005
Furniture Deliverer	ABC Furniture	2005

I asked Mr. Matisse which job he considers his most skilled or challenging, and he cited his current asset recovery worker job. "You have to actually use your mind. There's a lot of processes in it," he said. He reported Pools Only terminated his employment; no other job terminations were reported. He denied ever claiming workers' compensation benefits.

Mr. Matisse told me his lawyer, Todd Smerconish, is his employer. I inquired about his affinity for his asset recovery job, and he stated: "I do love it. I'm good at it. If it's dealing with computers and onlining, I'm pretty good at it." Several times during my clinical interview, Mr. Matisse expressed his desire to increase his work participation, but he indicated additional work hours are not currently available for him.

I asked Mr. Matisse about his federal tax returns, and he indicated he has filed some "after the fact [after my September 26, 2011, motor vehicle accident]." He advised me he most recently filed a tax return retroactively for 2013. He also expressed his belief he filed a tax return in 2009 or 2010.

Mr. Matisse conveyed he returned to work approximately 6 weeks after his March 12, 2013, surgery. "I've missed some days for doctor visits, or I couldn't get out of bed," he added. He volunteered that his employment is secure, and he informed me his performance appraisals have been positive.

When asked about his ability to resume his former driver job with Deluxe Car Interiors, Mr. Matisse assessed he is incapable of performing it. "The fast-paced walking, talking, sitting," he said about the bases for his opinion. I asked about his career plans before his 2011 accident, and he noted he had planned to continue his employment with Deluxe Car Interiors.

Regarding his present career plans, Mr. Matisse apprised me he intends to continue his present asset recovery job. "With my criminal history, it's hard to get a job, period," he stated. He went on to cite his limited education and lack of a GED. "It's up to me to make it just not another job," Mr. Matisse added. He expressed he is grateful to his lawyer for the work opportunity.

Mr. Matisse and I discussed viable, alternate employment for him to pursue, including sales. He replied, "Everyone says that's me." I encouraged Mr. Matisse to investigate online GED studies.

Currently, Mr. Matisse reported, he is not searching for another job. "I haven't searched for a job since I started with Smerconish [on July 19, 2012]," he said. He denied planning to begin a job search.

As for his financial situation, Mr. Matisse told me he is experiencing difficulties. Apart from his $1,000 per month in employment income, he indicated, he relies upon his parents for financial support. Mr. Matisse denied applying to the Social Security Administration for disability benefits.

Review of Medical Records

Results of Diagnostic Testing

11/02/11 *George Jefferson, MD*

MRI Lumbar
Impression:
1. Multilevel disc bulges including L3-4, L4-5, and L5-S1 and bilateral neuroforaminal narrowing at multiple levels.
2. Right paracentral posterior disc extrusion-type herniation at T12-L1 with superior migration of the herniated disc.

02/07/12 *Robert P. Wilson, MD*

MRI Cervical Spine without Contrast
Impression:
1. Central disc protrusion at C5-6 resulting in central spinal stenosis without cord compression.
2. Complete cervical spine straightening with rotation of the upper two-thirds portion of the spine, findings which are consistent with soft tissue injury/muscular spasm.

MRI of the Right Shoulder without Contrast
Impression:
Unremarkable examination. No evidence of a rotator cuff tear. No evidence of bony contusion or fracture.

02/20/12 *Gary Morris, MD*

Lumbar Spine MRI dated November 02, 2011
Impression:
Focal (R) T1-L1 herniated nucleus pulposus.

08/02/12 *Mike White, MD*

Nerve Conduction Study/EMG
Impression:
1. Repeat studies in 3-4 months if symptoms are progressive or not resolved.
2. The patient would benefit from an exercise program with a focus on stretching the lower back, along with core strengthening exercises. I would also include piriformis stretches to this regimen. Patient may also benefit injection therapy, including but not limited to, trigger point injections, facet injections, and epidurals.

12/11/13 *William D. Dixon, MD*

MRI of the Thoracic Spine without Contrast
Impression:
1. Disc bulges occur at C3-4, C5-6, and T11-T12.
2. Superior endplate compression fracture at T4.

3. Straightened thoracic kyphosis can represent muscle spasm or sprain.

Operations/Procedures

06/07/12 *Mike White, MD*

Procedure:
Lumbar epidural steroid injection under fluoroscopy.
Epidurogram under fluoroscopy.

07/19/12 *Mike White, MD*

Procedure:
1. Lumbar transforaminal epidural steroid.
2. Fluoroscopy.
3. Radiological examination and interpretation of lumbar epidurogram.

01/11/13 *Lori Boston, DO*

Procedure:
Right L4-5 selective nerve root block.

02/07/13 *Lori Boston, DO*

Procedure:
Right L4-L5 therapeutic transforaminal epidural steroid injection.
Right L5-S1 therapeutic transforaminal epidural steroid injection

03/12/13 *John Swift, MD*

Procedure:
Right side L4-L5 laminotomy and discectomy.

Assessments

09/29/11 *Mark O. David, DC*

Initial Evaluation
History of Present Illness:
Immediately following the collision, Mr. Matisse experienced headaches, and low back pain. He reports being dazed. He was not taken to the hospital. Mr. Matisse did not see any other doctor for treatment of injuries sustained in this collision prior to entering this office. The patient reports an increase in symptoms. Mr. Matisse has been able to work and has not lost a time at work since the collision. He reports not been able to perform normal work activities at this time because of pain, weakness, and stress.
Chief Complaint:
Left shoulder pain.
Lower back pain.

Neck pain.
Headache.
Recommendations:
Patient is scheduled for 4 visits per week for 2 weeks.

10/27/11 *Mark O. David, DC*

Recommendation:
Patient is scheduled for 3 visits per week for 3 weeks.

11/08/11 *Mark O. David, DC*

Comments:
Mr. Matisse reported a return of symptoms or increase of complaints since last visit. He stated: "I have been having pain in my jaw and a lot more headaches lately. The jaw pain had been there since the accident but up until now it was tolerable. It's been making clicking noises too."
Recommendations:
Mr. Matisse is to be referred to Dr. Samuel Jackson DDS for evaluation of his temporomandibular joint.

11/16/11 *Mark O. David, DC*

Comments:
Mr. Matisse reported a return of symptoms or increase of complaints since last visit. He stated: "My low back is on fire today. Everything since the accident has me depressed, my life just isn't the same anymore."
Assessment:
The patient is experiencing a slight exacerbation of their low back pain.

11/17/11 *Scott D. Jackson, DMD*

History of Present Illness:
Areas of immediate concern: Mr. Matisse's immediate complaints were of intermittent headaches, facial pain, chipped teeth, and pain while eating and speaking. The patient stated that the pain started as result of the accident and his jaw as locked open three times since the accident.
Assessment:
Clinical examination revealed three chipped front teeth on patient's upper arch.
Plan:
Orthotic splint therapy was ordered to stabilize the mandible.

12/09/11 *Francisco M. Gatwick, MD*

Initial Evaluation
Chief Complaint:
1. Low back pain with predominate right radiculopathy.
2. Bilateral shoulder pain, left greater than right.
3. Neck pain.

History of Present Illness:
The patient relates that most of his pain is in the middle and lower back. He rates this to be a 7/10. The patient states that the low back pain will radiate down his right lower extremity. He feels the

pain has worsened since the accident, particularly the low back and this is 70% worse than immediately after the accident.

The patient states the painful shoulder is the left, particularly the suprascapular area; however, on physical examination the abnormalities seem to be more on the right than the left but he states that on today's exam the right one does not hurt.

Conclusion:

I also explained that I'm a little puzzled about his shoulder condition. As on examination the right shoulder seems to have the bigger problem than the left but at this time I will hold off on any further MRI/diagnostic studies to see how this pans out and if indeed we are still having a discrepancy in complaints and findings on the next office visit, we may need to assess that at that time.

01/12/12 *Richard A. Hunter, Ph.D.*

Psychological Evaluation

Vocational History:

It was reported that the patient's first serious job was working for Pools Only. This lasted slightly less than year. He then spent a year working as a parking attendant in Ybor City. The patient reported that he worked nearly 80 hours a week in this capacity. He then worked for an asset recovery company briefly and worked briefly for a lawn service. He then was able to obtain employment with the mobile detailing company and has continued in this line of work despite his accident.

Conclusion:

His history indicates that he has had difficulty with the pain compromising his ability to concentrate and that this has impacted his ability to function efficiently at work and as a result has impacted his relationships with his girlfriend and with his parents. The parents apparently are allowing him to stay with them and becoming impatient with his lack of improvement. The patient reports that his concentration and ability to bend and stoop have been markedly impacted by the accident and resulting ongoing pain. He describes himself as much more socially withdrawn and having been a much happier, more energetic person prior to his accident. Independent verification of his reported status cannot be made based on the personality inventories. These suggest that while he is making indiscriminate endorsement of symptomatology, he does not appear to be exaggerating physical symptoms insofar as they were relatively less pronounced than the emotional distress that was endorsed. This same pattern was revealed for the posttraumatic stress inventory. His Multidimensional Pain Inventory, a measure administered to assess whether his response pattern is consistent with that of other chronic pain patients, would support the credibility of his complaints. Based on this, the history and the nature of the MMPI-2 that was produced, it is suggested that the patient is more likely to simply be emotionally out of control than to be trying to fabricate or exaggerate physical complaints.

Recommendations:

It is recommended that the patient be followed in outpatient psychotherapy with a psychologist or psychiatrist well experienced in the emotional effects of physical illnesses and injuries. This patient would likely need a very skilled therapist who is focused on helping the patient get himself back under control.

Diagnostic Impression:

Axis I Major Depressive Disorder (by clinical impression)

Axis II Not Applicable

Axis III S/P Motor Vehicle Accident of 09/26/11 with reports of left shoulder and lower back pain including reports of three bulging and one herniated lumbar disc (by patient report)
Pain Disorder Associated with Medical Condition

Axis IV Psychosocial Stresses:
Fears that he will not be able to earn a living and that the conflicts with his parents will

continue and exacerbate
Concerns that his lifestyle will be markedly compromised by his ongoing pain
Economic frustrations that he will never be able to move beyond assisting in a mobile car detailing company if he cannot get better control over his pain syndrome

Axis V Social and Occupational Functional Assessment Scaled Score = 52

01/17/12 *Fred Troy, MD*

Initial Examination

History of Present Illness:

He is working doing marketing for a law firm in the area, but he has had to decrease his number of hours.

He does have a previous history of back pain from an auto accident two years ago.

Assessment:

This is a 25-year-old black male with low back pain as a result of a motor vehicle accident that occurred September 26, 2011.

Conclusion:

He will have permanent restrictions of no heavy lifting, no frequent bending, and no prolonged sitting or standing.

01/18/12 *Robert Perez, MD*

Chief Complaint:

Low back pain.

History of Present Illness:

The patient has ongoing low back pain. The low back pain is his major complaint. It involves the muscles of the low back, left and right hand sides.

Work Status:

He does marketing work which is mostly talking, walking, and computer work.

Neurological Impression:

1. Chronic severe lower thoracic, lumbosacral sprain with palpable fibromyositis.
2. Chronic insomnia secondary to chronic pain syndrome.
3. Chronic pain syndrome.
4. Multiple level disc bulges at L3-4, L4-5, L5-S1 level with bilateral neural foraminal narrowing, right paracentral posterior disc extrusion type herniation at T12-L1 superior migration of the herniated disc.

Recommendations:

Do not believe any further neurodiagnostic testing is indicated.

In my opinion, he has by now reached maximum medical improvement and has suffered a permanent injury from the accident September 26, 2011. He will have symptoms indefinitely. He has to learn to live with his symptoms, adjust his lifestyle accordingly, periodically will require palliative physical therapy, medications and exercises.

He is permanently restricted from lifting greater than 20 pounds from a bent position, 10 pounds repetitively.

In my opinion this represents an overall 20% permanent impairment rating to the body as a whole.

02/20/12 *Gary Morris, MD*

History:

He has low back constant pain which on an average day is 8/10 which is associated with (R) lower extremity cramping.

Assessment:

He has a focal T12-L1 herniated nucleus pulposus, currently recommend continued symptomatic conservative care with a trial of trigger point injections. The patient will think about the injections and will call if he wishes to try them

03/05/12 *Francisco M. Gatwick, MD*

History of Present Illness:

He continues to complain of pain in the neck and low back area. He states that physical therapy really did not help that much.

Conclusion:

At this time, I think he has achieved maximum medical improvement from conservative treatment. The residual pain he has is something that he is going to have to learn to live with as it is permanent in nature and causally related to his MVA from 9/26/11.

06/01/12 *Mike White, MD*

History of Present Illness:

The patient presents today with complaints of lower back pain, which is constant in nature. He has pain radiating down the right lower extremity, which occurs daily.

Assessment:

1. Posttraumatic lumbar pain.
2. Posttraumatic lumbosacral radiculopathy.
3. Posttraumatic lumbar herniated nucleus pulposus.
4. Posttraumatic facet arthropathy.

Plan:

1. The patient will benefit from a lumbar epidural steroid injection help to alleviate his radicular symptoms. It is my medical opinion that the patient will benefit from a therapeutic epidural injection. The patient understands all risks associated with the procedure and wishes to undergo a lumbar epidural.
2. The patient will benefit from a right lower extremity EMG to better assess the etiology of his radicular pain.
3. The patient will bring in the actual MRI films of his lumbar spine at next visit.

07/11/12 *Michael G. Zelner, MD*

Neurological Evaluation

Work Status:

Upholsterer.

History of Present Illness:

This patient is 25-year-old male involved in a motor vehicle accident on September 26, 2011. Mr. Matisse was the restrained passenger sitting behind the driver when they were rear ended. As a result of this he had sudden onset of dizziness problems with attention, concentration, recent memory, nausea and vomiting and headaches. He has also been having neck pain radiating to the region of the right triceps. There has been low back pain radiating to the L5 dermatome.

He has had chiropractic care. The patient is not been on any medications for this condition.

Assessment:

1. Thoracic disc herniation.

2. Lumbar disc displacement.
3. Lumbar radiculitis.
4. Postconcussion syndrome.
5. Scalp contusion.

Plan:

1. Consider EMG and nerve conduction studies of the lower extremities.
2. MRI of the brain.
3. Neuropsychological assessment.
4. Obtain copy of cervical MRI.
5. Follow up in one month.

08/30/12 *Mike White, MD*

Final Report

History:

Today, he presents with complaints of constant lower back pain, which radiates down the right lower extremity. The leg pain is constant.

Assessment:

1. Posttraumatic lumbar pain.
2. Posttraumatic lumbosacral radiculopathy.
3. Posttraumatic lumbar herniated nucleus pulposus.
4. Posttraumatic lumbar facet arthropathy.

Plan:

Anderson Matisse presents with the above referenced objective findings, which are consistent with the complaints and mechanism of injury as a result of the September 26, 2011, accident. Anderson Matisse has reached maximum medical improvement as of August 30, 2012. In my opinion, the patient had a whole person impairment of 15% (15% lumbar) according to the American Medical Association Guides to the Evaluation of Permanent Impairment 6th Edition, it using the Diagnosis-Related Estimates Method.

11/15/12 *Joseph Simpson, MD*

History of Present Illness:

He complains of a low back pain with radiation into the sacroiliac joint regions, bilateral buttocks, and into the iliac crest areas. He still continues with this severe quite bothersome chronic discomfort.

The patient had a previous MVA in 2008. An MRI at that time revealed a possible disc bulge at that time.

Impression:

1. Chronic intractable lower back pain with intermittent sciatica of the right lower extremity secondary to herniated lumbar disc.
2. Lumbar paraspinous muscle spasm.
3. Lumbar facet joint mediated mechanically generated lower back pain

Recommendations:

A trial of a bilateral lumbar facet joint nerve block under x-ray needle fluoroscopic guidance.

12/05/12 *Francisco in. Gatwick, MD*

History of Present Illness:

The patient called a few days ago complaining of increased pain. He evidently had been going to a pain management facility because of persistent neck and low back pain. He states that his neck and shoulder pain seems to be a little bit better; however, the low back is just killing him and he cannot put up with the pain as obviously he works in a standing position and has to be up long hours filing. Because of the pain, it makes it very hard for him to do that and he was asked to come in.

Impression:

Exacerbation of low back pain secondary to multiple level disc protrusions and what seems to be a central disc herniation to the right of the midline at the T12-L1 level.

Recommendation:

At this time, we are going to go ahead and give him a prescription for gabapentin 100 mg once a day for 3 days, then increase to bid and eventually tid if he is tolerating it well with no side effects, omeprazole 20 mg while taking Naprosyn at total of #30 with one refill and oxycodone 30 mg q6-8h prn at total of #120.

12/12/12 *Robert M. Dunning, MD*

Assessment:

Sciatica.

Cervicalgia.

Sacroiliitis.

Low thoracic rib head displacement and resulting inflammation.

Plan:

1. Continue therapy.
2. Lumbar spine steroid epidural injection.
3. Sacroiliac joint injection.

01/04/13 *Francisco M. Gatwick, MD*

History of Present Illness:

The patient comes back still with similar complaints of low back pain. He states that he tried by all means to get his medication filled, but there was nobody that will refill his oxycodone and he is still having a significant amount of pain. He inquired about other medications. I explained to him that I would not do that. We elected to go ahead and try to see if we can find some Percocet to help him with the pain, but other than that I really do not feel that there is anything else that I can do to help his condition.

Plan:

We will go ahead and give him a prescription for #150 Percocet.

01/11/13 *Lori Boston, DO*

History of Present Illness:

The patient continues to have pain despite chiropractic adjustments, chiropractic massage, chiropractic modalities, lumbar epidural steroid injection and medication (Soma, hydrocodone, methadone and Roxicodone).

Plan:

Fluoroscopic spinal cortisone injection.

01/15/13 *Robert M. Dunning, MD*

Chief Complaint:

My low back pain going into my right leg went away for a couple of hours after I had that injection.

But, now the pain is back.

Assessment:

Sciatica: significant right-sided radicular pain into the right lower extremity.

Plan:

Based on the findings from the Selective Nerve Root Block, when the right L4-5 nerve root was anesthetized his low back pain symptoms radiating into his right leg disappeared. Since he has already exhausted all other forms of conservative medical therapy including Lumbar Epidural Steroid Injections, I believe that an Orthopedic Spine Surgery consult with Dr. John Swift would be beneficial to determine the surgical alternatives to him living with this pain.

01/23/13 *John H. Swift, MD*

Comments:

Today when he presented for evaluation, he did have complaints of back pain and therefore took a Percocet. He also feels in his feet are cold, and now has some complaints of left-sided numbness. He has only had this left-sided numbness once prior.

Plan:

At this time, his presentation may have changed as he just started on Percocet. There is patchy areas of numbness in the left leg and some mild weakness of the left leg that has not been previously identified. At this time, I recommend repeat right-sided L4-L5 selected nerve root locking. If he has significant improvement, he may be a candidate for limited foraminotomy on the right side at L4-L5.

Francisco M. Gatwick, MD

History of Present Illness:

He had some nerve root blocks or facet blocks and he got significant pain relief from this. Evidently, he is scheduled to have a second block done. This time evidently it was steroids and according to what he says if he gets significant pain relief they will then consider a surgical procedure. I assume that we are looking at denervation of the facet block.

As far as the medication is concerned, he states that the Percocet really does not seem to help him as well as the oxycodone and he would like to get back on the oxycodone program. The gabapentin he seems to be tolerating well and it does not seem to make him dizzy at all.

Plan:

At this time, we are going to go ahead and renew the medication. I am going to go ahead and do that now since I am going to be out of town next week and we are already rather busy, so I am going to post date the medication for the date that he is due for refills, which would be February 4th. We are going to give him oxycodone 30 mg q6-8h at total of #120, Naprosyn 500 mg 1 tablet po bid with meals at total of #60, omnipresent 20 mg at hs while taking Naprosyn at total of #30 and gabapentin 100 mg 1 tablet po tid at total of #100 with one refill.

02/21/13 *Robert M. Dunning, MD*

Plan:

Anderson Matisse will require a right L4-5 open surgical laminectomy, foraminotomy and discectomy. This will be scheduled.

03/06/13 *Francisco M. Gatwick, MD*

History of Present Illness:

He states that he has seen Dr. Swift, a spine specialist somewhere in Clearwater, and because of the persistence of the discomfort they have both decided it is probably best to go ahead and proceed with the surgical procedure.

Plan:

We are going to go ahead and renew the medication until his next office visit. In all likelihood, he will have the second procedure prior to seeing us again.

03/27/13 *John H. Swift, MD*

Comments:

2 weeks postop from foraminotomy on the right at L4-L5.

Recommendations:

At this time, he may slowly resume his exercise activities. He will be tapered off all his pain medications. He will not be prescribed any more narcotics.

He is to increase his activities as tolerated. No contraindications to heavy exercise after 6 weeks.

04/17/13 *Francisco M. Gatwick, MD*

History of Present Illness:

He states he did have his lumbar laminectomy surgery done on March 12, 2013 at Kirk Enterprise McCoy Hospital. He shows me in approximately 1 to 1 ½ inch scar on his back. He states that the surgery has helped quite a bit with his pain, but that he still has a significant amount of pain.

Impression:

Status post lumbar laminectomy and discectomy.

Plan:

We are going to go ahead and renew the medication of gabapentin 100 mg 1 tablet po tid, Percocet 10/325 mg 1 tablet q4-6h prn for pain a total of #120, omeprazole 20 mg at hs while taking Naprosyn a total of #30, gabapentin 100 mg 1 tablet po tid a total of #100 and Naprosyn 500 mg 1 tablet po bid.

05/29/13 *Francisco M. Gatwick, MD*

History of Present Illness:

The patient comes back in today for a follow up visit still with similar complaints. He states actually his back is starting to hurt again and he is again having pain down his right lower extremity. He had to wait awhile, but we finally were able to get operative notes from Kirk Enterprise McCoy Hospital where Dr. John Swift evidently performed a laminectomy. From what I can see on the records, it seems like the patient had a mini procedure. The remnant of the disc was then probed, found to be stable and no laminotomy per se was performed.

Impression:

Chronic low back pain syndrome with persistent right lumbar radiculopathy.

Plan:

We are going to go ahead and renew the medications a Percocet 10/325 mg 1 q4-6h prn for a total of #120, omeprazole 20 mg at hs a total of 30, gabapentin 100 mg tid a total of #100, Naprosyn 500 mg 1 tablet po bid a total of #60.

07/17/13 *Francisco M. Gatwick, MD*

History of Present Illness:

He has been complaining of increased pain in his back. We did a spot urinalysis, which was positive for marijuana and negative for the Percocet that we have been administering. When confronted, he did state that he did have to smoke a couple of weeks ago as he had ran out of medicine and he could not get rest and go to sleep, so the only source of palliation of his symptoms was pot.

Plan:

All this being said, the patient has been warned that we are going to go ahead and keep him in the practice. However, if this should occur again where he tests positive for marijuana or negative for the medication that we are prescribing him, we will have no other choice but to discharge him from the practice.

10/08/13 *Francisco M. Gatwick, MD*

History of Present Illness:

A spot urine test done today was negative for everything. When confronted, he stated that because he was taking the Percocet on a prn basis he ran out of medication this past Friday. He states that before he was taking the oxycodone around the clock, now he is just doing it on a prn basis and obviously he is consuming more that he went from 30 mg to 10 mg. I also explained to him that if he tests negative when he should be positive or tests positive when he should be negative again I will have no other choice but to discharge him from our practice.

11/07/13 *Francisco M. Gatwick, MD*

Comments:

A spot urinalysis was done. The patient tested positive for marijuana and THC. When confronted, he states that he has not smoked for months. He states he had a spot urinalysis done by his probation officer 2 days ago and tested fine. I explained to him that obviously in our test that we performed it is positive and it was conceivable that it could be an error. I will go ahead and give him the benefit of the doubt and send the urinalysis out for evaluation.

12/11/13 *Robert Perez, MD*

History of Present Illness:

The patient's symptoms have markedly deteriorated. He is currently having excruciating low back pain. It is a severe, burning, sharp pain, but it is predominantly in the right mid to lower back area. It radiates down the right posterior thigh and right posterior calf.

He is having marked difficulty sleeping.

Work Status:

He is currently mostly doing file work.

Neurological Impression:

1. Chronic severe lower thoracic, lumbosacral strain.
2. Chronic insomnia.
3. Chronic pain syndrome.
4. Chronic lumbar radiculopathy – mostly L5-S1 level with bulging disc at L3-4, L4-5, L5-S1 with a disc extrusion type herniation at T12-L1.
5. Status post surgery by Dr. Swift on March 12, 2013.

Recommendation:

Not to lift greater than 10 to 20 pounds from a bent position.

He is to remain off of work for the next couple of days until I get the MRI scan.

The patient is in excruciating pain at this time.

Results of Preinjury Diagnostic Testing

07/29/08 *Gargi S. Adams, MD*

Cervical Spine Series
Impression:
Straightening of the normal lordotic curvature suggesting muscle spasm or musculoligamentous strain.

Thoracic Spine
Impression:
No acute bony abnormality visualize. It symptoms warrant, evaluation with MRI is recommended.

Lumbar Spine Series
Impression:
No acute bony abnormality.

08/29/08 *Jon Clinton, MD*

MRI Cervical Spine without Contrast
Impression:
Moderate reversal of the normal cervical lordosis.
C5-6 disc desiccation with mild posterior annular bulging.

10/20/08 *Mark J. O'Hara, MD*

MRI of the Lumbar Spine
Impression:

1. L4-5 level: Posterolateral disc bulge in combination with facet arthropathy narrows neural foramina.
2. L5-S1 level: Slight posterolisthesis of L5 on S1. Facet arthropathy narrows bilateral neural foramina.

Preinjury Assessments

07/15/08 *Brian Garcone, DC*

History:
This is an Initial Medical Examination on the above captioned patient who was seen in my office on 07/15/08, for an automobile accident that occurred in April of 2008. The patient was the restrained front driver of a 2007 Scion TC that sustained a rear left and side impact. The patient reports, "My car was hit from the rear left and side swiped." The patient was looking straight ahead and was surprised by the impact his right shoulder and head struck the center console of the car. The patient did not go immediately to the hospital. The patient reports his pain has gotten worse since the accident.

Chief Complaint:
Chief symptoms at the time of this examination are neck pain of severe intensity, right shoulder pain of moderate intensity, upper back pain moderate intensity, low back pain of moderate inten-

sity, right hand and arm pain.

Work Status:

The patient is not employed at this time.

Recommendation:

The patient will be put on a course of conservative chiropractic care 3 times weekly for 6 weeks with continued reduction.

09/23/08 *Richard E. Standish, DC*

History:

Mr. Anderson Matisse was examined in my office on September 23, 2008, for the purpose of an independent medical examination.

Chief Complaint:

1. Low back pain.
2. Right leg pain one to two times weekly.
3. Neck pain on the right.

Recommendation:

It is my opinion the examinee needs further chiropractic care of one time per week for four weeks.

12/02/08 *Brian Garcone, DC*

Final Medical Examination

Diagnoses:

1. Status post vehicle accident with another vehicle (driver).
2. Late effects of MVA.
3. Cervical radiculitis.
4. Paresthesia.
5. Posttraumatic cervical sprain/strain-hyperflexion/extension.
6. Posterior neck lumbar sprain/strain-hyperflexion/extension.
7. Right shoulder pain in joint.

Recommendation:

I believe the injuries I was able to see on this examination were causally related to the accident in question on 04/30/08. I believe the patient has suffered severe structural weakness to the cervical, lumbar spine, and right rotator cuff. I believe the patient has suffered a permanent partial spinal/extremity impairment of 15% (cervical 5%, lumbar 5%, right shoulder 5%) of the body as a whole in accordance with 5th Edition AMA range of motion guidelines.

Results of Testing

On the Wahler Physical Symptoms Inventory, Mr. Matisse generated a score of 2.2. This score placed Mr. Matisse at the 9th decile in relation to a comparable normative group.

The Multidimensional Aptitude Battery-II (MAB-II) was used to assess Mr. Matisse's intellectual skills and abilities. Scores from this instrument are presented relative to a normative sample.

The MAB-II Verbal, Performance, and Full Scale scores are converted to deviation IQ scores that are based upon an average score of 100 with a standard deviation of 15. The scores express where an individual's score falls in relation to the average score. Additionally, the MAB-II subscales are converted to-scores that are based upon an average score of 50 with a standard deviation of 10. For example, a score of 60 on the MAB-II would indicate a performance that is one standard deviation above average relative to the individual's peer group, and a score of 40 would indicate a performance that is one standard deviation below average relative to the individual's peer group.

Overall, Mr. Matisse scored as follows on the MAB-II:

Verbal IQ	72
Performance IQ	85
Full Scale IQ	77

Mr. Matisse's performance placed him in the borderline range of mental functioning. His individual scores on the MAB-II subscales are summarized below:

Information	33
Comprehension	23
Arithmetic	40
Similarities	21
Vocabulary	34
Digit Symbol	44
Picture Completion	39
Spatial	49
Picture Arrangement	27
Object Assembly	44

The Wide Range Achievement Test – Revision 4 (WRAT4) is a test of basic skills. Mr. Matisse's performances on this measure are presented below in terms of grade level equivalents:

Reading	Grade 8.1
Spelling	Grade 12.2
Arithmetic	Grade 6.9

The Grooved Pegboard is a manipulative dexterity test used in the selection of employees for industrial jobs such as assembler, machine operator, and other manual jobs. This test measures finger and manual dexterity, and requires complex visual-motor coordination. Below are Mr. Matisse's scores:

	Score	Normative Comparison Data
Dominant Hand (R)	66 seconds	mean = 63.40 seconds (SD = 7.90)
Nondominant Hand	71 seconds	mean = 69.10 seconds (SD = 18.70)

On the Beck Depression Inventory-II, Mr. Matisse generated a total score of 43, which corresponds to the severe range of depression.

Results of personality testing from the MMPI-2 were invalid. According to a computer-generated interpretive report, Mr. Matisse responded to test items in an extremely exaggerated manner, endorsing a wide variety of rare symptoms and attitudes. His results may stem from several factors that include excessive symptom checking, falsely claiming psychological problems, low-reading level, a plea for help, or a confused state. His extreme score on a measure of psychopathology suggests that his responses are more extreme than people who are hospitalized for severe psychiatric problems.

On the Self-Directed Search Form R, Mr. Matisse scored highest on the Enterprising occupational theme. This theme is most often associated with business and self-gain occupations. He rated his teaching, sales, clerical, and math abilities; understanding of others; and managerial and office skills as very high. He also assessed his mechanical ability and manual skills are above average. The occupations Mr. Matisse noted interest in pursuing most recently were "typing," "Internet Explorer," "computer programing," "customer service," "driving," "sales," and "marketing." Among the occupations from the Self-Directed Search Form R that correspond with his profile are Production Supervisor (DOT #539.137-014), Furniture Assembly Supervisor (DOT #763.134-014), Jeweler (DOT #700.281-010), Locksmith (DOT #709.281-010), Chauffeur (DOT #913.663-010), Dental Ceramist (DOT #712.381-042), Safety Inspector, Truck (DOT #219.687-018), Estimator (DOT #169.267-038), Parcel Post Clerk (DOT #222.387-038), Credit Card Clerk (DOT #209.587-014), and Assembler, Electrical Accessories (DOT #729.384-010).

Summary and Impressions

1. Mr. Matisse presented an unimpressive scholastic and work history. He indicated he left school after the eighth grade and abandoned pursuing the GED after he obtained a job with Burger King, about which he stated, "I worked at Burger King for 2 days, and then I quit." His 2013 deposition testimony and Answers to Interrogatories identified several subsequent unskilled jobs he performed. Dr. Hunter, a psychologist, noted in a January 12, 2012, report that Mr. Matisse's employment with Pools Only Pool Supply was his "first serious job." Mr. Matisse told me he was terminated from his employment with Pools Only. The next job he secured was as a driver with Deluxe Car Interiors, the job he reported performing at the time of his September 26, 2011, motor vehicle accident. Based on my understanding of his job responsibilities, his driver job involved unskilled work that required sedentary/light exertion. Mr. Matisse reported he earned $12 per hour, worked from 40 to 60 hours per week, and earned from $500 to $2,500 per week; he noted he generated commissions based on jobs he secured. After his 2011 accident, Mr. Matisse recollected, he had "a few days" of work absences. Citing physician appointments that caused him to miss work, he conveyed, his employer became increasingly less tolerant of his work absences, and his work hours were reduced. "I took that as a hint," Mr. Matisse stated, expressing his presumption that Deluxe Car Interiors was planning to terminate his employment. In an attempt to be proactive, Mr. Matisse explained, he contacted his lawyer, and the firm representing him, Smerconish & Mustard, P.A., hired him as a file clerk. Apparently, Mr. Matisse had previous employment in this capacity with the Smerconish & Mustard firm. He informed me his file clerk job began in July 2012. He described unskilled, light-exertion tasks he was required to perform, noting his work involved extended walking and standing. "I couldn't do that," Mr. Matisse said, indicating his job responsibilities were incompatible with injuries he is associating with his September 2011 accident. Noting the Smerconish & Mustard firm accommodated him in an alternate position, asset recovery worker, approximately 9 to 12 months ago, Mr. Matisse reported his work hours were reduced from 37.5 to 25 per week. His present rate of pay is $10 per hour. As an asset recovery worker, he related, he performs semiskilled, sedentary tasks. "I like what I'm doing right now," Mr. Matisse said about his job satisfaction. He responded affirmatively when I inquired whether his job responsibilities are within his capacity. He provided inconsistent statements about his ability to increase his level of work participation beyond his current level of 25 hours per week. For example, Mr. Matisse made statements indicating that he desires to work longer hours; however, additional work is not available to him. Alternately, he made statements that expressed his reported physical problems preclude him from working more hours. He volunteered that his employment is secure and that his performance appraisals have been positive. The career plans Mr. Matisse presented were to continue his present asset recovery job. "With my criminal history, it's hard to get a job, period," he stated. He informed me he is not searching for another job, and he denied planning to do so. Regarding his former driver job with Deluxe Car Interiors, Mr. Matisse assessed he is incapable of resuming it. He cited, "The fast-paced walking, talking, sitting," as bases for his assessment. Mr. Matisse has had an unstable work history. He did not impress me as motivated to aggressively pursue vocational rehabilitation. I inquired about his activities when he is not working, and Mr. Matisse said, "I just stay in my room and play video games all day." I encouraged him to investigate online GED preparation programs. He expressed confidence in his learning ability, noting, "I'm a very quick learner." Mr. Matisse commented about his litigation, "I just want all this accident stuff to finish up before I pursue something else." His involvement in his present litigation appears to be inhibiting his motivation to pursue

vocational rehabilitation.

2. Mr. Matisse's medical history before his September 26, 2011, motor vehicle accident is significant from a vocational rehabilitation perspective. Records document injuries he sustained as a result of an April 2008 motor vehicle accident, and document complaints similar to those Mr. Matisse is associating with his September 2011 motor vehicle accident, including neck and lower back pain. Apparently, he struck his head in his 2008 accident. The last medical record I reviewed predating Mr. Matisse's September 2011 accident is Dr. Garcone's December 2008 report of a final medical examination. "I believe the patient has suffered severe structural weakness to the cervical, lumbar spine, and right rotator cuff. I believe the patient has suffered a permanent partial spinal/extremity impairment of 15% (cervical 5%, lumbar 5%, right shoulder 5%) of the body as a whole in accordance with the 5th Edition AMA range of motion guidelines," Dr. Garcone concluded. Interestingly, imaging of Mr. Matisse's lumbar spine on October 20, 2008, detected abnormalities at L4-5, the same level on which Dr. Swift operated on March 12, 2013. Additionally, imaging of Mr. Matisse's cervical spine on August 29, 2008, found abnormities at C5-6, and cervical spine imaging on February 7, 2012, also found abnormalities at this level. Quite likely, based on injuries predating Mr. Matisse's September 2011 accident, he would have had some limitations performing work-related activities.
3. Medical records postdating Mr. Matisse's September 26, 2011, accident indicates he initially pursued chiropractic treatment. During his initial examination by Dr. Gatwick, the physician commented about Mr. Matisse's left-shoulder complaints: "I also explained that I'm a little puzzled about his shoulder condition. As on examination the right shoulder seems to have the bigger problem than the left." Mr. Matisse apparently injured his right shoulder in his 2008 motor vehicle accident. Dr. Troy recommended on January 17, 2012, that Mr. Matisse "will have permanent restrictions of no heavy lifting, no frequent bending, and no prolonged sitting or standing." Mr. Matisse subsequently underwent an examination with Dr. Perez on January 18, 2012. The neurologist determined Mr. Matisse reached maximum medical improvement, and advised permanent restrictions including lifting greater than 20 pounds from a bent position, 10 pounds repetitively. "In my opinion, this represents an overall 20% permanent impairment rating to the body as a whole," Dr. Perez stated. In his March 5, 2012, office note, Dr. Gatwick opined that Mr. Matisse had reached maximum medical improvement; he reckoned Mr. Matisse would continue to experience residual pain, "as it is permanent in nature and causally related to his MVA from 9/26/11." Dr. White assigned a 15% impairment rating, secondary to Mr. Matisse's lumbar injuries, on August 30, 2012. On March 12, 2013, Dr. Swift operated on Mr. Matisse's L4-5 lumbar spine. In his only postoperative note, dated March 27, 2013, the orthopedic surgeon stated: "He is to increase his activities as tolerated. No contraindications to heavy exercise after 6 weeks." Subsequent notes by Dr. Gatwick include concerns about Mr. Matisse testing positive for THC and marijuana, but negative for Percocet, which he had been prescribed by Dr. Gatwick (please refer to Dr. Gatwick's notes dated July 17, October 8, and November 7, 2013). The most recent medical record I reviewed is Dr. Perez's December 11, 2013, office note. The neurologist recommended restrictions similar to those cited in his January 18, 2012, office note. Interestingly, despite his reported ongoing symptoms, Mr. Matisse has not returned to see Dr. Swift, the orthopedic surgeon who operated on his lower back on March 12, 2013. I am unaware of any medical advisement that restricts Mr. Matisse from full-time employment. My analysis of his medical records have led me to conclude that, at a minimum, he is capable of performing sedentary and light-exertion work full time. His medical records indicate he should be capable of resuming his prior driver job with Deluxe Car Interiors.
4. It should be noted that Mr. Matisse's MMPI-2 profile was invalid. A computer-generated interpretive report determined he responded to test items in an extremely exaggerated manner, endorsing a wide variety of rare symptoms and attitudes. As noted above, much of Mr. Matisse's time is consumed with nonproductive activity. His reported mood-related problems would likely improve if he focused his efforts on more productive activity including more aggressively pursuing vocational rehabilitation. In addition to other features of his vocational profile – including his limited education, unstable work history, and lack of transferable skills – other factors relevant to consider when evaluating Mr. Matisse's claim of loss of earning capacity include his criminal history and continued postaccident illicit drug use (please refer to Dr. Gatwick's office notes). The information I have had an opportunity to review does not support a claim of

loss of earning capacity attributable to Mr. Matisse's September 26, 2011, motor vehicle accident.

5. On as positive note, Mr. Matisse is a younger individual (age 27) who displayed a normal gait and did not use adaptive aids during my examination. His performance on tests of mental functioning were commensurate with my estimate of his preaccident level of intellect. Mr. Matisse demonstrated good performance on a test of manual speed and dexterity. Interpersonally, I found him skilled, confident, and outgoing. These factors are assets to Mr. Matisse, should he become more motivated to pursue vocational rehabilitation. I mentioned to him that, based on my analysis of his vocational profile, he would be well suited for sales and marketing occupations. Again, I encourage him to pursue GED studies, and I believe he is capable of passing the exam. This will further his work opportunities.
6. I have not reviewed any academic, employment, or earnings records, which are of interest to me. Additionally, I am interested in reviewing updated medical records including reports of compulsory medical examinations that I understand Mr. Matisse will be undergoing. Other records of interest include his dental and criminal records. If additional information I review causes a change in my opinions, I will make this known.

Michael Shahnasarian, Ph.D.
Certified Rehabilitation Counselor #3701
Certified Vocational Evaluator #58360
Certified Life Care Planner #258
Licensed Psychologist PY5644
Fellow, National Career Development Association
Fellow, International Academy of Life Care Planners

____
Date

Chapter 7

Assessment of Earning Capacity in Cases Involving the Americans with Disabilities Act

Synopsis

7.1 Introduction

The employment provisions of the Americans with Disabilities Act (ADA), introduced in 1992, aim to protect qualified persons with disabilities from discrimination. A person with a disability qualifies for the law's protection if he has a physical or mental impairment that substantially limits one or more major life activities, and the person has a record of such impairment or is regarded as having such an impairment.

The ADA defines a "qualified individual with a disability" as a disabled person who possesses the skill, experience, education, and other job requirements necessary to perform a position in question and can perform the essential functions of the job—with or without reasonable accommodation. A reasonable accommodation is any modification or adjustment to a job, an employment practice, or the work environment that makes it possible for a qualified individual with a disability to participate in the job application process, perform the essential functions of a job, or enjoy the benefits and privileges of employment equal to those employees without disabilities enjoy. The ADA does not require employers to extend accommodations if doing so will be an undue hardship (e.g., excessive cost; extensive, substantial, disruptive, or fundamentally altering the nature or operation of business).

7.2 Central Vocational Questions

Earning capacity assessments of persons pursuing claims under the ADA usually require vocational evaluators to address questions similar to those they address in cases involving a person with an acquired disability (please refer to Chapter 6). Besides customary vocational assessments—such as work history, acquired and transferable skills, and functional capabilities and limitations—disputed issues related to ADA claims often require vocational evaluators to address the following questions:

- Is the claimant capable of performing the essential functions of a job in question with or without accommodations?
- What types of accommodations may be available to enable the claimant to perform a job's essential functions?
- What alternate types of employment and earnings are available to the claimant? (This question has implications that may relate to back pay and front pay claims, discussed in more detail later in this chapter.)

A. Essential Job Functions

To assess whether an individual pursuing an ADA claim is in fact qualified to perform the essential functions of a job in question—with or without a reasonable accommodation(s)—a vocational evaluator must perform a thorough job analysis and appraise the individual's suitability for the job. A job analysis incorporates analyses of a job's functional requirements, mental demands, and work environment characteristics. This can be accomplished by:

- An on-site tour of the work premises and observation of the work being performed
- Review of job descriptions

- Interviews of employers and supervisors familiar with the job
- Interviews of present and/or prior job incumbents
- Review of descriptive job information promulgated by industry associations or other authoritative sources

Information obtained through a comprehensive vocational evaluation, as described in Chapter 4, and a thorough job analysis facilitates the vocational evaluator's appraisal of the subject's qualification to perform a job's essential functions—with or without an accommodation. The evaluator should analyze performance standards and expectations, unique job demands, and prevailing industry standards associated with the job.

B. Reasonable Accommodations

A primary issue in many ADA claims is whether an employer was remiss in not extending a reasonable accommodation to a qualified individual with a disability. The Equal Employment Opportunity Commission (EEOC) provided the following suggestions about how employers can extend reasonable accommodations:

- Make facilities readily accessible to and usable by individuals with disabilities
- Restructure jobs by reallocating or redistributing marginal job functions
- Alter when or how an essential job function is performed
- Offer part-time or modified work schedules
- Obtain or modify equipment or devices
- Modify examinations, training materials, or policies
- Provide qualified readers or interpreters
- Offer reassignment to a vacant position
- Permit use of accrued paid leave or unpaid leave for necessary medical treatment
- Provide reserved parking
- Allow employees to provide equipment or devices the employer may be unable or not required to provide

A vocational evaluator must thoroughly understand both a job's requirements—including the work milieu and the employer's business objectives—and an individual's assistive needs before analyzing possible accommodations. An assessment of viable job accommodations may require an evaluator to consult with vendors of adaptive equipment or devices, associations that represent individuals with specific disabilities, engineers, or other professionals who specialize in ergonomics.

In most cases, vocational evaluators should refrain from offering opinions about whether identified accommodations are reasonable for an employer to implement. Some accommodations may involve architectural modifications, disruptions in work processes, and costs that may not be readily apparent. A vocational evaluator can lose credibility by venturing into engineering, management, and economic discussions about whether identified accommodations are reasonable. Consequently, vocational evaluators should view their role as a purveyor of insightful, well-researched information that will help the trier of fact form opinions on reasonable accommodations.

Whether potential accommodations an employer may be able to implement are reasonable is quite often a legal decision. To this end, the trier of fact will likely find the following information helpful:

- Potential accommodations available to an employer
- Costs of accommodations and related logistical considerations
- Workplace consequences associated with implementing prospective accommodations

7.3 Back Pay and Front Pay

Back pay and front pay relate to a plaintiff's prospective loss of past earnings and future earning capacity caused by alleged failure of an employer to provide a reasonable accommodation to a presumably qualified plaintiff with a disability. Definitions of these damages follow:

back pay. Employment compensation to which a plaintiff may be entitled from the onset of an alleged failure to accommodate a qualified person with a disability to present.

front pay. Employment compensation that may be due a plaintiff as a result of any difference between prior earning capacity and future loss of earning capacity, beginning at present. In some cases, front pay damages extend over the remainder of the plaintiff's work life.

Defense counsel retained a vocational evaluator in a case in which an employee of a multinational business services organization alleged his employer's failure to reasonably accommodate him caused him to pursue his career development elsewhere, at a lesser rate of pay. The evaluator performed an analysis based on available information and research to provide opinions about job availability and earnings available to the claimant; however, defense counsel met resistance when introducing these opinions during trial. Below is the sidebar conversation that ensued when the defense attorney presented the vocational expert to offer testimony about the plaintiff's failure to mitigate alleged front pay and back pay damages. The plaintiff's attorney objected to the relevance of the expert's testimony. As indicated below, the defense attorney prevailed during the argument.

Plaintiff Attorney: I anticipate, Judge—but I could be wrong—that this particular witness is being called for the purpose of demonstrating that there were job opportunities in the Tampa area that Mr. Lincoln could perform within his limits. I'm willing to stipulate with the defendant, at this time, that Mr. Lincoln is not claiming that he is substantially limited in the major life activity of working. On that basis, if it saves the court a little time, I think maybe we can move on with the next witness.

Defense Attorney: I move to dismiss the case.

The Court: I don't think that gets it. I really don't.

Defense Attorney: I think we need the witness, Your Honor, to demonstrate both the elements of the case and the issue of—included in the elements of the case is the plaintiff's failure to seek and pursue employment opportunities that were within Mr. Lincoln's alleged limitations in the Tampa Bay area. We'll keep it as short as we can.

The Court: What's the relevancy of his failure to pursue employment activity?

Defense Attorney: It is at least for the purposes of evaluating his back pay, number one. Number two, it is certainly a question affecting Mr. Lincoln's credibility in the testimony. It is certainly his obligation . . . .

The Court: What about the back pay issue? He has a duty to mitigate. So, if this evidence showed that he didn't seek employment opportunities, wouldn't that affect the back pay issue?

Plaintiff Attorney: I'm going to enter argument here, Judge. I don't think it would under the circumstances. Under the circumstances, Mr. Lincoln was in fear of termination if he accepted alternate employment. He had paid for and received long-term disability payments and was working towards trying to get back to work with his employer. If Mr. Lincoln had been sitting on his hands doing absolutely nothing, I think that perhaps that might be relevant; but I think there's sufficient evidence that would obviate that. But I do understand that I'm crossing over and getting into argument at this point. Do they have a duty to mitigate? Yes, sir, they do. But could there be an exception? I think that there could be. I think this is going to be one of those cases.

The Court: All right. I'm going to overrule the objection.

After qualifying the vocational expert, the defense attorney elicited testimony about employment opportunities that had been available to the plaintiff. The expert identified records that he reviewed, provided a summary of the plaintiff's restrictions as outlined in medical records, reviewed the plaintiff's transferable skills, and then testified about jobs available to the plaintiff during the period in question. The vocational expert's testimony effectively demonstrated that the plaintiff had many opportunities to pursue alternate employment within his capacity. His lack of effort to do so led the jury to infer that he failed to mitigate his claimed loss of earnings damages. A synopsis of the vocational expert's testimony during direct examination follows. Cross-¬examination—which was nominal and concentrated on the expert's fees—proved to be ineffective and did not challenge the expert's assumptions or methods.

Defense Attorney: Based on the information available to you, were you able to evaluate the job opportunities available to someone in Mr. Lincoln's position as he described it?

Vocational Expert: Yes.

Defense Attorney: And what were those job opportunities?

Vocational Expert: Well, there are literally hundreds of thousands of jobs nationally that would have been available to him, thousands of jobs in the local economy. Mr. Lincoln has a background that includes completion of a two-year respiratory therapy program. He also has the equivalent of a college degree concentrating in business administration, and he has some business experience. I considered all of these factors and determined that there have been many opportunities available to him. Some of the fastest-growing areas are in the medical field and the computer field. An example of an occupation that Mr. Lincoln noted interest in pursuing was stockbroker. According to the Department of Labor, there were 3,845 stockbrokers employed in the area last year. The average wages for those individuals was $22.47 per hour. In the medical area, there've been many opportunities in medical sales positions. With Mr. Lincoln's background, for instance, I believe he has been qualified to pursue sales supervisor positions; the Department of Labor reported that there were 35,672 people employed in jobs of these types last year. Another job category that I believe would be well suited to Mr. Lincoln's background relates to the sales of business services. According to the Department of Labor, 7,499 individuals were employed in the Tampa Bay area last year selling business services of different types. The median, which is the middle-most wage, for those individuals was $15.61 per hour.

Defense Attorney: Dr. Expert, if you know, how many jobs are and will likely be available to Mr. Lincoln, given his twenty-pound lifting restriction?

Vocational Expert: There are several things to consider. He has a college degree, and that gives him a competitive edge, along with the other skills and factors I identified earlier. Another thing to consider is the labor market that has been available to him. I just reviewed a current report by the Department of Labor with projections about local job availability.

Plaintiff Attorney: Excuse me, Your Honor. I would just object to the witness' reference to this document on the grounds of speculation.

Defense Attorney: This is a document this witness read.

The Court: Overruled. Proceed.

Vocational Expert: This is a publication of the Department of Labor, and it's specific to Hillsborough County. It indicates that employment between now and 2016 is expected to grow substantially in a number of job categories. For instance, service jobs are expected to grow 22.9 percent during this period. Sales jobs are expected to grow 23.1 percent. Professional jobs, 28.4 percent. Those categories have jobs within that I believe Mr. Lincoln would be both able to pursue and be competitive for.

7.4 Noteworthy Considerations

In ADA cases with pending questions about reasonable accommodations, a worksite evaluation sometimes facilitates vocational evaluators' efforts. Preferably, the evaluator will also observe work associated with the job in question being performed. This inspection allows the evaluator to become more familiar with the job and its demands, the work environment, and the feasibility of implementing accommodations necessary to allow a person with a disability to perform the job's essential functions—with or without an accommodation. When providing testimony to a trier of fact, an evaluator's credibility may be enhanced if she has assessed the work environment firsthand.

Figure 7.1 summarizes a vocational evaluator's report of a worksite assessment at a machine shop. Because of complaints about the employer's selection practices, the Equal Employment Opportunity Commission (EEOC) pursued a claim on behalf of employees who alleged that a requisite medical examination for employment was unfair. The evaluator performed an on-site analysis of three jobs in question: machinist, mechanic, and fitter/welder. While reviewing the summary provided in Figure 7.1, note the evaluator's attention to the general work environment, nature of the work activities in question, specific functional requirements necessary to perform the essential functions of the three jobs, and references to modifying work processes to lessen the job's functional requirements such as installing lifting systems and automating welding processes.

Vocational evaluators will almost certainly draw an objection if they attempt to provide opinions about an employer's efforts to make reasonable accommodations. As always, it is imperative that evaluators restrict their opinions to the scope of their expertise and refrain from rendering opinions that require insight better provided by another professional such as an engineer or medical expert. Resources like the Job Accommodation Network (JAN), a nonprofit organization that offers counsel about workplace accommodations, can help identify options about how work tasks can be performed with different accommodations.

A vocational evaluator determined, for example, that an individual seeking employment as a shift supervisor was qualified to perform the job's essential functions, except for preparing daily production reports, because of a crush injury to the candidate's dominant hand. The evaluator identified accommodations the employer could have implemented to bypass the candidate's difficulty with writing and using a computer, such as providing to the candidate voice-activated software, dictation or transcription services, or a dictating machine. Additionally, the evaluator's analysis included information about costs and workplace logistics associated with implementing the various accommodations. The evaluator refrained from opining whether the accommodations were reasonable. This decision was deferred to the jury after the expert provided her opinion that (a.) the candidate was qualified to perform all but one of the job's essential functions, and (b.) accommodations were available for the employer to extend. With information about options, costs, and workplace logistics associated with potential accommodations, the evaluator probably gained credibility with the jury by not offering a legal opinion about the reasonableness of implementing available accommodations. With the aid of the evaluator's input, the jury became empowered to make a well-informed decision.

7.5 Conclusion

Vocational evaluations initiated in conjunction with ADA claims may require an in-depth analysis of specific job responsibilities and associated functional requirements, a worksite evaluation, and research about accommodations that could allow a qualified individual with a disability to perform a job in question. The vocational evaluator has a responsibility to discern and explain the implications associated with implementing prospective accommodations. Vocational evaluators may be tempted to offer an opinion

Report of Site Visit
Perfection Machine and Fabricating Corporation

During my tour of PMFC, I examined the workplace, observed the work of the three positions at issue (first class welders, machinists, and mechanics) being performed, and obtained supplemental information about the nature of the work environment and positions from Mr. Helpful. Based upon information obtained during my site visit on November 15, 2013; information in Mr. Helpful's deposition dated June 22, 2013; job descriptions published by PMFC; and descriptive information about the positions in question published by the U.S. Department of Labor, my assessment of the noteworthy physical demands associated with the work of fitters/welders, machinists, and mechanics follows:

1. Job responsibilities require exertion in the medium to heavy range.
2. Extended standing and walking are required.
3. Job incumbents must be able to perform the full range of body motions including contorting their bodies for extended durations.
4. The work environment has many hazards including exposure to moving machinery, loud and noisy machinery, loud and noisy work environment, occasional need to work at heights, exposure to extreme temperatures, and occasional exposure to vibration.
5. Job incumbents must be capable of the following physical activities: climbing, balancing, stooping, kneeling, crouching, crawling, reaching, handling, fingering, and feeling. Visual acuity is particularly important for work performed by welders, as is depth perception and accommodation.

I have begun an assessment of potential workplace modifications to reduce the functional requirements of the subject jobs. The site visit I conducted will facilitate my continued efforts.

Figure 7.1 *Summary of Onsite Work Evaluation*

about whether accommodations extended to a qualified individual with a disability are reasonable; however, the evaluator should refrain from rendering opinions that involve considerations beyond her expertise, and/or may call for legal conclusions.

Appendix 7.1: Sample Report of a Vocational Rehabilitation Evaluation in an Americans with Disabilities Act Case Prepared for Cheryl Marie Miller by Michael Shahnasarian, Ph.D., December 13 and 14, 2011

Approximately 10 years after being diagnosed with multiple sclerosis, a control room technician employed in an oil refinery filed an American's with Disabilities Act claim, alleging her employer failed to reasonably accommodate her and she was wrongfully terminated.

As the report in Appendix 7.1 indicates, evidence critical to the claim's evaluation included careful correlation of medical records documenting a progression of the claimant's disease and concomitant claimant job performance problems. The evaluator also considered accommodations extended to the claimant, viewed firsthand via a tour of the claimant's former workplace and supplemented by interviews of the claimant's former supervisors.

Pivotal to the vocational evaluator's assessment that the claimant was not qualified to perform her former job—even though numerous accommodations were extended to her—were two factors. First, she manifested significant performance problems, increasing in frequency and with accompanying dire implications for her and her coworkers' safety, rendering her incapable of performing her job's essential functions. Second, the performance problems correlated positively with medical records documenting a progression of the claimant's multiple sclerosis.

Overview

Cheryl Marie Miller was referred to me for a vocational rehabilitation evaluation. Ms. Miller testified in June 2009 that LMN, LLC, an oil refinery, employed her as an oil movement systems coordinator until November 17, 2010. According to her Third Amended Complaint, Ms. Miller alleges she has been discriminated against "as a result of her disability, sex, and race in her job assignments, promotions, pay, benefits, evaluations, and treatment." The Third Amended Complaint also alleges, "The actions of Defendant constitute intentional infliction of emotional distress."

On December 13 and 14, 2011, I conducted a vocational rehabilitation evaluation of Ms. Miller in a conference room in Miami, Florida. My examination consisted of a clinical interview, which required 4 hours and 15 minutes, and the administration of a battery of tests that required an additional 4 hours and 45 minutes for her to complete.

Approximately 90 minutes after my exam was scheduled to begin, Ms. Miller had not yet arrived, and I received a call from her lawyer, Sally Cook. Ms. Cook advised me of a miscommunication and noted her client was not aware of my scheduled examination. Ms. Cook went on to indicate that Ms. Miller would be attending, albeit late. Another 1 hour and 45 minutes elapsed before Ms. Miller arrived, and she was accompanied by a member of Ms. Cook's office; this person assisted Ms. Miller with walking. Ms. Miller accepted my offer of assistance at the end of my December 13, 2011, exam, and I assisted her with walking to her sister's vehicle.

I met alone with Ms. Miller. She informed me she was not aware of my scheduled exam on December 13, 2011. After my clinical interview, I began the testing portion of my exam. Ms. Miller conveyed she was beginning to have difficulties with fatigue and concentration. She requested that the testing be continued the following day, and I obliged her request. I completed the testing portion of my exam on December 14, 2011.

Ms. Miller reported she holds a valid driver's license. During her 2011 deposition, she indicated her motor vehicle had been modified with hand controls for operating brake and accelerator pedals. Ms. Miller provided similar information to me, advising me the modifications on her vehicle allow her to drive without problems.

In March 2000, Ms. Miller related, she was diagnosed with multiple sclerosis (MS). I asked whether she had any active symptoms at the time of her November 2010 termination; she responded affirmatively and elaborated about the following problems:

- Numbness throughout body, especially hands
- A "cutting" sensation in both sides
- Mobility difficulties

- Balance problems
- Right-side body weakness, "both limbs were very weak"
- Severe pain in right side of head
- Difficulty sleeping, "I would wake up screaming because of the pain in my head"
- Bladder control accidents, approximately three per week, "I had to start using Depends"
- Acid reflux, "I was vomiting, stuff like that"

Ms. Miller denied having any mental functioning problems near the time before her November 2010 termination. Further, she denied having mental functioning problems at any previous time; however, she acknowledged that stress worsened her symptoms.

Concerning her recent symptoms, Ms. Miller assessed her gait has worsened during the past year. During her September 2011 deposition, Ms. Miller presented the following problems:

- Unable to walk
- Bladder incontinence
- Bilateral weakness in hands, unable to hold a pen
- "Muscle spasms in my head"
- Unable to handle stress
- Trouble with focusing, concentration
- "Major headaches"

Ms. Miller informed me her disabling problems have continued. I asked about any change in her symptoms since her November 2010 termination, and she responded: "The pulling sensation in my head has gotten worse." Additionally, she conveyed she has memory and concentration problems she did not have previously. "That's affected my school work," Ms. Miller said, expressing her scholastic performance is less robust than it had been before her job termination.

Regarding mental functioning, Ms. Miller cited problems with memory and concentration. In addition to these problems, which she noted developing during the past year, she assessed her mental acuity has dulled. "I'm not as sharp [as I was in November 2010]," she stated.

Ms. Miller attributed her memory and concentration problems to "the stress of not working." Similarly, she associated the worsening of her headache problems since her severance with her termination-related stress. In her Answers to Interrogatories, Ms. Miller noted problems related to her 2010 termination: "I suffered severe stress and anxiety, which impacts my physical condition."

During her June 2009 deposition, Ms. Miller contended that her MS had been exacerbated by the alleged discrimination she suffered at LMN. "The kind of MS that I have, yes, MS does have progression, but I have been at this stage since 2000 when I was diagnosed with my sickness, and I have not had any major progression until I did not get the position," she testified. When asked whether she meant the supervisor or the superintendent positions, Ms. Miller replied, "Both positions." Regarding the superintendent position, she related:

> *Because of my disability, I am not able to go on board the ships, and stuff like that, to double check the inspectors. They wanted the superintendent to go on the tanks to double check that the inspectors were gauging the tanks properly. Not the ship tanks, the field tanks. And I couldn't pull the lines and stuff like that to tie up the vessels.*

According to a pretermination report from Dr. Clover dated June 2, 2010:

> *Ms. Miller complains of intermittent right-sided headaches of a pulling nature that radiate down into the neck, intermittent right-sided head pains (not headaches) that cause her to pound her head with her fist, constant painful tightness that feels like two balls concentrated in the center of the low back and right of center, constant painful tightness in the occipital region of the head, neck, and shoulders, constant sharp,*

cutting pains in both mid-thighs, preexisting constant weakness in both lower extremities and hands that has been exacerbated, and constant burning in the right knee and both ankles/insteps.

Vocational Activity

Ms. Miller reported she completed her high school education in 1983, and pursued studies at Robinson University in New Orleans and also at James University in Washington, DC. She noted she earned a certificate in paralegal studies at University of Miami in 1991 and an associate's degree in paralegal studies through Wright University in Wisconsin in 2007. Ms. Miller further apprised me she obtained a bachelor's degree in criminal justice through Wright University in 2008.

Currently, Ms. Miller told me, she is taking courses in nonprofit management through Eckerd University, and she anticipates completing master's degree requirements in February 2012. Additionally, she indicated she holds a real estate license in the U.S. Virgin Islands and has completed various computer-related courses.

During her 2009 deposition, Ms. Miller indicated she worked in various retail positions until 1988, when she became employed by LMN. She testified she was hired as a terminal dispatcher, explaining that she was cross-trained in computer applications as an oil movement coordinator.

Employment records indicate LMN hired Ms. Miller on July 5, 1988. Additionally, records note she held positions as a terminal dispatcher (1988 through 1992) and dock supervisor (1992 through 1994) before assuming her position as an oil movement coordinator (OMC) in 1994.

During her 2009 deposition, Ms. Miller testified she was in a motor vehicle accident in 1994, and, upon her return to work, she was placed in the position of oil movement coordinator. During my exam, she said that, after her 1994 motor vehicle accident, "I was demoted." She went on to say, "I could only do light duty, and my doctor did not want me to go back to dock foreman because of my injury." All of her employment with LMN from 1994 through the time of her November 2010 termination, she advised me, was as an OMC.

In the mid-2000s, Ms. Miller related, she was denied promotion opportunities as (a.) OMC documentation supervisor and (b.) documentation superintendent. She assessed she was discriminated against and cited reasons mentioned in her Complaint. Unfair treatment she received, she assessed, included notification that her physical problems precluded her from performing essential job tasks such as climbing ladders and steps on the side of tanks in the LMN refinery to oversee inspectors. Ms. Miller said:

Also going on vessels with the inspectors. The Superintendent at the time was not doing that. When I applied, they added that criteria. That criteria was not on the paperwork [job description] when I applied for that position. Back from the time I got injured [in 1994] I was not able to climb ships.

Ms. Miller conveyed her problems with MS have significantly affected her mobility.

Ms. Miller and I discussed the following events that occurred while she was performing her OMC job during the 2-year period before her November 2010 termination:

- A May 28, 2008, syncopal episode and subsequent leave of absence until September 2009
- Documentation of performance problems in spring 2010
- Incidents in March, September, and November 2010

Additionally, Ms. Miller and I discussed her Corrective Action Plan.

Ms. Miller apprised me she performed her job "alone, in a room alone surrounded by [approximately 12] computers [monitors]." She reported a high level of mental alertness was required to perform her job. Ms. Miller described sedentary tasks she performed while monitoring screens to ensure petroleum and related products were properly transferred to locations within the refinery. She told me she operated a keyboard and used a radio to communicate with field workers on transfer instructions. I toured Ms. Miller's former work environment on December 14, 2011; more information about this is later in this report.

Other job responsibilities Ms. Miller cited were inputting information into a computer about volumes of barrel transfers and monitoring computer-generated output to determine when tank capacities had been reached. She described various audible alarms she also tended while performing her job. Ms. Miller advised me her OMC job was quite safety-sensitive and that a high degree of vigilance was necessary to perform it.

I referenced documented performance-related problems near the time before Ms. Miller's November 2010 termination. She said about a September 2010 incident, "I was not feeling well, and I told them: I want to go home." Ms. Miller offered that her physical problems contributed to her performance problems exhibited in September 2010. She suggested to me that memory difficulties were interfering with her ability to accurately recall all events that transpired.

Ms. Miller did not recall an investigation in November 2010. "They sent me home on the 17th [of November] and called me back on the 30th [of November] to tell me I was terminated," she said. Before her termination, she conveyed, she worked 40 hours per week and was a salaried employee earning approximately $66,000 per year.

Since her severance in November 2010, Ms. Miller noted, she has not had any employment. She apprised me she has continued to pursue online master's degree studies in nonprofit administration. She reported she began the studies in September 2010, and she anticipated completing master's degree requirements in February 2012. Ms. Miller told me she is currently taking two courses.

Ms. Miller and I reviewed accommodations LMN had been extending to her (detailed later in this report), and I asked her whether she believes she is currently able to resume her former OMC job. She responded, "Yes, I could." Upon further inquiry, Ms. Miller assessed her cognitive and physical capacities, at present, are sufficient for her to perform the essential functions of her prior job.

Currently, Ms. Miller indicated, no physician is restricting her from working. She presented her career plans including completing a master's degree in nonprofit management in February 2012 and then pursuing a Ph.D. degree in nonprofit management.

Ms. Miller advised me she began searching for a job when her employment with LMN ended. "To get unemployment [compensation benefits, which I am receiving] you have to look for a job," she offered. Ms. Miller estimated she has applied for 20 jobs, and she cited positions as a paralegal, community coordinator of housing, and "some nonprofit jobs." She related she has not had any job interviews or job offers. She attributed her job-finding difficulties to the economic downturn. Ms. Miller assessed she is capable of holding full-time employment in a job with physical and cognitive demands similar to those required of her as an OMC.

When asked during her 2011 deposition whether she sought a return to her position with LMN, Ms. Miller responded, "No." She was asked if she sought to be reinstated, and she replied, "No." When asked whether she was seeking money, Ms. Miller replied, "Yes."

Ms. Miller stated during her 2011 deposition:

> *I believe everything that happened from that time of the lawsuit to my termination, that was the company's retaliation for me putting for the lawsuit. My termination was the way for the department to get rid of me due to the fact that I have made a fuss because of my disability and they have not done anything to – to – they took so long to accommodate my – my disability.*

Additionally, when asked during her 2011 deposition whether she believed her termination "had anything to do" with her race, Ms. Miller responded affirmatively.

Records Reviewed

Records from the following sources were reviewed with this evaluation:

- Complaint
- Answers to Interrogatories
- Deposition of Allen Roberts, September 29, 2011
- Deposition of Marvin Marks, September 15, 2011
- Depositions of Cheryl Marie Miller: June 22, 2009, and September 13, 2011
- Deposition of Hunter Smith, October 25, 2011

- Deposition of Bill Garcia, September 14, 2011
- Stewart Engineering and Risk Consultants
- Spine Institute
- Governor Crist Hospital and Medical Center
- MMP, Inc.
- MRI Center
- Happy Medical Center
- Neurologic Consultative Report
- Pride Emergency Medical Rescue
- Rehabilitation Center
- St. John Hospital
- St. Thomas MRI
- Frank Bryant, MD
- Chester D. Clover, Ph.D.
- Cora L. E. Cole, MD
- Marvin Eckstein, Ph.D.
- Caren B. Goshen, Ph.D.
- John G. Grant
- Claudius L. Hector, MD
- Charles Kingston, Ph.D.
- G. Hartley Mondae, Ph.D., December 5, 2011
- Douglas Moulin, MD
- Suren K. Miser, MD
- Walter Pennington, Jr., MD
- Arakere B. Pullert, MD
- Babu Stevens, MD
- David D. White, MD
- Education records
- LMN, employment records
- Wage and Tax Statements, 2007, 2009, and 2010
- Income Tax Returns, 2007-2010
- U.S. Equal Employment Opportunities Commission letter dated July 9, 2008
- OSHA file
- LMN in-house e-mails
- Investigation Report, Ms. Cheryl Miller, Denial of Promotions

Assessment Measures

The following assessment measures were used in this evaluation:

- Clinical Interview
- Client Intake Form
- Patient Pain Diagram
- Multidimensional Aptitude Battery-II
- Beck Depression Inventory-II
- Self-Directed Search
- MMPI-2

Background Information

The following background information was obtained from records and my clinical interview:

FULL NAME:	Cheryl Marie Miller
DATE OF BIRTH:	October 17, 1965
TERMINATION DATE:	November 17, 2010
RACE:	Black
DOMINANT HAND:	Right
HEIGHT:	5 feet 10 inches
CURRENT WEIGHT:	180 pounds
MARITAL STATUS:	Single/never married
NAMES AND AGES OF CHILDREN:	Richard L. Miller, 25
RESIDENCE:	Miami, Florida
PRESENTING PROBLEMS:	Unable to walk Bladder incontinence Bilateral weakness in hands, unable to hold a pen "Muscle spasms in my head" Unable to handle stress Trouble with focusing concentration "Major headaches"
TREATING DOCTORS:	Dr. Bryant, primary care Dr. Stevens, neurologist
MEDICATIONS:	Baclofen, for MS Betaseron injections, for MS Naltrexone, for MS Over-the-counter Aleve, MS-related pain Sanctura XR, MS-related bladder problems
EDUCATION:	High school diploma, 1983 Robinson University, 1983-84, no degree James University, 1984-85, no degree Paralegal certification, University of Miami, 1991 Obtained real estate license circa 1993 Computer Specialist Program, SPVS, 2006 AAS degree, paralegal studies/legal assisting, Wright College online, 2007 BA degree, criminal justice, Wright College online, 2008

	Currently pursuing online master's degree program in nonprofit management, Eckerd University, anticipates completing February 2012 Currently pursuing self-study Spanish language, Rosetta Stone software
EMPLOYER AT TIME OF TERMINATION:	LMN, LLC
JOB TITLE AT TIME OF TERMINATION:	Oil Movement Systems Coordinator
RATE OF PAY AT TIME OF TERMINATION:	$72,174 per year, 2010
PRESENT WORK STATUS:	1. Unemployed 2. Student, master's program in nonprofit management, Eckerd University online

Clinical Interview

Introduction

Cheryl Marie Miller presented as a black female who appeared younger than her stated age of 46. She had moderately long fingernails. Ms. Miller noted she has problems with cataracts that blur her vision and that she plans to undergo surgery to remove them. She did not relate her cataracts to her multiple sclerosis. Occasionally, she apprised me, she wears glasses for distance vision. Ms. Miller's presentation was similar on both occasions I met with her.

During my exam, Ms. Miller's gait was slow and labored. She used a cane and wore a long right-leg brace. She affirmed my observation that she had more difficulty with her right lower extremity than with her left lower extremity. A leg brace and a cane were the only adaptive aids Ms. Miller used during my exam. She told me she uses these devices "at all times, except when I'm home."

Ms. Miller indicated she is right hand dominant, 5 feet 10 inches tall, and that she weighs 180 pounds. She advised me her weight has been stable.

As for her marital status, Ms. Miller related she is single/never married. She informed me she has one child – a 25-year-old son. Apart from asthma, she conveyed, her son does not have health problems.

Concerning her home, Ms. Miller noted she lives alone in a single-story, three-bedroom house she owns in a residential area. "I bought the house when I was 24 [years old]," she said when asked how long she has lived in her home. She denied planning to relocate. Ms. Miller noted no disability modifications to her home. When asked about access limitations within her home, she said, "I can get around by holding onto the walls and everything else." She apprised me she has trouble accessing areas below her waist and that she uses a shower chair for this reason.

Physical Condition and Medical Information

Ms. Miller and I reviewed her multiple sclerosis (MS) symptoms near the time before her November 17, 2010, termination. She reported a medication prescribed for her at the time, Ampyra, "wasn't working. It made me depressed." Ms. Miller did not identify other medical problems near the time before her 2010 dismissal.

During her June 2009 deposition, Ms. Miller testified:

My leg is dragging more because of – I have multiple sclerosis, and I can say that from the time this case has happened, my leg has been starting dragging more. I'm having headaches. Went to Dr. Bryant about that. That's one of the reasons why he wanted me to have an MRI, to make sure there was no – nothing – no malignant, no tumor up there. And then he expressed to me that I was having stress. That's the reason for my headache. I'm having problems sleeping, 'cause the pain happens a lot at night.

Regarding preincident surgeries, Ms. Miller cited a tonsillectomy as a child and removal of uterine fibroids at age 32. She told me she had problems with asthma as a child. I inquired about other medical problems predating her November 2010 job termination, and Ms. Miller said, "I had diabetes when I was pregnant."

Ms. Miller also recalled "a couple of car accidents." We reviewed records from 1993 and 1994. Ms. Miller said, "From the 1993, I had neck problems; I got over that." She indicated the injuries associated with her 1994 motor vehicle accident involved her head and right lower extremity. She advised me she fully recovered from both motor vehicle accidents.

Further, Ms. Miller recalled a motor vehicle accident in the late 1990s. She related she injured her right knee and fully recovered. We reviewed other records predating her November 2010 job termination, and she did not recall any other significant medical problem. Ms. Miller did not identify unrelated postincident problems.

As for her understanding of diagnoses physicians have rendered to describe her condition, Ms. Miller said: "I was told [by Dr. Bryant] I have relapse/remitting [MS]. But I was also told by another doctor, someone I saw many years ago – I can't remember his name. He told me I have primary progressive [MS]." Apart from MS, she was unaware of any other current diagnoses.

I referenced prior brain MRIs, and Ms. Miller informed me she recently requested that Dr. Bryant schedule another one. "I asked him for a [brain] MRI and a mammogram," she stated. She surmised her last brain MRI was in 2008.

Concerning her primary problems, Ms. Miller said, "My mobility, and I can't write." She referenced trouble with right-hand weakness and conveyed she uses voice-activated software.

Ms. Miller noted her most intense pain is in the right side of her head. "It's always painful, worse at night, worse when I'm stressed," she said. She went on to apprise me she feels pain "at all times" throughout her body. Ms. Miller and I discussed a pain diagram she completed on which she referenced pain in the following body parts: head, neck, shoulders (more intense in the right side), lower back, hands, and legs down to her feet. She elaborated about burning, stabbing, and aching sensations.

Activities and conditions that exacerbate Ms. Miller's symptoms, she reported, are heat, stress, walking, bearing weight, and activity. She told me her symptoms worsen over the course of the day, and she elaborated about problems with fatigue. Further, the more tired and symptomatic she becomes, she indicated, the worse her quality of mental functioning.

I inquired about her reported diminished mental acuity and other cognitive difficulties, and Ms. Miller described problems with comprehension. "I have to read assignments over twice, so I can understand. That was the first time I had to get Dr. Bryant to do paperwork for me so I could get a disability extension," she said. She advised me Dr. Bryant completed documentation necessary for her to be granted additional time to meet deadlines associated with her studies through Eckerd University.

Ms. Miller recalled a prior occasion when Dr. Bryant also petitioned for her to be extended disability accommodations, while she pursued paralegal studies approximately 4 years ago. She informed me the accommodations related to her manual functioning difficulties. "That was because I had to do a semester of typing, and I couldn't do that. I got exempt from the class," Ms. Miller said.

When asked about syncopal episodes, Ms. Miller denied having any while performing her job after May 28, 2008. She also denied feeling faint since then.

Using a 0-to-10 scale, with a zero indicating no pain and a 10 representing the worst pain possible, Ms. Miller rated her pain intensities in the following body parts:

- Head – 9 to 10
- Right shoulder – 8
- Neck – "about 8"
- Lower back – "about 7"

Ms. Miller conveyed her pain is most severe in the preceding body parts. During my clinical interview, she characterized the pain she was experiencing as "very severe."

The only physician treating Ms. Miller, she noted, is Dr. Bryant – her primary care physician, whom she reported she last saw in October 2011. She apprised me her last contact with a neurologist, Dr. Stevens, was in November 2011. "My attorney sent me," Ms. Miller offered. No future medical appointments were identified. She denied undergoing surgery since her 2010 termination, and, apart from cataract surgery, she denied that future surgery has been scheduled or recommended.

I asked Ms. Miller whether she has participated in any treatment or therapy since her severance from LMN, and she responded, "I'm seeing Dr. Clover for this case, but he's not treating me." She told me she participates in an MS support group once per month. Ms. Miller indicated she uses the following adaptive aids: right lower-extremity braces, wheeled walker with a seat, shower chair, and cold packs.

Regarding medications, Ms. Miller advised me she takes baclofen, Betaseron injections, naltrexone, over-the-counter Aleve, and Sanctura XR. She related she was taking baclofen and Betaseron before her November 2010 termination. No current medication side effects were identified. Ms. Miller informed me she had taken her medication regimen during the 24 hours before my exam. She conveyed she began being prescribed naltrexone after her 2010 severance. "I heard about naltrexone from the support group [and] I told Dr. Bryant about it. He prescribed it to me," she said.

As for functional capacities, Ms. Miller noted she is able to safely handle, from a seated position, "probably less than 10 pounds." Again, she apprised me her right hand is stronger than her left hand, and she estimated she is able to handle from 3 to 5 pounds with her right hand. Ms. Miller reported that carrying any amount of weight is problematic because of her gait problems. "I'll lose balance," she said.

Ms. Miller demonstrated during my clinical interview that she could turn her head to either side and bend her head forward without problems. She told me leaning her head back exacerbates her neck pain. She recounted problems with use of either hand/arm and either foot/leg.

During her 2011 deposition, Ms. Miller testified, "My handwriting – I cannot hold onto a pen." Medical records indicate bilateral carpal tunnel syndrome was diagnosed in March 2000.

Ms. Miller demonstrated during my exam that she was able to touch each finger to her thumb on either hand, with difficulty. She demonstrated she could make a fist with either hand and extend her arms horizontally. Regarding overhead arm extensions, she cited pain in her right arm. Ms. Miller advised me her fine motor functioning is impaired in both hands. She related she cannot fasten buttons with only her fingers, and she explained she uses her teeth and fingers to accomplish this.

Concerning physical, everyday activities, Ms. Miller informed me walking and standing are problematic, even for short durations. She complained that extended sitting "hurts my back." She referenced the sitting associated with my exam and stated, "When I go home, I'm going to have to take something." Ms. Miller conveyed she avoids bending her waist and lower-extremity movements because of her balance problems.

Generally, Ms. Miller noted, she is able to sit comfortably for 2 hours. "I try not to walk because I'm afraid of walking. I try not to walk at all. That's [falling is] my biggest fear," she said. She apprised me she avoids bearing weight.

When asked about driving, Ms. Miller said: "I drive short distances, and I have two guys I can call any time. If I need to go shopping, they take me." She reported she does not shop alone. The individuals Ms. Miller referenced are friends and former coworkers. She told me she has a disabled-person parking placard. During her 2011 deposition, Ms. Miller testified her vehicle has been modified to include hand-operated brake and accelerator pedals.

Other physical problems Ms. Miller identified related to balance, falling, and exposure to hot temperatures. According to medical records, she reported falling at her place of employment in 1997, 2002, 2006, and 2007. We discussed other falls, and Ms. Miller indicated her most recent fall was approximately 4 months before my exam. "I was at home on the ground for 2 hours. I hurt my right shoulder," she stated. She advised me that, although her right-shoulder remains symptomatic, she has not pursued medical treatment for it. Ms. Miller informed me that her bladder problems she discussed during her 2011 deposition have resolved, since she has been taking Sanctura.

I asked Ms. Miller about physician-advised restrictions. She conveyed her doctors have apprised her to use good judgment in her activities.

Ms. Miller noted her condition during the past 3 months has been "getting worse. Even my hairdresser said she notices I'm dragging [my right lower extremity] more."

Activities of Daily Living

Ms. Miller apprised me she has difficulty sleeping every night. "I can't sleep because I get the spasms in my head. I wake up screaming, and it's hard to go back to bed," she said. Ms. Miller reported she began having difficulty sleeping "the same time I left LMN." Usually, she told me, she goes to sleep between 10:00 and 11:00 p.m., and awakens between 6:00 and 6:30 a.m. She denied napping, taking sleep-aid medication, or having problems with nightmares.

Regarding grooming and self-care, Ms. Miller indicated she is generally independent; however, she advised me friends help her with some tasks, and she related she has modified the way she performs other tasks. She informed me friends and members of her church assist her.

I inquired about her participation in household chores, and Ms. Miller said: "I try my best. It's a good thing to live alone." Occasionally, she conveyed, friends provide services such as washing her windows, mopping floors, and maintaining her garden.

Because of her problems with heat, Ms. Miller noted, she cooks only once per week. "After I finish cooking, I go to my room and put ice on my neck so I can get my body heat down," she stated. She described how she has modified the way she washes her clothes. Ms. Miller denied employing a housekeeper or other outside services apart from a yard maintenance service. "I used to do my own [yard] work many, many years ago, but I can't do that anymore," she said.

As for leisure activities before her November 17, 2010, termination, Ms. Miller apprised me she went to movies once or twice per month. She reported she last went to a movie "1 to 2 years ago. It's difficult for me to walk from where the parking lot is to the movie theater." Ms. Miller told me she previously volunteered at the Miami Care Center. "I did some volunteer work with them in January [2011], but they haven't called me back," she said. She described administrative work that involved calling clients to assess their satisfaction with services.

Concerning current avocational activities, Ms. Miller indicated she attends meetings at the Island Independence House on Thursday. She advised me she occasionally leads the meetings, and she described this as disseminating information about services to meeting attendees.

I asked Ms. Miller about her average day. After awakening, she related, she performs light housework, "and then I go outside on my exercise bike 20, 30 minutes. Then I go in and watch *Judge Mathis, the Price is Right,* and a soap opera. And then I study from 3:00 to 7:00 p.m." Then, Ms. Miller informed me, she watches more television.

I inquired how often she leaves her home, and Ms. Miller said, "If I don't have to, I don't leave." I probed further about the frequency, and she estimated twice per week: Thursday to attend a meeting at the Island Independence House and Sunday to attend religious services. Ms. Miller conveyed her excursions would likely be more frequent if not for her mobility problems.

Mental Health

Ms. Miller denied ever participating in mental health treatment. When asked about a family history of mental illness, she responded affirmatively, noting a maternal aunt committed suicide. Ms. Miller offered she attempted suicide when she was 12 years old. "I was tired of getting beat," she said about why she attempted to end her life. During her 2011 deposition, Ms. Miller reported she lost consciousness on June 28, 2008.

Recalling two emotional outbursts that occurred while at work, Ms. Miller indicated the first was in 2000 after learning about her multiple sclerosis diagnosis. She advised me the second occurrence was in 2007 or 2008. "That was during the time I got denied the promotion [I was pursuing], and the young man who got the job came to me and asked if I needed more training. I kept yelling, 'I've been doing this 19 f***ing[1] years. I don't need more train-

1 Out of respect for readers of this report, I have chosen not to spell out in entirety the expletive Ms. Miller spoke.

ing,'" Ms. Miller stated.

During her September 2011 deposition, Ms. Miller was asked whether she had treated with a psychologist or a psychiatrist since her 2010 termination. She replied: "Not treated, no. I thought I could handle it."

When asked about her current, overall psychological status, Ms. Miller said, "I'm trying to handle it." She went on to convey the causes of her mental health distress are "not working and my disability." She told me she believes she currently needs mental health treatment.

The primary mental health concerns Ms. Miller identified related to her physical health, depression, and finances. She expressed concern about her condition worsening as she ages. She denied having problems with anxiety. When asked about suicidal ideation, Ms. Miller stated: "I'm a Christian. I cannot do it."

During my clinical interview, Ms. Miller was pleasant and likable, and she projected a normal affect. Her memory was good/fair, and her concentration was good. She spoke softly, although clearly and coherently. I observed several instances when Ms. Miller exhibited word retrieval difficulties. She did not show evidence of a thought disorder.

Education and Special Training

Ms. Miller noted her scholastic performance had been very strong, until the past year. She did not recall her scores from prior standardized testing, and she denied ever repeating a grade. Ms. Miller apprised me she attended honors classes in English and Biology. She reported she graduated from Main High School in 1983.

After high school, Ms. Miller indicated, she attended Robinson University (1983 to 1984) and James University (1984 to 1985); she denied earning a degree from either institution. In 1991, she advised me, she earned a certificate in paralegal studies at University of Miami.

Ms. Miller informed me she obtained a real estate license in the Virgin Islands circa 1993. She conveyed she completed an online computer specialist program through SPVS in 2006.

In 2007, Ms. Miller noted, she earned an AAS degree in paralegal studies/legal assisting online through Wright College. In 2008, she apprised me, she earned a bachelor of arts degree in criminal justice online through Wright College.

Currently, Ms. Miller told me, she is pursuing a master's degree in nonprofit management, online through Eckerd University. She anticipates completing the program in February 2012. Further, Ms. Miller advised me she is pursuing self-study in the Spanish language using Rosetta Stone software.

I noted the education/training she has pursued is quite diverse, and Ms. Miller said, "Since high school, I wanted to be a lawyer," referencing her early career decision-making. When asked about her most recent pursuit of a master's degree in nonprofit management, Ms. Miller replied, "Because I have a disability, I decided that's something I can do with my condition." As for special skills, she related she has some patois language skills, and she recounted she is learning Spanish.

Ms. Miller informed me her real estate license is active and that her last sale was 4 or 5 years ago. Currently, she conveyed, she has two listings; she noted she secured her most recent listing 2 months before my exam. She apprised me she has a house sale pending. Ms. Miller reported all of her real estate experience has been with residential properties.

Discussing difficulty she has showing properties, Ms. Miller said, "When I do a showing, I take the two guys with me and they do the showing." She estimated she last earned income through her real estate work 4 or 5 years ago. Ms. Miller stated, "The license [I maintain] is just for me to write off taxes."

Regarding on-the-job training, Ms. Miller cited retail operations management, dispatching, and coordinating oil movements within a refinery. She told me she has never held a job as a paralegal.

Ms. Miller indicated she has access to a computer. She characterized her computer use skills as "very good," and she advised me she is proficient in using Microsoft applications.

Through training and work experience, Ms. Miller related, she has developed the following skills:

- Retail management including supervising up to 15 sales clerks
- Retail sales

- Customer service
- Ordering and inventorying merchandise
- Personnel administration including selection, training, and performance management
- Monitoring ship arrivals/departures
- Overseeing loading/unloading of petroleum and related products
- Using computers and radio devices to monitor product transfers and movement
- Overseeing worksite safety practices, she described as SHARP – Safety Health Action Reduction Process – a program in which she had been involved

As for retraining, Ms. Miller referenced her studies in nonprofit management through Eckerd University.

During her 2009 deposition, Ms. Miller stated about funding and continuing her education, "You don't have to pay back the federal government as long as you're in school, so I'm going to be 99 years old still in school."

Career Development

The following work history was obtained from records and my clinical interview:

Job Title	*Name of Organization*	*Dates*
Oil Movement Coordinator	LMN	1994 – 2010
Dock Supervisor	Liberteen	1992 – 1994
Terminal Dispatcher	Liberteen	1988 – 1992
Operations Manager	Marsha's Clothing Store	1987 – 1988
Accounting Clerk	Department of Interior	1986
Sales Associate	Dress Barn	1985 – 1986
Sales Associate	Beach Collection	1981 – 1983
Conservation Specialist	Forestry Commission	1981

Ms. Miller considers her oil movement coordinator (OMC) position with LMN to be her most skilled or challenging job. She denied having a job termination before her November 17, 2010, severance. Ms. Miller cited one claim for workers' compensation benefits – associated with a work-related fall in which she injured her lower back circa 2007.

I inquired about her job satisfaction as an OMC, and Ms. Miller responded affirmatively. Regarding sources of her job satisfaction, she cited, "Being in control, solving problems." About her performance appraisals before her documented September 2010 performance-related incident, Ms. Miller said, "I thought it was good."

During her 2009 deposition, Ms. Miller testified about the following accommodations LMN extended to her:

- After two motor vehicle accidents in 1 month in 2004, her leg was "starting to act up," and she requested placement on the day shift; she was accommodated and assigned to working with management on a training manual.
- She requested a ramp installed at the entrance to the computer room, "because my legs were tired." During 2003, ramps were installed both inside and outside the building; however, she noted she requested a ramp into the computer room and not anywhere else.
- Because of her history with falling, a scooter was made available for her to use, because she fell in the computer room while she was working. "The company decided I needed a scooter," she said.
- When she was provided the scooter, she requested a refrigerator and microwave be installed in the computer room, because space in the lunchroom was limited due to her use of a scooter; these were provided along with a wheelchair-accessible restroom, which was installed in 2007, and an automatic door opener into the restroom.
- Automatic door openers were also installed at entrances to the building.

- "I asked to use my vehicle, to drive in my vehicle. The company did not want that; that's why they, they got through with the taxi driver," she said. She confirmed that the provision of a cab to take her to the computer building accommodated her needs.
- "The motorized scooter [LMN provided July 25, 2007] came after my concern for the wheelchair. I wanted something, I wanted an apparatus for me to get out of the refinery."

In September 2011, Bill Garcia – manager of planning and performance at LMN – was deposed, and he testified about the accommodations LMN extended to Ms. Miller:

> *There were many discussions held with her and with management to make reasonable accommodation. For example, the ramp was already being installed north of the building. Now where I was involved was the ramp on the inside of the building, so there were many discussions with her and management to see that proceed. . . . An accommodation which was made for Ms. Miller with regard to having wheelchairs and vehicles. In the event of an emergency, to and from the NT Department and the Administration Parking Lot, that we have a wheelchair in a vehicle.*

After my exam of Ms. Miller, I toured her former place of employment and work environment. Appendix A includes photos of various accommodations LMN extended to Ms. Miller that are referenced in this report.

I asked Ms. Miller about her career plans before her November 2010 termination. She replied, "I wanted to continue with LMN and just do the nonprofit on the side."

Ms. Miller told me the last job for which she applied was a community coordinator position with a public housing project. She indicated she applied approximately 1 month before my exam.

Concerning sources of income, Ms. Miller cited unemployment compensation – $962 every 2 weeks. She expressed she is having financial difficulties. Ms. Miller indicated she has not applied for disability benefits through the Social Security Administration. She volunteered, "I was told [by my lawyer] I can't [apply for disability benefits] until this [pending litigation] is over." Then, Ms. Miller stated, "I shouldn't have said that."

Ms. Miller's W2s reflect the following wages:

2007	$78,680
2009	$65,300
2010	$72,174

The tax returns Ms. Miller filed indicate she reported the following wages:

2007	$75,355
2008	$71,796
2009	$60,760
2010	$67,213

Among the documents I reviewed were job descriptions written in 2006 for the following positions: superintendent – marine/terminal oil movements and documentation, and supervisor – marine/terminal oil movements and documentation. I also reviewed job descriptions for an oil movements system coordinator (one job description was written in May 2004, and one was written in September 2010). John Grant conducted an analysis on the criticality of the OMC position, the potential for storage tank overfill, the subsequent consequences of tank overfill, and an industry perspective of the discipline administered to Ms. Miller; his findings are in a December 17, 2011, report. Mr. Grant noted Ms. Miller was involved in two major incidents within a very short period (September 3 and October 17, 2010). "Both incidents demonstrated a lack of responsiveness and inattention to duty. A repeat incident, involving the same lack of attention and same types of errors, soon after placement on a corrective action plan (CAP) indicates that the corrective message and remedial supervision did not serve to change her work behavior," Mr. Grant stated. He went on to conclude:

There is a high degree of corporate and facility risk associated with inadequate performance in the OMC position. Miller's termination was an appropriate consequence given the magnitude and back-to-back frequency of her errors. There was no indication that additional training or other remedial action would improve her long-term performance in the role. Termination was consistent with industry practice and necessary to maintain safe operation given the tasks involved with the position.

Included in Ms. Miller's personnel file from LMN is a list of employment infractions. The list includes the following:

- 1/20/08 Improper monitoring of oil movements; failure to provide written statement
- 3/22/10 Poor job performance re: tank overfills; failure to act and escalate per procedure
- 4/23/10 Poor job performance re: tank overfills; failure to take appropriate action
- 9/3/10 Poor job performance re: CS left ill wo proper shift handover resulting in missed tank stop failed to report tank imbalance, report tank alarm, and to follow night instructions; hazardous conditions
- 9/7/10 Poor job performance re: CS "not fit for work" left multiple tasks undone; transfers unrecorded, CS claims had bad reaction to new meds and thought she could make it through shift
- 9/24/10 Poor job performance re: failure to follow procedure for monitoring of tank transfers
- 10/18/10 Poor job performance re: three missed tank transfer stops; set up tank transfer set improperly HR recommends termination. Poor job performance re: CS unresponsive; missed tank transfers and stops
- 11/30/10 Termination due to unsatisfactory job performance from 10/18/10; already on CAP for similar incident.

Tour of LMN Refinery, December 14, 2011

Upon entry at the LMN facility, I was required to view a safety video recording, and I was provided various safety-related written materials. Then, my photograph was taken, and I was issued a security entry card. A fire drill was conducted while I was on the premises. Further, I was issued a hard hat, steel-tipped shoes, and fire-retardant clothes.

Bill Garcia, manager of planning and performance monitoring, initially provided me information about the facility while we toured it. About Ms. Miller, Mr. Garcia said, "She had an unacceptable number of incidents that occurred during her shift that made it clear to us she was having unacceptable performance problems." He went on to disclose Ms. Miller's performance problems as an oil movement coordinator (OMC).

My tour included the building in which Ms. Miller had worked. Several ramps and other modifications within the building apparently were made for her. While at her former workstation, I also met with Allen Roberts, oil movements and documentation supervisor. He advised me an OMC is responsible for maintaining the approximately 200 tanks on the property, and he related from 50 to 75 tanks are active at any given time.

Mr. Garcia and Mr. Roberts expressed that marine transferring is especially critical. They discussed the attentiveness required when topping tanks and the safety measures associated with transfer movements.

The mental demands Mr. Garcia and Mr. Roberts associated with an OMC's job responsibilities included a high degree of vigilance, multitasking, prioritizing, and attention to detail. "It's a stressful job," Mr. Roberts added.

Both Mr. Roberts and Mr. Garcia noted Ms. Miller exhibited problems with mood swings within the year before her termination. "In the last year or 2 that she was here, these emotional things were more and more prevalent. You could see the trend," Mr. Garcia stated. He went on to say, "We didn't sleep well at night [because of safety concerns due to Ms. Miller's behavior and job performance]." Mr. Roberts added, "I can vouch for that," and he noted one of his colleagues, Mr. Green, apprised him about Ms. Miller, "She's not in the right mental state to do the job."

Mr. Roberts noted several employees complained that Ms. Miller's handwriting was faint and difficult to read. He went on to report that, over time, it became worse. Additionally, Mr. Roberts cited difficulty Ms. Miller intermittently had with pressing keys on a communication radio. He recalled: "One time, when she was having problems, I offered to change the battery. She said, 'No, it's not the battery. It's my hands. They get weak, and I have a hard time pushing it in.'"

Over time, Mr. Roberts indicated, he noticed Ms. Miller's physical condition was deteriorating. He went on to cite how she requested assistance with exiting vehicles. "Near the end, at times she couldn't get her leg in a vehicle, and she asked for assistance," Mr. Roberts said.

Mr. Roberts discussed various accommodations extended to Ms. Miller. "The falls were more frequent [over time] and we [accordingly] start giving her more accommodations," he said. Mr. Garcia and Mr. Roberts informed me LMN made the following accommodations available to Ms. Miller:

- Construction of outside concrete ramp
- Construction of internal hallway ramp
- Automatic external door
- Automatic internal door
- Automatic bathroom door
- Refrigerator – brand new feeder
- Microwave oven
- Purchase of scooter
- Purchase of two wheelchairs
- Transportation accommodations including taxi service and employee-assisted transportation

Mr. Garcia and Mr. Roberts discussed the May 2008 syncopal incident, and they both noted they were reluctant to have Ms. Miller return to work afterward. They went on to cite the human safety and environmental implications associated with errors. Mr. Roberts expressed that good judgment and "levelheadedness" were other essential qualities to perform the OMC position.

Review of Medical Records

Results of Diagnostic Testing

06/03/88 *Andre Ferris, MD*

Chest
Impression:
Within normal limits.

01/14/91 *Marvin Broderick, Ph.D.*

Hearing Test dated 11/06/90
Impression:
Speech frequency – within normal hearing both ears.
High frequency – within normal hearing both ears.

12/01/03 *Michael Z. Ferris, MD*

MRI Brain Pre & Post Gadolinium

Impression:
The randomly distributed white matter lesions are consistent with subacute and/or chronic changes of multiple sclerosis. No acute lesions are evident.

01/21/04 *Gary Kirtland, Jr., MD*

Skull Series
Impression:
Normal skull.

01/22/04 *Gary Kirtland, Jr., MD*

Facial Bones
Impression:
There is no evidence of a fracture nor subluxation.

04/28/05 *Michael Z. Ferris, MD*

Right Hip
Impression:
There is no evidence of a fracture nor other abnormality.

12/13/06 *Michael Z. Ferris, MD*

Mandible
Impression:
Normal mandible series.

Cervical Spine
Impression:
Normal radiographs.

05/07/07 *Angelo Ferris, MD*

Right Shoulder
Impression:
Normal right shoulder.

01/29/08 *Coralee Mondale, MD*

Bilateral Screening Mammogram
Impression:
No mammographic evidence of malignancy.

06/13/08 *Michael Z. Ferris, MD*

MRI of the Brain Pre and Post IV Contrast
Impression:

1. Bilateral demyelinating cerebral white matter disease due to multiple sclerosis or other demyelinating condition. The three enhancing white matter plaques represent active disease.

2. Mucous retention cyst in the left maxillary antrum

11/10/08 *Babu Stevens, MD*

EEG
Impression:
This EEG is abnormal. Localized slowing in the left temporal cortex suggests an underlying structural abnormity. Clinical and imaging correlation useful.

12/17/08 *Babu Stevens, MD*

EEG
Impression:
This awake and sleep deprived EEG is within the range of normal limits. No focal abnormality or seizure discharges were noted.

06/10/09 *David D. White, MD*

EEG
Impression:
Normal EEG. Slower waves noted during sleep. No clear cut epileptiform activity noted.

11/04/10 *Gary Kirtland, Jr., MD*

Pelvic Sonogram
Impression:
Fibroid uterus.

01/05/12 *George I. Dugan, MD*

MRI Brain or Pituitary w/wo contrast
Impression:
Multiple foci of signal hyperintensity within the periventricular and subcortical white matter. These findings are consistent with the patient's diagnosis of multiple sclerosis.
No masses or abnormal enhancement.

Assessments

06/03/88 *St. Paul Clinical Laboratories*

Conclusion:
Physically fit.

10/14/93 *Nerissa Hare, RN/LMN*

Comment:
MVA at 11:45 pm – truck hit pole. Seen at the Medical Unit at 12:05 am. States that as truck was backing up at Dry Cargo Dock, it hit a pole near a fire hydrant. States she hit her head against the steering wheel or the windshield(?). Has a little bump on the forehead. C/O headache, neck pain

and dizziness. BP-122/84, P-63 (R).

St. John Hospital Emergency Department

Work Status:
Miller, Cheryl has been under my care from 10/14/93 to 10/15/93 and is able to return to work on 10/16/93.

11/22/93 *St. John Hospital Emergency Department*

Work Status:
Miller, Cheryl has been under my care from 11/22/93 to 11/26/93 and is able to return to work on 11/29/93.

11/29/93 *Claudius L. Hector, MD*

Diagnoses:
Right shoulder, cervical, thoracic, and lumbosacral spine injuries.

Work Status:
Projected additional period of disability – 10 – 14 days. Additional disability period commences on 11/29/93.

01/12/94 *Linda Marie, RN/LMN*

Comment:
Apt return to wk.

01/19/94 *Claudius L. Hector, MD*

Diagnoses:
Low back problem. She has recovered sufficiently and may resume work activities on 1/24/94.

Recommendation:
Assignment to light duty for six weeks.

Work Status:
Heavy lifting, prolonged bending and prolonged standing not allowed.

02/04/94 *Claudius L. Hector, MD*

Diagnoses:
Low back problems.
Work Status:
She has recovered sufficiently and may resume her regular duties on 2/7/94.

02/07/94 *Cora Cole, MD/LMN*

Comment:

After getting clearance from Dr C, pt stated to nurse LRP "I wished the doctor would send me home, I don't want to go to work."

03/13/94 *Claudius L. Hector, MD*

Diagnoses:
1. Posterior dislocation of the R hip.
2. Cerebral concussion.

Symptoms:
Severe R hip pains.
Conclusion:
R hip adducted flexed and internally rotated.
The right lower extremity was also shortened.
Hospitalized 2/15/94 to 3/1/94. Closed reduction.

05/02/94 *Claudius L. Hector, MD*

Diagnoses:
S/P posterior dislocation of the right hip.
Work Status:
She has recovered sufficiently and may resume light duty for 4 months as soon as feasible.
Restrictions:
Prolonged standing, prolonged walking, climbing and squatting etc.

05/18/94 *Cora Cole, MD/LMN*

Comment:
28-year-old female post-MVA (Feb 15, 1994). Hospitalized under the care of Dr. C Hector from 2/15-3/1, 1994. States that she feels ok, uses the cane for better support and is undergoing therapy at home.
Work Status:
This is to certify the above may return to work as a terminal dispatcher.

01/16/96 *Jill Karman, RN/LMN*

History:
C/o numbness in left hand and numbness of fingertips of the rt hand since Aug 95. Pt states she has been to Dr. Merry her PMD, who has done lab work that was normal. Inquiry as to further tx. Advised to see another MD, possibly Neurologist.

08/06/97 *Cora Cole, MD/LMN*

Comment:
Pt presents to medical for suture removal from left upper eye lid – non job. Injury occurred at home. Fell in bathtub.

11/10/97 *Bob Miles, EMT/LMN*

History:

Employee walking from parking lot to south door of Admin Bldg. When I exited Bldg Jim Beane told me that a female Liberteen employee had fallen. I went to her and offered assistance.

Chief Complaint:

Had fallen at, aggravated rt ankle. Did not want medical assistance. Did not want to be seen by medical.

Assessment:

Employee stood up, limped a little, ascended steps. Again declined to be seen by medical. She then left Liberteen.

02/02/00 *Dona Oldham, RN/LMN*

History:

Pt presented to medical w/leg pain. Pt reports she was seen by a Neuro in PR on Monday. Pt has herniated disc. Pt had leg pain on Monday but it has gotten worse. Pt taking Rx med, but does not know name.

Pt advised to call PMD in PR. If not available to see Dr. Pennington.

02/10/00 *Bob Miles, EMT/LMN*

History:

Got out of chair to change paper in printer. She tripped when foot got tangled in floor mouse wire.

Assessment:

Asked if any injury. She said no. She refused any exam. Stated she was ok.

03/02/00 *Spine Institute*

Recommendation:

Physical therapy 3/wk, duration 4 wk.

03/03/00 *Spine Institute*

Comment:

May return to work.

Diagnoses:

Multiple sclerosis. Bilateral carpal tunnel synd. LLE Weakness.

Work Status:

Approved for regular duty. No lifting over 20 lbs. Infrequent bending at waist. Position changes every 30 minutes when sitting for prolonged periods of time. Difficult to climb stairs.

03/06/00 *Cora Cole, MD/LMN*

History:

Pt presents to medical with documents from spinal institute and RTW evaluation. Has restrictions of no lifting >20 lbs, bending at the waist q 30 minutes and frequent position changes. Taking Methylpred and Arthrotec. Pt was given dx of MS. Results for spinal institute to be sent to Dr. Pennington with recommendation for f/u with Dr. Richards for spinal tap. Discussed need to stay in St. Thomas following procedure. Pt had questions re: MS, given literature, advised to call EAP, MS foundation on Internet.

01/10/02 *Jill Karman, RN/LMN*

Comment:

Fell in hallway. "I am doing okay today, I am going to see Dr. Petersen this afternoon, I hope he pulled this tube out. I did not have any more fever or chills like I did two days ago."

Opening to shoulder almost closed.

Narrative:

Informed by H. Simon that "someone fell in hall and busted their mouth." To hall in front of cafeteria. Noted pt sitting on floor in no acute distress. G. Westhoff, EMT in attendance. Pt alert, 0x3. States she hit her chin on the floor and twisted her rt ankle. Denies hitting her head or LOC. Denies any other discomfort at this time. Request to C. George for nurse and WC. Pt states she was on her way home. She was "just walking and lost her balance falling to the floor."

Upon assessment, pt crying, states she is more embarrassed than anything else. Denies pain to any other part of body, besides small bruise to bottom of left side of lip. Minimal bleeding noted. Pt offered water and ice for same. Removed rt shoe and sock. Ankle examined, no bruising or edema noted. Pt denies pain of same. Noted hx of MS with ongoing treatment. States she saw a doctor in Martinique over the holidays who confirmed the MS is getting little worse and she has had more "dragging" of the rt leg. Pt very emotional re: MS and states it has been difficult dealing with all aspects of the disease. She has continued f/u with Dr. Bryant.

Pt rested in medical at least one hour with no further complaints. Sat and spoke with employee at length about MS and coping. Pt admits that times it is difficult emotional, however, she continues to do her job in addition to outside activities without difficulty.

Escorted pt to lobby and car. Ambulated with normal assisted (cane) gait to same. Noted cane to be in good condition with rubber on bottom. Pt verbalized that she has shift tonight at 8 p.m. Did not indicate at this time inability to work. Advised to RTM if any problems.

03/06/02 *Donna Oldham, RN/LMN*

History:

Pt inquired about referral for son with possible ADD. Pt inquired about counseling for her & her son.

01/21/03 *Babu Stevens, MD*

Work Status:

Is unable to return to work at this time because her condition. Is able to return to work on 2/4/03.

03/11/03 *Lauroline Gugenheim, RN/LMN*

History:

George Rumpelman came into the medical unit for a wheelchair, because an Emp fell in the hallway. Took wheelchair to the hallway to find Emp leaning against the wall with a cane and coworker Mark holding her up. Emp started crying saying no, she does not want to go into a wheelchair. Emp headed towards the exit using her cane and with the assistance of Bruce. Emp refuse treatment, saying that she wants to go home.

09/24/03 *Cora Cole, MD/LMN*

Comment:

C/o dizziness/ Non job. Another Emp came into the medical unit, stating that there is a lady outside that need some help, she needs some help.

Outside the west admin building door, Emp found sitting on the wall, alert and coherent.

Complain of dizziness. Emp states: "I was sitting here on the wall waiting for a ride to go down to terminal to start the shift. I am feeling dizzy and nauseated."

After 20 minutes, Emp states that she is ready to go back to work. BP 95/67. Call for ride take her to Terminal. No acute distress noted.

01/21/04 *Cora Cole, MD/LMN*

Comment:

Got a call from Frank Copland (16:45) who said there is an Emp on the 2nd floor in Terminal on the floor and we should come and get her. Asked Mr. Copland if the ambulance is needed. He repeated no.

Emp presented to the Medical Unit accompanied by EMT Montes and Frank Copland. Complained of falling down 2 steps in the Terminal building. Emp states: "I was coming down the steps outside my office. I missed the second step and fell face down. I hit the Rt side of my forehead and jerked my neck. I also hit my Rt knee. No one witnessed this incident. I am just feeling pain behind my neck. I kept telling my supervisors that a ramp need to be put in. They promise me that one would be put in after Christmas. Someone from Safety came and look at the area. I have not seen anyone since to put in the ramp."

Raised area noted to the Rt side of the forehead. Small abrasion noted to the Rt cheek and Rt side of back. Denies any dizziness or blurred vision. C/o pain to the back of neck.

Assessment:

Contusion to head secondary to fall.

01/26/04 *Cora Cole, MD/LMN*

Comment:

Emp presented to the Medical unit for f/u, fall. Emp states: "I am doing okay, but they still has not started building the ramp as yet. The only thing they have done is to put up four concrete polls. I have not heard anything else about it."

08/11/04 *Bonnie Perry, RN/LMN*

History:

Employee states that she was holding on to the door frame by the shift change room in Terminal and another employee closed the door on her little finger. Incident was reported to Marvin Todd.

The tip of her little finger over the nail bed was hit by the door. She has a small hematoma about 2 mm in diameter on her nail bed. She has good mobility of her finger and only complains of some tenderness across the nail. There is no edema noted at present. Ice pack applied to finger and instructed to continue to use ice intermittently through today. Advised to elevate hand if she notices throbbing. Given disposable ice packs to use. Advised to use NSAID for pain if needed. States she has Aleve which she can use. To return to Medical Unit if any problems or concerns.

08/28/06 *Suren K. Miser, MD*

Work Status:

From 8/29/06 to 8/30/06 – surgery.

12/13/06 *Lauroline Gugenheim, RN/LMN*

History:

An employee came to the unit stating that someone fell outside by the west door.

Went outside and saw employee on the sidewalk on her knees. Employee complains about pain to her chin. Got her in a wheelchair and brought her to the Medical Unit. To the brown recliner.

"My right leg give from under me causing me to fell forward and hit my chin on the sidewalk. I immediately felt pain to my chin. Pain rated 5/10. This incident was witnessed by a few employee."

Small open abrasion noted to the chin. Employee states: "If she can go do the X-ray later because she has been working 12 hour shift and she is very tired, that is probably one of the reasons why I fell. Everything I get tired I have to rest. Will go and do the x-ray later after I get some rest."

12/18/06 *Cora Cole, MD/LMN*

Comment:

During conversation, employee expressed that she feels the difficulties she is presently experiencing are physical manifestations of the emotional stressors in her life. Employee expressed that she is very angry and stressed about being overlooked for a job promotion.

Employee was given information re: EAP services available to her and she was also advised to f/u with a Physiologist for reassessment of leg brace and other assistive devices she is presently utilizing.

Brace on left leg. Knee of right leg – no apparent injury.

Plan:

Continue as is. Return if any difficulty. Spoke to patient about seeing a physiatrist for rehab and to get brace looked after since has not been seen since receiving brace. Also to contact the scooters that help with mobility. Patient given referral to EAP "for very angry at being passed over for a job for which I am qualified because of my disability." When asked if she spoke to HR, indicated she has started and was referred to Rick.

01/05/07 *Cora Cole, MD/LMN*

Work Status:

Non-job related. She is restricted from work 1/3/07 – 1/7/07.

01/12/07 *Cora Cole, MD/LMN*

Work Status:

Cleared to return to full duty 1/8/07.

05/03/07 *Pride Emergency Medical Rescue*

Chief Complaint:

Pt fell.

Narrative:

Pt fell in her office. Pt has had hx of MS. Pt stated she tripped on a tile and fell. Pt sustained swelling to R chin also c/o pain to R side of body.

05/04/07 *LMN*

History:

Employee with ho MS tripped on loose floor tile 2 nights ago and fell forward predominately hitting the R side her body and R chin.

05/07/07 *Dr. Sperry/LMN*

History:

Employee presents for follow up. Notes improved chin pain – not present significantly. Back pain has improved but persists. Previously was "sharp" now decreased in intensity. Hip pain and breast pain also decreased. Shoulder pain is only pain that has not significantly changed. Rated at 8/10. Also notes some forearm pain with supination/pronation movements. No sig effect of Aleve on arm sxs. Cont to ice. Patient did not work yesterday due to back pain. States tried to type this am and was unable to due to shoulder sxs.

Assessment:

S/P fall persistent shoulder pain.

Plan:

Will x-ray r/o fx ao acromial head. Cont ice.

05/09/07 *Dr. Randy/LMN*

History:

Employee presented to the Medical Unit for f/u lower back pain. Employee states: "The pain is not as bad as it was yesterday. Pain rated 5/10. I took two Aleve yesterday and again this morning.

Observation:

Mild tenderness in proximal area of right hip.

Assessment:

Restricting from sitting longer than 2 hours at a time. Advised to have a cushion on the seat. To be reevaluated in 7 days.

05/11/07 *?*

Surgeon's Report

History:

Employee stated that at approximately 12:30 a.m., she was walking in the computer room when her toe got caught in a lifted tile and she fell forward. She states that she landed on the Rt side of her body and hit her Rt chin. She complained of generalized body pain and pain to her Rt chest and back.

05/16/07 *Dr. Randy/LMN*

History:

Employee states that she is still experiencing a significant amount of pain to her Rt lower back and Rt flank area. She is still using cold compresses intermittently while at home.

05/21/07 *Cora Cole, MD/LMN*

History:

Employee presented to HMU for f/u of back pain. Escorted to exam room.

Employee states that she is still experiencing Rt lower back and Rt flank pain which she rates 9/10. She stated that she continues to take Motrin for the pain and she is also applying cold compresses to her back. She states that she is unable to use heat because when she uses heat she is unable to walk. She states that her legs become extremely weak. Explained to employee that since her pain is not being relieved with the current treatment, the next step for her is Physical Therapy.

Conversation ensued re: mobility within the plant. Employee was asked if she felt that her gait is unsteady. Employee states that she feels that her gait is very unsteady. Employee was asked what her feelings were about the possibility of using a Scooter in order to facilitate her mobility at work. Employee stated that she really did not want to be in wheelchair because she feels like that would make her "disabled." She stated that she is aware of the fact that she will eventually have to use a wheelchair, but she is and has been trying to avoid the use of a wheelchair for as long as she possibly can.

Observation:

Very unsteady gait using cane.

Assessment:

Fall; multiple sclerosis with ambulation complications.

Plan:

Employee eventually conceded to the use of a scooter for mobility while at work. Employee stated that although she is not happy about the use of a wheelchair, she is willing to try anything which will help protect herself from falling and the possibility of further injuring herself. Consultation for physical therapy given to take to Workers' Comp.

05/25/07 *Cora Cole, MD/LMN*

Work Status:

Job-related problem and will be reevaluated on 06/08/07. She is restricted from remaining seated more than 2 hours. Use pillows as a support for back while sitting. The above restriction ends 06/08/07.

06/13/07 *Cora Cole, MD/LMN*

History:

"I am concerned about the scooter and what the company is willing to do to help me. I know the scooter is very expensive and my car is not made to accommodate the ramp for the scooter. I do not feel comfortable using the scooter outside my job. I am okay going to the store without using a scooter. As long as I have a cart to hold on to at Cost U Less or K-Mart, I am good to go." Her employer is trying to assist her but understands the difficulty in all the possible approaches.

Employee was told that HR is looking into getting her a scooter to use on the job. She was advised to speak to Mr. Wise concerning getting her a van on term she can afford or to help make her present vehicle accessible to use a ramp.

Employee states: "I will think about this and speak to Mr. Wise. I really don't like the idea of getting help from the company. I don't want to be a burden to them."

06/18/07 *Cora Cole, MD/LMN*

Comment:

I am ready to go back to work. I miss the job and I miss the guys I work with, but don't tell them I said that."

Asked if the exercises are helping her being more stabilized on her feet? Employees stated: "no."

Explained to employee that Mr. Wise is working on getting her a scooter to use on her job. The scooter is very slim line and she will be able to maneuver it very easily. The idea of the scooter is to allow her to have more stability at work and not fall.

Employee was asked did she trip on the tile at her workstation? Employee states: "I tripped on the tile. PSM came down and did their investigation and they said nothing is wrong with the floor. Terminal said there is something wrong with the floor. I don't understand."

Employee was told that her restrictions are up as of June 6, 2007. A HDS was given to employee to have her PMD fill it out to determine when she is able to return to work.

06/27/07 *Cora Cole, MD/LMN*

Work Status:

Cleared to return to full duty 07/02/07.

06/28/07 *Douglas W. Moulin, DC*

Return to Work

Comment:

The above-named patient has been under our care since 5/29/07 for a musculoskeletal injury and has recovered sufficiently to resume work with no restrictions on 7/9/07.

07/02/07 *Lornah Watts, RN/LMN*

History:

Was informed by Mr. Hill that patient's scooter is on site. Examined scooter and drove it to test mobility. Nurse did the same. Scooter will be brought to patient at her car; she will be taken by LMN transportation to worksite and allowed to use scooter at worksite. Pt has seen and tested scooter and is pleased.

Work Status:

Pt cleared for duty on July 9, 2007.

09/06/07 *Frank T. Bryant, MD*

Comment:

Ms. Miller has been treated for relapsing-remitting multiple sclerosis since March 2000. Ms. Miller presently is on baclofen 20 mg four times a day orally along with every other day Betasone injections. Ms. Miller requires the use of a cane for assistance in walking. She requires a voice computer program for her to type due to her condition with multiple sclerosis. Ms. Miller's condition is permanent in nature and without a medical cure at the present time.

10/25/07 *Lauroline Gugenheim, RN/LMN*

Comment:

No answer at employee's house.

10/29/07 *Cora Cole, MD/LMN*

Comment:

Employee presented to the Medical Unit to discuss a new keyboard that will be installed at her work station in the Terminal building. The new keyboard was brought into the examination room. Employee states: "Presently I am using the mouse and I have no problem using the mouse I have trained myself to handle the mouse. I do not have strength in my left hand since I was diagnosed with multiple sclerosis (MS). My finger tips are numb. I have even had to learn to use the cane with my right hand although it should be in my left hand for I do not have strength in my left hand. The new system that is being put in by Honeywell is a closed system. There is no way a mouse could be plugged into the system. I have to use both hands in order to navigate the system. One hand to roll the track ball and the other to press one of the three buttons that is surrounding the tracking ball. Both action has to be done simultaneously. I don't think I can do this motion because I don't have strength in my left hand. I am not a very fast typist. I pick pick on the keyboard. Even to take the class online, there was a typing test that I had to complete, but could not. Dr. Bryant wrote a note to the school so I can be exempted from that part of the test. It is hard for me to complete any task with both hands."

Worked with patient to see what adjustments she could make like gripping a pen in the left hand and placing it directly on the tab to be pushed while using the right to roll the wheel. Pt was able to accomplish. Supervisors noted that the system cannot make any adjustment because it is a closed system. Will discuss with supervisors.

Told employee that she has to find some way to adapt to the use of the new keyboard. One way is to use something sturdy to grip in her palm and press down on the buttons surrounding the tracking ball. Employee said she will try and see if that will work.

02/18/08 *Cora Cole, MD/LMN*

Comment:

Employee escorted to the examination room. Employee requested Mr. Hill's presence. Explained to Ms. Miller that reason for this visit is because of the e-mail that was sent by her to Mr. Dost, stating that Medical was going to speak to Design Engineer to see if they could come up with something that would plug in the system to make it easier for her to use the tracking ball. Employee was told that this was not what was the final disposition in October when she came to the Medical Department. Employee was given the encounter to read from October 29, 2007. The encounter stated that her supervisor said the company who built the system said no adjustment can be made to the system. Employee states: "I did not know about this. The new system was installed and I was waiting to hear back from someone, Medical or Design Engineer what was going to be done to the system to make it easier for me to use the track ball." Informed employee the Medical Unit had spoken with management right after her visit and was told no adjustment could be made to the system. Medical Unit thought this was communicated to the employee. We apologize and will try to double check communications in the future.

Sean was asked, what is the next step in this process? Sean stated: "Employee needs to get documentation from her physician whether or not she can use the tracking ball. Then HR will consider how she will be accommodated on those restrictions."

Employee states: "I have a bad feeling about HR because of my previous experience. A couple years ago I was involved in a serious accident. When my paper work came in from my physician, I was told to go home because there is nothing for me to do on the job. At that time I was a dock foreman and was qualified for many different jobs. I am qualified as a dispatcher and can work the dispatcher room. I am afraid that once my physician write the note, I will be sent home and be out of a job."

Sean states: "Once the employee submit the note from her PMD to Medical then HR will go from there to see if any other jobs are available for her to do. If she cannot be accommodated."

05/20/08 *Frank T. Bryant, MD*

Work Status:

No modification needed.

06/02/08 *Cora Cole, MD/LMN*

History:

Employee was asked what happened on Wednesday, May 28, 2008. Employee states: "I was told to report here by my supervisor. Wednesday was not a good day for me. I had to come into the front lobby because I lost my badge. Sam Harding had to walk me down the hallway. Presently, I am moving from my mother's house to my house and the new house is very hot compared to my mother's house. On Wednesday, I was not functioning right and I told my supervisor Sheffield I was not feeling right. I got hysterical and went to the bathroom to cry. I returned my station. I did not hear the alarm go off because I know I gave the man a 20 minute stand by. I guess I was knocked out because I did not hear the alarm on the board. The last time I fainted was during my pregnancy, and I know I am not pregnant. The other dispatcher heard the alarm and came into the room where I was. He called me by name and I sat up. I knew where I was when I caught myself. I looked at Billy Dern for a minute and did not recognize him at first. He asked me if I did not hear the alarm. Billy then told the guy to make the switched so that the vessel did not overflow. I started crying and trembling because I thought that I overflowed the tank. That is one thing in Terminal, you do not overflow the tank. I was aware what was happening. Billy then called Robert who was the TSS. Robert asked me if I could continue my shift? I told him yes. I was able to finish up my shift and go home. I have not been back to work since. My supervisor told me that I have to come to Medical before I can return to work." When I asked again if she knows what happened, she stated that there was a period of time where she believes she was "knocked out" for there are things she does not remember.

Asked employee if she went to see her private doctor as yet? Employee said: "I went to see my doctor and he told me that I had an "exacerbation" of my illness. He did some blood test and will do an MRI.

Employee was told that she needs to supply medical with a result of the MRI and clearance from her physician so that she can return to work. Sean Hills was asked to provide Medical with employee's job task description so that she can take to her physician for him to see whether or not she is capable of doing the tasks her job requires.

06/26/08 *Cora Cole, MD/LMN*

Work Status:

Is cleared to return to full duty on 6/23/08.

08/06/08 *Cora Cole, MD/LMN*

Comment:

Consultation with Laurine Miller. Telephone conversation with Laurine Miller concerning sending employee for an IME. Laurine was informed that finding a neurologist in Puerto Rico is not easy due to the language barrier. Laurine asked: "Why can't employee go to St. Thomas? Employee cannot go St. Thomas because the planes are not equipped with a lift. She would have to go to Puerto Rico first and then to St. Thomas. Sending a nurse along with the patient would benefit the company and to ensure that the questions about employee's fit for duty are answered.

Laurine was told that the Mr. Dost came up with the idea of having someone actually sit with her like a "baby sitter" to make sure that she does not fall asleep at her work station, or find another position for her in a different department. It would not be fair to send her to another department because that will be sending a problem to someone else.

09/17/08 *David D. White, MD*

Independent Medical Exam

Impression:

There really is no clear-cut obvious explanation for the patient's syncope. Certainly, she does not suffer from epilepsy because from a medicolegal standpoint, one must have multiple episodes of seizures. This patient had only one episode of syncope of which we do not know the etiology. Therefore, in light of the fact that there is no new neuro-focal complaint. Her exam is stable and does not suffer from epilepsy per se, I do see any reason why she should not be able to return to work in her normal position as an Oil Movement Coordinator. Nonetheless, to be certain, one might consider doing an electroencephalogram just to be more thorough in our belief that she does not suffer from epilepsy. This option was given to her.

In addition, because of her neurological condition, she will need a handicapped accessible bathroom.

12/08/08 *Babu Stevens, MD*

History:

5/28/08 – 1 episode of syncope @ work. "Slumped" in a chair. + LOC approx 5 minutes.

04/18/09 *David D. White, MD*

Work Status:

I have reviewed the record of this pt of mine with job description and see no reason why she should not return to work.

05/20/09 *Cora Cole, MD/LMN*

Comment:

Dr. White was asked if he had a chance to review these documents. Dr. White said yes, and his opinion is the same. When he examined employee there were no neurological changes to show that there was a period of syncope. He would like her to get an EEG to show if she has syncope or a seizure disorder/epilepsy. If the EEG is negative then, in his opinion, there is no reason as to why she cannot return to work.

Dr. White states: "If she has a problem with syncope, he does not think she can return to work in the same position. If she does not have a problem with syncope, then she can return to work. A patient can pass out from being sleepy, suffering with the flu, a vagal stimuli, or epilepsy. An EEG needs to be done on the employee. If the result is negative, she can return to work. If the result is positive, she should not return in that job.

David D. White, MD

Comment:

This statement clarifies my note dated April 18, 2009, concerning Cheryl Miller, in which I stated that I "see no reason why she (Cheryl Miller) should not return to work."

Pt will need electroencephalogram. If EEG is negative for seizure disorder then I see no reason why she should not return to work as she does not have seizures.

04/28/10 *Cora Cole, MD/LMN*

Comment:

Laurine Hamburg stated: "some time ago in a crowd employee, Ms. Cheryl Miller, stood up and asked what happened to her if the refinery or the building where she works has to be evacuated?" Ms. Hamburg stated that she understood Hunter Smith told Ms. C. Miller that she did not need to worry – she would be taken care of and her supervisor Mr. Roberts said that he would take care of her. Ms. Hamburg reported that the taxi vans that used to take Ms. C. Miller from in front of the Admin building to the Terminal Building do not want to conduct that service anymore. Ms. C. Miller's coworkers are now responsible for taking her to and from the Terminal Building. The Company needs to come up with a plan as to how Ms. C. Miller is going to be evacuated in an emergency situation.

05/03/10 *Lauroline Gugenheim, RN/LMN*

Comment:

Hit on wrist with a wall picture. Employee presented to the Medical Unit via wheelchair accompanied by Steven Beale. Employee states: "About 1620, I was in a safety meeting in the Terminal Building on the 4th floor. I was sitting in my scooter with my hands on the handle of the scooter. There was a picture on the wall and I was sitting close to the wall. The picture fell off the wall and hit me on the left hand, close to my wrist. I did not feel any pain instantly. A short time after I felt some pain to my hand. Pain rated 5/10. Right now the pain is still the same."

Right wrist measure 15.5, left wrist measure 15.5. C/o pain to left hand. CMS intact. Apply cold compress to left hand. Advil given for pain. Instruct employee on use of ice and Advil. Also if there is any problem with the hand throughout the night, let her supervisor know so that the on-call nurse can come in and evaluate her.

05/04/10 *Lauroline Gugenheim, RN/LMN*

Comment:

Employee presented to the Medical Unit for f/u. Employee states: "My wrist is doing much better. I took two Advil last night. I did not use any more of the ice. The pain is not as much as it was. The area is still a little tender."

10/09/11 *Babu Stevens, MD*

Chief Complaint:

The patient is a 45-year-old right-handed female who is known to me from her prior evaluation on 10/15/2002 relating to the management of MS (Multiple Sclerosis) locally on St. Paul. The evaluation on 10/27/2011 was requested by her attorney to address the extent of disability pertaining to multiple sclerosis and to address the impairment(s) in activities of daily living, her capacity to perform work, etc.

History:

Ms. Miller was formally diagnosed with multiple sclerosis in March 2000 at the Spine Institute. The patient who sustained multiple motor vehicle accidents, notably in 1993 sustained a significant head trauma when she struck her head against the steering wheel and possibly the windshield. She noticed insidious onset symptoms of weakness in the right lower extremity described as "dragging" of her foot in mid 90s to perhaps as late as 1999. The patient also had suffered back injury from a fall at work. Multiple sclerosis was diagnosed in March 2000 after evaluation at the Spine Institute. Following confirmation of multiple sclerosis, the patient was started on baclofen 20 mg two tablets qid and Betaseron 0.3 mg injected subcutaneously on alternate days.

Impression:

1. Chronic relapsing remitting multiple sclerosis, diagnosis made in March 2000.
2. UMN type RLE monoparesis with right foot drop requiring AFO.
3. Central disequilibrium due to past MRI evidenced posterior fossa (pontine) white matter plaque.
4. Gait impairment due to # 1 & 3.

5. Neurogenic UMN type bladder dysfunction due to #1.
6. History of isolated syncope, 5/28/08 likely vasovagal. Work-up is negative for paroxysmal disorder such as epilepsy or seizure disorder.

Conclusion:

Ms. Miller has proven to be an asset to the oil refinery having performed remarkably well despite her disability and lack of proper support from the employer. Further, it is evident that the employer has consistently remained negligent, providing a hazardous workplace for Ms. Miller over many years.

The employer proceeded to involuntarily terminate Ms. Miller in spite of professional opinions rendered by two physicians, who felt that Ms. Miller was safe to return to her job. LMN, in order to justify their ill action cited the potential for catastrophic accidents at the refinery, stated that the job was complex to perform and yet the records showed of no gross errors that occurred while Ms. Miller worked at LMN over two decades. She performed the required complex tasks vigilantly all these years monitoring over 200 tanks in 20 systems. Ms. Miller in spite of suffering from a chronic, progressive neurodegenerative disorder showed up for work, didn't abuse her sick leave and yet was reprimanded for taking time off when she felt ill. On 5/28/08, she reported that she was not feeling well, but was allowed to stay at work. Later, she experienced the blackout. This could have been easily prevented if the employer allowed the employee to take time off or intervened with proper medical evaluation and recommended treatment.

The syncopal episode that occurred on 5/28/08 would have warranted no limitations or modifications to Ms. Miller's job. I concur with Dr. White and Dr. Bryant releasing and returning Ms. Miller back to her baseline job. Syncope can be triggered by several etiologies. In the case of Ms. Miller the cause was probably due to poor oral intake, volume contraction and dehydration. As stated above, the EEG was normal in my office and the one read by Dr. White. Ms. Miller does not suffer from paroxysmal seizure disorder or epilepsy that would have precluded her returning to her job.

Ms. Miller does have physical impairments that substantially limit one or more major life activities. She remains capable of working in her prior employment and related employment with reasonable accommodations.

Results of Testing

I administered tests to Ms. Miller over 2 days: December 13 and 14, 2011. Her handwriting was quite faint and difficult to read.

The Multidimensional Aptitude Battery-II (MAB-II) was used to assess Ms. Miller's intellectual skills and abilities. Scores from this instrument are presented relative to a normative sample.

The MAB-II Verbal, Performance, and Full Scale scores are converted to deviation IQ scores that are based upon an average score of 100 with a standard deviation of 15. The scores express where an individual's score falls in relation to the average score. Additionally, the MAB-II subscales are converted to T-scores that are based upon an average score of 50 with a standard deviation of 10. For example, a score of 60 on the MAB-II would indicate a performance that is one standard deviation above average relative to the individual's peer group, and a score of 40 would indicate a performance that is one standard deviation below average relative to the individual's peer group.

Overall, Ms. Miller scored as follows on the MAB-II:

Verbal IQ	82
Performance IQ	82
Full Scale IQ	80

Ms. Miller's performance placed her in the low average range of mental functioning. Her individual scores on the MAB-II subscales are summarized below:

Information	40
Comprehension	40
Arithmetic	34
Similarities	34
Vocabulary	43
Digit Symbol	45
Picture Completion	34
Spatial	34
Picture Arrangement	38
Object Assembly	42

On the Beck Depression Inventory-II, Ms. Miller generated a total score of 49, which corresponds to the severe range of depression.

Results of personality testing from the MMPI-2 were invalid. A computer-generated interpretative report indicated that Ms. Miller's results may stem from several factors that include excessive symptom checking, falsely claiming psychological problems, low-reading level, a plea for help, or a confused state. Her extreme score on a scale measuring psychopathology suggests that her responses are more extreme than people who are hospitalized for severe psychiatric problems.

On a Self-Directed Search Form R, Ms. Miller scored highest on the Enterprising and Social occupational themes. The Enterprising theme is most often associated with business and self-gain occupations. The Social theme is usually associated with occupations that involve promoting the health, education, and welfare of others. Ms. Miller rated her teaching and sales abilities, understanding of others, and managerial skills as very high. She also assessed that her artistic, clerical, and musical abilities, and office skills are above average. The occupations Ms. Miller noted interest in pursuing most recently were "lawyer," "non-profit mg," "OMC supervisor," and "dock supervisor." Among the occupations from the Self-Directed Search Form R that correspond with Ms. Miller's profile are Social Welfare Administrator (DOT #195.117-010), Association Executive (DOT #189.117-010), Housing Project Manager (DOT #186.167-030), Community Organization Director (DOT #187.167-234), Case Worker, Family (DOT #195.107-018), Public Service Director (DOT #184.117-010), and Equal Opportunity Representative (DOT #168.167-014).

Summary and Impressions

1. A 1983 high school graduate, Ms. Miller reported she earned a certificate in paralegal studies and then an associate's degree in paralegal studies in 2007. Additionally, she noted completing a bachelor's degree in criminal justice in 2008, and she informed me she is enrolled in an online program in which she is pursuing master's degree requirements in nonprofit management. Ms. Miller cited several computer-related courses she completed, and she indicated she also holds a real estate license in the U.S. Virgin Islands. Before beginning her employment with LMN in 1988, she worked in various retail positions. Initially, Ms. Miller's service with LMN had been as a terminal dispatcher (1988 through 1992); she then worked as a dock foreman (1992 through 1994) before assuming a position as an oil movement coordinator (OMC; DOT #914.167-014). Based on my understanding of Ms. Miller's job responsibilities, she performed skilled tasks that required sedentary exertion. A high degree of mental alertness, vigilance, and judgment is required. Because of her problems with multiple sclerosis (MS), LMN extended several accommodations to Ms. Miller; over time, the types of accommodations extended to her apparently increased. Records document a May 28, 2008, syncopal episode; she subsequently had a leave of absence until September 2009. Employment records document several significant performance-related problems that Ms. Miller had

upon her return to work and through the time of her severance in November 2010. Errors an OMC makes, according to information I reviewed, can have significant economic, human, and environmental consequences. Since her severance in November 2010, she apprised me, she has not had any employment. The job search efforts she initiated have been unsuccessful, and she has continued to pursue online master's degree studies in nonprofit administration. Currently, Ms. Miller assessed, she is capable of resuming her former OMC job; she also assessed she is capable of holding full-time employment in a job with physical and cognitive demands similar to those she performed as an OMC. She volunteered, "I was told [by my lawyer] I can't [apply for disability benefits with the Social Security Administration] until this [pending litigation] is over." After providing this response, Ms. Miller stated, "I shouldn't have said that." Bill Garcia, manager of planning and performance monitoring at LMN, told me Ms. Miller had an unacceptable number of incidents that occurred during her shift and unacceptable performance problems. Allen Roberts, oil movements and documentation supervisor, provided a similar assessment.

2. Medical records document various medical problems Ms. Miller had been experiencing before her diagnosis of MS in 2000. The records indicate Ms. Miller's gait progressively worsened. Dr. Bryant diagnosed relapsing-remitting multiple sclerosis in September 2007. After her syncopal episode in 2008, Dr. White determined on April 18, 2009, "I reviewed the record of this patient of mine with job description and see no reason why she should not return to work." The most recent medical record I reviewed is Dr. Stevens' report dated October 9, 2011. He concluded: "Ms. Miller does have physical impairments that substantially limit one or more major life activities. She remains capable of working in her prior employment and related employment with reasonable accommodations." I understand Ms. Miller will be undergoing an examination with Dr. Gil, a neurologist, and Dr. Weisbond, a psychiatrist. My assessment of Ms. Miller's vocational capacities continues to be in a formative state.
3. Ms. Miller scored in the low-average range (Full Scale IQ = 80) on testing I administered. On a measure of mood-related problems, Ms. Miller generated a score that indicates she is experiencing severe depression. Her MMPI-2 profile was invalid. She has obvious difficulties with her gait, and she required assistance when walking more than nominal distance on both occasions I met her. Her hand strength appears quite weak, as evidenced by difficulties she had with writing. Also evident were problems with fatigue. Ms. Miller presented several medical problems including pain in various body parts (she noted her pain is exacerbated by stress), mobility difficulties, upper-extremity weakness, and fatigue. She apprised me increased levels of activity, stress, and fatigue impair her mental functioning. Ms. Miller conveyed her symptoms worsen over the course of the day. Additionally, she discussed significant sleep problems. Her memory was good/fair during my examination, and she exhibited several instances of word-retrieval difficulties. My analysis has led me to conclude, from a vocational rehabilitation perspective, Ms. Miller is not capable of performing her former OMC job responsibilities.
4. Ms. Miller reported experiencing several active MS symptoms at the time of her November 2010 termination, including numbness throughout her body (especially her hands), a "cutting" sensation in both sides, mobility difficulties, balance problems, right-side body weakness ("Both limbs were very weak"), severe pain in the right side of her head, significant sleep difficulties ("I would wake up screaming because of the pain in my head"), approximately three bladder-control accidents per week, and acid reflux ("I was vomiting, stuff like that"). The work errors and performance problems Ms. Miller had been exhibiting before her severance are well documented. My analysis has led me to conclude that, even with reasonable accommodations, Ms. Miller was not capable of performing the essential functions of her OMC job at the time of her severance.

Michael Shahnasarian, Ph.D. Date
Certified Rehabilitation Counselor #3701
Certified Vocational Evaluator #58360

Certified Life Care Planner #258
Licensed Psychologist PY5644
Fellow, National Career Development Association
Fellow, International Academy of Life Care Planners

Appendix A
Photos Showing Accommodations
LMN Extended to Ms. Miller

1. Exterior ramping installed to ease the claimant's access from her vehicle to work environment.

2. Exterior door opening device, accessible from a wheelchair, installed for the claimant's use.

3. Interior door opening device, accessible from a wheelchair, installed for the claimant's use.

4. Grab rails and ramp installed for the claimant's use.

5. The claimant's control room work environment.

6. Microwave and refrigerator made available to claimant, allowing her access from a wheelchair.

Chapter 8

Assessment of Earning Capacity in Employment Law Cases

8.1 Introduction

Title VII of the Civil Rights Act of 1964 prohibits workplace discrimination and makes it unlawful for an employer to create a hostile work environment. Vocational evaluators become involved in employment law disputes when plaintiffs claim allegations of a Title VII offense and earning capacity damages. Wrongful termination or workplace discrimination alleged as a product of retaliation, along with sexual harassment, and discrimination based on sex, age, sexual orientation, or national origin are the most common employment law cases involving vocational evaluators.

In addition to questions generally pending in disputes involving earning capacity, vocational evaluators in employment law disputes sometimes address how alleged inappropriate employment practices may have adversely affected and will affect an individual's career development. These analyses range from potential employer stigmatization due to a record of involuntary dismissal—and in some cases, media coverage—to limitations in future promotion and career advancement an employer's alleged improper conduct caused. Astute vocational evaluators assume a broad, analytical perspective when evaluating how disputed events can affect an individual's career development and earning capacity. Supplemental research and analysis can help address how unique circumstances, such as sensationalistic media coverage related to a whistleblower's wrongful termination claim, affects a claimant's current and future vocational prospects. Heitzman, Amundsen, Gunn, and Christensen (2014) also address consultation in employment law.

8.2 Central Vocational Questions

Vocational evaluations associated with claims of employment law violations generally address the following questions:

- Have alleged incidents associated with employment by the defendant caused the plaintiff to acquire vocational handicaps that could impair future career development and earnings?
- What, if any, back-pay and front-pay damage has a plaintiff sustained?
- Has the plaintiff made reasonable efforts to mitigate claimed vocational damages?
- Was an alleged negative employment experience sufficiently severe to cause the plaintiff to acquire compensable mental distress damage?

Only vocational evaluators who possess a sufficient background in mental health counseling or psychology should address the latter question. Damages assessments related to allegations of mental anguish typically involve analyses of causal relationships between disputed events and acquired mental health problems, along with how residual mental health problems have affected and will likely affect future career development. Shahnasarian (2004b) addressed vocational experts' assessments of front-pay damages and psychological considerations in employment law cases.

A. Disruption of Career Development

Vocational experts attempt to quantify damages that earning

capacity issues in dispute, including disruptions to career development, may cause. These disruptions could include search time to secure new employment after a job termination, differentials in earnings upon workplace reentry, and length of time required to reach parity with prior levels of compensation.

While assessing earning capacity damages attributable to a disruption of a subject's career development, vocational evaluators—as in all earning capacity assessments—should examine the demand for subjects' experience and skills, available job opportunities within accessible labor markets, industry and marketplace projections and trends, and case-specific circumstances. Keen insight of subtleties embedded in disputed issues relevant to earning capacity damages also enhances evaluators' analyses.

In one case, a plaintiff alleged a defendant employer wrongfully terminated her, and then hampered her ability to become reemployed by providing defamatory and slanderous appraisals of her character and job performance when prospective employers conducted background checks. The plaintiff had been a corporate training manager working in a mid-size city, and the vocational evaluator's research detected that the local community of training professionals was small and cohesive. Within it, a reputation (whether founded or unfounded) of being a controversial, disgruntled employee undermined efforts to secure employment; associations of these types would likely be deleterious in any job candidate's efforts. During trial testimony, the evaluator described how defamatory comments made in unfair, poor job references could extend the plaintiff's job search time and unfairly exempt her from consideration of positions for which she qualified. This analysis, amplified via the evaluator's testimony, became an additional element for the jury's assessment of earning capacity damages.

B. Back Pay and Front Pay

The concepts of back pay and front pay as elements of loss of earning capacity were presented in Chapter 7 and are considerably important in damages claims in employment law cases. When addressing earning capacity damages, plaintiff counsel's strategy often relies on highlighting disparate compensation levels associated with previous earnings and future earning capacity. Defense counsel's strategy often relies on analyzing the plaintiff's mitigation efforts and presenting favorable opportunities to realize prior earnings levels.

Again, caution is in order: Each case involving an earning capacity assessment is unique and requires independent investigation and analysis. In some cases, an individual may possess substantive transferable skills that are in high demand, allowing a career transition with comparable near-term earnings and, occasionally, a higher level of earning capacity. In other cases, a vocational evaluation may yield information that leads the evaluator to conclude that few previously available career opportunities remain viable to a plaintiff, and these opportunities offer levels of compensation lower than previously realized levels. This analysis often forms an important predicate for the evaluator's appraisal of earning capacity damages.

A vocational expert's analysis in a case in which a plaintiff developed medical problems after an alleged wrongful termination complicated the assessment. The plaintiff, a former truck driver employed by a large building products corporation, had problems with hypertension that predated his job termination. These problems escalated after his termination, and he suffered a cerebrovascular accident; however, the plaintiff was unable to causally relate his medical problems and his allegations of wrongful termination. Because of his apparently unrelated medical problems, the vocational evaluator concluded, the plaintiff's employment with the defendant likely would have ended regardless of any alleged wrongful termination. This conclusion led the defense counsel to argue that any front-pay damages owed the plaintiff should be restricted. An excerpt from the evaluator's report follows:

> Mr. Daley had longstanding problems with hypertension that predated his termination from Big Builders in October 2011; medical records indicate these difficulties have persisted. In March 2013, Mr. Daley experienced a cerebrovascular accident that temporarily rendered him unable to pursue work activity.
>
> Because of his problems with hypertension, Mr. Daley has had periods when he would have been unable to satisfy medical standards established for commercial motor vehicle operators. Dr. Herman's recent deposition testimony suggests stress causes Mr. Daley's hypertension to escalate, and Mr. Daley represented that his prior employment with Big Builders caused him high levels of stress. As a vocational rehabilitation counselor, I cannot endorse work as a commercial truck driver for Mr. Daley. If he chooses to maintain his current part-time employment as a school bus driver, I recommend that he be very closely monitored. In any event, it is in his best interest from a vocational rehabilitation perspective to pursue alternate employment. Even if his employment with Big Builders did not end in 2011, Mr. Daley's career development as a commercial truck driver would likely have been trun-

> cated because of his hypertension problems.
> Based on statements made during his recent deposition, Mr. Daley appears content with his current employment situation. He denied intending to pursue alternate employment, retraining, or other vocational rehabilitation initiatives.
>
> I do not believe Mr. Daley's reported earnings since his employment with Big Builders ended in October 2011 represent his earning capacity. In my opinion, he would have been capable of obtaining employment representative of his demonstrated earning capacity within three to six months after his employment with Big Builders ended. Fleet maintenance and inside sales positions are among those Mr. Daley could have pursued. A reasonable estimate of his annual earning capacity at that time is from $30,000 to $33,000. Within three to five years after becoming reemployed, Mr. Daley likely would have realized a rate of pay comparable to what he would have earned at Big Builders if his employment had continued—assuming he initiated reasonable attempts to realize his career development potential.

C. Mental Distress Damages

Many plaintiffs allege feeling embarrassment, humiliation, and other types of mental anguish after their employment with a defendant ended. Accordingly, some seek compensation for mental distress damages their alleged inappropriate employment experiences caused. As an illustration, the following excerpt from a Complaint details a plaintiff's allegations of work-related events affecting her mental health.

> This is a sexual, racial, and national origin discrimination and retaliation action brought by Wendy Lou Pouzet, a punch press operator employed by Abracadabra Corporation since 2004. The plaintiff was subjected to a sexually hostile atmosphere by her coworkers and supervisors, which included unwelcome touches and offensive comments. The plaintiff was required to perform duties that her male coworkers were not required to perform. Ms. Pouzet was also subjected to a harassing environment based on her race and national origin. Several of her coworkers had made comments such as "Go back to Haiti." The plaintiff complained about the discrimination and was retaliated against by the defendant's agents while acting within the scope of their employment. Subsequent to plaintiff's complaints, she was denied promotions and scheduled pay raises, subjected to heightened discipline, false and malicious written warnings, false and malicious performance appraisals, increased scrutiny of performance, reprimands and threats of dismissal from her supervisors, retaliatory harassment, and ultimately dismissal. The defendant's conduct proximately caused plaintiff to suffer severe emotional distress, mental anguish, indignation, shame, and despair. In addition to these injuries, defendant's conduct has proximately caused the plaintiff to suffer pecuniary losses and lost employment opportunities. The plaintiff seeks damages, including punitive damages, under Title VII of the Civil Rights Act of 1964, as amended by the Civil Rights Act of 1991.

Cases that involve mental anguish claims require a vocational expert (who is also qualified to render opinions about issues related to mental health) to investigate and render opinions about how events in dispute have affected an individual psychologically. Accordingly, the expert may investigate a potential causal relationship between alleged workplace improprieties and a plaintiff's alleged psychological symptoms—especially if there is a suggestion that these symptoms correspond to front-pay damage. This investigation may require developing a composite subject profile from psychological testing, focused clinical interviews, psychological profiling based on collateral information, and other methods necessary to address specific referral questions. As always, vocational experts must contain their opinions to their scope of competence and not venture into investigations or opinions beyond their expertise.

8.3 Noteworthy Considerations

Although disability-related problems are generally not the focus of vocational evaluations undertaken in employment law disputes, the vocational evaluator should ascertain whether a subject possesses physical or mental health impairments that in any way threaten career development and earning capacity. The evaluator should also be attuned to considerations such as effects of notice extended to an affected employee about impending severance of employment, mitigation efforts, provision and uses of severance pay and outplacement services, entitlement sentiments, and postseverance vocational behavior.

A. Notice Extended to Affected Employee

An axiom career counselors who provide guidance to job seekers often cite is, "The best time to find a job is when you have a job." The gist of this statement is that job seekers are in a more powerful position to negotiate with prospective employers about issues such as compensation, job title, and job responsibilities when they are employed than when they are unemployed. This is especially the case when a job seeker is employed and is being recruited for a new job.

Job seekers in this position are also able to better discern opportunities they pursue. Perceptions about a job seeker's need and availability for employment are often factors that both the job seeker and prospective employer consider during the job recruitment process. When pertinent, the vocational evaluator should consider the following questions:

- What, if any, advance notice did the former employer provide the plaintiff regarding the termination of her employment?
- If the plaintiff received notice of impending job elimination, what efforts did she undertake to mitigate earning capacity damages by initiating a job search at the earliest possible opportunity?
- In cases where the plaintiff voluntarily left her employer, what job search efforts were made before giving notice of termination?

B. Mitigation

An analysis of a plaintiff's efforts to expediently resume his career development after termination should include assessment of job search efforts (e.g., number of job applications initiated, appropriateness of jobs pursued, time and effort committed to becoming reemployed, perseverance), initiatives to enhance skills in order to enhance employability and increase earning capacity through activities such as retraining or self-study, and use of time since separation from the defendant employer. It is often helpful to review records that document mitigation efforts, such as job applications, rejection letters from prospective employers, and advertisements of jobs for which the plaintiff applied. The absence of these types of records can also be enlightening. Career counselors advise individuals in search of employment to approach their job search as a job; that is, commit forty or more hours per week to activities related to becoming employed. The vocational evaluator should assess the plaintiff's efforts compared with a standard of this type. When pertinent, the vocational evaluator should consider the following questions:

- What efforts has the plaintiff expended to mitigate vocational damages?
- Have the plaintiff's efforts been consistent and suggestive of an individual making a good faith effort to resume prior levels of career development?

C. Severance Pay

In some cases, plaintiffs and defendant employers negotiate severance pay to coincide with the ending of an employment relationship. Inferences about a plaintiff's mitigation efforts can sometimes be made by examining how the plaintiff used this and other benefits extended upon termination. Uses of severance benefits tend to vary significantly. Some plaintiffs view severance pay like a windfall, squander money they have been provided, and defer their career development because of the short-term financial comfort the severance pay has afforded. Conversely, other plaintiffs may allocate a portion of severance monies toward mitigation to pay for retraining or financing a self-employment venture. When pertinent, the vocational evaluator should consider the following questions:

- How has money extended to the plaintiff in the form of severance pay been used?
- Has a plaintiff applied any severance pay benefits to further career development?

D. Outplacement

Outplacement services are occasionally provided to employees upon separation. These services aim to minimize disruption to career development that an unanticipated ending of employment may cause. The scope of outplacement services varies widely and may include relatively brief interventions such as a workshop on résumé preparation and job search techniques, personalized services in the form of private career counseling, or long-term assistance that includes providing clerical support and office space from which an individual can conduct a job search. When pertinent, the vocational evaluator should consider the following questions:

- Did the plaintiff take advantage of outplacement services made available?
- What specific career development practices has the plaintiff implemented from those offered through outplacement services?

E. Entitlement Sentiments

Some plaintiffs contend entitlement to a level of treatment above their coworkers for reasons that they had been extraordinarily loyal and/or had made significant, unappreciated contributions. These sentiments can interfere with mitigation efforts and career development focus. Entitlement sentiments are most common in situations that involve plaintiffs who have had long tenures of employment with an employer, plaintiffs who were one of the first employees hired by an organization and consider themselves to have been instrumental in the organization's growth and development, and plaintiffs who perceive they have greatly contributed to the financial success of the organization or to the career development of individuals who have subsequently allied against them. When pertinent, the vocational evaluator should consider the following questions:

- Is the plaintiff manifesting symptoms of entitlement?
- If present, how have these sentiments affected vocational behavior—both before and after severance?

F. Postseverance Vocational Behavior

An analysis of career-related actions—or a lack thereof—a plaintiff initiates after employment problems have commenced can yield information material to an assessment of earning capacity. For instance, consider a person who, after being terminated, expended the minimum level of effort necessary to satisfy requirements for obtaining unemployment compensation and then took an international vacation before beginning an aggressive job search. Postseverance behavior of this type should raise suspicions about the reasonableness of job search efforts. Or, after an analysis of a plaintiff's job applications, a vocational evaluator may learn that the plaintiff has chosen not to pursue employment within the industry in which her skills are most directly transferable and command the highest level of compensation. This may lead the evaluator to deduce the plaintiff's current level of compensation—offering a lower rate of pay than previous positions in an unrelated position and industry—may be related to the plaintiff's decision to change careers for reasons other than inability to secure employment in a position related to prior experience. That is, the plaintiff may be voluntarily suppressing his earning capacity; this may account for a differential between postseverance earnings levels and should be a component of the vocational evaluator's focus.

Changes in work values, such as valuing discretionary time more than in the past, are among the reasons some plaintiffs voluntarily suppress their earning capacity. A myriad of personal factors can also affect postseverance career decision-making. The evaluator should be sensitive to voluntary and involuntary factors that may be contributing to a plaintiff's postseverance vocational behavior. When pertinent, the vocational evaluator should consider the following questions:

- How has the plaintiff applied her time and efforts since employment-related problems began to mitigate alleged career development problems?
- What deductions can be made about incentives, disincentives, and other motivations that may be operating and influencing the plaintiff's vocational behavior?

8.4 Conclusion

Many factors beyond back pay, front pay, and mitigation may be relevant to an earning capacity assessment in cases that involve employment disputes. Vocational evaluators should assume a broad, analytical approach, tending to vocational behaviors that may provide insight germane to assessing the extent of claimed earning capacity damages.

Appendix 8.1: Sample Report of a Vocational Rehabilitation Evaluation in an Employment Law Case Prepared for Lucas Theo Roumain by Michael Shahnasarian, Ph.D., August 1, 2013

A vocational evaluator reviewed records and conducted labor market research to analyze economic damages claims in a case of alleged wrongful termination for reasons including discrimination because of national origin. While the evaluator did not examine the claimant, he offered to do so if the case did not settle.

Briefly, the case involved a restaurant kitchen supervisor who, after a period of unemployment when he collected unemployment compensation, secured two line-cook jobs. He was unemployed at the time of his deposition, approximately 4 years after his alleged wrongful termination.

The vocational evaluator reviewed job search records and conducted labor market research to arrive at an opinion about the reasonableness of the claimant's job search efforts after the alleged wrongful termination. This analysis included an opinion about a reasonable time for the claimant to have been able to secure new employment. Although the evaluator assessed the claimant's workplace reentry wage rate would have been lower than his rate at the time of his severance, he prognosticated a timeframe when he anticipated the claimant would have been able to realize his former pay level.

By addressing (a.) a reasonable job search period, (b.) workplace reentry wage rate, and (c.) time necessary for the claimant to reach his prior earnings level, the vocational evaluator provides the bases necessary to compute front pay and back pay damages.

Overview

Lucas Theo Roumain was referred to me for a vocational rehabilitation analysis. A Charge of Discrimination dated May 12, 2009, alleges Mr. Roumain was wrongfully terminated on April 10, 2009, in retaliation for reporting to OutSideBar management that he was verbally abused by his supervisor, Sonny Angun. Mr. Roumain further charges that he has been discriminated against because of his national origin (Haitian).

Records Reviewed

Records from the following sources were reviewed with this analysis:

- Complaint
- Answers to Interrogatories, July 2, 2013
- Deposition of Lucas Roumain, July 5, 2013
- Southern Diagnostics
- Chandler Medical Center
- Gilbert Anthony, MD
- Medical Certification for Disability Exceptions, July 7 and 23, 2012
- Defendant's Response to Request for Information, June 29, 2009
- Charge of Discrimination, May 12, 2009
- Unemployment Compensation Decision of Appeals Referee, December 3, 2009
- Equal Employment Opportunities Commission, Letter of Determination, February 23, 2011
- OutSideBar, employment records
- W-2 Wage and Tax Statements, 2008 and 2009
- Individual Income Tax Returns, 2010
- Internal Revenue Service Wage and Income Transcript, 2007 and 2008
- Employment Search file

Vocational Activity

Mr. Roumain reported during his deposition testimony on July 5, 2013, that he completed the sixth grade in Haiti. He denied obtaining any additional education or certifications. Interestingly, Mr. Roumain's resume represents he earned a high school diploma and attended Pierre College in Port au Prince. He represented to the Agency for Workforce Innovation that, after he left OutSideBar, he intended to attend Hemmingway High School to obtain training in English on December 2, 2009.

During his deposition, Mr. Roumain testified that he sought political asylum in the United States, having moved from Haiti on July 16, 1994. He reported that his first position after arriving in Miami was a factory job, as an extractor for Buford Company, for 11 months. Mr. Roumain noted he moved to Key West and began employment with Zayre's, unloading trucks for approximately 1 month, when he became employed by OutSideBar as a line cook.

According to his deposition testimony, Mr. Roumain was employed as a line cook from 1997 to approximately January 2009, earning $14 per hour, working 40 to 50 hours each week. He reported he was promoted to a kitchen supervisor position in January 2009 by Chef Angun, had a $1.00 per hour raise, and his pay increased to $15 per hour.

Included in Mr. Roumain's employment file from OutSideBar is a job description for a culinary supervisor. Also included is a Personnel Action Form noting Mr. Roumain's last date worked was March 21, 2009. He was involuntarily terminated because of a policy violation. The following comment is noted: "Termination is due to inappropriate behavior in the work place, insubordination to management, and false allegations against management." His termination was recommended by the home office.

In April 2010, after leaving his position with OutSideBar, Mr. Roumain testified, he became employed by the Seafood Haus as a line cook in April 2009; he earned $13 per hour. He conveyed that his job ended in July 2009 when the restaurant closed. Mr. Roumain testified he then collected unemployment for 2 years, during 2010 and 2011. On his 2010 income tax return, he reported earning more than $18,000. He testified his next employment was in May 2012, as a line cook at Cromwell's British Pub.

Background Information

The following background information was obtained from records:

FULL NAME:	Lucas Theo Roumain
DATE OF BIRTH:	April 14, 1960
INCIDENT DATE:	March 23, 2009, wrongful termination
RACE:	Black
MARITAL STATUS:	Married, Raquel Alcine
NAMES AND AGES OF CHILDREN:	Theo Roumain, 28 Carin Roumain, 14 Raymonde Roumain, 9 Marguaritte 21, daughter of Ms. Alcine
RESIDENCE:	Key West, Florida
PRESENTING PROBLEMS:	Dizziness
EDUCATION:	Sixth grade, Haiti

EMPLOYER AT TIME OF INCIDENT:	OutSideBar Restaurant
JOB TITLE AT TIME OF INCIDENT:	Kitchen Supervisor
RATE OF PAY AT TIME OF INCIDENT:	$15 per hour
PRESENT WORK STATUS:	Unemployed

Physical Condition and Medical Information

Mr. Roumain testified on July 3, 2012, that he suffers from dizziness because of losing his position at OutSideBar. "Before I was fired from that job I was normal, but now I have some sort of a disease in my head that sort of affects my memory," he stated. He reported that he was seen by Dr. Anthony and noted, "Tests were performed and it was found that my disease is very high." Mr. Roumain was unable to recall the name of the disease, although he said: "It's a dizziness disease. Sometimes it precludes me from driving, and, when I have those symptoms, I have to stop driving." He further testified: "It's not the medication that is affecting my memory. It's the fact that I've been thinking about being fired, always thinking about it, and it's a disease."

When asked about the basis for his claim of emotional distress during his deposition, Mr. Roumain testified:

> *The disease, the stress, the thoughts and it causes me to shake sometimes, for my body to shake and many other symptoms. The shaking started more or less around the same time when the disease started. When it happens, I experience dizziness. My head spins.*

When asked whether he has seen any mental health professionals, Mr. Roumain responded, "No." He elaborated, "It's because of all the thinking, the stress, and I realized that my children have been having difficulty even feeding themselves."

Career Development

The following work history was obtained from records:

Job Title	*Name of Organization*	*Dates*
Line Cook	Cromwell's British Pub	5/12 – 11/12
Line Cook	Seafood Haus	04/09 – 07/09
Kitchen Supervisor/Prep Cook	OutSideBar	1997 – 3/21/09
Stocker	Zayre's	1997
Extractor	Buford Company	1997

Mr. Roumain's employment-search file documents e-mail correspondence and job opportunities he apparently pursued between September 9, 2010, and June 9, 2013, Figure 1 summarizes his efforts.

Date	Employer	Job Title	Employer's E-mail Response
9/9/10	Southern Casino	24 Hour Cook	Position Filled
3/6/12	Big Supermarket	Dairy/Frozen Food Manager	Received Application
4/24/12	Big Supermarket	Asst Meat Manager	Chose other candidates
5/23/12	City of Deerfield: Public Works	Chief of Maintenance Operations	Received Application
5/23/12	International Hotel Miami Airport	Cook	Received Application
5/25/13	Bayside Miami Eats	Dishwasher	Received Application
5/27/13	Sandy Shore Hotel	Line Cook	Received Application
6/9/13	The Strand Hotel & Spa	Dishwasher/Line Cook	Received Application
6/9/13	Sunny Miami Beach Hotel	Dishwasher	Received Application

Figure 7.1. Documented E-mail Correspondence

Mr. Roumain's employment search file also identified 10 additional positions he apparently pursued (please refer to Figure 2); however, there is no e-mail correspondence related to these efforts.

Mr. Roumain testified during his deposition that he is limited to working within 3 miles of his home and conveyed, "Yes, because of my disease I can't drive further than that."

When asked about information contained in his resume reporting that he was employed by Smokey Jim's from January through May 2012, Mr. Roumain testified:

> *Yes. I did it so I could find a job. Because once you've been terminated in the past I wasn't sure if they would be still willing to give a good reference, so I had to think of a way to be creative and find a way to get a job because I'm a hard worker and I spent 4 years without work, so I had to find a way to get a job. It's all incorrect. No, that is not correct.*

Date	Employer	Job Title	Mr. Roumain Wrote
	Jagger's		Interviewed or Response
	Music Café		Interviewed or Response
	Long Key Resort & Marina		Interviewed or Response
	Fancy Suites		Interviewed or Response
	Over Easy		Not interviewed, received application
	M Hotel		Applied
	The Shore House		Applied
	Lots-O-Meat	Cook	"Recent"
5/27/13	Happy Chicken		"Recent"
6/2/13	Café Brunch	Line Cook	"Recent"
6/9/13		Line Cook (Craigslist)	"Recent"

Figure 7.2. No E-mail Correspondence

Mr. Roumain reported the following income to the Internal Revenue Service:

Year	Wages, Salaries, Tips, Etc	Business Income or Loss	Unemployment Compensation
2007	$40,450		
2008	$37,280		
2010		$2,934	$15,850

Earnings records from W2 Wage and Tax statements. These documents indicate Mr. Roumain was paid the following Medicare wages and tips:

2008	$37,280
2009	$19,712 (he also received unemployment compensation in the amount of $4,500
2012	$ 960

Review of Medical Records

Assessments

05/13/09 *Gilbert Anthony, MD*

Chief Complaint:
Dizzy x 3-4 days.
History:
Dizziness when standing to lying.

06/06/11 *Gilbert Anthony, MD*

Chief Complaint:
C/o dizziness with movement.

03/08/12 *Gilbert Anthony, MD*

Chief Complaint:
URI, dizziness, nausea.
History of Present Illness:
52-year-old male presents dizziness x 1 day.
Assessment:
Allergic rhinitis.
Vertigo.
Plan:
Meclizine 25 mg 1 po tid.

04/18/12 *Gilbert Anthony, MD*

Chief Complaint:

C/o vertigo, nausea, gait instability.

Assessment:

Nystagmus, vertigo.

Vertigo.

07/13/12 *Gilbert Anthony, MD*

Chief Complaint:

Dizziness on/off months.

07/17/12 *Gilbert Anthony, MD*

Chief Complaint:

Vertigo/labyrinthitis.

Symptoms of vertigo nystagmus.

07/23/12 *Gilbert Anthony, MD*

Medical Certification for Disability Exceptions

Comments:

Melissa Impalloneri, ARNP-BC, nurse practitioner, who was employed by Chandler Medical Center until March 2011. She is now working for the Veterans Affairs Clinic. There are multiple providers in the family walk-in setting. Mr. Roumain has been evaluated by two providers and MD Raymond Dixon.

Has the applicant's disability and/or impairment(s) lasted, or do you expect it to last, 12 months or more? Yes.

The etiology of vertigo/labyrinthitis cause, onset, duration can be related to inflammatory, viral, or bacterial causes as well as closed head injury. On two separate occasions exacerbation of symptoms preceded by an upper respiratory infection.

Results of Preincident Diagnostic Testing

10/17/05 *Mark Miller, MD*

Chest

Impression:

No acute process.

Preincident Assessments

02/11/08 *Gilbert Anthony, MD*

Comments:

Patient having pain in both ears. He had this pain 2 months ago, and it resolved. Now it has come back for the last 3 days. Pain is burning in nature and it hurts when he touches the outside.

EtOH 12/week.

Summary and Impressions

Born in Haiti, Mr. Roumain testified he immigrated to the United States in July 1994. Although he testified that he completed the sixth grade in Haiti and has no other education or credentialing, he represented on a resume that he has a high school education and attended college in Haiti. From 1997 through the time of his termination in March 2009, OutSideBar employed Mr. Roumain; his terminal position was kitchen supervisor, and he was compensated $15 per hour.

The only posttermination employment Mr. Roumain identified during his July 5, 2013, deposition were jobs as a line cook at Seafood Haus from April through July 2009, when the restaurant closed; and Cromwell's British Pub, from May through November 2012. Mr. Roumain indicated he collected unemployment compensation during the time between his employment with Seafood Haus and Cromwell's British Pub. He was unemployed at the time of his July 2013 deposition.

Mr. Roumain was able to secure a line cook job soon after he left OutSideBar. His employment with Seafood Haus, the restaurant that hired him in April 2009, ended for reasons unrelated to his March 2009 severance from OutSideBar.

Mr. Roumain described a "disease" he is associating with his severance from OutSideBar. The primary symptom he described is dizziness. I am unaware of any specific work-related medical restrictions specified for Mr. Roumain, age 53.

The job search records I reviewed are scant, unimpressive, and not supportive of one who has conducted a good-faith job search. Assuming Mr. Roumain conducted a good-faith job search, I would have expected him to be capable of securing a food service job within a period of 1 to 3 months, as he did after his severance from OutSideBar. Mr. Roumain received considerable unemployment compensation, and he is also pursuing a claim in which he is seeking monetary damages. These types of factors are disincentives to resuming employment and adversely affect one's motivation to secure reemployment.

Labor market research I conducted included use of job availability data compiled by Wanted Analytics and the Bureau of Labor Statistics. I also independently researched current job opportunities for which Mr. Roumain is qualified.

Briefly, my research determined approximately 50,000 job postings for positions in the restaurant industry were announced in South Florida between April 10, 2009, and January 5, 2013. Additionally, during the period of March 4, 2010, through January 31, 2011, there were approximately 29,800 job postings in South Florida for positions in the restaurant industry. Examples of the types of jobs announced for which Mr. Roumain would have been qualified to pursue included first line supervisor of food preparation and serving workers; waiters; combined food preparation and serving workers including fast food; cooks, restaurant; food preparation workers; baristas; dining room and cafeteria attendants and bartender helpers; and cooks, short order.

As noted above, Mr. Roumain secured a job as a line cook within a month of his severance from OutSideBar. Assuming he conducted a good-faith job search effort in July 2009, when his employment as a line cook with Seafood Haus ended, within a reasonable degree of vocational rehabilitation probability, he would have been able to secure new employment within a period of 1 to 3 months. I estimate his earning capacity at the time of workplace reentry in 2009 would have been in the range of $13 to $15 per hour. Further, assuming Mr. Roumain would have reentered the workplace in late 2009 at a rate of pay less than $15, I believe he would have been able to fully mitigate any differential between his earnings and what his earnings would have been, had his employment with OutSideBar not ended, within a period of 1 to 2 years.

Michael Shahnasarian, Ph.D. Date
Certified Rehabilitation Counselor #3701
Certified Vocational Evaluator #58360
Certified Life Care Planner #258
Licensed Psychologist PY5644
Fellow, National Career Development Association
Fellow, International Academy of Life Care Planner

Chapter 9

Assessment of Earning Capacity in Family Law Cases

Synopsis

9.1 Introduction

Family law disputes are generally argued to a judge, grand master, or arbitrator who serves as the sole trier of fact. In this forum, the trier of fact rules on alimony; a partial basis for this determination often relates to the earning capacity of one or both spouses. Occasionally, a judge will need to impute or ascribe an earning capacity for a spouse. This situation generally arises when evidence suggests spouses have not fully converted their earning capacity.

A vocational evaluation in a family law case may involve either spouse. Its purposes include establishing a baseline earning capacity for a judge's reference when (1) determining alimony and (2) adjusting alimony the higher wage earner or financially advantaged spouse will be ordered to pay. Occasionally, vocational evaluations commence after a marriage's dissolution, pursuant to a spouse's petition for an adjustment of a previously determined alimony. These petitions generally emanate from a claim that the preestablished alimony amount is unfair and unduly burdensome because it was based on an earning capacity standard that no longer represents a spouse's current earning capacity.

9.2 Central Vocational Questions

Vocational evaluations in family law disputes typically address the following questions:

- Considering family responsibilities and other personal factors assessed when developing a vocational profile, what is the earning capacity of the spouse who is the subject of an earning capacity assessment?
- Would retraining increase the earning capacity of a spouse who is the subject of an earning capacity assessment? If so, what is the length and cost? What type of employment and commensurate earnings would be available after retraining?

A. Earning Capacity Determination

Like other evaluations undertaken to determine earning capacity, the methods outlined in Chapter 4 apply in family law cases. The earning capacity considerations listed in Chapter 5 also relate to assessments of a spouse's ability to pursue future career development.

Because of the cost of a vocational evaluation and the relative values at stake, assessments of earning capacity in family law cases occur most often in cases involving families with above-average net worth. Correspondingly, the vocational evaluator often finds that the subject of an earning capacity assessment has not had recent employment, or has had some form of employment or work activity that underrepresents earning capacity. In cases where a spouse has not fully participated in the workplace proximate to the time of a vocational evaluation, the evaluator should take a broader perspective of the spouse's vocational profile by assessing previously demonstrated abilities, transferable skills, and latent vocational capacity. As in all assessments of earning capacity, the vocational evaluator should consider how availability of financial resources may be affecting a spouse's vocational behavior. Financial motivations, like other external influences, can range widely in degree—from potential disincentives to highly motivating influences.

Occasionally, a vocational evaluation is initiated when one spouse petitions for an adjustment in alimony after a divorce has been finalized. The adjustment request, which typically occurs years after a marriage's dissolution, is often advanced because a spouse claims to have experienced a diminution in earning capacity since the judge initially imputed an alimony amount. For example, an executive who divorced while earning approximately $350,000 was later terminated during a corporate downsizing. He was subsequently unable to secure employment at a compensation level commensurate with the earnings he generated while married. His counsel argued for an alimony adjustment to reflect his current compensation—approximately two-thirds less than what he previously earned. Alternately, his ex-wife's counsel argued the former husband's earning capacity was greater than it had been during the marriage, and that the ex-husband was not motivated to maximize his earning capacity because he became remarried to a woman with considerable wealth. Both the ex-husband's counsel and the ex-wife's counsel retained vocational experts to assess the ex-husband's earning capacity.

After a divorce, some spouses relocate. Evaluators should consider how wages and labor demands vary by locale. A decision to relocate after becoming divorced is an example of a voluntary decision that may have implications relating to an assessment of earning capacity (please refer to the discussion in Chapter 8 on voluntary and involuntary factors that can affect earning capacity). An evaluator who does not consider such labor market nuances risks losing precision and credibility.

B. Retraining Considerations

Vocational evaluators generally develop scenarios that involve retraining when subjects (a) have suboptimized their career development, (b) have experienced an erosion of previously developed skills for reasons including absence from the workplace, and/or (c) lack substantive skills. Depending on the evaluee's background and vocational profile, assessments of potential for retraining include analyses of previously developed skills and work experiences, educational and vocational accomplishments, and latent abilities.

Assessments of earning capacity in family law cases occasionally concern rehabilitative alimony, a period during which the spouse with the higher earning capacity or greater financial wealth provides financial support to the other spouse to facilitate that spouse's vocational rehabilitation. During the rehabilitative alimony period, the recipient has the burden of converting financial resources awarded into outcomes (e.g., an enhanced career portfolio, job placement) that facilitate maximizing earning capacity. The vocational evaluator contributes to decisions about rehabilitative alimony by identifying viable career goals for the subject, specifying a training plan and costs, and estimating earnings after retraining. Vocational evaluators typically outline the following information in training plans:

- Retraining options
- Time required to complete training
- Costs of training
- Earning capacity at time of labor market entry or reentry
- Career development opportunities after retraining
- Potential employers (when possible to identify)

An excerpt from a report about proposed rehabilitative alimony follows. The subject's career portfolio included a two-year, hospital-based ophthalmic technician training program, an occupation she performed for approximately fourteen years before she chose to withdraw from the workplace and focus on family activities and volunteer work. Her certification had lapsed, and she had not been employed for approximately five years.

> Ms. Mahanian is a high school graduate who completed a bachelor of arts degree in art history and a two-year ophthalmic technician preparatory program at Yerevan Hospital. She subsequently became certified in this capacity and worked as an ophthalmic technician for fourteen years. The credentials Ms. Mahanian reported attaining as an eye care professional have lapsed. Based on her presentation and my research, she does not possess current skills or credentials that qualify her for employment within the eye care industry. Ms. Mahanian is a younger individual (age 40) who has no known physical or psychological problems that interfere with her ability to pursue her career development. She impressed me as a self-assured, articulate, confident, and optimistic individual. Results of testing indicate Ms. Mahanian's level of mental functioning is in the bright normal range. The Joint Commission on Allied Health Personnel and Ophthalmology awards the ophthalmic medical assistant credential at three levels: Certified Ophthalmic Assistant, Certified Ophthalmic Technician, and Certified Ophthalmic Medical Technologist. Recertification is on an individual basis and can be accomplished through approved courses, self-study programs, reviewing video recordings, and reading articles. Ms. Mahanian would likely require six to twelve months of training to reactivate the credentials she previously held. According to the Bureau of Labor Statistics, median wages for ophthalmic technicians with one to five years of experience in 2014 ranged from $39,088 to $46,162, annually. This data is based on a wage survey specific to Denver, Colorado. Ophthalmic technicians with

ten years' experience reportedly had annual earnings of $58,948.

9.3 Noteworthy Considerations

Assessments of earning capacity in family law disputes are often among the most emotion-laden (from an evaluation perspective) and contentious (from a legal perspective) that vocational evaluators perform. Intense emotions frequently surface during family law evaluations. Feelings of anger, vindictiveness, guilt, shame, indignation, and fear often arise from common causes of marital discord: infidelity, family-unit breakup, manipulation of children, battles over marital possessions and money, fear of ability to survive and thrive as before, and mental or physical abuse, to name a few.

While issues contributing to the dissolution of a marriage are typically immaterial to a vocational evaluator's earning capacity assessment, the evaluator may encounter manifestations of the marital rift, obliquely or directly. Resistance from a subject during a vocational evaluation, or an evaluee's inordinate focus on the pending divorce, for instance, can signal preoccupation with the marital dissolution and associated dynamics.

Within the context of these broader issues, a vocational evaluator must focus on evaluating earning capacity while placing in perspective subjects' reactions to emotional issues secondary to a divorce and its precipitating events. For example, an evaluator may conclude that a spouse's problems with depression emanate from the situational stress of a pending divorce, and present psychological distress will not affect future career development. Conversely, an evaluator may conclude that longstanding problems with alcoholism and associated personality disorders—central factors related to marital conflict and contributors to a spouse's erratic work history and underachievement—will continue affecting that spouse's future career development. Vocational rehabilitation analyses of these types should integrate available behavioral information.

Entitlement sentiments (discussed in Chapter 8) may also emerge during divorce proceedings; again, this can affect a spouse's motivation toward career development. Emotions fueled by a pending divorce can magnify entitlement sentiments, which vocational evaluators most often encounter in cases of long-term marriages. These sentiments manifest in references to commitments made early during marriages about promised roles and responsibilities, suggestions that one spouse made significant personal or financial sacrifices to facilitate the other's career development, and statements of a spouse's indignation about possibly lowering a standard of living. Vocational evaluators should recognize how entitlement sentiments may affect a spouse's participation in an examination, vocational behavior, and willingness to maximize earning capacity. As in all vocational evaluations, evaluators should assess secondary gain motivations.

Because a divorce usually disrupts the balance of household chores—including child custody and childcare responsibilities—the expert should also assess how proposed vocational activities could affect custody-related responsibilities. Childcare responsibilities can be particularly relevant in instances where children have special needs that restrict a spouse from furthering career development.

In cases where one spouse has been away from the workplace for an extended period, experts should assess skills that may have been developed through alternate activities such as participation in volunteer work, or household chores like managing the family budget. A vocational evaluator, for instance, determined that a spouse who had been quite active in developing educational programming as a volunteer in her church cultivated significant transferable skills in training and development, nonprofit administration, and program development. The evaluator further opined that these skills had value in the local labor market and, accordingly, identified job openings the spouse was qualified to pursue.

9.4 Conclusion

Vocational evaluations in family law cases often include assessments of retraining options and viable career opportunities. Outlining a specific retraining plan can be particularly helpful. Family law evaluations sometimes involve embittered relationships, and subjects' participation in a vocational evaluation is particularly unwelcome.

Appendix 9.1: Sample Report of a Vocational Rehabilitation Evaluation in a Family Law Case Prepared for Daphne Dharma Wilrich by Michael Shahnasarian, Ph.D., May 30, 2014

The sample report that follows facilitated a judge's imputation of a soon-to-be ex-wife's income in a marriage dissolution case. Her approximately 14-year absence from the workplace and age (56) were significant inhibitor factors affecting her vocational rehabilitation. The vocational evaluator's analysis, however, also identified several facilitative factors including a strong, diverse educational background; previously developed transferable skills; high-average performance on a measure of intellectual development; maintenance of credentialing through continuing education; lack of physical, cognitive, or emotional problems; and opportunities to apply previously developed skills in the local workplace.

Included in the vocational evaluator's assessment is a plan to facilitate the examinee's vocational rehabilitation. The plan features a recommendation for retraining including the duration and cost, and identifies jobs the soon-to-be ex-wife would be qualified to pursue after retraining. Wage information is also cited.

A review of this report reveals how the vocational evaluator integrates information from a clinical interview, transferable skills analysis, review of available records, and interpretation of standardized testing. This analysis, supplemented by labor market research, culminates in a plan—with identified timeframes, identification of bona fide job opportunities available to the examinee upon retraining, and wage information—to enable the examinee to optimize her earning capacity.

Overview

Daphne Dharma Wilrich was referred to me for a vocational rehabilitation evaluation. Before my exam, I was informed that Ms. Wilrich and her husband are dissolving their marriage.

On May 21 and 24, 2014, I conducted a vocational rehabilitation evaluation of Ms. Wilrich at my office in Tampa. My examination consisted of a clinical interview, which required approximately 2 hours and 45 minutes on May 21, 2014, and the administration of a battery of tests that required an additional 3 hours and 35 minutes for her to complete. Aaron Hill from my office assisted with the testing portion of my exam.

I met alone with Ms. Wilrich on May 21, 2014. She noted she has a valid driver's license and that she drove from her home in Wesley Chapel to my office. Ms. Wilrich denied having physician-advised driving restrictions or any problems with driving.

Ms. Wilrich apprised me she is unemployed and that her last full-time employment was on July 3, 1995, when she worked as a recovery nurse in a medical center in Arlington, Virginia. She reported she subsequently worked intermittently as a recovery nurse until March 1998. Ms. Wilrich denied having any subsequent employment. "I did do a lot of volunteer work at Tampa Palms," she added.

Although Ms. Wilrich did not identify any medical problem that would prohibit her from working, she told me she has spinal stenosis. "It's not a daily thing. Every once in a while it flares up," she said. She elaborated she occasionally experiences neck pain with left-upper-extremity radiculopathy, "like once every couple months, and then it will resolve on its own. Sometimes a heating pad will help with it." Ms. Wilrich also advised me, "I do have high blood pressure." Again, she denied that her problems with spinal stenosis affect her ability to work.

Ms. Wilrich denied having a cognitive impairment. I inquired whether she has any psychological or emotional difficulties that would restrict her ability to work, and she responded negatively.

Vocational Activity

I reviewed with Ms. Wilrich information about her educational background and work history, obtained from a copy of her resume. She verified the information was accurate and conveyed she completed a bachelor's degree in nursing in 1979 and a master's degree in nursing in 1986.

Additionally, Ms. Wilrich noted she earned a juris doctorate degree in 1992. "I just wanted to go to law school to learn more, to be an educated person," she said about her law school studies. Ms. Wilrich went on to offer, "I never dreamed to be a lawyer," apprising me she never practiced as one. Despite her law school education, she informed me, she has never used it in a job.

Other training Ms. Wilrich completed, she reported, related to real estate. "The real estate was purely because of our real estate investments. It was on the advice of our accountant," she said. She told me she became a licensed realtor in 2005.

Ms. Wilrich indicated her only activity as a realtor involved "finding renters for our property [a house in Wesley Chapel]." She went on to advise me she listed the property she owned but never had a customer. Ms. Wilrich conveyed her real estate license remains active; however, she noted her experiences as a realtor have been nominal.

Again, Ms. Wilrich's last employment, which was part time, was as a recovery room nurse in 1998. Although she apprised me she has maintained her RN licenses in Indiana and Wisconsin through continuing medical education, she reported she has not maintained her clinical nursing skills. Ms. Wilrich told me she has never held an RN license in Florida.

Regarding her absence from the workplace since March 1998, Ms. Wilrich cited her "kids" and noted the birth of her children in 1995 and 1998. She indicated she has focused her efforts on raising her children and that her husband's time was consumed with his surgical practice; hence, she noted, his contributions to child development activities were sparse.

Ms. Wilrich advised me she had not considered returning to work before the onset of her marital difficulties and that she prefers not to reenter the workplace at this time. She conveyed that her preference is to remain at home, focusing her efforts on raising her children. "Sir, that's all I've ever done," she said during this discussion.

During my exam, Ms. Wilrich acknowledged she is capable of working. I inquired whether she believes, if retrained, that she could resume her prior job as a recovery room nurse, and she said, "I believe so, yes sir."

I engaged Ms. Wilrich in a discussion about career options that are viable for her to pursue. She said, "I don't know if I really want to study for the Bar exam again." She went on to cite her age of 56 and her understanding about a surplus of lawyers in the local labor market.

We also discussed Ms. Wilrich's prior career development as a nurse, and she stated, "That's all I know." She informed me she has not considered other career options.

Ms. Wilrich did not recall her terminal rate of pay when she left the workplace in March 1998. She noted her highest annual earnings were approximately $40,000 circa 1995. I asked her what she believes she is currently capable of earning, presuming she pursues retraining as a nurse, and she replied, "I don't know."

At the conclusion of my clinical interview, I discussed with Ms. Wilrich alternate occupations that would make use of her composite skills, such as a medicolegal nurse records reviewer, risk management administrator, and occupational health nurse. She expressed interest in all of these occupations.

Records Reviewed

Records from the following sources were reviewed with this evaluation:

- Resume
- Registered nurse, professional development records
- Supreme Court of Indiana Attorney Registration card
- Realtor, professional development records

Background Information

The following background information was obtained from records and my clinical interview:

FULL NAME:	Daphne Dharma Wilrich
DATE OF BIRTH:	February 16, 1958
REASON FOR EXAM:	Dissolution of marriage
RACE:	Caucasian
DOMINANT HAND:	Right
HEIGHT:	5 feet 9 inches
MARITAL STATUS:	Separated/dissolving, Robert Wilrich, MD
NAMES AND AGES OF CHILDREN:	Olivia, 18 Caleb, 15
RESIDENCE:	Wesley Chapel, Florida
PRESENTING PROBLEMS:	Spinal stenosis, occasional flare-ups Occasional neck pain with left-upper-extremity radiculopathy
SURGERY:	Removal of ovarian cyst, 1990 Growth removed from left lower extremity, spring 1993 Dilation and curettage (D & C), October 1994 Cesarean-section deliveries, November 1995 and September 1998 Hernia repair and hemorrhoidectomy, spring 2001 Laparoscopic hysterectomy, 2005
PRESENT TREATMENT:	None
TREATING PROFESSIONALS:	Dr. Cunningham, ophthalmologist Dr. MacArthur, internist Dr. Jane, gynecologist Dr. Rachel, retina specialist Ms. Jefferson, physician assistant specializing in dermatology
MEDICATIONS:	Lipitor, elevated cholesterol Hydrochlorothiazide, hypertension Quinapril, hypertension Low-dose aspirin Vitamin D
EDUCATION:	BS degree, nursing, Saint Leonard University, 1979 Registered Nurse license (IN), 1979, currently active, IN and WI MS degree, nursing, Watson University of Chicago, 1986 JD degree, Baxter University, 1992 Passed Indiana Bar exam, 1992, IN attorney's license inactive

Ron White School of Real Estate, Inc., Florida Real Estate Sales Associate Licensing, Post-Licensing Education, and Continuing Education, 2005 to Present
Continuing medical education

PRESENT WORK STATUS: Unemployed, Homemaker

LAST EMPLOYMENT: Part-time Recovery Room Nurse, 1998; last full-time employment: Recovery Room Nurse, July 1995

Clinical Interview

Introduction

Daphne Dharma Wilrich presented as a Caucasian female who has brown hair and brown eyes. She appeared younger than her stated age of 56. Ms. Wilrich noted she was wearing contact lenses, and she apprised me her corrected vision is clear.

During my exam, Ms. Wilrich had a normal gait and repositioned normally while seated. Contact lenses were the only adaptive aid she used during my exam.

Ms. Wilrich reported she is right hand dominant and 5 feet 9 inches tall. She told me she "put on a tremendous amount of weight after I had children."

In September 1991, Ms. Wilrich indicated, she and Robert Wilrich, MD, married; she advised me this has been her only marriage. Again, they are dissolving their marriage. Ms. Wilrich conveyed that Dr. Wilrich is employed as a cardiac surgeon.

As for children, Ms. Wilrich noted she has two: an 18-year-old daughter and a 15-year-old son. She apprised me her children are healthy and do not have disabling problems. "They're National Honors [Students]," Ms. Wilrich stated, reporting her children have demonstrated strong scholastic performance.

I inquired about child custody arrangements, and Ms. Wilrich said, "There's nothing formalized," although she told me she is the primary custodial parent. She indicated her son stays with his father every Friday and Saturday night, and every other Monday night. Ms. Wilrich anticipated she will continue to be the primary custodial parent after her divorce has finalized. During this discussion, she offered, "I have raised these kids single-handed."

Ms. Wilrich advised me she lives in the marital home and plans to remain there. After her son turns 18 years old, she noted, she may consider relocating to the Chicago area, where many of her family members reside. She described her home as a two-story, approximately 3,200-square-foot house where she lives with her two children.

Physical Condition and Medical Information

Again, Ms. Wilrich denied having any medical problems or restrictions that affect her work capacity. Regarding her medical history, she identified the following surgeries: removal of ovarian cyst (1990), growth removed from the distal area of her left lower extremity (spring 1993), dilation and curettage procedure (October 1994), two cesarean-section deliveries (November 1995 and September 1998), hernia repair and hemorrhoidectomy (spring 2001), and a laparoscopic hysterectomy (2005).

Ms. Wilrich recounted her diagnoses of spinal stenosis and hypertension. She conveyed a retina specialist she saw in summer 2013 found she has elevated intraocular pressure, "and that's when they found I had cotton ball spots [affecting my vision], but that's since resolved."

In July 2013, Ms. Wilrich informed me, her physicians suspected she was experiencing renal failure, and she underwent a renal ultrasound. "That came back OK. They thought it was maybe stress, and I wasn't drinking enough water; that was affecting my creatine levels," she said.

I presented a pain diagram to Ms. Wilrich near the onset of my exam, after she apprised me of her problems with spinal stenosis. She noted she was not experiencing pain while conversing with me and that the document was irrelevant.

Ms. Wilrich apprised me the following medical professionals are treating her: Drs. Cunningham (ophthalmologist), MacArthur (internist), Jane (gynecologist), and Rachel (retina specialist), and also Ms. Jefferson (physician assistant specializing in dermatology). As for future medical appointments, Ms. Wilrich reported she would see Dr. MacArthur next on January 29, 2014. She denied participating in any active treatment or therapy, and no adaptive aids were identified.

Concerning medications and supplements, Ms. Wilrich told me she takes Lipitor, hydrochlorothiazide, quinapril, low-dose aspirin, and vitamin D. She did not identify any medication side effects. Ms. Wilrich indicated she had taken her medication regimen during the 24 hours before my exam.

When asked about physical capacities, Ms. Wilrich advised me she is able to safely lift and carry at least 50 pounds. She denied having physician-advised lifting restrictions or problems with lifting.

Although Ms. Wilrich did not cite problems with any cervical spine movements, she conveyed she occasionally has crepitation in her neck. She denied having limitations with using any of her limbs.

During my exam, Ms. Wilrich demonstrated she could touch each finger to her thumb on either hand, make a fist with either hand, and extend her arms horizontally and overhead without problems. She informed me her fine motor functioning is intact in both hands.

Ms. Wilrich referenced her large body habitus and said, "My limitations are what someone my size would have." She denied being exempt from any functional activity. Ms. Wilrich offered: "If I'm sitting for a couple of hours, after I get up, my knees are stiff for awhile, and then they get better. It's not bad. It's just [body] size-related." She went on to express she tends to lag behind her children when walking, for example, at theme parks.

Generally, Ms. Wilrich noted, she is not limited in the duration she is able to walk, stand, or sit comfortably. She apprised me she operates a motor vehicle daily.

The only other physical problem Ms. Wilrich identified related to her sense of smell. She stated, "I don't think I smell as good as my kids." She specifically denied having problems with balance or fatigue. Ms. Wilrich did not cite any physician-advised restrictions. She assessed that her condition is stable.

Activities of Daily Living

I inquired about difficulty sleeping, and Ms. Wilrich replied: "I wake up a lot. My husband always used to say I have sleep apnea." She went on to state, "I think my sleep has improved since he's gone."

Usually, Ms. Wilrich reported, she goes to sleep between 9:00 and 10:00 p.m., and awakens at 5:30 a.m. She told me she naps infrequently, and she denied taking sleep aid medication.

Ms. Wilrich indicated she has problems with nightmares. I asked about a recurrent theme, and she cited structural problems with her home, "and a lot of people from my past, like friends and stuff." Ms. Wilrich advised me she tends to have nightmares more frequently "when I have court stuff." She conveyed she is independent in grooming and self-care.

Regarding household chores, Ms. Wilrich informed me she is able to perform the full range without problems. She noted she previously employed a housekeeper, although she apprised me she terminated the service in July 2013 "for financial reasons." Ms. Wilrich reported she employs yard and pool maintenance services.

As for hobbies and leisure activities, Ms. Wilrich said, "I read a lot." She told me she enjoys reading magazines and nonfiction, especially biographies. Ms. Wilrich responded negatively when I inquired whether she reads professional materials. She indicated that transporting her children to their extracurricular activities consumes much of her time.

I asked Ms. Wilrich about her average day. She advised me that, after awakening, she helps her children with preparing for their school days. She conveyed she drives her daughter to her school and her son to where he meets a carpool for school.

Ms. Wilrich informed me her marriage dissolution consumes much of her time. Other activities of daily living she identified involved housekeeping activities. "I leave the house at 2:00 p.m. to get in the carpool line at Plant IB," she said, noting, "I pick up my daughter at 3:00 p.m. on my carpool days."

Concerning how she spends her afternoons and evenings, Ms. Wilrich said, "It's kid-related." She went on to say, "This is a stressful time for them, so I want to be there for them." Ms. Wilrich apprised me she prepares the dinner meal. She reported she has a supportive network of friends.

Mental Health

Ms. Wilrich told me she saw a psychologist when she was approximately 28 years old and that the treatment related to the dissolution of a relationship while she was in law school. No other mental health treatment was identified. Ms. Wilrich denied ever being prescribed antidepressants or other psychotropic drugs. She expressed her belief that she does not currently need mental health treatment.

I asked Ms. Wilrich about the onset of her marital difficulties, and she specified February 2013. She denied participating in any mental health treatment associated with the dissolution of her marriage.

Regarding her overall psychological status, Ms. Wilrich said: "It's good he's out of the house. He was very hostile and destructive." She became tearful and emotional during this discussion.

I inquired whether she is experiencing any mental health concerns or problems, and Ms. Wilrich replied: "At times, mild anxiety. I guess it's external events, just the process of it [dissolving my marriage]."

Ms. Wilrich was pleasant, personable, and likable. She was also cooperative, well spoken, and interpersonally skilled. Her cognition was intact, and her memory and concentration were good. Ms. Wilrich spoke clearly and coherently. She did not display problems with either expressive or receptive language, and she showed no evidence of a thought disorder.

Education and Special Training

Ms. Wilrich said about her scholastic performance: "I did well. I worked full time and went to law school at night. The same thing with the master's [degree], too." She did not recall her scores from prior standardized testing.

In 1979, Ms. Wilrich noted, she earned a bachelor of science degree in nursing at St. Leonard University and became a registered nurse (RN) in Indiana the same year. She apprised me she currently holds active RN licenses in Indiana and Wisconsin, and she reiterated she has never been licensed as an RN in Florida. We reviewed documentation of continuing medical education Ms. Wilrich completed in April 2013.

Ms. Wilrich reported she earned a master of science degree in nursing at Watson University of Chicago in 1986. In 1992, she indicated, she earned a juris doctorate degree at Baxter University and passed the Indiana Bar exam the same year; she advised me her Indiana attorney's license is inactive.

Beginning in 2005 and continuing to date, Ms. Wilrich advised me, she has attended Ron White School of Real Estate, Inc., and obtained a Florida real estate license. Further, she conveyed she has had post-licensing and continuing realtor education.

Regarding work-related credentials, I inquired about the possibility of obtaining a reciprocal RN license in Florida, and she stated: "I began an application process." She expressed her understanding she will likely be required to take a nurse refresher course and stated, "I think it's mandatory because I've been out [of clinical practice as a nurse] for so long."

A Supreme Court of Indiana Attorney Registration card notes that Ms. Wilrich was inactive in 2013. A State of Indiana Department of Financial and Professional Regulation document indicates that Ms. Wilrich is a registered professional nurse; the license expires on May 31, 2014.

When asked about on-the-job training, Ms. Wilrich cited general patient care and monitoring patients after various surgeries, for example, related to transplants, orthopedics, and burn injuries. The preoperative and postoperative experiences she described involved pediatric and adult patients. She informed me she has access to a computer, and is able to correspond by e-mail and browse the Internet. Ms. Wilrich noted she is not familiar with Microsoft programs.

Ms. Wilrich denied possessing skills as a lawyer or realtor. "My skills as a realtor are: I can fill out a lease," she said. Because she has not worked as a nurse since March 1998, she recounted, she has not maintained her clinical nursing skills.

I inquired about work-related skills she currently possesses, and Ms. Wilrich responded, "I think I do well socially." She went on to report she tends to be well organized and has good attention to detail. "I have a good memory. I'm generally pretty easy going. I'm pretty adaptable," Ms. Wilrich added.

Ms. Wilrich recalled possessing the following skills as an RN:

- Starting IVs and administering medications
- Preparing patients for surgeries
- Catheterizing patients
- Charting
- Monitoring medical equipment including pulse oximeters and body fluid output
- Transporting patients

As for retraining, Ms. Wilrich expressed interest in enhancing her computer skills. She told me she is also investigating obtaining an RN license in Florida. She expressed that raising her children supersedes any of her career development aspirations. "I don't feel like I'm done raising my kids yet. They're doing well in school because of me," Ms. Wilrich stated.

Career Development

The following work history was obtained from records:

Job Title	*Name of Organization*	*Dates*
Part-time Registry Nurse, Recovery Room Nurse	Arlington Medical Center	Intermittently, 1995 – 3/1998
Staff (Recovery Room) Nurse	Arlington Medical Center	1994 – 7/3/1995
Nursing Instructor	University of Virginia	1994
Nurse Clinician	General Hospital	1992 – 1994
Staff Nurse	University Medical Center	1981 – 1992
Staff Nurse	County Hospital	1979 – 1981

Ms. Wilrich denied ever being terminated from a job or claiming workers' compensation benefits. "My husband never encouraged me to work until all of this [onset of our marital problems]. Our accountant said it wasn't financially worth it [for me] to work. The reason I'm here today is because he [Dr. Wilrich] doesn't want to pay me alimony," Ms. Wilrich said. She went on to reiterate she had been quite active in her children's activities throughout her marriage.

Apprising me she never aspired to reenter the workplace, Ms. Wilrich noted she intended, after her children left for college, "to do more volunteer work." She responded affirmatively when I inquired about her prior job satisfaction as a nurse. "Right out of nursing school I went into ICU. I liked the intensity of it. I liked just having one or two people you could really focus on," Ms. Wilrich stated. She reported her prior performance reviews were positive.

Ms. Wilrich expressed uncertainty about her vocational rehabilitation. She told me she has not applied for a job since leaving the workplace in March 1998. She indicated her realtor license is affiliated with 20th Century Realty in Clearwater. Ms. Wilrich denied having current plans to begin a job search.

Concerning her financial situation, Ms. Wilrich described it as strained. I inquired about her sources of income, and she advised me her estranged husband provides her $1,200 per month in addition to paying her mortgage and utilities.

Results of Testing

The Multidimensional Aptitude Battery-II (MAB-II) was used to assess Ms. Wilrich's intellectual skills and abilities. Scores from this instrument are presented relative to a normative sample.

The MAB-II Verbal, Performance, and Full Scale scores are converted to deviation IQ scores that are based upon an average score of 100 with a standard deviation of 15. The scores express where an individual's score falls in relation to the average score. Additionally, the MAB-II subscales are converted to T-scores that are based upon an average score of 50 with a standard deviation of 10. For example, a score of 60 on the MAB-II would indicate a performance that is one standard deviation above average relative to the individual's peer group, and a score of 40 would indicate a performance that is one standard deviation below average relative to the individual's peer group.

Overall, Ms. Wilrich scored as follows on the MAB-II:

Verbal IQ	112
Performance IQ	123
Full Scale IQ	117

Ms. Wilrich's performance placed her in the high average range of mental functioning. Her individual scores on the MAB-II subscales are summarized below:

Information	54
Comprehension	60
Arithmetic	54
Similarities	59
Vocabulary	59
Digit Symbol	56
Picture Completion	55
Spatial	64
Picture Arrangement	65
Object Assembly	69

The Grooved Pegboard is a manipulative dexterity test used in the selection of employees for industrial jobs such as assembler, machine operator, and other manual jobs. This test measures finger and manual dexterity, and requires complex visual-motor coordination. Below are Ms. Wilrich's scores:

	Score	*Normative Comparison Data*
Dominant Hand (R)	80 seconds	mean = 68.10 seconds (SD = 9.42)
Nondominant Hand	76 seconds	mean = 74.70 seconds (SD = 10.51)

On the Beck Depression Inventory-II, Ms. Wilrich generated a total score of 10, which corresponds to the minimal range of depression.

Results of personality testing from the MMPI-2 were valid. Ms. Wilrich's clinical scale scores were within normal limits. She appears to have an average interest in being with others, and she is not socially isolated or withdrawn. No diagnostic considerations are warranted on the bases of Ms. Wilrich's profile. She scored within normal limits on measures of depression and anxiety.

On the Self-Directed Search Form R, Ms. Wilrich scored highest on the Social occupational theme. This theme is most often associated with occupations the involve promoting the health, education, and welfare of others. Ms. Wilrich rated her scientific and teaching abilities, understanding of others, and managerial and manual skills as above average. The occupations she noted interest in pursuing most recently were "mom," "RN," and "risk management." Among the occupations from the Self-Directed Search Form R that correspond with Ms. Wilrich's profile are Nurse, Instructor (DOT #075.124-018), Nurse, School (DOT #075.124-010), Nurse, Head (DOT #057.137-014), Nurse, Supervisor (DOT #075.167-010), Nurse, Staff, Occupational Health Nursing (DOT #075.374-022), Psychometrist (DOT #045.067-018), Industrial Relations Director (DOT #166.117-010), and Health Officer, Field (DOT #168.167-018).

Summary and Impressions

1. Along with bachelor's and master's degrees in nursing, Ms. Wilrich holds a juris doctorate degree. Ms. Wilrich informed me she has never applied her law school education in the workplace. Most of her work experiences relate to clinical nursing in hospital environments. Ms. Wilrich's last full-time employment, a job as a recovery room nurse, was in 1995, and her last part-time employment was as a recovery room nurse in 1998, she conveyed. Although she has since performed volunteer work, Ms. Wilrich advised me she has not had any gainful employment since 1998, and her efforts have concentrated on raising her two children. She continues to hold active RN licenses in Indiana and Wisconsin, which she has maintained through continuing medical education. Additionally, Ms. Wilrich holds an active Florida Realtor license; she noted her experiences as a realtor have been nominal. Based on my understanding of the type of hospital-based nursing work she formerly performed, she performed skilled, light/medium exertion tasks. The highest annual earnings she generated, she recalled, were approximately $40,000 circa 1995. Ms. Wilrich expressed interest in enhancing her computer skills, and noted she is investigating obtaining an RN license in Florida. She conveyed that she had not planned to reenter the workplace, and she expressed her desire not to have to do so. Ms. Wilrich noted she had intended, after her children left for college, "to do more volunteer work."
2. Ms. Wilrich did not present any physical, cognitive, or emotional contraindications to resuming her career development. She is well educated and continues to hold credentials of value in the workplace. Ms. Wilrich demonstrated high average intelligence (Full Scale IQ = 117) on testing administered during my examination. She scored particularly well on measures of visual analysis, social insight, and mental organization and planning. On a personal level, I found Ms. Wilrich pleasant, personable, likeable, and interpersonally skilled. She noted she does not need mental health treatment. Along with her education, training, work experiences, and previously developed transferable skills, these factors are assets to Ms. Wilrich in her career development.
3. Although Ms. Wilrich has a strong, diverse educational background, she has been absent from the workplace for several years and, at age 56, is in an age category the Social Security Administration recognizes as a person of advanced age. Considering her vocational profile and presuming she were motivated to aggressively pursue her career development, I encourage her to consider occupations such as risk management administrator and occupational health nurse. Employment as a medicolegal nurse records reviewer would also be viable. From a practical perspective, my assessment has led me to conclude that Ms. Wilrich's best opportunities to resume her career development would be to return to work as a nurse in areas comparable to her prior employment. To facilitate her vocational rehabilitation, I recommend she pursue a one-semester RN refresher/remediation course offered by St. Petersburg College; the cost of this course is $1,395. Ms. Wilrich will need to secure a Florida RN license. Because she has an active out-of-state RN license, she will need to apply for endorsement with the Florida Board of Nursing; the application and licensing fee is $175. Once Ms. Wilrich completes the requisite retraining and obtains a Florida RN license, she will become a candidate for hospital-based nurse positions. According to the Florida Department of Economic Opportunity, the mean salary for a registered nurse in Hernando, Hillsborough, Pasco, and Pinellas counties in 2013 was $30.78 per hour. The U.S. Bureau of Labor Statistics reported that hourly wages for registered nurses in Tampa/St. Petersburg/Clearwater in 2012 were $30.01. The labor market research I conducted successfully identified several current job opportunities similar to employment Ms. Wilrich previously held. For example, I identified an intensive care nurse position in St. Petersburg offering compensation of $29.71 per hour, and a pre-op/PACU/recovery nurse position at HRC Physicians Group offering $30.00 per hour. I also identified current job opportunities for an RN MICU nurse at Southside Hospital, and a RN ICU position at Bay Area Hospital.

Michael Shahnasarian, Ph.D. Date
Certified Rehabilitation Counselor #3701
Certified Vocational Evaluator #58360
Certified Life Care Planner #258
Licensed Psychologist PY5644
Fellow, National Career Development Association
Fellow, International Academy of Life Care Planners

Chapter 10

Assessment of Earning Capacity in Cases of Long-Term Disability Insurance

Synopsis

10.1 Introduction

Two major economic trends have contributed to increased sales of long-term disability (LTD) insurance products: the longer working life of baby boomers compared with their predecessors, and employers' ongoing cost-containment efforts including curtailing employee benefits such as disability insurance. As the percentage of working Americans over age fifty continues to increase, by extension, a need to extend income protection to older ages has arisen.

An individual's ability to pursue career development—what disability insurance is actually underwriting—is predicated on both health and career-related factors. The primary consumers of individual LTD products have above average employment incomes and typically include physicians, professionals, and business owners.

10.2 Central Vocational Issues

Most LTD providers require medical and financial documentation to validate coverage limits before underwriting policies. To qualify for an LTD benefits claim, policyholders must meet an insurance carrier's standards. Typically, eligibility for a claim has two requirements. First, for a predetermined period (generally twenty-four months), policyholders' disabling problems must be of sufficient severity to preclude them from returning to their regular occupations (sometimes referred to as "own occ"). Then, after the "own occ period," to maintain LTD benefits, a second standard generally applies: Policyholders must be deemed unable to pursue any occupation (sometimes referred to as "any occ") for which they are reasonably capable of pursuing by training, education, or experience. These standards are detailed below.

A. Ability to Pursue Own Occupation

Knowledge of an occupation's requisite work tasks and associated functional requirements is fundamental to any vocational evaluation. When evaluating the merits of a claim for LTD benefits, this analysis is especially important. Because those privately paying to protect their income individually procure LTD policies, determinations about eligibility for benefits tend to be more case-specific than those in other forums.

Disputes about LTD benefits often involve a claimant's essential or important job responsibilities associated with the occupation for which she was insured; several examples presented below highlight this. The crux of a dispute about whether a claimant meets the definition of disabled as defined in an LTD policy often involves interpreting a policyholder's job responsibilities at the time a policy was issued. The importance of a vocational evaluator obtaining as precise an understanding as possible of the job functions a policyholder performed before making a claim for LTD benefits cannot be overstated. As in other cases associated with a claim involving acquired disabilities, a claimant's ability to engage in an occupation's essential or important job responsibilities must be considered with respect to factors such as residual functional capacities and ability to implement workplace modifications.

In a case involving an invasive cardiologist who pursued an LTD claim after a lower-back injury, defense counsel aggressively interrogated a vocational expert about the plaintiff's residual functional capacities and attempts to pursue accommodations. While performing invasive procedures in a cauterization laboratory, the plaintiff conveyed, he was required to wear a twenty-pound lead apron to protect him from harmful radiation used during procedures he conducted. Additionally, he noted he stood with his arms extended for lengthy, unpredictable periods, and contorted his body for unpredictable periods. These working conditions, he related, exacerbated symptoms associated with his lower-back injury and compromised his ability to meet patient standard of care requirements. Accordingly, he asserted that his disabling problems exempted him from performing his occupation as an invasive cardiologist.

Below are excerpts from the vocational expert's deposition, during which he testified that the invasive cardiologist was not a candidate to return to his own occupation. Defense counsel's interrogation focuses on job accommodations—namely use of a lighter lead apron—and assessment of the plaintiff's residual functional capacities. Vocational experts can expect inquiries of these types, discussed in greater detail in preceding chapters, when providing opinions about a subject's ability to perform an occupation at the time LTD insurance was underwritten.

Q. What research did you conduct to help you arrive at your opinions?

A. I consulted some Department of Labor sources just to get some generic information about cardiologists, and I did some research on lead aprons.

Q. Okay. Well let's break that down. What type of research did you do on lead aprons?

A. Some Internet research; that was before meeting Dr. Xiang, because I knew that part of the issue, after reviewing the records, related to the weight of the apron.

Q. And what specifically did you do?

A. I went to the Internet and found suppliers of lead aprons to determine what products were available. I was specifically interested in the weight of the aprons and the protection they offer.

Q. What is your understanding of the weight of the aprons?

A. My understanding is that they vary, depending upon several factors. One is the size of the apron, the length of the apron, and so forth. The lightest one is 2.5 kilograms. I understand they go beyond that weight, as well.

Q. Okay. Now is it your understanding that these aprons come in different sizes and shapes, and makes?

A. Yes.

Q. And it wouldn't surprise you that these aprons could even be customized to a specific individual?

A. No. I know that from my research.

Q. What, if any, efforts did Dr. Xiang make to get one tailored to his needs?

A. He suggested that his ability to do that was limited because of the type of X-ray that he was using and the type of radiation to which he was exposed. So, what he suggested to me is that he did not have that much flexibility concerning reducing the size or bulk of his apron. And he actually brought his lead apron with him to my office. He didn't put it on, but he had it in a bag. He told me wearing his lead apron was especially problematic when he had to hold his arms in front of him. He discussed some things he tried to do during procedures to reduce the mechanical strain on his back, including sitting whenever possible and modifying how he performed his procedures. But it's not just the weight of the apron that he's indicating worsens his back problems. It's also the need to assume contorted positions for indeterminate periods, and then, of course, the unpredictability of a surgery. If there's a complication during surgery, and you think a surgery might take an hour, but it takes much longer than that, Dr. Xiang doesn't have the latitude of taking his lead apron off and resting.

Q. Do you agree that functional capacity evaluations are an accurate way in which to evaluate and objectify claimed physical impairments?

A. They can be helpful, but they have to be considered in toto. For instance, Dr. Xiang could demonstrate, theoretically, in a functional capacity evaluation that he's able to lift and carry twenty pounds. But whether he could do that for several half-hours or hours, or whatever may be required if he has a complication in a surgery is another matter. Or whether he could do that with a lead apron around his neck that alters mechanical strain on his back while in a contorted position is another matter. So, results from a functional capacity evaluation can be helpful, but you have to place the results in a broader perspective that considers the unique functional demands of a job in question.

B. Ability to Pursue Any Occupation

Some LTD policies require policyholders to meet a second standard either to begin receiving LTD benefits or to continue receiving them beyond a specified period (again, policy details tend to vary): this standard usually focuses on whether a subject can perform any occupation. It applies when there is a consensus that the subject cannot return to his own occupation—the occupation recognized as the policyholder's occupation when the insurance was underwritten.

Chapter 6, which relates to conducting assessments of earning capacity in cases of acquired disabilities, includes detailed discussions about assessing work capacity in cases involving people with disabilities. These guidelines (e.g., conducting transferability of skills analyses, evaluating the feasibility of job accommodations, assessing potential for retraining) also apply to cases involving LTD insurance.

Unlike other legal forums involving assessments of earning capacity, several considerations otherwise relevant are either immaterial or less important in a case involving adjudication of a LTD insurance claim. For example, there is generally no pending "onset date" as is customarily associated with personal injury and medical malpractice cases—dates that require a vocational evaluator to obtain precise medical and vocational histories, and involve parsing out preexisting and commingled disabling problems. In a case involving LTD insurance, the vocational evaluator's task is to assess the subject's capacity to pursue work activity while considering the claimant's constellation of presenting problems and associated functional limitations—physical, cognitive, and psychological. The etiology of the disabling problems is generally less important than it is in other legal forums.

The concept of earning capacity remains pertinent in cases involving LTD insurance, but more so as a matter of reference than a matter of compensatory damages. For example, a commercial airline pilot with a head injury and significant visual impairments—while unequivocally incapable of resuming his prior job—may remain capable of unskilled, telephone-based work. While the trier of fact may appreciate that other occupations remain within the former pilot's capacity, the perceived hierarchical difference in skill-set requirements between the occupational categories, along with associated wages, is likely to be too great to treat as a viable "any occupation" when deliberating an LTD insurance policy's parameters.

10.3 Noteworthy Considerations

Like vocational issues pending in other forums, every analysis involving an LTD claim has its nuances and requires perspective. Many issues—including career-related, health-related, and personal issues—can affect an analysis. A vocational expert retained to evaluate a claim for LTD benefits must consider the factors enumerated in the previous discussion about the Earning Capacity Assessment Form-2 (ECAF-2). The methodology prescribed in Chapter 4 is recommended to fully elucidate issues germane to an analysis and to facilitate experts' abilities to transcend superficial vocational issues accompanying a claim. Many concepts presented in previous chapters about assessing earning capacity (e.g., evaluating job requirements and functional capacities, extending workplace accommodations, reengineering work processes, identifying transferable skills, evaluating mitigation efforts) apply to assessments involving claims for LTD benefits.

The following examples are from litigated cases. These examples illustrate several factors, including the diffuse nature of disabling problems that can spawn a claim for LTD benefits and the varied backgrounds of claimants, and how a range of factors not readily apparent—including disincentives to pursue career development and career dissatisfaction—may be affecting a claimant's vocational behavior. Because many policies emphasize ability to pursue one's "own occupation," it is imperative for the vocational evaluator to obtain a thorough understanding of the policyholder's career development and occupation at the time insurance was underwritten and afterward.

- A forty-three-year-old manager of a financial services firm alleged sustaining various orthopedic injuries from a motor vehicle accident. He did not return to work after the accident, and he claimed permanent total disability. Medical support for the claimant's symptoms was weak, and defense counsel generated damaging surveillance information and damaging testimony about the claimant's avocational activities such as regularly playing golf and participating in pornographic movies. Interestingly, the claimant's wife was earning more than $400,000 per year. The claimant had been receiving LTD benefits for three years before his claim was challenged. During a vocational examination, the evaluator constructed a claimant vocational profile that included an irregular earnings history, gaps in employment and mediocre preaccident work propensity, an erratic pattern of career development, and multiple job terminations.
- A fifty-six-year-old dentist practicing in a rural area had been unsuccessfully attempting to sell his practice for nine years before incurring multiple orthopedic injuries when a rack of heavy building materials fell on him while he was a patron in a hardware store. He sold his practice approximately nine months before the incident. Other pertinent details that emerged during a vocational evaluation undertaken with his claim for LTD benefits included the fact that he underwent a radical prostatectomy, with a significant amount of radiation therapy and chemotherapy concomitant with his transition after the sale of his practice, and that he had a noncompete agreement with the buyers of his former practice. After the hardware store incident, he made a claim for LTD benefits and represented his loss of earning capacity as the amount of his highest earnings year as a dentist.
- A forty-year-old internist alleged he was too anxious to perform his job at a veterans hospital and,

therefore, was entitled to LTD coverage because he was unable to pursue his "own occupation." None of the mental health professionals who examined him diagnosed more than an adjustment disorder, which appeared situational and associated with several life stressors he encountered within a twelve-month period. These stressors included his wife's bilateral mastectomy, a cross-country move, and beginning a new job. The claimant took a three-month leave of absence under the Family and Medical Leave Act after his wife's surgery, and then returned to work for less than two weeks before he alleged he was too anxious to perform his job as an internist. He cited patient standard of care concerns associated with his alleged anxiety impairment as a reason he believed himself unable to perform his occupation, and claimed he was owed LTD benefits. The claimant ultimately returned to part-time (less than twenty hours per week) employment in an outpatient rehabilitation clinic; he alleged this level of work participation represented his work capacity. An examiner conducting a vocational assessment determined the claimant had been miscast in his occupation as an internist. That is, his decision to pursue his career development as a physician was not compatible with his vocational profile. The claimant, academically, was a poor high school student who dropped out of school to pursue a GED. He then attended a community college where he buttressed his grade-point average; he was subsequently admitted to an unaccredited medical school. His transcripts revealed marginal performance in the sciences, and occupational interest testing indicated his highest areas of interest were in social services rather than healthcare. Personality testing revealed hypochondriacal and histrionic features. The vocational expert concluded the claimant was likely dissatisfied with his career as an internist and was quite likely attempting to leverage pending circumstances to obtain LTD benefits.

- A restaurant owner in his mid fifties reported a slip-and-fall accident in his bathtub. His restaurant employed twenty to thirty workers, seated 150 patrons, and generated annual revenues of $800,000. The claimant underwent lumbar surgery, and, although no physician determined he was unable to pursue light-duty work, he alleged that he was unable to pursue his "own occupation" as a restaurant owner. Specifically, the claimant alleged that, despite the size of his restaurant, the "important functions" (this was the language used in his policy) of his occupation essentially involved work as a cook, which required standing for extended periods and lifting up to fifty pounds of food. He argued that his culinary talent was key to the success of his restaurant, and he could neither trust nor afford replacement labor to engage in the meal preparation tasks he performed before he became injured. Litigation followed and the case was subsequently tried. Defense counsel argued the insurance company extended an LTD policy to a restaurant owner, not to a cook, and the claimant remained able to perform the "important functions" of a restaurant owner. The claimant exhibited great charisma with the jury during his trial and he prevailed.
- Similar to the case described above, a forty-year-old attorney (interestingly, specializing in insurance defense) made a claim for LTD benefits after undergoing a lumbar procedure. He was riding a bicycle when a dog crossed his path, causing an accident in which he injured his back. Again, a key issue in dispute involved whether the claimant could perform his "own occupation." The claimant alleged he was a "trial lawyer." Because of lumbar problems that precluded him from maintaining either a seated or a standing position for extended periods, as required during trials, he alleged, he was unable to perform the "important functions" of his job. After undergoing surgery, the claimant returned to his law firm and worked twenty hours per week. He alleged that this level of work participation represented his capacity, he was no longer able to engage in trial practice, and that his career advancement opportunities were greatly curtailed. An analysis of the claimant's work history revealed that during his fifteen-year career as an attorney he only tried nine cases, and the longest case was five days. The LTD carrier maintained that their insured was not a "trial lawyer." In fact, the insurer asserted this occupational classification, contrary to what the claimant suggested, does not exist. A vocational expert testified during an acrimonious deposition that the claimant could perform the "important functions" of the occupation for which he was trained and in which he had been working. The case settled three days into the trial.

10.4 Conclusion

Vocational assessments in cases involving LTD insurance claims tend to focus on subjects' ability to return to their "own occupation"—the policyholder's occupation at the time a policy was underwritten. Most policies also include a clause concerning the policyholder's ability to pursue "any occupation"; this latter condition often applies after a specified period during which a policyholder has been deemed unable to pursue one's "own occupation." Many methodological procedures associated with this latter determination are similar to those related to conducting vocational assessments in cases involving acquired disabling problems. Appendix 10.1 contains a sample report in a case involving a claimant pursuing LTD insurance disability benefits.

Appendix 10.1: Sample Report of a Vocational Rehabilitation Evaluation in a Long-Term Disability Insurance Case Prepared for Dean Weisbond by Michael Shahnasarian, Ph.D., February 12, 2010

A dermatological surgeon complained that ongoing, progressively worsening neck, back, and headache problems, along with secondary sequelae, impaired his ability to safely practice his occupation. Accordingly, he ceased performing surgical dermatology and, before pursuing a claim for long term insurance disability benefits, his lawyer referred him to a vocational expert for an assessment.

The vocational evaluator concluded the surgeon was not capable of performing the material and substantial tasks related to his own occupation. Important in reaching this determination was a careful understanding of the surgeon's essential work functions. This information enabled the evaluator to then juxtapose medical assessments and evaluate the compatibility between worker capacities and job requirements.

Some readers may question the need for the vocational expert's analysis, since a neurologist previously assessed the surgeon was not capable of working (please refer to the Review of Medical Records section in the sample report). Opinions related to employability, judges typically rule, fall under the purview of vocational experts rather than physicians; hence the need for a qualified vocational expert opinion on the question of whether the surgeon could perform his own occupation.

Overview

Dean Weisbond, MD, was referred to me for a vocational rehabilitation evaluation. He reported his symptoms, described below, began circa 1996 or earlier. Dr. Weisbond was not aware of any trauma that caused his symptoms. He told me he has been self-employed as a dermatological surgeon specializing in skin cancer since he became board certified in 1978.

On December 27, 2011, I conducted a vocational rehabilitation evaluation of Dr. Weisbond at my office in Tampa. My examination consisted of a clinical interview, which required 2 hours and 15 minutes, and the administration of a battery of tests that required 3 additional hours for him to complete. Aaron Hill from my office assisted with the testing portion of my exam. Dr. Weisbond independently completed an intake form, relying solely upon memory.

I met alone with Dr. Weisbond. He indicated he drove an automatic transmission SUV from his home in Dunedin to my office; he advised me his commute required 1 hour. Dr. Weisbond related he holds a valid driver's license and does not have physician-advised driving restrictions. When asked whether he has problems with driving, he responded affirmatively, citing, "Back, neck pain and headache if long drive; difficulty looking over left shoulder to change lanes."

Dr. Weisbond informed me he experiences the following problems:

- Pain in neck, mid back, and lower back, "not at the same time," and headache with nausea aggravated by bending head forward or backward, stooping, jarring movements, and prolonged standing
- Difficulty sleeping
- Need to take naps during the day due to "constant, extreme" fatigue
- Irritability
- Poor concentration

Regarding mental functioning, Dr. Weisbond cited problems with memory, concentration, mental alertness, and attention span. He elaborated about these problems: "Often can't remember something I read in medical journal several days ago. Often loss of attention when someone speaks. Often fall asleep or mind wanders when watching movie or when pain increases, keep trying to change my posture." Dr. Weisbond conveyed his physicians attribute his cognitive difficulties to his sleep problems.

Vocational Activity

Dr. Weisbond noted he graduated from high school in Quebec, Canada, in 1963. He apprised me he continued his education at Davis University, where he earned two degrees: a bachelor's degree and a medical doctorate degree. Also at Davis, Dr. Weisbond reported, he completed a 3-year internal medicine residency. Then from 1976 to 1978, he told me, he completed a residency in dermatology.

In 1978, Dr. Weisbond indicated, he became board certified as a dermatologist. He advised me he moved from Columbus, Ohio, to Dunedin, Florida, in 1979 and was thereafter self-employed as a surgical dermatologist until mid-December 2010, when he sold his practice.

Dr. Weisbond described how his work participation began to diminish in 2008 or 2009 because of his symptom progression. He related neck, back, and head pain contributed to his reduced work activity.

As for the work tasks he performed, Dr. Weisbond identified taking patient histories, prescribing diagnostic tests (biopsies, blood tests and cultures), interpreting diagnostic test results, diagnosing causes of skin rashes, prescribing interventions (including medication, surgery, and injections), and providing patient education. "I did the bookkeeping. I paid the checks," he said, reviewing other job responsibilities.

Dr. Weisbond informed me he performed his job in a 3,500-square-foot office in Dunedin. Additionally, he conveyed he had a 1,500-square-foot branch office in Ozona, where he worked 1 day per week. He noted he was the only dermatologist in his office. Dr. Weisbond apprised me he employed an office manager, receptionist, two or three medical assistants, and two part-time transcriptionists. Before he began decreasing his work participation, he reported, he worked "45 or 50" hours per week.

Concerning the time demands associated with his self-employment as a surgical dermatologist, Dr. Weisbond estimated 85% of his time involved performing surgeries such as skin cancers, and removal of cysts, moles, precancerous lesions, and skin tags. He told me the remainder of his time involved practice administration and medical dermatology such as conducting skin exams.

Dr. Weisbond indicated the surgeries he performed were quite physically demanding. He advised me he stood over a surgical field for up to 60 minutes while flexing or extending his neck with his arms outstretched. He related he operated daily and would schedule up to three patients "back to back." Occasionally, Dr. Weisbond informed me, he encountered complications while performing surgeries. He conveyed the weight of instruments he handled was usually nominal.

Continuing to perform his job, Dr. Weisbond noted, exacerbated his symptoms. Despite restricting his work participation to 20 to 25 hours per week, he apprised me, he was unable to manage his symptoms. "I even took some time off, doing nothing. I got somewhat better, but the moment I started back, there it was again," he said.

As a dermatological surgeon, Dr. Weisbond reported, his problems with neck pain particularly impaired his ability to work. He went on to reference secondary problems, including fatigue and concentration difficulties, that further reduced his ability to perform his job.

Dr. Weisbond told me he began developing concerns about his patients' safety. He said: "It's a bad sign when you start to think about: What can I do to get comfortable? How can I get out of here as quick as possible?" Dr. Weisbond indicated his concerns about his patients' welfare was a major factor in his decision to leave his practice in December 2010. "It was only a matter of time until something bad would've happened," he said.

Dr. Ronstadt and Dr. Pickford have contraindicated Dr. Weisbond performing surgical dermatology, he advised me. He indicated he has not pursued any work activity since December 2010. "I'm sure I could do something if I could get some sleep and my concentration would improve," he said.

Records Reviewed

Records from the following sources were reviewed with this evaluation:

- Arthritis Center, P.A.
- Gulf Pain Group
- Joint Diseases Medical Center

- Monroe Imaging Center
- New Hampshire School of Medicine
- Stand Up MRI of Maryland
- Lynne Hepburn, DO
- Robert Pickford , MD
- Anthony Ronstadt , MD
- Gary Streep, MD
- Bruce Taylor, MD, Ph.D.
- Big Insurance Disability file
- Big Insurance Denial of Disability Claim letter

Assessment Measures

The following assessment measures were used in this evaluation:

- Clinical Interview
- Client Intake Form
- Patient Pain Diagram
- Wahler Physical Symptoms Inventory
- Grooved Pegboard Test
- Beck Depression Inventory-II
- Self-Directed Search
- MMPI-II
- Shipley Institute of Living Scale

Background Information

Dr. Weisbond provided the following background information:

NAME:	Dean Weisbond
DATE OF BIRTH:	March 14, 1946
ONSET OF DISABLING PROBLEMS:	Symptoms began circa 1996 or earlier
RACE:	Caucasian
DOMINANT HAND:	Left
HEIGHT:	5 feet 10 ½ inches
CURRENT WEIGHT:	165 pounds
MARITAL STATUS:	Single/divorced
NAMES AND AGES OF CHILDREN:	Matthew, 28 Kelly, 26

RESIDENCE:	Dunedin, Florida
PRESENTING PROBLEMS:	Pain in neck, mid back, and lower back, "not at the same time," and headache with nausea aggravated by bending head forward or backward, stooping, jarring movements, and prolonged standing Difficulty sleeping Need to take naps during the day due to "constant, extreme" fatigue Irritability Poor concentration

REPORTED ABILITIES WITH THE FOLLOWING DEFINITIONS:

Never	– Cannot do for any amount of time
Occasionally	– Up to 33% of the time (0.0 - 2.3 hrs/day)
Frequently	– From 34% to 66% of the time (2.3 - 5.5 hrs/day)
Constantly	– More than 67% of the time (5.5 + hrs/day)

Walking	Frequently
Standing	Frequently
Sitting	Frequently
Bending at waist	Occasionally
Squatting	Occasionally
Kneeling or getting on hands/knees	Occasionally
Climbing stairs	Occasionally
Pushing/pulling	Occasionally
Reaching with right hand	Constantly
Reaching with left hand	Constantly
Handling	Constantly
Gripping right hand	Constantly
Gripping left hand	Constantly
Right-arm extension overhead	Occasionally
Left-arm extension overhead	Occasionally
Right-arm extension horizontal	Occasionally
Left-arm extension horizontal	Occasionally
Driving	Occasionally

SURGERY:	Appendectomy, age 4
TREATMENT SINCE ONSET:	Physical therapy Massage therapy Chiropractic treatment Prescribed home exercise Pain management including injections
PRESENT TREATMENT:	Enbrel injections
TREATING DOCTORS:	Anthony Ronstadt, MD, rheumatology Robert Pickford, MD, neurology Seth Blanchet, DPM, podiatry

MEDICATIONS:	Enbrel, joint/back inflammation, psoriasis Excedrin Migraine, headaches Prilosec OTC, gastritis from Excedrin Verapamil, hypertension Tekturna HCT, hypertension Lipitor, cholesterol Tetracycline, rosacea MetroLotion, rosacea Nizoral shampoo, psoriasis Elidel cream, psoriasis Claritin, nasal allergies and sinusitis Nasonex, nasal allergies and sinusitis Avodart, prostatic hypertrophy
EDUCATION:	High school diploma, Quebec, Canada, 1963 BS degree, physiology, Davis University, 1967 MD degree, Davis University, 1971 Ophthalmology residency, 1973-74, did not complete Completed internal medicine residency, 1976 Completed dermatology residency, Toledo University, 1978 Various continuing education courses in dermatology
LAST EMPLOYER:	Self-employed, Dean Weisbond, P.A.
LAST JOB TITLE:	Dermatological Surgeon
LAST RATE OF PAY:	More than $300,000 per year
PRESENT WORK STATUS:	Disabled/unemployed, last employed in mid-December 2010

Clinical Interview

Introduction

Dean Weisbond, MD, presented as a clean-shaven Caucasian male who had graying hair and hazel eyes. He appeared his stated age of 65. Dr. Weisbond told me he wears eyeglasses for distance vision, and he said his corrected vision is "20/20."

During my exam, Dr. Weisbond affirmed my observation his gait was normal. He elaborated, "I can walk without any problems, as long as it's [the surface is] level, and not too fast." Dr. Weisbond did not use adaptive aids during my clinical interview. "The only adaptive aid I use is in the car – it's a lumbar support [pillow]," he said, indicating his physical therapist recommended he use the device. "It has helped a little bit with my driving," he added.

Dr. Weisbond advised me he is left hand dominant, almost 5 feet 11 inches tall, and weighs 165 pounds. He conveyed his weight has been stable. Dr. Weisbond informed me he was born in Germany and that he is a U.S. citizen.

When asked about his marital status, Dr. Weisbond noted he is single/divorced with two prior marriages. He apprised me he has two children: a 28-year-old son and a 26-year-old daughter. He reported his children are healthy.

Regarding his home, Dr. Weisbond indicated he lives in a two-story, 2,100-square-foot condominium he owns.

He advised me he has lived in this home during the past 16 years and does not plan to relocate. Dr. Weisbond related he uses an elevator within his home, and he denied having accessibility limitations in his home environment. He informed me he lives alone and does not have pets.

Physical Condition and Medical Information

As for his understanding of diagnoses physicians have rendered, Dr. Weisbond identified:

- Psoriatic spondylitis and arthritis
- Osteoarthritis in neck and back
- Ruptured discs in back
- Spinal stenosis

Dr. Weisbond conveyed Dr. Ronstadt and Dr. Streep rendered these diagnoses. We reviewed Dr. Pickford's assessments, which are similar.

Other significant medical problems Dr. Weisbond identified were high cholesterol, hypertension, psoriasis, rosacea, enlarged prostate, and sinusitis. The only surgery he identified was an appendectomy at age 4.

Dr. Weisbond conveyed a neurosurgeon, Dr. Bremmer, recommended a cervical fusion circa 1996. He noted no other surgical recommendations have since been made.

Concerning his primary problem, Dr. Weisbond cited: "Pain – made it difficult and dangerous to perform dermatological surgery, made it necessary to retire from my profession (dermatological surgery)."

Dr. Weisbond described how his neck, back, and head pain correlate with his level of activity, and he said, "The more I do, the worse my pain." Using a 0-to-10 scale, with a zero indicating no pain and a 10 representing the worst pain possible, Dr. Weisbond rated his pain intensities:

- Neck – "2 to 9"
- Mid back – "2 to 7"
- Lower back – "2 to 9"
- Head – "1 to 10"

Among the activities and conditions that exacerbate Dr. Weisbond's symptoms, he apprised me, are activities that jar his body, bending his back or neck for more than brief periods, maintaining a position, and stooping/twisting his torso, which he described as particularly problematic. He reported his cervical spine pain radiates into his upper back but not into his upper extremities. Dr. Weisbond described aching sensations he feels. He told me his neck is generally his most symptomatic body part.

Dr. Weisbond described aching pain associated with his headaches. "When the neck pain is bad, I get headaches as well, and when the headaches are real bad, I get nauseated as well. I have a headache every day, but it's mild unless I do something I shouldn't be doing," he said. I inquired about headache triggers, and he replied, "Besides the neck, no." Dr. Weisbond indicated Excedrin Migraine effectively alleviates his headaches, although he added, "It upsets my stomach."

Occasionally, Dr. Weisbond advised me, his mid-back and lower-back pain is so severe it masks his neck pain. "It usually comes on posturally, when I'm doing something I shouldn't be doing [like] bending, stooping. I often have the back pain when I wake up; that's what wakes me up," he said.

The doctors treating Dr. Weisbond, he related, include Drs. Ronstadt, Pickford, and Blanchet. He informed me he saw Dr. Blanchet most recently – in November 2011. As for future medical appointments, Dr. Weisbond conveyed he has a follow-up appointment with Dr. Ronstadt in January 2012. He denied that future surgery has been scheduled or recommended.

When asked about treatment and therapy, Dr. Weisbond noted he has participated in physical therapy, massage therapy, chiropractic treatment, prescribed home exercise, and pain management including injections for his headaches. Currently, he apprised me, he is administered Enbrel injections once per week.

Dr. Weisbond reported using the following adaptive aids: TENS unit, traction device, cervical collar, and a lumbar support pillow. He indicated he is considering obtaining a grabber.

Dr. Weisbond advised me he takes/applies the following medications:

- Enbrel
- Excedrin Migraine
- Prilosec OTC
- Verapamil
- Tekturna HCT
- Lipitor
- Tetracycline
- MetroLotion
- Nizoral shampoo
- Elidel
- Claritin
- Nasonex
- Avodart

Regarding medication side effects, Dr. Weisbond related, "Grogginess, sleepiness, constipation and fecal impaction, 'stupidity' caused by pain medication in past, upset stomach (abdominal pain and gastritis) caused by Excedrin Migraine." He informed me he had taken his medication regimen during the 24 hours before my exam.

As for functional capacities, Dr. Weisbond estimated he can safely lift and carry between 10 and 20 pounds. When asked about physician-advised lifting restrictions, he conveyed Dr. Ronstadt recommended he avoid lifting that causes pain, as much as possible. Dr. Weisbond complained of pain in his neck, back, and head when lifting.

Dr. Weisbond cited problems with essentially all cervical spine movements, noting limitations in all directions, especially when turning his head to the right or leaning his head forward. He did not identify problems with using either hand/arm or either foot/leg. During my clinical interview, Dr. Weisbond demonstrated he could touch each finger to his thumb on either hand, make a fist with either hand, and extend his arms horizontally and overhead.

Although he apprised me his fine motor functioning is intact in both hands, Dr. Weisbond reported repetitive movements with his arms outstretched cause him neck pain and headaches, for example, when suturing, cauterizing, undermining skin, and performing biopsies and cryosurgeries. "Sometimes the back [symptoms are exacerbated], too," Dr. Weisbond added.

Concerning physical, everyday activities, Dr. Weisbond denied being exempt from any; however, he told me many are problematic. He cited no problems with walking or standing. While seated during my clinical interview, he repositioned normally. Dr. Weisbond indicated he avoids bending his waist. He advised me he is able to climb stairs, although he said, "If it's a lot of stairs, it'll be a problem."

Generally, Dr. Weisbond related, he can drive 1 hour, sit 2 hours, and walk or stand 30 minutes before overexerting himself or needing to rest. He indicated he operates an automatic transmission vehicle, daily, and he denied having a disabled-person parking placard. He recounted using a lumbar support pillow when driving. As for problems with driving, Dr. Weisbond conveyed: "Pain in back, neck, headaches. If prolonged driving, difficulty in changing lanes, especially on right due to limited neck mobility."

Other physical problems Dr. Weisbond identified related to hearing, fatigue, and exposure to cold temperatures and dampness/high humidity. He informed me these environmental conditions cause him to experience stiffness and increase his pain. He noted he tires easily with nominal activity. No falls were identified.

When asked about physician-advised restrictions, Dr. Weisbond apprised me Dr. Ronstadt and Dr. Pickford contraindicated performing dermatological surgery. He reported Dr. Ronstadt also recommended: "Avoid as much as possible activity that aggravates neck, back pain, headache, and jarring, stooping, twisting activities."

Dr. Weisbond opined that his condition is worsening, and he cited neck and back pain. He expressed his understanding he has reached maximum medical improvement. "The thing is to hold the fort, hopefully," he stated.

Activities of Daily Living

Dr. Weisbond recounted difficulty sleeping, and he estimated pain awakens him from two to three times per night. He noted he sleeps 6 or 7 hours per night. Dr. Weisbond apprised me he naps 1 or 2 hours during the afternoon. He denied taking sleep aid medication or having problems with nightmares.

Regarding grooming and self-care, Dr. Weisbond reported his podiatrist cuts his toenails. He cited difficulty lacing his shoes and putting on his socks. Dr. Weisbond complained that shaving and brushing his teeth exacerbate his neck pain.

As for household chores, Dr. Weisbond told me his condominium is far less tidy than he prefers. "I can't take care of it," he said. He indicated he launders his clothes. Dr. Weisbond advised me he often dines out or prepares light meals.

Before the onset of his symptoms, Dr. Weisbond related, he enjoyed the following leisure activities: "Jogging, weight lifting, tennis, skiing, ping-pong. All have been discontinued. Only exercise I now do (for cardiovascular system) is upright stationary bicycle at low speeds."

Dr. Weisbond described how he spends a typical day:

> *[Use] exercise bicycle in morning (try), then shower, groom. Read newspapers/sometimes difficult, restaurant for breakfast or lunch. Nap, sometimes Nook, book, watch TV, some computer (limited), dinner (out of cans or preprepared), telephone (talk with friends), sometimes go out, TV movie, sleep.*

Mental Health

Dr. Weisbond denied participating in mental health treatment, being prescribed antidepressants or other psychotropic drugs, losing consciousness, or having a family history of mental illness. He opined he does not currently need mental health treatment.

Concerning his overall psychological status, Dr. Weisbond described how his self-image as a physician has changed since he ceased practicing dermatology in December 2010. "I feel kind of useless, to say the least," he stated.

The primary mental health concerns Dr. Weisbond identified related to anxiety and stress management, his physical health, loss of employment income, legal issues (he noted his dispute with Big Insurance), and sexual activity. As for sexual problems, Dr. Weisbond apprised me his neck and back pain makes sexual intimacy "almost impossible."

Dr. Weisbond was pleasant and likable, and his affect ranged from normal to somewhat anxious. His memory and concentration were good. He spoke clearly and coherently. Dr. Weisbond did not display problems with either expressive or receptive language, and he showed no evidence of a thought disorder.

Education and Special Training

Dr. Weisbond indicated he performed "well," scholastically. He did not recall his scores from prior standardized testing, and he denied ever repeating a grade. Dr. Weisbond advised me he attended honors classes and graduated from high school in Quebec, Canada, in 1963.

In 1967, Dr. Weisbond related, he earned a bachelor of science degree in physiology at Davis University. Also at Davis, he informed me, he earned a medical doctorate degree in 1971. From 1973 to 1974, Dr. Weisbond conveyed, he was an ophthalmology resident, which he did not complete. "I didn't like it," he said.

Dr. Weisbond noted he completed residency in internal medicine in 1976. In 1978, he apprised me, he completed a dermatology residency at Toledo University. Further, he reported, he has completed various continuing education courses in dermatology.

When asked about work-related credentials, Dr. Weisbond indicated he is board certified in dermatology (active status) and board certified in internal medicine (uncertain of status). He advised me he has access to a computer and has some basic PC skills in Windows 7, Excel, and Photoshop.

Dr. Weisbond expressed he considers himself most skilled in excisions of skin cancers. He informed me that all surgeries he performed were outpatient in his office. "My office manager took care of everything, from A to Z," Dr. Weisbond replied when I inquired about his practice management skills. Occasionally, he conveyed, he prescribed surface treatments such as chemotherapy for patients. He noted he had privileges at Monroe Hospital. "I'd be called in on consultations very infrequently," Dr. Weisbond said. He denied considering retraining.

Career Development

Dr. Weisbond provided the following work history:

Job Title	*Name of Organization*	*Dates*
Dermatological Surgeon	Self-employed, Dean Weisbond, P.A.	4/79 – 12/15/10

Dr. Weisbond said about his job satisfaction as a self-employed dermatological surgeon: "I loved it. It's really a fun job, most of the time. You help people, solve problems." Dr. Weisbond noted his job's physical requirements included "extended standing, stooping, twisting, bending."

Informing me his practice had "been doing very well," Dr. Weisbond said: "It went down with the economic downturn, but it was still a nice practice. As I started feeling worse, I did less to promote the practice."

Dr. Weisbond cited the following organizations in which he participates:

- County Medical Association
- National Academy of Dermatology
- U.S. Society of Dermatological Surgery
- Statewide Society for Dermatological Surgery
- West Coast Association of Dermatology

Regarding his career plans before his condition continued to deteriorate, Dr. Weisbond conveyed he had planned to continue working until age 75. "It's a relatively low-stress practice, and it's fun," he said. He expressed uncertainty about his present vocational rehabilitation plans. Dr. Weisbond denied searching for a job since December 2010.

Dr. Weisbond noted his employment earnings before closing his practice were $300,000 per year. He apprised me his highest earnings during his work career were $450,000 in 2006. As for current sources of income, Dr. Weisbond cited his savings account and also rental income of $12,000 per month.

Review of Medical Records

Results of Diagnostic Testing

01/29/09 *Amy Madonna, MD*

MRI Elbow without Contrast Left

Impression:

1. Flexor tendinopathy.
2. Mild osteoarthritic changes.
3. Subcutaneous edema over the triceps may suggest site of direct blow. Recommend clinical correlation.

04/05/11 *Stephen John, MD*

MRI Scan of the Cervical Spine
Impression:
C2-3 and C4-5 disc bulges which impinge upon the thecal sac.
C5-6 and C6-7 disc bulges causes small ventral impressions upon the thecal sac.
Mild C5-6 and C6-7 spinal stenosis.
Degenerative disease.

MRI Scan of the Lumbar Spine
Impression:
T11-12 extruded disc herniation causing a small ventral impression upon the thecal sac.
L1-2, L3-4, and L4-5 disc bulges which impinge upon the thecal sac.
L2-3 disc bulge causing a small ventral impression upon the thecal sac and partially compromising the L2-3 neural foramina bilaterally.
Mild L2-3 spinal stenosis.
Straightening of the lumbar spine probably secondary to muscular spasm and/or strain.
Degenerative disease.

Assessments

07/13/09 *Gary Streep, MD*

Second Opinion
Comment:
Dr. Weisbond came for a second opinion regarding the management of psoriatic arthritis.

He states that at the age of 53, he developed the subacute onset of severe neck pain associated with frontal headache and nausea. He was evaluated by multiple specialists including a physiatrist and a neurosurgeon and was treated with physical therapy. Nonsteroidal anti-inflammatory agents all produced gastritis and indeed an endoscopy revealed erosive gastritis. He has needed to take them in restricted fashion. He did obtain significant relief from the headache component, but not the neck pain with Excedrin Migraine.

He has gone on to develop mild psoriasis involving the alar area as well as the scalp and the eyebrows and he has had intermittent nail pitting. He has gone on to develop peripheral arthritis involving his heels, elbows and hands as well as pain in the lower back with associated morning stiffness. There has been a dramatic los of motion in the neck.

Impression:
Based on the assessment, I fully concur with the diagnosis of psoriatic arthritis with a prominent axial component. I am concerned about the possibility of a secondary occipital neuralgia and to better evaluate this I suggested a CT scan with special views to look at the C1-C2 facet articulations.

With regards to his basic problem, that is psoriatic arthritis, I believe as I am sure you do too that Remicade is the gold standard for this disorder and I would put him back on Remicade perhaps at a higher dose either 6 or 7 mg/kg in combination with methotrexate at a dose of at least 20 mg per week given via IM injection.

09/24/09 *Bruce Taylor, MD, Ph.D.*

Letter addressed To Whom It May Concern

Comment:

I currently treat Dr. Dean Weisbond in my practice at New Hampshire University Department of Dermatology. Dr. Weisbond is a 63 year old man with both psoriasis and psoriatic arthritis. He relates to me in the past that his psoriatic arthritis and psoriasis respond to the medications Remicade and Humira. He came to me on September 22, 2008, essentially off all medication after having been denied receipt of Humira by his insurance company. His arthritic and skin conditions at that visit were currently flaring.

Given his exam and history, it is clear to me that Dr. Weisbond suffers from psoriasis with associated psoriatic arthritis. Keeping in mind that he has responded to a TNF inhibitor previously, I think it is medically necessary that he be restarted on a TNF inhibitor such as Humira as soon as possible so that he may regain better disease control and a more normalized quality of life.

11/20/09 *Lynne Hepburn, DO*

Physical Therapy Evaluation

History:

Neck pain started 8 years ago, mid and low back pain a few years ago. Is a surgeon and spends many hours in surgery in a flexed forward head position.

Chief Complaint:

Constant neck and lower back pain. daily suboccipital to frontal headaches, also has psoriatic arthritis and is on Humira and methotrexate.

Recommendation:

Patient to be seen 1 times per week (frequency) x 2 weeks (duration).

03/03/10 *Lynne Hepburn, DO*

History of Present Illness:

Dr. Weisbond returns today for a follow up visit. He states that he had some abdominal pain, went to see his gastrointestinal doctor, he had a CT of the abdomen which checked out ok, per patient. Patient has been benefiting from physical therapy but is becoming very desperate for other options.

Diagnoses:

Neck pain.
Cervical spondylosis.
Psoriatic arthritis
Cervical degenerative disc disease.
Migraines versus occipital neuralgia.
Low back pain.

Plan:

We will continue with physical therapy for now. He does not wish to have an MRI of the T/L spine and is not a candidate for epidural steroid injection due to skin breakout from the steroids. I have offered to start a low dose opioid such as Norco/T3, wishes to hold off until physical therapy is done.

04/28/10 *Lynne Hepburn, DO*

Comment:

Dr. Weisbond presents today for follow up regarding his chronic neck pain and headaches, which are the worst when he stands and tries to do surgeries. He feels low back pain and thoracic pain when he stands for a while. He has tried multiple medications and is looking for something that won't affect his cognition.

Diagnoses:

Neck pain.
Cervical spondylosis.
Psoriatic arthritis
Cervical degenerative disc disease.
Migraines versus occipital neuralgia.
Low back pain.

Plan:

I think that Dr. Weisbond should be on a continuous release medication for his pain. I have recommended that he try Ultram 200 mg/day.
We discussed the possibility of Botox for his headaches to try to cut down on his Excedrin usage.
Continue with physical therapy directed towards his neck.
The patient states that their current treatment has helped improve their quality of life and helped in psychosocial functioning.
The current treatment regimen is needed to decrease the patient's pain symptoms, improve the quality of life, improve his ability to function and improve sleep and mood symptoms.

06/25/10 *Lynne Hepburn, DO*

Comment:

Presents for reevaluation after physical therapy sessions completed. Says that he needs more pain intervention/modalities that physical therapy can offer. Explains that he had some improvement with physical therapy but minimal. His chief complaint is still a decrease in range of motion of the neck and head. This condition affects his ability to perform duties in his dermatology practice. He verbalized the rosacea and daily antibiotics he uses to treat it prevent him from receiving epidural steroid injection or spinal injections for his pain symptoms.

Diagnoses:

Neck pain.
Cervical spondylosis.
Psoriatic arthritis
Cervical degenerative disc disease.
Migraines versus occipital neuralgia.
Low back pain.

Plan:

Advised patient to use Ultram extended release.
Informed patient on possible drug-drug interactions with tramadol.
Verbalized understanding of seizure implications with tramadol and that he will call if any problems occur.

08/11/10 *Anthony Ronstadt, MD*

Letter addressed to Norman Carter , MD

Comment:

Dr. Weisbond undoubtedly has psoriasis, documented by Bruce Taylor, MD, Ph.D. at NHU who is confirmed psoriasis and distal onycholysis. (He has a strong family history of psoriasis including a father and brother).

Dr. Weisbond has difficulty functioning at both a personal and professional level. I personally have seen him getting out of his car, a process which took him a minute or two, due to axial pain largely.

He is either unable to tolerate or has not responded to, muscle relaxants, anti-inflammatories, methotrexate, Lyrica, steroids, or sulfasalazine. Unfortunately, I think he has to modify his life to accommodate his current level of functioning. I don't see any improvement likely in the foreseeable future, symptomatically, and again unfortunately it is more likely than not that there will be progression of his axial disease.

09/08/10 *Lynne Hepburn, DO*

Diagnoses:

Neck pain.
Cervical spondylosis.
Psoriatic arthritis
Cervical degenerative disc disease.
Migraines versus occipital neuralgia.
Low back pain.

Plan:

Schedule for physical therapy.
Consider trigger point injections to back without steroid – focus on needling if therapy does not improve symptoms.
He will give this clinic a copy of the lower back x-rays Dr. Streep has recently ordered.
Lidoderm patches today.

12/16/10 *Lynne Hepburn, DO*

Comment:

He is having a lot of trouble with his energy. He isn't sleeping at all. He falls asleep a lot during the day. He is having a lot of trouble at work as a dermatologist because of his fatigue.

Plan:

I recommended that we start physical therapy concentrating on pain modalities, TENS unit, ultrasound, spine stabilization, and range of motion techniques.
We discussed using Botox for his headaches. He is going to call as needed for the injections.

01/03/11 *Robert Pickford, MD*

History of Present Illness:

This is a 64 year old, left-handed physician. He is actually a dermatological surgeon doing predominantly cancer surgery. He has had to quit. He is just simply unable to do the work. His symptoms have been progressive now for over ten years.

This patient has some rather serious medical issues. Consequently, they prevent him from being able to work due to chronic severe pain.

Neurological Impression:

1. Chronic severe cervical, thoracic, and lumbosacral strain with palpable fibromyositis.
2. Chronic insomnia secondary to chronic pain syndrome.
3. Chronic pain syndrome.
4. Chronic neck pain, cervical spondylosis, cervical psoriatic arthritis, cervical degenerative disc disease.
5. Migraines versus occipital neuralgia.
6. Chronic low back pain.
7. Psoriatic spondylosis and arthritis.
8. MRI scan demonstrating C5-6 disc protrusion with osteophytes and neural foraminal narrowing at

multiple levels.

Recommendation:

1. In my opinion, this patient is 100% permanently, totally disabled, unable to work, unable to function, unable to compete in a competitive job environment.
2. Follow up with the rheumatologist.
3. Follow up with chronic pain management.
4. May consider epidural steroid injections.
5. Should consider surgery with Dr. Marcus or Dr. Sheila .
6. Williams' exercises for the neck and back to be done 3 times daily and at night after hot showers.
7. May do low impact.
8. Avoid high impact.
9. Not to lift greater than 10 to 20 pounds.
10. May change positions frequently.
11. In my opinion, this patient is definitely 100% permanently, totally disabled, unable to work, unable to function, unable to compete in a competitive job environment. In fact, it would be dangerous to any patients if he were to try to practice surgery. I do agree with the rheumatologist, Dr. Ronstadt, that I do not foresee him getting better in the foreseeable future. In fact, these symptoms tend to get progressively worse.
12. I have reviewed extensive medical records.
13. Return to see me in follow-up on a prn basis.

06/16/11 *Robert Pickford, MD*

Conclusion:

After reviewing these additional medical records and MRI scans, my opinions remain chronic severe cervical, thoracic, and lumbosacral strain with palpable fibromyositis, migraines versus occipital neuralgia and cephalgia, chronic insomnia secondary to chronic pain syndrome, chronic pain syndrome, cervical and lumbar spondylosis, psoriatic spondylosis and arthritis and cord stenosis and neural foraminal narrowing at multiple levels. After reviewing these, in my opinion it confirms my original opinion that this patient is 100% permanently, totally disabled, unable to work, function or compete in a competitive job environment. Certainly he would not be able to work as a dermatological physician. He probably would not be able to work under any capacity.

Results of Testing

On the Wahler Physical Symptoms Inventory, Dr. Weisbond generated a score of 1.5. This score placed Dr. Weisbond at the 9th decile in relation to a comparable normative group.

The Shipley Institute of Living Scale was used to assess Dr. Weisbond's intellectual skills and abilities. Dr. Weisbond attained an estimated WAIS-R IQ score of 124 on the Shipley Institute of Living Scale. This performance placed him in the superior range of mental functioning.

The Grooved Pegboard is a manipulative dexterity test used in the selection of employees for industrial jobs such as assembler, machine operator, and other manual jobs. This test measures finger and manual dexterity, and requires complex visual-motor coordination. Below are Dr. Weisbond's scores:

	Score	Normative Comparison Data
Dominant Hand (L)	84 seconds	mean = 82.70 seconds (SD = 18.70)
Nondominant Hand	77 seconds	mean = 87.55 seconds (SD = 26.20)

On the Beck Depression Inventory-II, Dr. Weisbond generated a total score of 13, which corresponds to the minimal range of depression.

Results of personality testing form the MMPI-2 were valid. Somatic concerns were a prominent feature of Dr. Weisbond's profile. Correspondingly, Dr. Weisbond appears to be experiencing problems with his psychological adjustment; however, he does not appear to be having difficulty with depression or anxiety. His results indicate that he tends to be an introverted person.

On the Self-Directed Search Form R, Dr. Weisbond scored highest on the Investigative occupational theme. This theme is most often associated with science and healthcare occupations. Dr. Weisbond rated his scientific ability and manual skills as very high. He also assessed his teaching and math abilities, and understanding of others as above average. The only occupation he noted interest in pursuing was "physician." Among the occupations from the Self-Directed Search Form R that correspond with Dr. Weisbond's profile are Anesthesiologist (DOT #070.101-010), Biochemist (DOT #041.061-026), Dentist (DOT #072.101-010), Dermatologist (DOT #070.101-018), Ophthalmologist (DOT #070.101-058), Osteopathic Physician (DOT #071.101-010), and Mechanical Engineer (DOT #007.061-014).

Summary and Impressions

1. Dr. Weisbond completed his high school education in Quebec, Canada, and continued his college studies at Davis University, where he earned a bachelor's degree in physiology and a medical doctorate degree. Then, Dr. Weisbond completed a 2-year internal medicine residency and a 2-year residency in dermatology. All of his employment since 1978 has been as a dermatologist (DOT #070.101-018), he reported. He advised me he was self-employed from April 1979 through December 15, 2010. Based on my understanding of his work activities, Dr. Weisbond performed highly skilled, light exertion tasks. Much of his time involved performing surgeries, he conveyed. He described several very physically demanding tasks such as standing over a surgical field for extended periods while flexing or extending his neck with his arms outstretched; at times, complications arose, he noted. Dr. Weisbond described how performing his job exacerbated his neck, mid-back, and lower-back symptoms, and he discussed his attempts to contain his symptoms. Despite restricting his work participation to 20 to 25 hours per week and taking time away from work, Dr. Weisbond related, he was unable to manage his symptoms. Neck and back pain were particularly problematic, he recalled, while also citing secondary problems that included fatigue and concentration difficulties, further reducing his ability to perform his job. Concern about his ability to safely provide dermatologist services to his patients was a major factor in his decision to leave his practice in December 2010, Dr. Weisbond noted. He has not pursued work activity since December 2010. Before his condition began to deteriorate, he related, he planned to continue working until age 75. Dr. Weisbond is 65 years old.
2. Medical records provide objective support for Dr. Weisbond's presenting problems. Imaging of his cervical, thoracic, and lumbar spine areas showed several abnormalities, and degenerative disease is noted. Dr. Ronstadt commented in August 2010: "I think he has to modify his life to accommodate his current level of functioning. I don't see any improvement likely in the foreseeable future, symptomatically, and again unfortunately it is more likely than not that there will be progression of his axial disease." The most recent records I reviewed are from Dr. Pickford, a neurologist. In his January 3, 2011, report, Dr. Pickford opined that Dr. Weisbond "is 100% permanently, totally disabled, unable to work, unable to function, unable to compete in a competitive job environment." Dr. Pickford restated this opinion in a report dated June 16, 2011. My analysis has led me to conclude, within a reasonable degree of vocational rehabilitation probability, that Dr. Weisbond is not capable of performing the material and substantial tasks related to his own occupation.

Michael Shahnasarian, Ph.D. Date
Certified Rehabilitation Counselor #3701
Certified Vocational Evaluator #58360
Certified Life Care Planner #258
Licensed Psychologist PY5644
Fellow, National Career Development Association
Fellow, International Academy of Life Care Planners

Part III

Forensic Practice Issues

Chapter 11

Testimony

Synopsis

11.1 Introduction

A vocational opinion, regardless of its validity, has little if any value unless the trier of fact understands and believes it. Further, incredulous, offensive, or otherwise ill-received testimony can cast a pallor over the witness that has adverse, carryover effects on those perceived aligned with him. Withstanding adverse, manipulative, and self-serving counterattack hallmarks effective vocational expert testimony.

The vocational expert's testimonial objective is straightforward: to offer comprehensible, credible professional opinions resilient to unfair attack. Many obstacles during the dispute resolution process, however, can undermine an expert's efforts. This chapter focuses on delivering effective expert witness testimony.

11.2 The Trial Environment

Providing professional and candid testimony—which skilled lawyers subject to intense, filtered, and engineered cross-examination in an adversarial, often emotionally charged environment—poses a unique test to vocational experts. Not only should experts anticipate intense challenge, they should assume foundations undergirding their opinions—as well as every scintilla of input applied to formulate opinions—will undergo calculated, intense analysis, criticism, and attack. The expert's qualifications, methods, conclusions, and presentation provide opposing attorneys fodder to discredit, distort, and otherwise manipulate opinions not favorable to their cases.

Maintaining a professional demeanor under intense pressure, communicating clearly and concisely, professionally matching an adverse attorney's tactics and responding appropriately, and remaining resolute when mettle and resolve are persistently tested—these skills transcend the technical skills and knowledge necessary to sustain an expert's opinions. While a vocational expert may be quite adept technically, this expertise has little value in a legal forum unless the trier of fact comprehends the expert's opinions and perceives them as valid after intense challenge.

Effective testimony requires insight and perspective into the trial environment. Parties to the lawsuit—the attorneys trying the case, the trier of fact, witnesses, insurance adjusters and the general trial environment including the jurisdiction, courtroom, and issues of the day—influence a trial's dynamics.

The parties to a lawsuit, typically with significant stakes in the trial's outcome, are often emotionally involved in the litigation process. From a claimant's perspective, for example, years of denigrating experiences—including intrusive surveillance, lawyer-engineered harassment, financial burden, various threats, and major lifestyle changes—can cloud objectivity.

A father who believed his child became severely disabled because of a physician's negligence, for instance, lost objectivity after months of financial hardship and unwelcome lifestyle changes, evidenced by his yearning to "teach [the physician] a lesson for what he's done to us." The father declined a formidable settlement offer that would have sufficiently provided for his child's special needs, and he persisted in trying the case because of his desire to punish the physician. The jury found no evidence of medical malpractice and the family received no compensatory award.

Other examples of individuals who lose objectivity during the litigation process include vengeful spouses in the midst of a divorce, a displaced executive with entitlement sentiments after many years of service, and a person angry and humiliated by acquired disabilities. Vocational experts should discern how litigation-related events affect subjects' emotions and motivations, and, correspondingly, vocational behavior.

Opposing attorneys have competing interests—including their financial incentives, career-related objectives, sense of responsibility to their clients, and ego—that can drive their behavior at trial. Their interactions with a vocational expert will depend on factors that include individual style, trial developments and strategy, and a case's facts. The attorney who has retained an expert will present him as a highly qualified professional with standards beyond reproach. The opposing attorney's treatment of the expert, conversely, may be hostile and contemptuous, with undercurrents that the expert is inept, biased, and financially motivated to mislead the trier of fact. Many opposing attorneys outwardly assert or subtly imply—through theatrically embossed and manipulated information and underhanded tactics—that triers of fact should distrust a vocational expert witness.

The trier of fact—whether a judge, jury, an arbitrator, or arbitration panel—brings to jurisprudence a unique blend of life experiences and worldviews. Of course, the climate and culture in which a case is being tried may influence how a vocational expert is viewed. An expert with a personal style perceived as indigenous to the locale, for instance, may be better received than an expert perceived as out of sync with the community in which a case is being tried.

As a trial evolves, triers of fact may experience a range of feelings including boredom, anger, skepticism, empathy, contrition, and sympathy. When an individual such as a judge or chairperson of an arbitration panel presides, rulings made during the proceedings can establish norms that set the trial's tenor. An expert's sensitivity to the trier of fact's mood can affect how testimony is received and weighed.

Witnesses who precede a vocational expert can also influence a trier of fact's receptiveness to testimony. An incredulous witness who testified immediately before a vocational expert and faltered under cross-examination, for instance, may cause the trier of fact to look askance at the vocational expert for attempting to extrapolate an opinion on shaky-at-best testimony. Views and dispositions of triers of fact develop as a trial evolves; it behooves the vocational expert to gauge a trial's tempo and course before testifying.

Even the composition of the gallery may have significance to a vocational expert. Commonly, attorneys scout experts who frequently testify and are involved in cases other than the pending case; these attorneys often seek information to use against the expert in future cases. Occasionally, members of the media attend trial and, by their very presence, introduce yet another influence on a case's tenor.

Within an environment laden with paradoxes and an accompanying mesh of human dynamics, vocational experts present and defend technical opinions about earning capacity. Of course, they are also bound to adhere to their profession's ethics. Barros-Bailey, Carlisle, and Blackwell (2010) discussed forensic ethics and indirect practice for the rehabilitation counselor. The codes of ethics most applicable to vocational rehabilitation experts' work include:

- The American Board of Vocational Experts' *Code of Ethics* (2007)
- The American Counseling Association's *Code of Ethics* (2014)
- The American Psychological Association's *Ethical Principles of Psychologists and Code of Conduct* (2010)
- The American Psychological Association and American Board of Forensic Psychology's *Specialty Guidelines for Forensic Psychology* (2012)
- The Commission on Rehabilitation Counselor Certification's *Code of Professional Ethics for Rehabilitation Counselors* (2010)
- The International Association of Rehabilitation Professionals' *Code of Ethics, Standards of Practice, and Competencies* (2007)
- The National Board for Certified Counselor's *Code of Ethics* (2012)

11.3 Trial Preparation

Testimony at trial requires vocational experts to integrate information considered while conducting analyses and arriving at opinions. Presenting these opinions for a trier of fact's deliberation is another challenge. Trial preparation typically includes:

- Reviewing written reports.
- Reviewing deposition testimony.
- Reviewing extant records and file materials.
- Analyzing new records generated after a previous exam or file review.

- Conducting an update examination if a significant amount of time has elapsed or significant changes in a subject's status have occurred since any prior exam.
- Conducting updated labor market research.
- Consulting with other experts.
- Preparing trial exhibits.
- Consulting with the attorney who will conduct the vocational expert's direct examination at trial.

Trial preparation challenges vocational experts to distill complex analyses into concise, understandable, and credible presentations in anticipation of strong opposition. Details associated with trial preparation are more fully discussed below.

A. Reviewing Written Reports

Occasionally, considerable time lapses before a trial's onset and the time when an expert's opinions were initially formulated and committed to a report. A review of key documents underlying opinions, as well as all reports written, can help refresh an expert's recollection about how vocational opinions were formulated. Refamiliarizing oneself, before trial, with subject-specific information (e.g., names of employers, earnings history, job titles and responsibilities, treatment providers) and reviewing the chronology of a case's events is recommended.

Vocational experts should presume opposing attorneys, in preparation for cross-examination, would have culled all reports the expert has authored. A lack of familiarity about information contained within one's own report can be embarrassing and foster trier of fact perceptions that the expert is ill-prepared and/or uses sloppy methods. These types of attributions detract from value placed on an expert's opinion, regardless of the opinion's validity. Before trial, the expert should also review all reports—including those that provide contrary opinions and the foundations for contrary opinions—and adjust assessments as necessary.

B. Reviewing Deposition Testimony

Expert witnesses should expect that, besides reviewing all reports the vocational expert has authored, opposing attorneys will have read deposition testimony provided in the pending case—as well as in other cases—in preparing for cross-examination. Opposing attorneys attempt to identify inconsistencies and other information to impeach an expert at trial. During cross-examination, the vocational expert commonly encounters questioning such as, "Dr. Knowitall, do you recall when I took your deposition last week, and you testified under oath that your final opinion was ABC? Today, you're telling this jury something radically different, correct?"

Familiarity with previously rendered testimony is essential to correcting statements taken out of context during trial. Since the trier of fact typically does not know what actually transpired during depositions, the expert should anticipate and circumvent attempts to misrepresent information conveyed through prior testimony.

Experts should ask to review, during cross-examination, references from which attorneys derive their attempted impeachment, imposing context and perspective as needed. Triers of fact respect witnesses who detonate a lawyer's manipulative, underhanded tactics by correcting misrepresentations, half-truths, and other untoward defaming initiatives.

C. Reviewing Extant Records and File Materials

A vocational expert has little control over questions posed during a deposition or cross-examination. Experts should expect to be questioned about all opinions, how opinions were formulated, and any report or evidence incorporating expert opinions. Experts often undergo lengthy inquiries about records in their possession, as well as documents they have not reviewed. An opposing attorney, as a product of this exercise, may infer that lacking knowledge about information in a document introduced as evidence renders an expert's opinion incomplete and/or deficient, and, accordingly, the trier of fact should discount its value.

The importance of an expert's knowledge and proper maintenance of a litigated file's contents cannot be overstated. General familiarity with all records in one's possession—especially those that address pending referral questions—enhance perceptions of the expert as thorough and well prepared, and may thwart embarrassing insinuations and inferences that analyses are cursory or haphazard.

D. Analyzing New Records Generated After a Previous Examination or File Review

As noted in the preceding discussion, a vocational expert's lack of access to records may lead to insinuations that opinions are incomplete or inaccurate because the expert did not consider all information necessary to arrive at a fair, informed opinion. It is impossible for an expert to know the universe of records pertinent and available for analysis. Experts should inform retaining attorneys of the types of records necessary to address referral questions and request updated records as they become available. New information provided through updated records may be irrelevant, reinforce previously developed opinions, cause the expert to modify an earlier opinion, or prompt the expert to conduct additional research or request an update exam. Chapter 4 discussed how experts should communicate to referral sources when new information causes opinions to change.

E. Conducting an Update Examination

Occasionally, a vocational expert determines an update exam, before trial, is needed. Changes in a subject's medical condition, occurrences in the subject's career development, or the passage of considerable time since the expert's prior examination may drive this decision. Conducting an update exam may not be an option; an expert's access to the subject, for example, is restricted when defense counsel retains an expert. The retaining attorney should initiate all requests for update examinations. Experts should communicate immediately to the retaining attorney new or revised opinions formed from an update exam; otherwise, the new opinions may not be admissible at trial.

F. Conducting Updated Labor Market Research

Changes in labor market conditions, or a subject's vocational status or personal situation may require updated labor market research before trial. Just as subjects' vocational profiles are dynamic, so are the labor markets that relate to them. A vocational expert should assess labor market vicissitudes relevant to the subject. An opinion based on outdated or irrelevant information has little or no value.

G. Consulting with Other Experts

Vocational experts consult with other experts, including physicians and mental health professionals, to obtain information necessary to formulate their opinions. They also consult with experts, such as economists and accountants, who may be basing their opinions on the vocational expert's opinion. For instance, a vocational expert may need to consult with a subject's physician to obtain specific information about lifting or carrying restrictions and other exertion limitations. On the other hand, an economist or accountant, using a vocational expert's opinion to calculate past wage loss and/or future value of a subject's earning capacity, may seek the vocational expert's input on specific vocational questions. An economist sought a vocational expert's input in an Americans with Disabilities Act case, for example, in which a disabled subject alleged wrongful termination because of his employer's alleged failure to extend a reasonable accommodation to enable him to continue performing his job. While projecting future damage scenarios, the economist sought guidance on the interval required for the subject to secure posttermination employment, compensation at the time of reentry into an alternate position, and the likely period required to reach a compensation level commensurate with the pretermination compensation level (converted to future value). Consultations with other experts can help a vocational expert refine opinions and ensure opinions have been accurately interpreted.

H. Preparing Trial Exhibits

Vocational experts should prepare exhibits to aid their trial testimony. Well-prepared exhibits help focus the trier of fact's attention to salient testimony points and can communicate information difficult to fully grasp or comprehend via oral presentation. For instance, verbally reciting to a jury a subject's ten-year earnings history while simultaneously presenting a trend chart of the subject's earnings history compared to people with a similar background helps emphasize takeaway points. Preparing and using exhibits is detailed later in this chapter.

I. Consulting with Attorney About Direct Examination

A pretrial conference between the vocational expert and the attorney who will conduct direct examination is advised. This conference can update the expert on case developments and coordinate how to best present expert opinions. A more detailed discussion about the pretrial conference follows.

11.4 Pretrial Conference

Although the vocational expert and the retaining attorney may have had a pretrial conference, developments during a trial may necessitate an update conference. Commonly, experts meet with the attorney in a witness waiting room as late as a few minutes before entering the courtroom. Once an expert witness' testimony has begun, however, most jurisdictions prohibit communication between attorneys and witnesses about the case at hand. For instance, if an expert has begun to testify and the court recesses before the expert has completed his testimony, most courts do not allow any communication between the expert and legal counsel on matters relating to the pending case.

During the pretrial conference, the vocational expert should learn how upcoming testimony relates to testimony anticipated from other witnesses. For example, an economist may rely on a vocational expert's opinion about the time required for a plaintiff in a wrongful termination dispute to reach parity with previous earnings after reentering the labor market. Knowing how other witnesses may rely on a vocational expert's opinion can facilitate the expert's presentation of testimony.

Lawyers are required to brief experts on motions in limine that may restrict their testimony. For instance, a judge may rule at a pretrial hearing that certain evidence—like a plaintiff's sources of income, criminal record, or history of substance abuse—is inadmissible because of its irrelevance to matters in dispute and/or potential to bias the trier of fact against the plaintiff. Experts who disclose inadmissible evidence at trial risk causing a mistrial or having their testimony stricken.

In addition to discussing vocational experts' opinions and how to elicit these opinions during trial, experts and attorneys should also (1) discuss records particularly important to the vocational expert's opinions, (2) identify relevant records the expert has yet to review, and (3) determine the need to conduct additional work before trial, including conducting an update exam of the plaintiff if a considerable amount of time has elapsed or significant changes have occurred since the expert last examined the plaintiff. The pretrial conference is also opportune to review anticipated cross-examination questions and all trial exhibits the expert contemplates using to explain key testimony points.

A vocational expert can facilitate direct examination by providing proposed questions to elicit testimony as concise and organized as possible. Efforts of these sorts are a courtesy to the trier of fact and promote expeditious judicial proceedings.

A sample set of proposed direct examination questions appears in Appendix 11.1. Three categories delineate the questions: qualifying questions, methodology, and substantive questions.

The proposed questions are from a case in which a senior bank executive pursued earning capacity and life care plan damages after a medical incident. Also a certified life care planner, the expert witness opined the claimant was not a candidate for vocational rehabilitation and that he would require significant, lifelong rehabilitation intervention. At trial, while testifying about future care needs, the expert left the witness box and stood near the jury while referencing enlarged boards (exhibits) showing her life care plan.

Invariably, counsel opposing the lawyer who hired the expert will inquire about fees. Among the reasons for this questioning is to imply to triers of fact that the expert's objectivity may be compromised due to compensation from the retaining lawyer. Many experts prefer to deal with fee-related questions during direct examination, thereby rendering additional questioning during cross-examination redundant.

As noted earlier, in some cases, vocational experts serve exclusively as consulting experts and their retention source does not disclose the expert's opinions to opposing counsel. These retentions generally emanate from lawyers representing a defendant(s). The consulting expert's engagement typically centers on evaluating the merits of an assessment opposing counsel's expert prepared. Reviewing the expert's reports, reading and critiquing deposition testimony, and providing cross-examination questions are the types of services consulting experts provide. Additionally, a consulting expert's input can help determine the value of damages claims, which facilitates decisions on settlement offers and lawyers' representations to triers of fact on awarding damages.

11.5 Depositions of Testifying Experts

Vocational experts are subject to being deposed during the discovery phase of litigation. Deposition questions focus on opinions to be offered at trial, the bases for these opinions, the expert's credentials, fees, litigation experience, and other related questions. Occasionally, the attorney who has retained the expert will take the deposition; this usually occurs when the expert anticipates being unavailable to attend the trial, or the attorney plans to submit the expert's deposition transcript to the trier of fact in lieu of live testimony.

Depositions of vocational experts typically require from one to two hours. Experts are often served subpoenas before their depositions that denote the deposition's time and location, and lists records mandating the expert to make available. Appendix 11.2 is a vocational expert's predeposition letter sent to the lawyer taking the deposition. The letter clarifies deposition conduct details. Before the deposition, the vocational expert should specify fee requirements, amount of time reserved, and any other pertinent arrangements or requirements including exhibit copying costs and special logistics related to details such as transmittal of standardized test data.

Lawyers' aims in taking vocational experts' depositions vary. In some cases, depositions elucidate opinions and their bases. In other cases, opinions are evident, and attorneys aim to secure information to impeach expert opinions during trial. Developing an impression of how the trier of fact will respond to the expert and using the deposition as an opportunity to subtly communicate with the opposing side are other reasons lawyers conduct depositions. Sometimes, there is no logical reason to explain why an attorney took a deposition, and the vocational expert is left with the impression that the attorney simply followed through on a job assignment or unnecessarily generated fees.

Often, the attorney who retained the expert schedules a predeposition conference. This conference typically includes a review of the expert's opinions, a briefing on case developments, and a review of the expert's file to ensure receipt of records necessary to offer complete opinions.

In most cases, the opposing attorney deposes a vocational expert. Occasionally, the attorney who has retained the expert will take the deposition; again, this is most often the case when the expert will be unavailable during the trial, or the dispute will be tried by a bench trial in which allotted time is limited. In these instances, the expert's deposition, or selected parts of it, will be either read into the record at trial or introduced as an exhibit into evidence.

Questions posed to a vocational expert during depositions a retaining attorney takes tend to be straightforward and concise, and generally address the scope of retention, qualifications, methods used to formulate opinions, results from all testing conducted, and opinions. After this direct examination, the opposing lawyer cross-examines the expert; redirect examinations and cross-examinations may follow.

Depositions opposing counsel take, on the other hand, are far less predictable. Questions posed often depend on attorney-related characteristics including familiarity with the vocational expert, overall trial strategy, experience, intent in taking the deposition, and personal style. During opposing counsel's depositions, the expert can anticipate:

- File review and copying of documents not already in the attorney's possession.
- Questions intended to elicit information for potential impeachment at trial. These questions often include queries about the percentage of time the expert spends in litigation-related activities, previous deposition and trial testimony, fees, percentage breakdowns of litigation work performed on behalf of plaintiff counsel versus defense counsel, and number of previous retentions by the retaining attorney.
- Questions about qualifications.
- A test of knowledge of the case via records and the expert's evaluation.
- The expert's methods, assumptions, opinions, and bases for opinions.

The opposing attorney will muster any evidence—either real or contrived—to suggest the vocational expert is biased, inconsistent, unqualified or less qualified than the opposing expert; uses deficient methods; or has relied on faulty assumptions. More discussion on how lawyers use these types of evidence during cross-examination at trial is presented later in this chapter.

Opposing attorneys' styles during depositions, as well as during trials, vary widely: from charming to brusque, intimidating to obnoxious, superficial to obsessive-compulsive, and unsophisticated in knowledge of vocational rehabilitation to highly knowledgeable. The vocational expert should assume that, regardless of style, the opposing attorney will be well prepared. Attorneys gather information about experts by:

- Consulting with counsel familiar with the expert
- Researching the expert's trial history using LexisNexis or a similar source
- Consulting with other vocational experts
- Investigating the expert's professional background
- Observing the expert testify at another trial
- Reading reports the expert prepared in other cases
- Reading deposition and trial transcripts of testimony the expert provided in other cases

Attorneys often compile dossiers about vocational experts who testify frequently; experts should assume that a compendium of information about them has been archived for reference and circulated among law firms within their communities. They should also prepare for questions—often taken out of context and with a bullying overtone or undertone—that may attempt to exploit a lawyer's perceptions of what will cause a jury or other trier of fact to discount their testimony. A lawyer, for example, could harangue an expert for presenting a lecture on forensic testimony at a professional conference with innuendo that the expert is skilled in teaching other experts how to present manipulative, dishonest testimony. The expert's challenge is to correct the record in the face of half-truths and remain composed when dealt ethical, professional, and personal insults.

A vocational expert learned the importance of carefully responding to all questions during a case in which she was deposed by telephone; the case was ultimately tried in a rural, southern jurisdiction. At the onset of the deposition, before the expert was sworn-in and testimony began, the opposing attorney engaged the expert—who was from a major urban area—in a seemingly innocuous, disarming dialogue about life in a small, rural area. The opposing attorney carefully selected words to seemingly joke with and bait the expert about her planned commute from an urban area to attend the trial; the expert responded in kind, and made in jest some stereotypical comments about rural lifestyles. During his opening statement to the jury, the opposing attorney read selected portions of the expert's deposition testimony about traveling to their community; the expert's comments, taken out of context, sounded offensive and cast an unfavorable image of the expert before the jury had an opportunity to meet her or hear her testimony. Some might regard a tactic like this as a "dirty trick"; others regard it as smart lawyering. In any event, the message to the vocational expert is clear: Never let your guard down while involved in litigation, even during a seemingly innocuous, rapport-building conversation.

Vocational experts, of course, cannot control either questions posed to them or how opposing attorneys will garner and use evidence. By remaining wary about each question and action an opposing attorney initiates and maintaining a vigilant guard, however, an expert may be able to preempt the types of manipulative tactics described above.

When providing deposition testimony, the vocational expert should approach the deposition as if it were the trial. Avoid being lulled into conversations that deviate from a professional discourse, and remain mindful that a small portion of any testimony rendered could be read to a trier of fact.

Questions posed to an expert may seek to elicit information not necessarily pertinent to a matter specific to the expert's retention, but related to some other disputed matter—such as the mechanism of injury in a workers' compensation case, a spouse's psychiatric history in a family law case, or a subject's compliance with treatment in a medical malpractice case. An attorney's efforts to present to the trier of fact a theory or develop a profile of a plaintiff, for instance, may be accomplished by weaving pieces of information elicited from various witnesses through well-crafted questions. Questions that do not appear related to the expert's analysis could have significant importance on a case's outcome. Again, experts are advised to exercise caution when responding to all questions including those that have little apparent relevance to their opinions.

11.6 Testifying at Trial

When necessary, vocational experts testify about disputed vocational issues at a trial. If their testimonies are to be considered and accepted, they must be perceived as well-qualified, objective professionals who have applied appropriate methods to arrive at opinions within a reasonable degree of probability. Experts' sound preparation and ability to communicate well under stress at trial are essential to this.

Vocational experts generally serve as damages experts and testify near the end of a case's damages presentation. An expert's testimony begins with a direct examination conducted by retaining counsel and is followed by opposing counsel's cross-examination. Then, the lawyer who retained the vocational expert has the option of conducting a redirect examination. Typically, a redirect examination occurs if counsel who retained the expert perceives a need to clarify the expert's testimony. The redirect examination also provides an opportunity to "rehabilitate" the expert; that is, if cross-examination damaged the integrity of the expert's opinion, redirect examination offers an opportunity to rehabilitate the damaged opinion.

A. Direct Examination

Direct examination typically consists of three parts: qualifying questions, methods, and substantive questions. Qualifying questions intend to feature the expert as highly competent and beyond reproach to offer opinion testimony. To demonstrate this, the retaining counsel begins direct examination by inquiring about the expert's education and background, focusing on areas particularly relevant to the case at hand. Besides academic accomplishments, specialty credentials, and professional work experience, common areas of inquiry include published works, presentations at professional meetings, college-level teaching experience, leadership experience in professional associations, and experience providing testimony in legal forums.

Whenever possible, the attorney conducting the direct examination will elicit testimony that allows an expert to present experiences or specialized knowledge particularly germane to vocational issues in dispute. For instance, if the expert has had considerable experience related to high-tower crane operators, and the trial involves a plaintiff who had been employed in this capacity, the expert's specialized experience and knowledge will likely be brought to light.

Opposing counsel has an opportunity to voir dire or question the expert witness about qualifications after the qualifying portion of a direct examination. Opposing attorneys sometimes choose to reserve voir dire for cross-examination or submit that the vocational expert is qualified to offer opinion testimony. During voir dire, the opposing attorney may challenge the expert's credentials and suggest to the trier of fact that the expert is (a) less qualified than a vocational expert whom he is offering, (b) lacking expertise in an area pertinent to the pending vocational issues, or (c) is biased. For example, opposing counsel in a family law case may attempt to demonstrate that an expert's engagements have been predominantly on behalf of husbands, and, accordingly, some type of bias against wives is operating. Opposing attorneys' voir dire objectives aim to detract from the expert's qualifications, thereby attempting to diminish weight the trier of fact places on the testimony.

After presenting the expert's qualifications, direct examination typically proceeds with questions about methods the expert applied to conduct the vocational evaluation. The expert should be prepared to testify about documents reviewed, examination protocol (when applicable) including tests administered or reviewed, independent research, consultations, and any other input that contributed to opinions. Vocational experts should employ methods outlined in Chapters 4 and 5 to nullify cross-examination attacks implying use of improper practice standards to formulate opinions.

Direct examination typically concludes with substantive questions that elicit the expert's opinions, along with reasons supporting those opinions. During this testimony, experts typically respond to questions about the plaintiff's education and work history, acquired skills, and assets/impediments to career development. The areas included in the Earning Capacity Assessment Form-2 (ECAF-2), introduced in Chapter 5, may also be questioned. Of course, the type of testimony elicited will depend on the facts of the case and damages sought. Finally, the direct examination typically concludes with questions that elicit opinions in the following areas:

- Present earning capacity
- Prognosis for future earning capacity
- Presence of any vocational handicap(s) and associated deleterious affect on career development
- Effects on earning capacity caused by preexisting problems
- Appropriateness of efforts to mitigate vocational damages

The vocational expert should respond directly to questions posed, without advocating for either of the adverse parties, and communicate effectively, avoiding technical, complex presentations that would be difficult for triers of fact to comprehend. Directing discourse to the trier of fact and being aware of nonverbal indicators about how testimony is being received allows the expert to pace and adjust testimony as needed, thereby promoting the trier of fact's comprehension and receptivity.

Below is an excerpt from a trial transcript in which a vocational expert provided opinions about a work-related injury that caused a construction worker a loss of earning capacity. Two scenarios, which serve as a predicate for an economist's calculations about the value of lost wages, are enumerated.

Q. Do you have any final opinions regarding Mr. Green?
A. Yes.
Q. Okay. Could you tell me your final opinions?
A. I presented my opinions in a report I authored after my exam of Mr. Green and my analysis of his case. The Summary and Impressions section of my report notes my analysis of his work history as a carpenter. I indicated that the work a carpenter performs is classified as skilled by the U.S. Department of Labor. In terms of the exertion demands, the Department of Labor classifies a carpenter's work as medium, which means it involves work requiring lifting/handling up to 50 pounds. The medical records indicate that Mr. Green has not been released by his physician, Dr. Yellow. Based on my understanding of the medical records, Mr. Green will be unable to return to his preinjury work as a carpenter. Dr. Yellow is of the opinion that Mr. Green reached maximum medical improvement on August 11, 2013. He gave him restrictions that included occasionally lifting/carrying up to 10 pounds, occasionally bending and squatting. I am also aware of a workers' compensation report that indicates Mr. Green has been deemed permanently, totally disabled.
Q. Okay.
A. My opinions include two vocational scenarios. The first scenario is based on Dr. Yellow not releasing Mr. Green to return to work, although he determined that he has already reached maximum medical improvement with significant restrictions, the workers' compensation opinion that Mr. Green is totally disabled, and Mr. Green's complaints of chronic pain problems and functional limitations. Those things in concert lay a foundation for a scenario that this man is unable to go back to work, and he has lost his entire future earning capacity.
Q. Okay.
A. My second opinion is a best-case scenario. This is a scenario that apparently does not have a foundation at present, but it is a best-case scenario suggesting that Mr. Green will be able to pursue at least some type of sedentary employment in the future—assuming, of course, that Dr. Yellow does release him to return to work at some future date. Under this scenario, what I would foresee for Mr. Green would be for him to return to work in a part-time capacity, which I'm defining as 20 hours per week. Of course, this would be restricted to sedentary employment. After three to six months, he should be reexamined to determine whether he's capable of increasing his work participation to full-time employment. I don't believe he would be capable of earning more than the minimum wage rate, again under this best-case scenario.
Q. Anything else?
A. I've also identified several vocational handicaps that Mr. Green has acquired because of the industrial accident, which would further reduce his future earning capacity under the best-case scenario. These include extended search time between jobs, lessened opportunity for overtime work, periodic exacerbations of his physical problems that would affect his work participation, and likelihood of a reduced work life. I believe that the conjoint effect of these vocational handicaps under this best-case scenario would result in a further diminution of 30% to 40% of Mr. Green's future earning capacity over the remainder of his work life.

Q. Anything else?
A. Yes. I believe Mr. Green is experiencing depression. He is having difficulty with his disability adjustment, and I recommend 15 to 20 sessions of psychotherapy. The cost of this treatment is $150 to $200 per hour.
Q. You said that the second situation is the best-case scenario. That's the optimum he could ever achieve?
A. Yes. Within reasonable vocational rehabilitation probability, at this point, that's my opinion.
Q. Does that opinion take into account any new training or his ability to acquire new skills?
A. This is an optimistic scenario; there is not a foundation for this opinion at this time. His primary doctor has not released him to return to work, and the Division of Workers' Compensation has determined he is permanently totally disabled. He has a lot of hardware in his neck, and he has chronic pain and physical problems that, in my view, are particularly problematic when considering his work capacity and ability to maintain employment, so I'm looking at a best-case, optimistic scenario. Getting this man back to work will be challenging, even under the best-case scenario.

B. Cross-Examination

Opinions offered during direct examination are often aggressively challenged during cross-examination. Before trial, opposing counsel learns of a vocational expert's opinions, along with the bases for these opinions, through reports an expert authors, responses to expert interrogatories, and deposition testimony. The cross-examining attorney will have had an opportunity to thoroughly prepare, and occasionally will have consulted with another vocational expert for technical assistance in attacking the opposing expert's opinions. To withstand the scrutiny of intense cross-examination and remain a credible, objective source of information on which the trier of fact can rely, the vocational expert must show confidence and conviction when expressing opinions, prepare thoroughly, and respond to cross-examination in a professional manner—regardless of how inappropriate cross-examination interrogation may be.

Lawyers most often apply the following strategies during cross-examination to undermine the credibility of a vocational expert's opinions:

- Attacking the expert's competence (e.g., suggesting the expert is not fully qualified to render the opinions presented, or that the expert's testimony should be given less weight than the testimony of a vocational expert the opposing attorney presents; suggesting the expert is testifying outside the scope of his competence and venturing beyond the domain of vocational rehabilitation)
- Accusing the expert of bias (e.g., having a financial incentive to render opinions favorable to the party who has retained and paid her and/or tending to be retained more frequently by either defense counsel or plaintiff counsel and, therefore, having a biased perspective)
- Attacking the expert's methods or assumptions for being faulty or incomplete (e.g., suggesting the expert lacks important documents or information and, therefore, has formulated opinions without full information; overreliance on information supporting the side that has retained the expert; suggesting the expert's methods depart from generally accepted standards)
- Suggesting serious errors are inherent in the expert's analysis (e.g., suggesting test results have been incorrectly interpreted; inaccurate information has been relied on)

Attempts to impeach the credibility of a vocational expert's testimony can include efforts to portray an expert as inconsistent. In this impeachment attempt, the attorney conducting cross-examination may refer to the expert's deposition testimony in a pending case and imply inconsistency between it and prior testimony. The attorney may also refer to testimony the expert provided in other cases with similar facts and suggest testimony in the present case is at odds with previous testimony. Quite often, the method and style of attack an opposing attorney employs during a deposition will be similar to the approach employed at trial; this is another reason experts should reread and be thoroughly familiar with deposition testimony before a trial.

As previously noted, a professional who regularly provides expert witness services can expect that a dossier of her deposition and trial transcripts, reports, and professional works (e.g., books and articles authored, statements made at professional meetings, website information, public records that summarize past trial participation) will be culled and circulated among the legal community. Opposing counsel regularly peruses these sorts of records to obtain information to impeach an expert's testimony. Submitting to service as an expert witness is also submitting to the likelihood of intense scrutiny and aggressive cross-examination. Those aspiring to longevity as an expert witness must be consistent in every facet involved in arriving at an opinion committed to testimony and permanent records.

During cross-examination, vocational experts should remember that opposing attorneys aggressively advocate on behalf of their clients. No matter how vigorous or improper the cross-examination, the expert should avoid personalizing the attack, remain objective, and maintain a professional demeanor. This can be quite challenging, especially when the expert is fully aware that the opposing attorney is employing tactics intended to confuse the jury or distort factual information averse to the attorney's position. Redirect examination affords the attorney who has called the expert to trial an opportunity to clarify testimony that may have been contorted or needs clarification after cross-examination.

Additionally, the vocational expert should avoid any perception of evasiveness during cross-examination and concede issues when appropriate. The expert should not argue, under any circumstance, while being cross-examined or become emotionally involved in a position.

In preparation for cross-examination, the vocational expert should anticipate opposing counsel's attacks. During direct examination, the expert should raise and dispel the strongest points counter to his own opinion to blunt opposing counsel's attempt to discredit the expert's opinion during cross-examination. This communicates to the trier of fact that the expert has thoroughly analyzed all relevant perspectives, including points that may not support the expert's position, and desensitizes notions that the expert failed to earnestly consider reasonable alternate analyses. A vocational expert exemplified this approach in a case involving a fifty-four-year-old individual who was self-employed in a residential lawn service business. The plaintiff injured his left lower extremity and consequently became limited in his ability to perform many work tasks he performed before his injury, including edging and using a blower to clean walkways and driveways. He remained capable of operating a riding lawnmower.

Because of the incompatibility between his injuries and the requirements of his job, the expert testified that the plaintiff's most promising vocational option was to pursue alternate employment in a sedentary capacity. This change of employment, accordingly, would cause the plaintiff a loss of earning capacity. In anticipation of cross-examination testimony, the vocational expert testified during direct examination about the plaintiff's absence of any substantive transferable skills, and she discussed other vocational alternatives she entertained and ruled out before arriving at an opinion about the plaintiff's most promising work options. For instance, the expert testified that the plaintiff's employment of replacement labor to perform work tasks he was unable to perform was not viable because of reasons that included added workers' compensation insurance costs the plaintiff would incur (thereby making self-employment no longer profitable), problems with reliability of entry-level labor, and the plaintiff's modest level of intellect that would likely restrict him from functioning effectively as a supervisor.

Occasionally, the attorney conducting a cross-examination will pose questions that reinforce or punctuate key points in support of the position he is advocating; this type of inquiry may not challenge the expert's opinions or elicit any new information. Rather, the attorney's aim in this case is to use the expert as a conduit to introduce or restate favorable testimony to the position being advocated. For example, during cross-examination in a medical malpractice case, plaintiffs' counsel may pursue a laborious line of inquiry, one document at a time, about whether the expert is aware of multiple treatment records that followed an incident in dispute—even though the attorney has full knowledge of the expert's file.

Although an attorney's objectives will likely be apparent, the expert should avoid fostering a perception of resistance to any question posed, and should refrain from attempts to redirect attention to the core of the expert's testimony—lest the expert risk being perceived as an advocate of the side who has called him to testify. Perception of a vocational expert as an advocate rather than an objective professional can destroy an expert's credibility.

The opposing attorney, during cross-examination, may also appropriate portions of a vocational expert's opinion that favor her position, while ignoring or dispelling portions that oppose it. This can frustrate a vocational expert, especially when the expert is not allowed to explain how selective portions of a composite opinion taken out of context compromise the integrity of the opinion as it was formulated.

An opposing attorney can apply numerous tactics during cross-examination to discredit an expert's opinion. The actual tactics employed generally derive from the attorney's overall trial strategy and her assessment of how the trier of fact will react to the expert's analysis and testimony.

Triers of fact evaluate an expert on factors beyond testimony proffered. Demeanor in addressing lawyers, and even the way an expert enters and exits a courtroom can foster attributions that affect the weight ascribed to testimony.

Thorough preparation, an unflappable sense of conviction in opinions rendered, talent in accurately surmising trial tactics, and an unshakeable sense of resolve are essential to withstanding cross-examination.

C. Redirect Examination

After direct examination, the attorney who called an expert to testify has the option of conducting a redirect examination. This option may be forfeited, for instance, in cases where the attorney is satisfied that the expert has adequately withstood cross-examination, or in cases when the retaining attorney makes a decision not to dignify points made by opposing counsel. In cases such as these, the attorney will signal to the court after cross-examination that he has no further questions.

Redirect examination is usually brief and does not go beyond the scope of cross-examination. The attorney's questions typically allow the expert to clarify points that may have been muddled by cross-examination, or give the expert an opportunity to explain points the opposing attorney may have prohibited from being fully presented. As noted above, redirect examination provides the retaining attorney an opportunity to repair damage to an opinion that may have occurred during cross-examination.

D. Trial Exhibits

Trial exhibits can greatly enhance a vocational expert's presentation of key points and opinions. Effective use of exhibits requires some creativity in determining how to visually present both the basis for opinions and actual opinions to enhance oral presentations. Information presented through exhibits must be well integrated and coordinated with expert testimony. Both the expert and examining attorney should be aware of how exhibits can supplement and enhance testimony.

Well-selected and well-presented exhibits can accomplish several objectives including better illustrating key points, summarizing a vast amount of information, retaining the trier of fact's focus and interest, and aiding recollection. The trier of fact can also refer back to exhibits admitted into evidence after the vocational expert has departed and deliberations have begun. In effect, an exhibit can serve as the expert's voice after testimony has been proffered.

Potential exhibits for trial include:

- The vocational expert's curriculum vitae
- Reports the vocational expert authored
- Diagrams the vocational expert prepared to illustrate or emphasize points
- Relevant documents (e.g., employment records citing job performance problems before event in question)
- File records (e.g., a completed pain diagram)
- Photographs and video recordings

Exhibits can be developed from extant records or information generated during the discovery phase of the litigation process, or they can be developed from an amalgamation of records and research for presentation at trial. Several examples of the use of exhibits at trial are included in the following discussions.

1. Exhibits from extant records and information

Any record or information collected during the discovery phase of litigation can serve as the basis for a trial exhibit. Visual reinforcement of facts and evidence developed in a case through strong exhibits can significantly enhance a trier of fact's understanding and receptivity to opinion evidence.

An interesting example of how a vocational expert used an opposing attorney's exhibit to support his own opinion arose in the following case. During a clinical interview that opposing (plaintiff's) counsel video-recorded, a defense-retained vocational expert elicited information from the plaintiff that was inconsistent with the case's facts. At trial, the defense expert showed portions of the videotape spotlighting various inconsistencies. This evidence, along with results from testing that suggested symptom magnification and other plaintiff inconsistencies, highlighted to the jury the plaintiff's credibility problems. The video recording, initiated by—and obviously backfired on—the plaintiff's counsel, added to the jury's consideration of it as objective admissible evidence, rather than potentially offensive evidence procured in a clandestine manner.

In an Americans with Disabilities Act case involving a passenger service agent a global airline employed, during trial, a vocational expert referenced a blueprint of the airport in which the claimant worked to explain how the physical layout of the work environment and job demands (including standing for extended periods, walking long distances, needing to occasionally ascend and descend stairs, and frequently lifting and carrying more than 25 pounds) were incongruent with a subject's physician-advised restrictions. Further, the vocational expert learned that the airline's staffing at the airport was minimal, and job incumbents performed multiple functions at various workstations dispersed throughout the airport. Given the job responsibilities, physical layout of the airport, and the plaintiff's restrictions, the vocational expert concluded he could not identify how the airline could have extended reasonable accommodations to the plaintiff to enable him to maintain his employment in his previous capacity. The use of a blueprint as an exhibit, along with photographs of the various airport workstations in question, focused the jury on a discussion that otherwise may have been dry and uninteresting. The expert's analysis of how the plaintiff's restrictions were incompatible with the prevailing work environment, coupled with images familiar to jurors, made the expert's analysis and testimony more personal and convincing.

Exhibits an opposing expert introduces that include inaccurate data can discredit that expert. To demonstrate to a jury how an adverse vocational expert incorrectly used test data to support her assessment that a plaintiff alleging injuries from an automobile accident was not magnifying symptoms, for instance, an expert showed the jury slides of her counterpart's raw test data while pointing out numerous scoring errors. During this presentation, the expert demonstrated how the errors led her counterpart to several incorrect conclusions. The expert used enlarged images of the actual data generated by the adverse expert to make an understandable, coherent explanation, and a persuasive presentation.

In a case involving a seventeen-year-old who sustained a severe head injury in a motorcycle accident, the presentation of academic transcripts—apparently overlooked by the opposing side—helped dispel the argument that, if not for the accident, the plaintiff likely would have graduated from college and earned wages commensurate with this standard. Referencing slides of the plaintiff's high school transcript, the expert cited low standardized test performance, low class rank, poor academic performance, and chronic attendance problems to discredit the opposing expert's assessment that the plaintiff would likely have completed college if not for accident-related injuries.

2. Exhibits developed by the expert

Well-developed exhibits can help encapsulate a vocational expert's testimony and improve communication of opinions with triers of fact. Both attorneys and experts should consider how opinions offered through testimony can be visually represented to aid in communicating them.

Exhibits proved to be important in a family law case that involved an ex-husband seeking a reduction in alimony. The expert developed several exhibits to support testimony that the ex-husband's job-search efforts were insufficient. These exhibits compared the ex-husband's actual efforts to become employed with the expert's declaration of reasonable efforts. The ex-husband had been a senior executive who lost his job after divorcing; he represented to the court that his attempts to become reemployed three years after losing his job were unsuccessful, and he petitioned for a reduction in alimony he paid. After analyzing job search records the ex-husband maintained, the expert consolidated the data and prepared several graphics comparing the ex-husband's efforts with those the expert defined as consisting of a good-faith job search. The graphics included a bar chart that compared the number of job applications the ex-husband initiated with efforts the expert determined were reasonable over the three-year period the ex-husband was unemployed. The expert also developed several pie charts contrasting the job search methods the ex-husband initiated with job search methods the expert deemed reasonable over the three-year period. In each case, the disparities the exhibits visually illustrated reinforced the expert's testimony that the ex-husband had not been making an earnest effort to become employed. After this presentation, the expert provided testimony about the length of time that likely would have been required for the ex-husband to become reemployed, along with testimony of the ex-husband's earning capacity.

A vocational expert developed the exhibit in Figure 11.1 to help illustrate a plaintiff's preinjury earnings history and postinjury earning capacity. This case involved a thirty-seven-year-old construction superintendent who sustained a below-the-knee injury requiring amputation. During trial, the expert referenced the exhibit to highlight the plaintiff's earnings history during the fifteen-year period preceding the accident, a one-year postinjury rehabilitative period, and potential earnings in four different postinjury occupations the vocational expert determined viable for the plaintiff, based on a transferability of skills analysis. The exhibit effectively illustrated to the jury the following points: The plaintiff had been underachieving his earning capacity before the accident; the plaintiff's preinjury earnings history demonstrated a downward trend; and the plaintiff retained transferable skills after the accident, allowing him to pursue employment within his restrictions that would have enabled him to generate earnings commensurate with his demonstrated preinjury earnings history.

11.7 Conclusion

Vocational experts, savvy in the dynamics of the trial process, can mitigate lawyers' tactics that threaten to compromise their opinions' integrity. Effective testimony requires robust analysis, credible presentation of opinions, deft handling of cross-examination, and consideration about how to best present opinions at trial. Well-conceived exhibits can augment testimony, and enhance how triers of fact comprehend and process opinions.

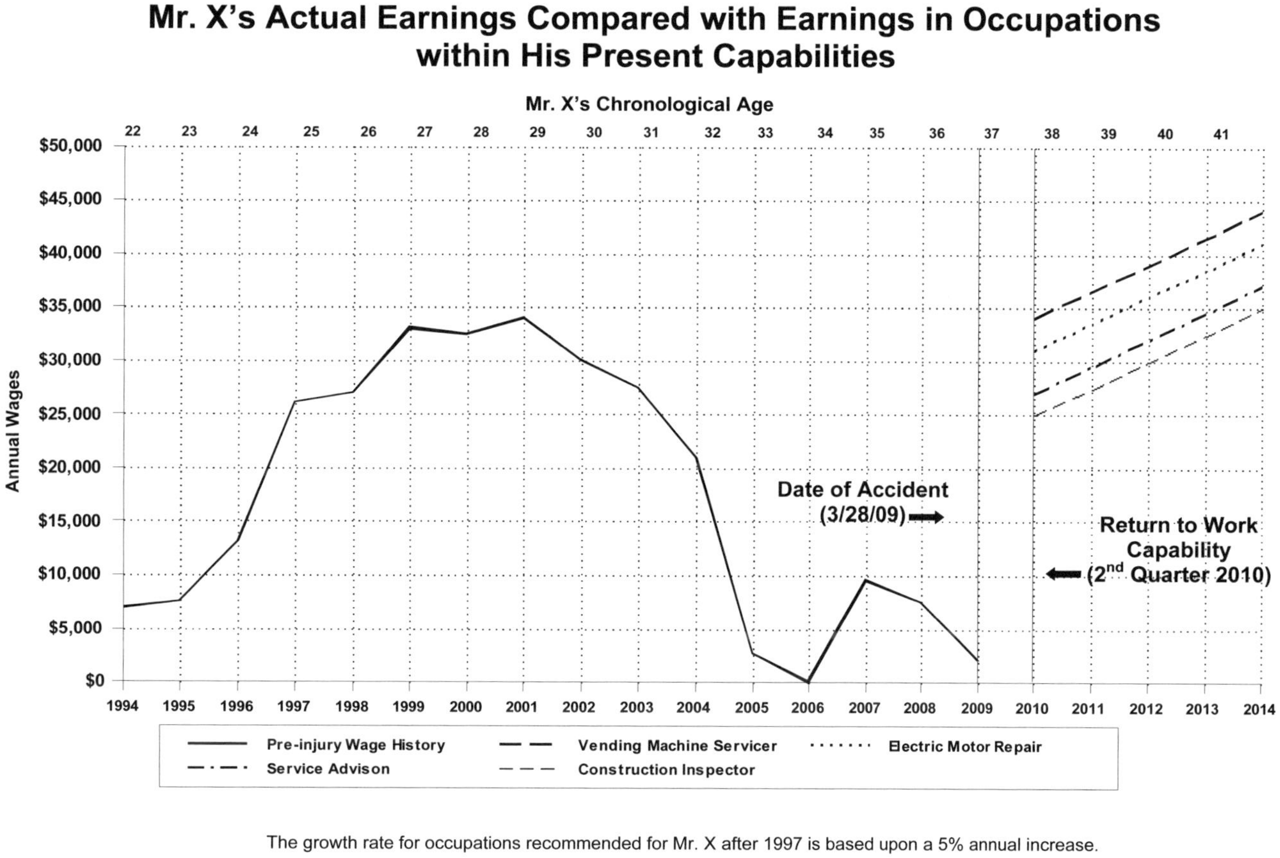

***Figure 11.1** Sample trial exhibt showing historical earnings record.*

Appendix 11.1: Sample Proposed Direct Examination Questions for a Vocational Expert Richards v. County Hospital

Direct examination begins with a retaining attorney presenting a witness as a vocational expert qualified to provide opinion testimony. Occasionally, the attorney will feature aspects of the vocational evaluator's background particularly germane to the case at hand (e.g., the evaluator's specific experience with an industry or type of disability), or features of the witness' background that suggest she is better suited to render opinions in the case than the counterpart vocational expert. The considerations that lead to the expert's retention (please refer to discussion from Chapter 1) are among those often noted during the qualifying portion of the direct examination. Overall, the attorney's aim is to establish the witness' credibility—typically through questions that elicit the following information:

- Educational background
- Specialty credentials
- Professional experience
- Publication record
- Professional recognition
- Leadership and service in professional associations
- Testimony experience

Qualifying Questions:

1. Dr. __________, tell the jury about your areas of specialization.
   — Vocational Rehabilitation
   — Life Care Planning
   — Career Counseling
   — Human Resources Consultation

2. Describe for us, please, the professional practice of vocational rehabilitation.
   — Assisting individuals with various types of disabilities on career related problems to realize their highest potential level of vocational functioning.

3. Please provide us with your educational background.
   — Bachelor's degree in Psychology from Indiana University
   — Master's degree in Psychology, with a specialty in Clinical Psychology, from Texas A&M University
   — Doctorate (Ph.D.) in Counseling Psychology from Florida State University, with a specialty in Rehabilitation Psychology
   — Postdoctoral residency completed at Florida State University and the University of Wisconsin

4. What licensures or specialty certifications do you hold?
   — Licensure as a Psychologist
   — Licensure as a Mental Health Counselor
   — Board Certification as a Rehabilitation Counselor
   — Board Certification as a Life Care Planner
   — Board Certification as a Vocational Evaluator
   — Board Certification as a Career Counselor

5. Please tell us about your practice.
   - I founded Career Consultants of America, Inc., in 1986 and continue to serve as president.
   - The practice employs 10 professionals in a 3,200-square-foot building in Tampa and has been the training site of graduate interns from several universities.
   - Career Consultants of America, Inc., has provided services to over 200 different business organizations and several thousand individuals throughout Florida, the United States, and North America.

6 Do business organizations or public organizations utilize your services as a consultant? Give us some examples.
   - Selection work for companies such as AmeriSteel Corporation, Cemex Corporation, and Florida Tile Corporation
   - Outplacement work after downsizing for organizations such as Moffitt Cancer Center
   - Consultation on issues specific to the Americans With Disabilities Act for organizations such as Honeywell and Kash 'n Karry
   - Surveys for organizations such as Snelling International (placement firm)
   - Training on career development issues throughout North America.

7. Your curriculum vitae indicates that you have privileges at 2 hospitals – is that correct, Dr. __________? Tell us about your hospital-based rehabilitation practice

8. Have you had university level teaching experience?
   - Assistant Professor in the Department of Neurology at the University of South Florida Medical School (consult on life care planning)
   - Doctoral and master=s level supervisor of students in my practice
   - Adjunct Psychologist at the University of South Florida
   - Prior teaching experience at the graduate level at Florida State University

9. Dr. __________, are you an author of any professional publications?
   - Published approximately 46 articles in refereed journals (many articles on the topic of computer assisted career guidance, initially, and during the past 10 to 15 years I have concentrated on topics related to assessing earning capacity)
   - Published eight books
   - One book—*A Decision Time: A Guide for Career Enhancement*—was translated into Italian@
   - Last book, published in January 2006, includes a Foreword written by General Schwarzkopf

10. Tell the jury topics you have addressed in your publications.
   - Articles relate to career development and vocational rehabilitation
   - Published books on use of a popular vocational test, career decision making, and assessment of earning capacity in forensic matters
   - One publication, *The Earning Capacity Assessment Form-2,* is an assessment measure other vocational evaluators throughout North America use. It sold 2,400 copies last year.

11. Have you served on any editorial boards related to publications in your profession?
   - Served two terms on the *Journal of Career Development* and one term on the *Journal of Counseling and Development*
   - Guest editor and invited author on numerous occasions
   - Presently a member of the following editorial boards, *Journal of Applied Rehabilitation Counseling, The Rehabilitation Professional, The Career Development Quarterly,* and *Estimating Earning Capacity.*

12. Dr. _________, during your career, have you received any special recognition or awards from your professional peers?
    - Selected *Practitioner of the Year* by the Florida Career Development Association (1992)
    - Selected *Outstanding Graduate of the Year* in Business and Industry (College of Education, Florida State University, 1991)
    - Selected *Outstanding Graduate of the Department of Psychology* for the first 25 years of the department at Texas A&M University (1995)
    - Selected *Rehabilitation Counselor of the Year* (1998) by the American Rehabilitation Counselor Association.
    - Selected *Outstanding Career Development Practitioner* in 2002 by the National Career Development Association
    - Presented 2005 *W. F. Faulkes Award* by the National Rehabilitation Association

13. Your resume identifies a number of professional leadership positions you have held. For sake of brevity, please tell the jury about your experience as Chairman of the Board of the Multiple Sclerosis Society and President of the National Career Development Association. This is all in addition to your private practice work - correct?
    - Served as Chairman of the Board of the Gulfcoast Chapter of the National Multiple Sclerosis Society (1993-1995) a 5,000 member organization
    - Served as President of the National Career Development Association (1997-1998). This organization was founded in 1913 and includes 10,000 members

14. Dr. _________, your resume indicates that you have also served as a vocational expert with the Social Security Administration - correct? Please tell the jury what that involves. In addition to your work at disability hearings, have you performed any other vocational rehabilitation services for the Social Security Administration?
    - On the request of Administrative Law Judges, have testified in approximately 400 disability hearings since 1987
    - Career Consultants of America was previously one of four pilot test sites in the United States for a return-to-work program sponsored by the Social Security Administration

15. Dr. _________, have you on previous occasions testified in Courts of Law as a vocational rehabilitation expert? Do you have some idea about the number of times? Have you testified in Courts throughout the state of Florida? Have you testified elsewhere? For example where?
    - Have consulted and testified as an expert witness throughout Florida, the United States and internationally.

16. Dr. _________, have you served in an official capacity to the State of Florida on rehabilitation-related issues?
    - Appointed by the Governor Chiles to the Florida Rehabilitation Council in 1998
    - Reappointed by Governor Bush, and served in this capacity through June 2002

17. Your curriculum vitae indicates that you served as a columnist for USA Today --correct? Tell the jury what this involved. Have you had any other experience as a consultant to the media?
    - Became a columnist for the *USA Today* Website in September 1998 and continued through 2003
    - Responded to disability-related questions submitted by readers and offered tips on job finding
    - Have been interviewed for articles in numerous publications, including *Business Week, The Wall Street Journal,* and *Forbes.*

18. Dr. _________, have you on prior occasions been invited to speak at national conferences related to serv-

ing as an expert witness? In this capacity, were you a member of a panel composed of other leaders including Federal Court Judges? What specific topics did you address?

— Dr. __________ has, on prior occasions, served as a panelist along with Federal Court Judges, Circuit Court Judges, and others.
— The topics Dr. __________ has addressed include withstanding cross-examination in which opposing attorneys employ techniques that include bullying, taking information out of context, manipulation, distorting testimony, and other related tactics.

Methodology

1. When did you become involved in Mr. Richards' case, Dr. __________? Who requested that you become involved? What did I specifically ask you to do?

2. Are there generally accepted standards of practice within the profession of vocational rehabilitation evaluation to assess whether an individual has sustained a loss of earning capacity? Did you observe these practice standards, Dr. __________? Briefly, tell us what is involved in conducting a professional evaluation to determine whether an individual has sustained a loss of earning capacity.

3. You indicated that the second part of your involvement in Mr. Richards' case relates to determining future rehabilitation needs he has acquired because of his May 4, 2008, medical incident – correct, Dr. __________? Again, are there professional standards of practice that are recognized in the rehabilitation profession to conduct an evaluation of future care needs a person is reasonably expected to require? Did you observe these practice standards? Briefly, tell us about the methodologies professional life care planners apply when determining a patient's future care needs.

4. Did you have an opportunity to review any records to facilitate your analysis? Briefly, Dr. __________, tell the jury what records you reviewed and how they contributed to your evaluation of Mr. Richards' disabling problems from his May 4, 2008, medical incident.

5. As part of your evaluation, did you have an opportunity to examine Mr. Richards? Tell us about the exam protocol you implemented when you met with him on September 20, 2012. What was the purpose of the standardized testing you administered? I will ask you about Mr. Richards' test results later.

6. In addition to reviewing Mr. Richards' records, conducting your clinical interview of him, and administering and interpreting a battery of standardized tests, did you have an opportunity to consult with physicians who have been treating Mr. Richards since his May 4, 2008, medical incident? Tell us with whom you consulted and the reasons for your consultations.

7. Did your analysis also include any independent research, Dr. __________? Tell us about this and how your research contributed to the formulation of your opinions.

8. Ultimately, Dr. __________, did you develop any reports that described the methods you applied in your assessment of Mr. Richards' damages from his May 4, 2008, medical incident, along with your analyses and opinions? Tell us about the reports you authored.

9. After you authored your reports, Dr. __________, did the defense lawyers in Mr. Richards' case have an opportunity to question you about your opinions during a November 28, 2012, deposition?

10. After your examination of Mr. Richards and the reports you subsequently authored, did you have an oppor-

tunity to review updated records? What types of updated records did you review? Did the new information you reviewed cause any change in your opinions?

11. Dr. __________, you have been involved in Mr. Richards' case since August 2012 – correct? If I understand your testimony, since you became involved in Mr. Richards' case you reviewed a volume of records including records postdating your exam – correct? Additionally, you conducted a full-day examination of him – including a 3.5-hour clinical interview and administration and a battery of tests, and you consulted with his physicians – correct? You also conducted considerable research to profile Mr. Richards' prior work activities and to obtain costs of medical treatment reasonably expected for him – correct? Did your work also include authoring a 37-page report dated October 2, and a 17-page report dated October 9, 2012? You gave a 2-hour deposition at the request of defense counsel – correct? Your testimony at the time of your deposition was that the total fees you billed for your services were approximately $14,200 – correct, Dr. __________? You told the jury today that you have continued to work on Mr. Richards' case – correct? Approximately how much have your fees been to date, including the extra work you performed since your deposition was taken?

Substantive Questions – Vocational Rehabilitation

1. Briefly, Dr. __________, what is your understanding of the disabling problems Mr. Richards acquired because of his May 2008 medical incident. Of his disabling problems, what did he communicate to you was his major or primary disabling problem?

2. Are you aware of any significant medical problems Mr. Richards experienced before May 2008? Tell us about these, including your understanding of how they had been affecting Mr. Richards near the time before his May 2008 medical incident.

3. Please summarize for us Mr. Richards' educational background and work history. Tell us your understanding of his job responsibilities as a service director with Western Bank, the job he had been performing at the time of his 2008 medical incident. Did Mr. Richards have any difficulty performing his job responsibilities before his April 2008 admission at County Hospital?

4. Tell the jury about Mr. Richards' efforts to work and pursue vocational rehabilitation after his discharge from County Hospital.

5. Did you discuss with Mr. Richards his opinion about his ability to return to work? What did he tell you?

6. How old is Mr. Richards, Dr. __________? What do you know about his family and living situation? Did he tell you about any disability modifications made to his home? Tell us about this.

7. Earlier you provided some information about Mr. Richards' medical history before his April 30, 2008, hospital admission. Do you know anything else about Mr. Richards' medical history?

8. You testified earlier that Mr. Richards related to you that his loss of independence is his primary disabling problem – correct? Did you have an opportunity to discuss with Mr. Richards his pain problems? What did he tell you? From your review of Mr. Richards' medical records, do you understand that he was diagnosed with incomplete paraplegia? Did you review any documentation of surgery he underwent on his thoracic spine?

9. Because of his mobility and other disabling problems, does Mr. Richards use any adaptive aids? Tell us

about this. You told us earlier that you had an opportunity to consult with Dr. Theo, Mr. Richards' physiatrist – correct? Did Dr. Theo discuss with you the types of medications he is prescribing for Mr. Richards? What did he tell you?

10. Dr. __________, do you recognize the term "functional capacity" as a term of art in the rehabilitation profession? What does this mean? Did you discuss this with Mr. Richards when reviewing his medical records? Briefly, summarize these for us.

11. Do Mr. Richards' limitations related to 2008 medical incident pose any problems to his ability to perform housework? Please explain. Who has been providing Mr. Richards housekeeping and other chores that he is no longer able to perform?

12. Can Mr. Richards perform light housework such as preparing light means and wiping off tables and countertops?

13. Before his 2008 medical incident, do you know whether Mr. Richards had been maintaining his yard? Can he do this now? Who has assumed this chore for him?

14. Have Mr. Richards' recreational activities changed since he became injured in 2008? Please summarize these for us.

15. At the time of your exam of Mr. Richards, what did he tell you about his activities during an average day?

16. Dr. __________, earlier you testified that you hold a doctorate in psychology and that you are a licensed psychologist – correct? During your clinical interview and examination of Mr. Richards, did you conduct any type of mental health status exam? What types of mental health concerns and problems did Mr. Richards disclose to you? Tell us about any clinical impressions you generated while interacting with Mr. Richards.

17. You provided us a summary of Mr. Richards' educational background earlier. Through his education, training, and work experiences, did Mr. Richards acquire any substantive work-related skills? Please summarize these for us.

18. You told us earlier that the records you reviewed included documentation of Mr. Richards' prior earnings – correct? Please tell us what you learned from your review of these records.

19. Dr. __________, you told us earlier that your examination of Mr. Richards included administering various standardized tests to him – correct? Are the results of this testing contained in your October 2, 2012, report? Please summarize for us what you found to be significant in Mr. Richards' test results.

20. Dr. __________, I would like to refer you to the last two pages of your October 2, 2012, report. Do these pages include four major areas of opinion regarding the affect of Mr. Richards' May 4, 2008, medical incident on his ability to work and earn wages? Please summarize the opinions you presented.

21. You told us that, since you authored your report, you have had an opportunity to review updated records and information – correct? Has the updated information/records you reviewed in any way changed the opinions to which you just testified?

Substantive Questions – Life Care Plan

1. Dr. __________, I would like to now move on to the second area in which you told us you were asked to provide expert opinions. The first area had to do with Mr. Richards' ability to work and earn wages, secondary to disabling problems he acquired in May 2008 – correct? If I understand your former testimony correctly, the second area in which you were retained to provide opinions had to do with future rehabilitation needs Mr. Richards acquired because of his May 2008 medical incident – correct?

2. You told use earlier that your work in Mr. Richards' case included developing a life care plan for him – correct? Briefly, tell the jury what a life care plan is, and how a certified life care planner performs the task of assessing what a disabled person is reasonably expected to require over his/her lifetime? Again, if I understand your earlier testimony, you applied standards of practice to guide your evaluation of Mr. Richards' future care needs – correct?

3. Dr. __________, you earlier told the jury about your professional credentialing including your certification as a life care planner. Do you hold any additional distinction as a certified life care planner? Apart from yourself, do you know how many other practitioners have been recognized as a Fellow by the International Association of Life Care Planners?

4. You already told us about your consultations with Mr. Richards' physicians. After you consulted with them and you developed your life care plan, did you transmit it to them for their review and approval? Tell us about this.

Note: At this time, invite Dr. __________ to come out of the witness box and present to the jury pages 3 through 17 of his October 9, 2012, life care plan. Ask him to present the contents at a high level. After his presentation, invite Dr. __________ to return to the witness box.

5. You developed, with Mr. Richards' physicians, the life care plan you just presented to us in late 2012 – correct? You told us earlier that you have continued to review updated records to date – correct? Dr. __________, has any of the new information you reviewed caused any change in your opinion about future care needs that are reasonably anticipated for Mr. Richards?

6. Have all of the opinions you provided today been within a reasonable degree of rehabilitation probability, Dr. __________?

Redirect Examination Questions

1. Dr. __________, I retained you on behalf of Mr. Richards, whom I represent – correct? Is your professional work as an expert witness exclusively at the request of plaintiff lawyers, like me? Tell us about this.

2. Does it matter to you, Dr. __________, whether a plaintiff lawyer or defense lawyer retains you? Why not?

3. The defense lawyers here today are from the firms of Smythe & Westin and the Law Office of Kim Carmichael. Has either of these firms retained you as their expert witness in the past?

4. Dr. __________, I would like you to assume for the purpose of this question that either one or both of the defendant firms retained you as their expert witness. Would the methods you applied to conduct your

analysis in Mr. Richards' case be any different? Would the opinions to which you testified today be different? Would your fees be different?

Appendix 11.2:
Sample Scheduled Deposition Letter
August 9, 2013

Lisa Haines, Esquire
The Law Office of Lisa Haines, P.A.
Suite 222
345 Bayshore Boulevard
Tampa, FL 33606

Re: Todd Allen

Dear Ms. Haines:

This letter is regarding the taking of my deposition in the above-styled matter, scheduled for October 19, 2013, at 8:00 a.m. at Career Consultants of America, 11019 North Dale Mabry Highway, Tampa, Florida.

My policy in scheduling a deposition is to block off 2 hours of time. If you anticipate that less or more time will be required, please notify my office in advance, and I will attempt to accommodate you. I require a prepayment in the amount of $990.00, 48 business-day hours before the onset of the deposition. I will not make myself available for the deposition unless I receive this prepayment by October 17, 2013. Costs associated with any copies that you may request during or after the deposition will also be billed to you. Pursuant to Florida Administrative Rule FS-64B8-10.003, costs of reproducing medical records shall not be more than $1.00 per page.

Shipping is accomplished via FedEx (or Choice, if local) for the amount we are charged. The cost for our personnel to handle copying is billed at $50.00 per hour. Note: We require a purchase order or authorized signature before beginning the copying process.

Concerning my cancellation policy, I will provide you with a full refund if the deposition is cancelled 48 business-day hours in advance. If the deposition is cancelled between 24 business-day hours and 48 business-day hours in advance, I will refund one-half of your prepayment. No refund will be provided for cancellations less than 24 business-day hours before the scheduled deposition.

Please contact me if you have any questions.

Sincerely,

Michael Shahnasarian, Ph.D.
President
MS/taw

Chapter 12

Case Studies

Synopsis

12.1 Introduction

This chapter features expert analyses of three cases. The first case involves an evaluation undertaken in the process of a dissolution of marriage, and the other two cases that follow involve acquired disabling problems with accompanying claims of loss of earning capacity. Each case includes an overview and a vocational chronology that a vocational expert assembled via clinical interview, records review, and other information. Expert analyses, and summaries and impressions follow.

The case overviews outline facts specific to the dispute, including the evaluee's presenting problems, thereby providing a context for a vocational analysis. Next, vocational chronologies provide a review of evaluees' educational backgrounds and work histories.

In the cases involving injuries, specific information follows about vocational activity—including skill and exertion demands, along with work participation and compensation information—proximate to the time disabling problems onset. Then, postinjury vocational activity is discussed; these discussions identify rehabilitation and vocational initiatives, and contentions of changed capacities to pursue career development. The vocational chronology section incorporates facts, claimant perspectives on injuries and vocational damages, and chronological events necessary for the vocational expert to frame an analysis of a claim.

In the summary and impressions sections, while recapping a claimant's vocational background, expert analyses comment on vocationally relevant issues such as exertion and skill requirements necessary to perform prior and proposed work, assessments of career development stability, and viability of expressed preinjury career objectives. When relevant, the analyses incorporate discussions of preincident issues including work, medical, psychological, and personal considerations. The analyses conclude with an expert's earning capacity appraisal.

The summary and impressions sections employ analytical processes, integrating subjective and objective data with test results, clinical impressions, labor market research, and clinical judgment necessary to formulate expert opinions. Analyses focus on factors outlined in Chapters 4 and 5.

12.2 Case Study 1

The wife is the subject of a vocational rehabilitation evaluation in this divorce case. She had been unemployed during the 7-year period preceding her husband's petition for the dissolution of their marriage; however, her work history, skill set, earnings record, and scope of job responsibilities had been impressive.

Based on his vocational profile of the wife, the vocational evaluator advised an initial period of retraining. The details associated with this recommendation include the identification of specific types of retraining, duration of retraining, and costs.

The vocational evaluator cites labor market research, including identifying current job opportunities, he conducted to help formulate an estimate of the wife's earning capacity. Additionally he projects the time anticipated for the wife to realize her prior levels of compensation.

Overview

Kelly AnneMarie Franklin was referred to me for a vocational rehabilitation evaluation. A Petition for Dissolution of Marriage from Christopher Dickson, spouse, is dated February 12, 2013. Ms. Franklin reported during her October 14, 2013, deposition that she was unemployed at the time of the 2013 petition for dissolution of marriage.

On April 14 and 15, 2014, I conducted a vocational rehabilitation evaluation of Ms. Franklin at my office in Tampa. My examination consisted of a clinical interview, which required 3 hours and 30 minutes on April 15, and the administration of a battery of tests that required 5 hours and 15 minutes for her to complete on April 14, 2014. Aaron Hill from my office assisted with the testing portion of my exam.

Ms. Franklin independently completed an intake form, although she apprised me she accessed her LinkedIn account to aid her memory of her work history. During my clinical interview, she used a tablet computer to provide information to me.

I met alone with Ms. Franklin. She reported she traveled from her home in Longwood, Florida, to Tampa on April 13, 2014, to participate in my exam on April 14 and 15. Her arrival was one day early, which she noted was due to her scheduling error. Ms. Franklin took notes during my clinical interview.

Ms. Franklin told me she drove an automatic transmission auto to my office. She indicated she holds a valid driver's license, and does not have physician-advised driving restrictions or problems with driving.

Ms. Franklin advised me she is unemployed and that her last employment was in June 2006. She conveyed she had been the owner of an auto body collision repair business, Best Body Repair, which had two locations in Orlando. Ms. Franklin informed me the business had 27 employees and generated annual sales of $3.4 million.

Noting she sold Best Body, Ms. Franklin explained, "I didn't have to work with his [my husband's] job, so we agreed to do that." She went on to apprise me she did not financially need to work and that she opted not to resume her career development. Further, she reported she and Mr. Dickson traveled extensively and that she was caring for her daughter, who is now age 13. "We ended up with four homes. That kept me busy. I kept busy doing things to build our life," Ms. Franklin said.

Ms. Franklin indicated she experiences the following physical problems:

- Left foot bunion
- Left foot hammertoe
- Pinched nerves in cervical spine and lumbar spine resulting in radiating pain in legs and hip, and occasional tingling in hands and forearms
- Mild arthritis around lumbar discs
- Dental veneers needed due to enamel erosion and chipped front tooth

Ms. Franklin advised me she is a candidate for left foot bunion and hammertoe procedures. "The only thing with that as far as a job is the surgery and the need to wear closed-in shoes in a professional environment," she said. I inquired whether she believes her reported physical problems prevent her from working, and she responded negatively. "As long as I don't wear closed-toe shoes right now," Ms. Franklin added.

Regarding mental functioning, Ms. Franklin did not cite problems. She specifically denied having trouble with memory, concentration, or mental alertness.

Vocational Activity

Ms. Franklin conveyed she completed her high school education in 1984 and pursued college studies, eventually earning a bachelor of science degree in information technology at the University of Ohio in 1995. "A lot of times I worked two jobs and went to school at night," she said, recollecting her educational experiences.

Reviewing her work history, Ms. Franklin informed me her early career development involved providing computer systems support services. Then, she noted, she developed expertise related to installing management information systems while employed with Ernst & Young, LLP. Further, Ms. Franklin apprised me she developed specialized skills and knowledge specific to the auto collision industry during her 10 years of service with ABC Coatings, Inc., and CarMax, Inc.

Ms. Franklin reported her highest earnings were $157,000, when she was 34 years old and employed as national director of collision repair operations with CarMax in 2002. She recalled her employment in a Fort Lauderdale office of CarMax when her job ended in 2002 due to a reduction in force. Her resume provides the following description of her former job responsibilities:

> Responsible for evaluating and business planning for CarMax's 105 collision centers across the country. Developed and implemented standard operating procedures and a comprehensive program to create a "certified" national collision network. Developed a national rollout for these initiatives utilizing a base staff of six district collision managers. Utilized the size of our collision repair network to form new relationships with auto insurers. During this time I was awarded as one of the 10 Most Influential Women in Collision Repair. Due to several changes in corporate priorities, my national initiatives were put on hold.

After Ms. Franklin left CarMax, she told me, she and a partner purchased Best Body Repair in June 2002. "Just the business side. I leased the buildings," she said. Ms. Franklin indicated she bought out her partner in 2004 and continued to operate the business until June 2006. Ms. Franklin's resume provides the following description of her job responsibilities as the owner of Best Body Repair:

Owned and operated all aspects of two auto collision repair locations in Orlando. Responsibilities included marketing and developing relationships with insurers, managing bank relationships, HR, accounting, tax and licensing compliance, implementation of SOP's and ensuring customer satisfaction.

Ms. Franklin explained she sold Best Body Repair in 2006 after she became married; she estimated the sales price was $550,000. She advised me her wages were $60,000, and she conveyed she had personal expenses the business absorbed. She denied holding any employment since June 2006. Ms. Franklin cited remodeling projects at her personal residences, and she stated, "I just kept busy with projects and kept busy with personal affairs."

In early 2014, Ms. Franklin conveyed, she began searching for a job; more information about this is in the Education section of this report. She informed me she has been pursuing operations management positions with profit and loss responsibility, along with sales management and business planning positions. Although she has been out of the workplace since 2006, Ms. Franklin assessed she possesses a strong skill set.

Ms. Franklin denied having any physical or emotional problems that prohibit her from pursuing her career development. I asked her opinion about what level of earnings she is capable of generating, and she stated: "I'm a lot more mature now. I think that's a huge benefit. I would like to start at the $100,000 range."

Summary and Impressions

1. A 1984 high school graduate, Ms. Franklin reported she earned a bachelor of science degree in information technology in 1995. She reported a 5-year tenure of employment as an information technology audit manager/consulting associate with Ernst & Young, LLP, before she pursued her career development in the auto collision industry. From June 1994 through December 1998, Ms. Franklin conveyed, she served as national account manager with ABC Coatings, Inc. Then CarMax, Inc., employed her as national director of collusion repair operations from December 1998 through June 2002. Ms. Franklin advised me her employment with CarMax ended due to a reduction in force, and she pursued self-employment when she purchased Best Body Repair, LLC, in June 2002; she advised me she continued to operate the business until June 2006 when she sold it for approximately $550,000. The highest earnings Ms. Franklin noted to have generated were in 2002, at the time she left CarMax; she recalled she was 34 years old and her earnings were $157,000, annually. Ms. Franklin described a broad scope of job responsibilities she performed before she left the workplace in 2006; she indicated she has not had subsequent employment, although she began a job search in early 2014. Ms. Franklin informed me she has been pursuing operations management positions with profit and loss responsibility, along with sales management and business planning positions. She expressed confidence in her skillset, and, when asked about her assessment of her earning capacity, she stated: "I'm a lot more mature now [than when I left the workplace in 2006]. I think that's a huge benefit. I would like to start at the $100,000 range." Ms. Franklin demonstrated an impressive record of career development before she withdrew from the workplace in 2006. The job responsibilities she noted as a self-employed owner of an autobody collision repair business included supervising 27 employees at two locations and generating $3.4 million in annual sales. Although Ms. Franklin has contemplated resuming her studies and pursuing a master's degree in business administration, she noted she will more likely focus her efforts on obtaining a job. Her job search efforts have included initiating approximately 20 job applications and participating in interviews with two employers: CarMax and Reliance Consulting. Ms. Franklin estimated her compensation with CarMax could be up to $100,000, and she estimated Reliance Consulting would offer pay in the range of $60,000 to $120,000, annually.
2. Ms. Franklin is a younger individual (age 48) who demonstrated average performance on a measure of intellectual functioning. She scored particularly well on measures of general fund of information, word use, and ability to quickly learn, retain, and apply new information. "As long as I don't wear closed-toe shoes right now," Ms. Franklin stated, she does not feel her physical problems prevent her from reentering the workplace. On a personal level, I found her poised, professional, confident, and well spoken. Ms. Franklin possesses education, training, work experiences, and skills as previously delineated. These factors are assets to her in her vocational rehabilitation.

3. The labor market research I conducted in Ms. Franklin's Longwood locale successfully identified several current positions she is competitive to pursue. These positions include sales management trainee, RV sales professional, sales manager, software development project sales, and IT supply chain application analyst. These jobs offer compensation commensurate with Ms. Franklin's stated earnings goals; however, she has been absent from the workplace for approximately 8 years. Considering her vocational profile, it would be reasonable to anticipate a 6-to-10-month period for her to secure new employment. During this time, I recommend that Ms. Franklin pursue retraining to enhance her skillset. In particular, computer use and general business management training would benefit her. A reasonable budget for retraining is in the range of $2,000 to $4,000. For sake of reference, below are median earnings data for the Orlando, Kissimmee, and Sanford, Florida, area; this information was published by the Florida Occupation Employment and Wages, Department of Economic Opportunity, and is from 2013:

General and operation mangers	$45.07 per hour
Marketing managers	$48.21 per hour
All other managers	$46.37 per hour

I appreciate Ms. Franklin's confidence in assessing that she is capable of securing a position that would allow her "to start at the $100,000 range," and I cannot rule this out; however, conservatively, my analysis has led me to conclude that she should be capable of earning $60,000 to $80,000, annually. Her stated earnings goals, again conservatively, should be attainable within 2 to 3 years, if not sooner.

12.3 Case Study 2

A building manager pursued a claim of loss of earning capacity after a motor vehicle accident. Complicating the case were (a) both the claimant's preaccident and unrelated postaccident medical history, (b) the claimant's continued postaccident employment in the same job, and (c) the fact that the claimant's employment ended when his employer sold the building he had been managing. The claimant did not pursue subsequent employment.

While the vocational evaluator concluded the claimant's postaccident severance was not associated with accident-related problems, she also determined he was not capable of resuming his former employment due to the constellation of his physical problems including preexisting and unrelated postaccident problems. Regardless of any injuries associated with the accident, she also reasoned, continued employment as a building manager would have been contraindicated from a vocational rehabilitation perspective due to preexisting problems. Further, the evaluator opined that the claimant remained a candidate for vocational rehabilitation, albeit at a lower earning capacity.

Overview

Keith Eldon Dillinger was referred to me for a vocational rehabilitation evaluation. A Complaint documents allegations of injuries he sustained as a result of a February 27, 2012, motor vehicle accident. Mr. Dillinger reported University Medical Center employed him as a building manager at the time of the 2012 accident.

On April 17, 2014, I conducted a vocational rehabilitation evaluation of Mr. Dillinger at my office in Tampa. My examination consisted of a clinical interview, which required 3 hours and 35 minutes, and the administration of a battery of tests that required an additional 3 hours and 50 minutes for him to complete. Aaron Hill from my office assisted with the testing portion of my exam.

As requested by Mr. Dillinger's lawyer, Malcolm Maxwell, my exam was video recorded. Mr. Dillinger arrived with his wife, Miranda, whom I met. Mr. Dillinger told me his wife transported them from their home in Seffner to my office, and he estimated the commute required 40 minutes.

Mr. Dillinger indicated he holds a valid driver's license and does not have physician-advised driving restrictions. When asked about problems with driving, he referenced trouble with sitting, which he said restricts his ability to drive "for long periods." He also advised me his hands "go numb," after holding a steering wheel from 30 to 35 minutes. Mr. Dillinger conveyed he most recently operated a motor vehicle the day before my exam. I asked him why his wife transported him to my exam, and he informed me, "She wanted to come with me, and if I ride with her, she drives."

Concerning his 2012 accident, Mr. Dillinger denied striking his head or losing consciousness. In his September 5, 2013, Answers to Interrogatories, when asked to describe each injury for which he is claiming damages in this case, he reported: "To the best of my knowledge, I did receive injuries to my neck and back."

During my exam, Mr. Dillinger identified the following problems:

- Headaches
- Neck pain
- Ongoing burning pain and numbness in arms, prominent in the left side, "and it moves around"
- Ongoing lower back pain radiating bilaterally, more problematic in right lower extremity
- Occasional left foot drop
- Lower extremity weakness

I asked Mr. Dillinger whether he experienced the aforementioned problems before February 27, 2012, and he responded, "Yes, but not to this extreme." I reviewed with him his presenting problems. Mr. Dillinger said about his prior headaches, "I did get headaches, but not as often as I get them now."

Acknowledging he experienced neck pain before his February 2012 accident, Mr. Dillinger denied having restrictions because of preexisting neck trouble. I inquired about neck symptoms near the time before his 2012 accident, and he responded, "Every once in a while I had a little pain."

Mr. Dillinger denied having bilateral arm problems near the time before his 2012 accident. "Mostly it was in my right side, my right arm. It was nothing like it is now, though," he stated.

Further, Mr. Dillinger acknowledged having lower back pain near the time before his 2012 accident. "It would come and go," he said. I asked about radicular symptoms, and he replied, "The right leg a little bit."

I inquired about preexisting left foot drop problems, and Mr. Dillinger said, "Not that I know of." When asked about prior problems with lower extremity weakness, he said, "There was a little bit every once in a while."

As for mental functioning, Mr. Dillinger cited trouble with concentration. I asked him about memory problems, and he said: "I think so. My memory is not as good as it used to be." When asked whether he believes his reported cognitive difficulties are accident-related, he responded, "I don't know." During this discussion, Mr. Dillinger apprised me his hand numbness frustrates him.

Dr. Connors stated in a November 1, 1995, record that Mr. Dillinger had "cervical myelopathy, rule out H&P C5-6 and status post anterior cervical discectomy C4-5."

In a May 28, 1998, record, Dr. Connors stated:

> In the thoracic spine he has degenerative changes with hemangioma at approximately T8. In the cervical spine, he is status post fusion C5-6, C6-7, with instrumentation and a prior older fusion at C4-5. He does have some spinal canal impingement at C4-5 but I do not feel surgical intervention is indicated. I feel that he should be treated conservatively.

Dr. Gross stated in a July 24, 1998, record, "The patient has a suspicion of mild spinal cord impingement that may account for some of his symptoms including the jerking at night."

In a November 9, 2003, record, Mr. Dillinger was diagnosed with a lumbar strain. A September 27, 2004, record from Dr. Urich diagnosed Mr. Dillinger with an upper back strain. Dr. Mench diagnosed Mr. Dillinger with a lower back strain in a June 13, 2005, record. Dr. Connors stated in an August 19, 2005, record:

> About one and a half years ago he moved a table which was small, however, he bent over the back of a couch to pick it up and when he did so, he felt a sharp pain in his back. An hour later, he could not walk because of severe pain. He tried to get EMS to take him to the ER. They would not. He was eventually taken to TRH ER, evaluated, treated conservatively and discharged. By Monday, he returned to work. With his back pain, he also had a burning sensation, but his symptoms finally resolved. Three months later his symptoms developed again when he picked up his leg as he tried to get into his truck. He could not move because of severe pain and again he was taken to TRH, again treated conservatively and his symptoms gradually resolved. Then three weeks ago, he was taking his daughter to daycare, was walking up the steps, opened the door and again had severe back pain. Again, he went to TRH and was treated conservatively.

Vocational Activity

Mr. Dillinger reported he left school during the 10th grade. Most of his work experiences have involved vehicle maintenance, primarily with the Bay Area Tribune for approximately 10 years, and building maintenance, mostly with University Medical Center.

In August 2002, Mr. Dillinger indicated, he began his service with University Medical, where he continued to work as a building manager through the time of his February 27, 2012, motor vehicle accident. At the time of his accident, he worked at least 40 hours per week, he advised me. "I was the only employee there [performing building maintenance]," Mr. Dillinger said. He conveyed he was a salaried employee and paid between $62,000 and $67,000 per year

Mr. Dillinger informed me University Medical is approximately 55,000-square-feet with physician offices and a pharmacy. He noted his job responsibilities involved maintaining the premises. He apprised me he was required to perform repair and maintenance work as needed, including janitorial work, general grounds maintenance, minor plumbing and drywall repairs, and painting. Occasionally, Mr. Dillinger reported, when larger scale construction was required for projects such as build-outs, he hired and oversaw contractors.

The heaviest weight Mr. Dillinger handled, he told me, was up to 150 pounds – air-conditioning compressors and electric motors. He indicated he was required to climb ladders and occasionally access confined areas. He performed the full range of body motions and engaged in bimanual tasks throughout his workday, he advised me. Mr. Dillinger estimated 80% of his job involved "hands on" work.

Noting his preexisting neck and lower back problems, I asked Mr. Dillinger when he realized aggravation of his symptoms after his February 2012 accident. He replied, "As soon as I was hit, I felt something in my neck." He conveyed his back felt "tight, but at that time I was more concerned about my neck." I referenced Dr. Miller's February 29, 2012, office note, and Mr. Dillinger recalled this was his first post-accident medical treatment.

Regarding his postaccident work participation, Mr. Dillinger informed me he had a work absence the day of the accident; thereafter, he did not recall any other accident-related work absences until his employment with University Medical ended in July 2012.

Mr. Dillinger apprised me his job responsibilities as a building manager after February 27, 2012, were the same as his preaccident responsibilities. He denied that University Medical extended accommodations to him after his 2012 accident. "If I needed to, I could hire [someone to perform a task beyond my capacity]," Mr. Dillinger said.

Over time, Mr. Dillinger reported, performing his job became increasingly difficult. "My left arm started dying," he stated when asked how his injuries specifically affected his job performance. He went on to cite his lower back and headache problems.

Noting his worsening condition, Mr. Dillinger told me Dr. Miller advised him before July 2012 that "I would not be able to work anymore." Mr. Dillinger did not recall when the neurosurgeon made this proclamation.

Dr. Timberlake stated in a University Medical Center record:

> I was the employer/supervisor for Keith Dillinger during the 10 years from August 2002 until August 2012. Mr. Dillinger began to work for UMC as an assistant to our former building manager, whom he eventually replaced. . . . In July, 2012, University Medical Center was purchased by a large real estate investment trust. As such, Mr. Dillinger's employment with University Medical Center Associates came to an end.

Mr. Dillinger recounted that his building manager job with University Medical ended in July 2012. "They sold the building," he said about the reason and added: "The new owners, they offered me a job. They wanted me to continue to take care of University Medical Center and another one of their buildings two doors down."

Initially, Mr. Dillinger conveyed, he accepted his new job offer. "It was verbal," he said about the offer. He informed me his new annual compensation would have been from $10,000 to $20,000 less than it was with University Medical and that his job responsibilities would have been enlarged. "Then I realized I couldn't do the job," Mr. Dillinger stated, noting he declined the new job offer. "You can't take something you can't do," he said.

Mr. Dillinger denied holding any employment since he left University Medical in 2012. Further, he denied having any subsequent retraining, searching for a job, or initiating other vocational rehabilitation efforts.

I discussed with Mr. Dillinger the possibility of resuming his former building manager job, and he said, "There's no way." He apprised me Drs. Miller, Smythe, Nacco, and Jules are restricting him from working.

As for alternate employment, I discussed sedentary jobs with Mr. Dillinger that would allow him to reposition as needed, such as a security guard at a stationary post. He said, "It's possible," and he referenced his difficulty sleeping, pain, and need to take medications.

Mr. Dillinger opined that he is incapable of maintaining any employment on a regular basis. He said this is also "the doctors' opinion." Mr. Dillinger reported he is appealing the Social Security Administration's denial of his application for disability benefits.

Summary and Impressions

1. The work history Mr. Dillinger reported after he left school during the 10th grade related mainly to vehicle maintenance and building maintenance. Dr. Ellis Timberlake, former managing partner of University Medical Center Associates, indicated Mr. Dillinger was employed by the organization from August 2002 through August 2012. Mr. Dillinger began as an assistant to the former building manager, and then transitioned to the building manager position when his predecessor retired.

Mr. Dillinger indicated he performed general building maintenance tasks at the 55,000-square-foot facility, and occasionally contracted others to perform larger scale construction work. Based on my understanding of his job responsibilities, Mr. Dillinger performed semiskilled tasks that, at times, involved heavy and very heavy exertion. He estimated 80% of his job involved "hands-on" tasks. Apart from a 1-day absence after his accident, Mr. Dillinger recollected, he did not have any other accident-related work absences until his employment ended with University Medical in July 2012. He advised me his preaccident and postaccident job responsibilities were the same, and he denied that any accommodations were extended to him after his accident; however, Mr. Dillinger indicated performing his job became increasingly difficult. He expressed that his surgeon, Dr. Miller, told him before July 2012, "I would not be able to work anymore." According to a January 30, 2014, letter by Mr. Dillinger's former supervisor at University Medical (Dr. Timberlake), his employment with University Medical ended in July 2012 when the building was purchased by a large real estate investment trust; the letter makes no mention of any difficulty Mr. Dillinger may have had performing his job. It appears that his severance from University Medical was not associated with accident-related problems. Although he reported the new owner of University Medical Center offered him employment, he declined it. I am not aware of any documentation supporting Mr. Dillinger's representation that he had an opportunity to continue his job. He apprised me he declined the offer because "you can't take something you can't do." He denied holding employment since he left University Medical. Likewise, he advised me he has not initiated any subsequent efforts to further his vocational rehabilitation. Mr. Dillinger assessed he has been incapable of resuming his former building manager job. Regarding alternate employment, such as a sedentary job that would allow him to reposition as needed, Mr. Dillinger stated, "It's possible [I could perform work of that sort]." He went on to opine that he has been incapable of maintaining any employment on a regular basis. The Social Security Administration denied Mr. Dillinger's application for disability benefits; he informed me he is appealing the decision. He denied planning to begin a job search. He did not impress me as motivated to pursue vocational rehabilitation.

2. Medical records predating Mr. Dillinger's February 27, 2012, motor vehicle accident are significant from a vocational rehabilitation perspective. He had longstanding cervical spine and lumbar spine problems that are well documented. He underwent an anterior cervical discectomy and fusion at C4-5 on November 5, 1992, and an anterior cervical fusion at C5-6 and C6-7 in December 1995. Mr. Dillinger subsequently continued to pursue treatment for his neck symptoms. A July 24, 1998, office note by Dr. Gross describes difficulty Mr. Dillinger had obtaining employment because of his previous medical history. According to preaccident medical records, Mr. Dillinger's cervical spine complaints continued. There is also documentation of multiple occurrences when he sought treatment for lumbar spine problems. Additionally, in a September 16, 2011, office note, Dr. Miller commented on Mr. Dillinger's muscle wasting involving predominantly his triceps. Mr. Dillinger was prescribed physical therapy in October 2011; this treatment ended in December 2011 "due to patient's busy schedule." Regardless of any additional injury he may have acquired as a result of his February 27, 2012, motor vehicle accident, his preaccident medical history likely would have had implications on his employability. From a vocational rehabilitation perspective, based on Mr. Dillinger's preaccident medical history, work involving more than light/medium exertion would have been contraindicated. As he described his former building manager job, it would not have been compatible with his preaccident medical problems, and an occupational change would have been in order. Even if Mr. Dillinger's employment with University Medical would have continued, absent the sale of the building, he likely would have had a truncated work-life expectancy as a building manager had he persisted in his former job. Additionally, when considering his employability as a building manager, it should be noted that he experienced an apparently unrelated postaccident medical problem involving his right knee. Mr. Dillinger advised me he underwent right-knee surgery 2 weeks before my April 17, 2014, examination. I have not had an opportunity to review any documentation associated with his operation or subsequent treatment; of course, this information has relevance to my analysis including an assessment of his capacity to work as a building manager in view of his preaccident medical

problems and unrelated postaccident medical problems.

3. The first medical record postdating Mr. Dillinger's February 27, 2012, motor vehicle accident is an office note by Dr. Miller dated February 29, 2012; she had been treating him before his February 2012 accident. In her initial postaccident record, Dr. Miller stated: "K. D. apparently sprained his neck. I do not feel that there are any new problems." She subsequently performed a C4-T2 posterolateral fusion from C3-T2 on October 15, 2012. Although Dr. Miller initially determined Mr. Dillinger did not acquire new problems because of his February 27, 2012, accident, in a March 6, 2013, note, she opined otherwise and stated, "I believe his symptoms did begin following the auto accident which occurred in February of 2012." She also noted Mr. Dillinger's back problem was progressing. In her March 22, 2013, office note, Dr. Miller commented on Mr. Dillinger's "long history of labor-intensive work." Dr. Jules stated in a May 6, 2013, report: "The only work that the patient could do previously was manual labor. The patient is unable to do any manual labor." Dr. Miller authored a May 24, 2013, statement in which she declared, "He is at MMI and is in my medical opinion, permanently disabled." Dr. Jules stated on August 5, 2013, "The patient is unable to hold any type of meaningful work." Dr. Nacco, a neurologist, examined Mr. Dillinger in September 2013 and assigned a 23% permanent impairment rating, with restrictions that included no lifting greater than 20 pounds from a bent position, 10 pounds repetitively. The neurologist added, "He is permanently disabled." Mr. Dillinger underwent a functional capacity evaluation on November 15, 2013; the physical therapist determined, "Mr. Dillinger is able to perform activities within the light DOT category for short periods of time. He fatigues quickly which causes him to demonstrate unsafe behaviors such as lateral bending and twisting to handle a load and dragging his right foot causing him to lose his balance." The first reference I am aware of that addresed Mr. Dillinger's right-knee problems is a record by Dr. Devine dated December 20, 2013; the orthopedic surgeon diagnosed a medial meniscal tear. As noted above, Mr. Dillinger underwent surgery on his right knee 2 weeks before my April 17, 2014, examination.

   The most recent records I reviewed are from Dr. Newell. In his April 10, 2014, report, the orthopedic surgeon concluded that, based on his analysis of preaccident and postaccident MRIs of Mr. Dillinger's cervical spine, there was no significant change and no objective evidence of any permanent injury caused by the February 27, 2012, accident. Dr. Newell also cited Dr. Miller's February 29, 2012, note in which she felt the accident did not cause new problems. Regarding Mr. Dillinger's lumbar spine, Dr. Newell likewise determined that comparisons of Mr. Dillinger's preaccident and postaccident lumbar MRIs did not show significant changes. Based on my analysis of Mr. Dillinger's medical records, it is my opinion that he is not capable of resuming his preaccident job as a building manager; however, as noted above, from a vocational rehabilitation perspective, this employment would have been contraindicated due to his preexisting medical problems. Additionally, his apparently unrelated postaccident right-knee problems further disqualify him from his former employment.

4. Mr. Dillinger, age 51, is in an age category the Social Security Administration recognizes as a person approaching advanced age. His measured basic skills were at low levels, and he did not perform well on a test of mental functioning administered during my exam. Mr. Dillinger's options for retraining will be limited.

5. On a positive note, Mr. Dillinger is cognitively intact, and he possesses work experiences and skills as previously delineated. Psychologically, he assessed he is well adjusted and does not need mental health treatment; I concur. On a personal level, I found Mr. Dillinger pleasant and likeable. These factors are assets to him should he become motivated to pursue vocational rehabilitation.

6. As indicated above, a functional capacity evaluation Mr. Dillinger previously underwent defined his capacities/restrictions. Subjectively, he assessed he is capable of safely handling from 5 to 8 pounds, driving 30 minutes, sitting and/or standing from 15 to 30 minutes, and walking no more than 200 yards. Under his physicians' supervision, I believe Mr. Dillinger is a candidate for vocational rehabilitation – again, should he become motivated to pursue this. At this time, I would restrict him to part-time (no more than 20 hours per week), unskilled work with sedentary/light exertion require-

ments. After a 30-to-90-day trial period, his condition should be reassessed to determine whether he is capable of increasing his level of work participation. Examples of jobs I believe Mr. Dillinger could attempt include caregiver to a person who does not require physical assistance, courier, card swiper, and telephone answerer. His earnings in positions of these sorts would be at the minimum wage rate. While considering alternate employment for Mr. Dillinger, it should be noted that an occupational change would have been in order for him regardless of any injuries he may have acquired because of his February 27, 2012, motor vehicle accident.

7. Based on my review of Dr. Newell's assessments, Mr. Dillinger's February 27, 2012, motor vehicle accident did not cause him to acquire any new treatment needs; therefore, a life care plan attributing treatment needs to Mr. Dillinger's 2012 accident is unmerited.
8. Mr. Dillinger was less than fully compliant with me during my April 17, 2014, exam. On the instruction of his lawyer, Mr. Dillinger conveyed, he refused to complete a pain diagram I presented to him at the onset of my exam. As noted above, he has a significant preaccident medical history, and he has had unrelated postaccident medical problems including a right-knee surgery near the time before my exam. I am unaware of a court order restricting me from requesting Mr. Dillinger to complete a pain diagram or elicit from him other pertinent information.
9. I have requested an opportunity to review several updated/additional records. My opinions continue to be in a formative state.

12.4 Case Study 3

Because of a motor vehicle accident that involved a fatality, the claimant in this case sustained multisystem injuries—including a head injury and spinal cord injury—and had not returned to work at the time of his vocational rehabilitation evaluation. He previously worked as a forklift operator.

The vocational evaluator rendered opinions related to the claimant's likely preaccident career path, residual postaccident employability, and prospects for vocational rehabilitation including potential for retraining. Noting the claimant had preexisting lower back and right elbow problems, the evaluator also comments on how these would have impacted the claimant's employability and earning capacity in the absence of the motor vehicle accident.

Other opinions the vocational evaluator presented related to future need for rehabilitation intervention and the claimant's disability adjustment. The accident occurred approximately one year before the evaluation, and the evaluator notes that he planned to review updated records. Stating he is "not optimistic" about the claimant's prospects for vocational rehabilitation, the evaluator intended to write an update report near or at the time the claimant reached maximum medical improvement.

Update reports provide an expert witness an opportunity to integrate additional information into analyses and refine opinions preliminarily rendered. Courts often prohibit new, previously undisclosed opinions during the discovery period from being admitted into evidence. Even if update records do not change opinions and/or provide additional support for previously rendered opinions, it can be helpful to make this known. In one case, a judge restricted an expert from testifying about updated records he reviewed—and that supported but did not change his opinions—after authoring his report because he did not provide an update report during discovery identifying the updated records and noting that they supported his opinion.

Overview

Carlo Montana, Sr. (also known as Carlo Montana Perez, Sr.), was referred to me for a vocational rehabilitation evaluation. A Complaint outlines allegations of injuries he sustained as a result of a motor vehicle accident on May 27, 2013. Mr. Montana reported BigSugar Corporation employed him as a forklift operator at the time of his accident.

On June 9, 2014, I conducted a vocational rehabilitation evaluation of Mr. Montana in a conference room in West Palm Beach, Florida. My examination consisted of a clinical interview, which required approximately 5 hours, and the administration of a battery of tests that required 50 additional minutes for Mr. Montana to complete.

Mr. Montana arrived with his son, Carlo Montana, Jr., who was present during my clinical interview, as was Marcus Iglesias, who provided English/Spanish translation services. Mr. Montana advised me his English language skills are nominal.

Mr. Montana informed me he lives in Moore Haven, Florida, and that his son transported him to the exam site. "I haven't driven [since my February 20, 2014, cervical spine operation]," Mr. Montana said. He complained of problems with vision, dizziness, and restricted cervical spine range of motion. During this discussion, Mr. Montana's son described an incident, before his father's February 2014 operation, when he was driving, became confused and disoriented, and arrived at an unfamiliar retail store location. Mr. Montana reported he has a valid driver's license and does not have physician-advised driving restrictions.

Records indicate the driver of the vehicle in which Mr. Montana was a passenger was killed in the May 2013 accident. Records also note Mr. Montana struck his head and lost consciousness in the accident.

In his February 27, 2014, Answers to Interrogatories, when asked to describe each injury for which he is claiming damages in this case, Mr. Montana reported:

> I sustained numerous orthopedic injuries, including but not limited to severe bruising abrasions, lacerations, injuries to my nose, face, knee, ribs, chest wall and spine. I was also knocked unconscious during the accident and sustained a traumatic brain injury which has left me with residual cognitive deficits, including, but not limited to, severe headaches, memory problems and dizziness. I also have to relive Klaus' death on a daily basis as he was killed through no fault of his own while seated directly next to me.

Mr. Montana told me he tends to feel particularly weak in the morning. He indicated he often has difficulty getting out of bed.

I reviewed with Mr. Montana documentation from medical records predating his 2013 accident, including documentation of preexisting lower back problems. He recalled a lower back operation while in Cuba in the early 1970s. "Everything was fine after that," he stated. Mr. Montana discussed the physical nature of work he performed before his 2013 accident and conveyed he had periods of situational lower back pain. He denied having any lower back symptoms near the time before his accident.

I asked Mr. Montana whether he ever injured his neck before May 27, 2013, and he responded negatively. I inquired about preaccident cognitive difficulties, and he said, "Not to my knowledge."

Regarding current mental functioning, Mr. Montana cited problems with memory, concentration, and attention span. He gave examples of being reminded by his wife that he asks questions repeatedly and forgetting activities he intended to pursue while in the midst of engaging in them.

Vocational Activity

Mr. Montana informed me completed 9 years of schooling Cuba. He noted BigSugar Corporation, a sugar manufacturer in Belle Glade, hired him as a utility worker in 1991 and that his service with the organization continued through the time of his May 27, 2013, motor vehicle accident. Mr. Montana apprised me he transitioned into a forklift operator position 14 or 15 years before he became injured.

As a forklift operator, Mr. Montana told me, he performed his job inside a warehouse. "I used to load containers sometimes, so I had to change the attachment [on my forklift]," he said. Mr. Montana indicated his job responsibilities included selecting pallets in a warehouse for shipment and loading pallets into trucks. He denied having any mechanical repair or maintenance responsibilities.

I asked Mr. Montana about the physical demands associated with his forklift operator job. He conveyed his job generally required nominal lifting, apart from when he changed attachments. "My thing was to sit on the forklift and operate the forklift," he said, informing me he performed repetitive movements with all four limbs and frequently moved his cervical spine. Mr. Montana also noted he was exposed to considerable jarring.

Mr. Montana apprised me he was a union employee of BigSugar and worked more than 40 hours per week. He reported he earned approximately $17 per hour. We reviewed documentation of his earnings.

Since his May 2013 accident, Mr. Montana told me, he has not returned to work. His son indicated that, since he was unable to resume his forklift operator job, BigSugar terminated his father's employment on January 1, 2014. Records indicate Mr. Montana underwent cervical spine surgery on February 20, 2014.

I inquired whether he believes he has been capable of resuming his forklift operator job, and Mr. Montana responded, "I don't think so." He discussed his pain, functional limitations, and cognitive difficulties as reasons for his assessment, and he surmised that his acquired disabling problems are incompatible with the demands of his former job.

Mr. Montana's son advised me that Dr. Alman and Dr. Dartmuth continue to restrict Mr. Montana from returning to work. He conveyed his father is applying for Social Security Administration disability benefits.

Summary and Impressions

1. Born in Cuba, where he attended 9 years of school, Mr. Montana reported he immigrated to the United States in 1990 or 1991. He became employed with BigSugar Corporation in 1991, and his service with the organization continued through the time of his May 27, 2013, motor vehicle accident. Mr. Montana apprised me that, during the last 14 or 15 years of his tenure with BigSugar, he worked as a forklift operator (DOT #921.683-050). Based on my understanding of his job responsibilities, he

performed semiskilled tasks that required light/medium exertion. A letter from a BigSugar administrator indicates Mr. Montana's employment was terminated on January 1, 2014, because he did not return to work, and the prospects of him doing so were uncertain. Mr. Montana informed me that he has not had employment since he became injured, and he opined that he has not been capable of resuming his forklift operator job. Before he became injured, Mr. Montana reported, he enjoyed a high level of job satisfaction, had been meeting his employer's performance expectations, and his job had been secure. The preaccident career plans he presented included continuing his employment with BigSugar as a forklift operator. I am unaware of a reason he would not have been able to pursue his stated preaccident career plans if not for his accident-related problems.

2. Preaccident medical records document a history of lower-back pain complaints Mr. Montana presented. There is also documentation of injury to his right elbow secondary to a work-related mishap in June 2008. It does not appear that either Mr. Montana's preaccident lower-back problems or his right elbow injury adversely affected his ability to work as a forklift operator. The last medical record I reviewed predating his May 27, 2013, motor vehicle accident is an office note dated February 11, 2013. The note indicates Mr. Montana was capable of continuing full-duty work.
3. Postaccident medical records provide objective support for Mr. Montana's presenting problems. Apparently, bystanders at his May 27, 2013, accident scene found him nonresponsive, and, upon the arrival of emergency medical service workers, his Glasgow Coma score was 11. Mr. Montana experienced polytrauma including injury to his head and spinal cord. He underwent surgery to his cervical spine on February 20, 2014. My analysis of medical records has led me to conclude that Mr. Montana has not been capable of resuming his preaccident forklift operator job or alternate employment.
4. Mr. Montana, age 57, is in an age category the Social Security Administration recognizes as a person of advanced age. He is 1 year status postaccident and remains symptomatic as noted. His education is limited, and he lacks substantive transferable skills. Mr. Montana's English language skills are nominal, and he lives in a rural area. He is not a good candidate for retraining. As noted above, Mr. Montana is not capable of resuming his preaccident forklift operator job or alternate employment. I am not optimistic about his future prospects for vocational rehabilitation.
5. Consistent with my clinical impression, Mr. Montana exhibited severe depression on testing I administered. He also evidenced indicia of cognitive dysfunction during my clinical interview.
6. Because of injuries and associated disabling problems Mr. Montana acquired as a result of his May 27, 2013, motor vehicle accident, he will require significant rehabilitation intervention. I am developing a life care plan for him.
7. I understand Mr. Montana underwent a neuropsychological evaluation with Dr. Beso in April 2014. I am interested in reviewing updated medical records. Depending on his progress, an update rehabilitation evaluation may be in order.

12.5 Conclusion

Competent evaluators add value to jurisprudence by applying the science of the vocational rehabilitation profession to gather relevant information, analyze pertinent evidence, interpret test results, conduct and evaluate labor market research, document findings and analyses, and integrate information to formulate opinions. Opinions developed via peer-reviewed methodology, undergirded by the profession's literature and empirically tested, can best serve triers of facts' efforts to decide on disputed vocational issues. This also helps to contain opposing lawyers' allegations of bias and attacks on an evaluator's analysis.

Bibliography

American Board of Vocational Experts. (2007). Code of ethics. Aptos, CA: Author.

American Counseling Association. (2014). Code of ethics. Alexandria, VA: Author.

American Medical Association. (2009). AMA guides to the evaluation of permanent impairment, sixth edition. Chicago: Author

American Psychiatric Association. (2013). Diagnostic and statistical manual of mental disorders, fifth edition (DSM-5). Arlington, VA: American Psychiatric Publishing

American Psychological Association. (2010). Ethical principles of psychologists and code of conduct. Washington, DC: Author.

American Psychological Association and American Board of Forensic Psychology. (2012). Specialty guidelines for forensic psychology. Washington, DC: Author.

Athanasou, J. A. (2013). The use of the earning capacity assessment form-2 in a medico-legal setting: An australian experience. Paper presented at the 2013 annual conference of the American Board of Vocational Experts in Scottsdale, AZ.

Austin, T., Barzegarian, B., Ciddio, M., Cottle, R., Diaz, F., Ferra, K., . . . Winn-Boaitey, K. (2009). White paper: IARP-DFEC work group. The Rehabilitation Professional, 17 (3), 14 –150.

Bacallo v. Dauphin, 963 So. 2d 962, page 2 (Florida 3rd District Court of Appeals, 2007).

Barros-Bailey, M., Carlisle, J., & Blackwell, T. L. (2010). Forensic ethics and indirect practice for the rehabilitation counselor. Rehabilitation Counseling Bulletin, 53, 237–242.

Barros-Bailey, M. & Heitzman, A. M. (2014). Labor market survey. In R. H. Robinson (Ed.), Foundations of forensic vocational rehabilitation (pp. 167–201), New York: Springer Publishing Company.

Barros-Bailey, M. & Karman, S. (2014). Occupational and labor market information. In R. H. Robinson (Ed.), Foundations of forensic vocational rehabilitation (pp. 203–237), New York: Springer Publishing Company.

Ceaser, K. (2014). Book Review: A claimant's guide to understanding and presenting injury damages: A damages expert's perspective. The Rehabilitation Professional, 22, 141 – 143.

Commission on Rehabilitation Counselor Certification. (2010). Code of professional ethics for rehabilitation counselors. Schaumburg, IL: Author.

Deutsch, P. & Sawyer, H. (1986). A guide to rehabilitation. New York: Mathew Bender. Dillman, E. G. (1998). Interfacing the economic and vocational in personal injury cases. Journal of Forensic Vocational Assessment, 1, 19–39.

Dillman, E.G. (1998). Interfacing the economic and vocational in personal injury cases. Journal of Forensic Vocational Assessment, 1, 19–39.

Dunn, P. (2014). Introduction to the American legal system and rules of civil procedure: A primer for vocational experts. In R. H. Robinson (Ed.), Foundations of forensic vocational rehabilitation (pp. 239–259), New York: Springer Publishing Company.

Field, J. & Field, T. F. (2001). Labor market access 2000 (software program). Athens, GA: Elliott & Fitzpatrick, Inc.

Field, T. F. (2008). Estimating earning capacity: Venues, factors, and methods. Estimating Earning Capacity, 1, 5–40.

Field, T. F., Choppa, A. J., & Weed, R. O. (2009). Clinical judgment: A working definition for the rehabilitation professional. The Rehabilitation Professional, 4, 185–193.

Field, T. F. (2012). Review of the ECAF-2. The Rehabilitation Professional, 20, 147 – 148.

Field, T. F. (2014). Adverse situations encountered by vocational and economic experts. The Rehabilitation Professional, 22, 31 – 36.

Field, T. F. & Dunn, P. L. (2014). Transferability of skills: Historical foundations and development. In R. H. Robinson (Ed.), Foundations of forensic vocational rehabilitation (pp. 133–143), New York: Springer Publishing Company.

Gibbs, R.L. & Crtalic, A.K. (2013). Test review: The earning capacity assessment form- 2nd edition. Rehabilitation Counseling Bulletin, 57, 57 – 59.

Heitzman, A. M., Amundsen, C., Gann, C., & Christensen, D. (2014). Consultation in employment law. In R. H. Robinson (Ed.), Foundations of forensic vocational rehabilitation (pp. 363–377), New York: Springer Publishing Company.

International Association of Rehabilitation Professionals. (2007). Codes of ethics, standards of practice, and competencies. Glendale, IL: Author.

Kohlenberg, B. (2014). Consultation in marital dissolution and family law. In R. H. Robinson (Ed.), Foundations of forensic vocational rehabilitation (pp. 341–361), New York: Springer Publishing Company.

National Board for Certified Counselors (2012). Code of ethics. Greensboro, NC: Author.

Neulicht, A. T. (2011). Book review: Assessment of earning capacity (3rd ed.). The Rehabilitation Professional, 19, 39- 40.

Paquette, S. & Heitzman, A. M. (2014). Job analysis. In R. H. Robinson (Ed.), Foundations of forensic vocational rehabilitation (pp. 145–165), New York: Springer Publishing Company.

Parker, R. M. & Schaller, J. L. (1996). Issues in vocational assessment and disability. In E. M. Szymanski & R. M. Parker (Eds.), Work and disability (pp. 127–164). Austin, TX: Pro-Ed.

Pomeranz, J., Yu, N. & Robinson, R. H. (2014). Introduction to life care planning. In R. H. Robinson (Ed.), Foundations of forensic vocational rehabilitation (pp. 391–399), New York: Springer Publishing Company.

Robinson, R. H. (2014). Forensic rehabilitation and vocational earning capacity models. In R. H. Robinson (Ed.), Foundations of forensic vocational rehabilitation (pp. 33–61), New York: Springer Publishing Company.

Robinson, R., Young, M. E., & Pomeranz, J. (2009). Content analysis of factors identified in vocational evaluation analysis reports. The Rehabilitation Professional, 17, 163–174.

Robinson, R. & Pomeranz, J. (2011). The vocational and rehabilitation assessment model (VRAM): Introduction of an empirically derived model of forensic and rehabilitation assessment. The Rehabilitation Professional, 19 (4), 91 – 104.

Robinson, R. H. & Drew, J. L. (2014) Consultation in civil injury litigation. In R. H. Robinson (Ed.), Foundations of forensic vocational rehabilitation (pp. 325–339), New York: Springer Publishing Company.

Robinson, R. H. & Drew, J. L. (2014) Psychometric assessment in vocational rehabilitation. In R. H. Robinson (Ed.), Foundations of forensic vocational rehabilitation (pp. 87–131), New York: Springer Publishing Company.

Shahnasarian, M. (2001). Assessment of earning capacity. Tucson, AZ: Lawyers and Judges Publishing Company.

Shahnasarian, M. (2004a). Assessment of earning capacity (2nd ed.). Tucson, AZ: Lawyers and Judges Publishing Company.

Shahnasarian, M. (2004b). Front pay damage assessment: A summary of vocational and psychological considerations. Journal of Forensic Economics, 16, 177–184.

Shahnasarian, M. (2004c). The earning capacity assessment form. Athens, GA: Elliott & Fitzpatrick.

Shahnasarian, M. (2008). A review of recent, circulated publications on earning capacity assessment. The Rehabilitation Professional, 16 (1), 39–42.

Shahnasarian, M. (2009a). Perceptions of plaintiff or defense retention source as a confounding variable in the assessment of earning capacity: A reliability study of the earning capacity assessment form. Estimating Earning Capacity, 2, 85–98.

Shahnasarian, M. (2009b). The litigation process and the truth: Meditations of a forensic expert. The Rehabilitation Professional, 17, 201–212.

Shahnasarian, M. (2009c). Video recordings in forensic examinations. The Rehabilitation Professional, 17, 175–184.

Shahnasarian, M. (2010a). Earning capacity assessment: Operationalizing a theory. Forensic Rehabilitation & Economics, 3 (2), 111–124.

Shahnasarian, M. (2010b). The earning capacity assessment form – 2. Tampa: Psychological Assessment Resources, Inc.

Shahnasarian, M. (2010c). Professional manual for the earning capacity assessment form – 2. Tampa: Psychological Assessment Resources.

Shahnasarian, M. (2011). Assessment of earning capacity (3rd ed.). Tucson, AZ: Lawyers & Judges Publishing Company.

Shahnasarian, M. (2012). A claimant's guide to understanding and presenting injury damages: A damages expert's perspective. Chicago: ABA Publishing.

Shahnasarian, M. (2013). Justice indicted. Johnson City, TN: OverMountain Press.

Shahnasarian, M. (2015). Consultation in litigation. In P. J. Hartung, M. L. Savicas, & W. B. Walsh (Editors-in-Chief), APA handbook of career interventions (pp. 521–534). Washington, DC: American Psychological Association.

Shahnasarian, M., Kaiser-Ulrey, C., & Lassiter, D. (2006). The MMPI-2 and other personality measures in forensic vocational assessment. The Rehabilitation Professional, 14 (2), 39 – 46.

Shahnasarian, M., & Leitten, C. L. (2006). The earning capacity assessment form: An exploratory factor analysis. The Rehabilitation Professional, 14, 39 – 45.

Shahnasarian, M. & Leitten, C. L. (2008). A longitudinal study of claimants' return to work and vocational factors. Estimating Earning Capacity, 1, 123–130.

Shahnasarian, M. & Leitten, C. L. (2009). The earning capacity assessment form: An exploratory study to assess the feasibility of establishing cut-off scores to determine impairment to earning capacity ratings. The Rehabilitation Professional, 17, 85 – 96.

Shahnasarian, M., Leitten, C. L., & Tremp, R. P. (2010). The earning capacity assessment form-2: An exploratory study of its inter-rater reliability. The Rehabilitation Professional, 18, 213 – 218.

Shahnasarian, M. & Hill, A. (2014). The earning capacity assessment form-2: A status report. The Rehabilitation Professional

Sleister, S. L. (2000). Separating the wheat from the chaff: The role of the vocational expert in forensic vocational rehabilitation. Journal of Vocational Rehabilitation. 14, 199–129.

Slesnick, F. (2012). Book review: Assessment of earning capacity (3rd ed.). Journal of Forensic Economics, 23, 91 – 96.

Super, D. (1957). The psychology of careers: An introduction to vocational development. New York, NY: Harper & Row.

Tate, D. G., Heinrich, R. K., Paasuke, L., & Anderson, D., (1998). Vocational rehabilitation, independent living, and consumerism. In J. A. Delisa & B. M. Gans (Eds.). Rehabilitation Medicine: Principles and Practice (3rd ed.). Philadelphia: Lippincott-Raven Publishers.

Van de Bittner, E. E., Wallace, A., Cottle, R. B., & Simon, S. (2012). Comparison of a consensus methodology for evaluating employability and earning capacity by the CA-IARP DFEC work group with published, peer-reviewed methodologies. The Rehabilitation Professional, 20, 75–86.

Weed, R. O. (1999). Forensic issues for life care planners. In R. O. Weed (Ed.). Life care planning and case management handbook (pp. 351–357). Washington, DC: CRC Press.

About the Author

Michael Shahnasarian, Ph.D., author of *Assessment of Earning Capacity, Fourth Edition*, authored previous editions of this work in 2001, 2004, and 2011. His publication record includes approximately 70 articles, book chapters, and monographs, along with 11 books. Additionally, Dr. Shahnasarian developed a standardized test, the Earning Capacity Assessment Form, which vocational experts worldwide have been using since 2001. This instrument is the only peer-reviewed measure of claims of loss of earning capacity.

Dr. Shahnasarian is president of Career Consultants of America, Inc., a private practice he founded in Tampa, Florida, in 1986. The practice provides services related to vocational rehabilitation and career development, rehabilitation psychology, human resources consulting, and life care planning. Dr. Shahnasarian has rendered consulting services to global manufacturing, financial services, business consulting, and healthcare organizations. Part of his practice is hospital-based, and he makes rounds to provide bedside rehabilitation psychology services to catastrophically disabled and end-stage patients.

After completing undergraduate studies in psychology at Indiana University and a master's degree in psychology at Texas A&M University, Dr. Shahnasarian earned a doctorate in counseling psychology at Florida State University. A licensed psychologist, he also holds certifications as a rehabilitation counselor, vocational evaluator, career counselor, and life care planner.

Dr. Shahnasarian has more than 30 years' experience as an expert witness evaluating thousands of damages claims related to vocational, life care planning, and rehabilitation psychology issues. His litigation work has been evenly divided between retentions from plaintiff and defense counsel, and he has provided expert witness services—evaluation, consulting, research, and testifying—throughout the United States and abroad.

Two organizations—the National Career Development Association and the International Association of Life Care Planners—appointed Dr. Shahnasarian Fellow status. Other major recognition Dr. Shahnasarian has received includes selection as Rehabilitation Counselor of the Year in 1999 by the American Rehabilitation Counselor Association, and Outstanding Career Practitioner of the Year in 2002 by the National Career Development Association. The National Rehabilitation Association presented Dr. Shahnasarian the W. F. Faulkes Award in 2005 for his research and development of the Earning Capacity Assessment Form.

Leadership in professional and civic organizations has also been a feature of Dr. Shahnasarian's career development. He served as 1998 president of the National Career Development Association, a 10,000-member professional organization established in 1913. Former Florida Governor Lawton Chiles appointed Dr. Shahnasarian to the Florida Rehabilitation Council in 1998, and former Governor Jeb Bush reappointed him in 2000. His record also includes service on numerous editorial boards, presentations at national and international conferences, and membership on boards of directors. Dr. Shahnasarian was selected as a "Healthcare Hero" in his community (Tampa, Florida) in 2009.

Index

R

S

T

V

W

X

Other quality products available from

Lawyers & Judges Publishing Company, Inc.

2014 Future Damage and Present Value Calculator

by Steve Weintraub

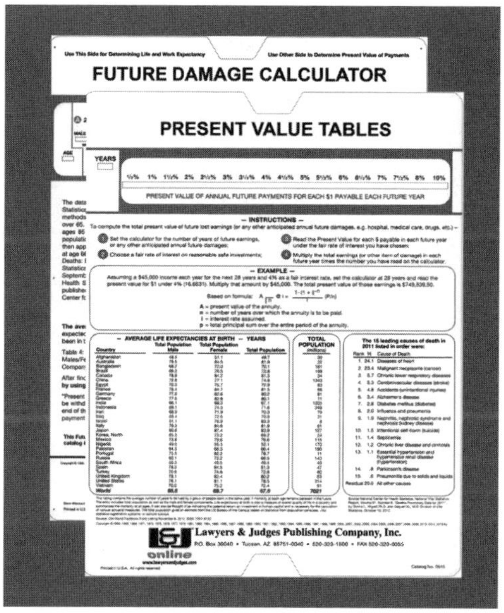

Whatever type of case you're working on, you will find the exact information you need without wasting hours on research. The 2014 Future Damage Calculator breaks down the life expectancies of men and women by gender, age, education level, and ethnic background. It also gives their worklife expectancies, including the average number of remaining years of labor force participation.

Additionally the calculator contains the average life expectancies for twenty-nine countries, more than ever before! Countries featured on the 2014 calculator include the United States, Canada, Afghanistan, Australia, Austria, Bangladash, Brazil, China, Egypt, France, Germany, Honduras, India, Indonesia, Iran, Iraq, Ireland, Israel, Italy, Japan, North Korea, South Korea, Lebanon, Libya Mexico, Nigeria, Pakistan, Russia, South Africa, Turkey, United Kingdom, and World as well as a worldwide average life expectancy. The new calculator also reflects annual changes in life expectancies for the male and female populations, as well as the total population size, of the countries listed. All life expectancy data has been updated for 2014 for White, Black, Hispanic and Total males and females. Four new 2014 tables are included for White, Black, Hispanic, and Total Population with the most recent figures.

The flip side of the calculator provides the Present Value Tables sorted by a wide range of interest rates showing the present value of future lost earnings or any other anticipated annual future damages. The 2014 calculator contains expanded Present Value Tables, which are important for calculating worker's compensation claims. This calculator is ideal for use in trial, for research, settlement conferences, and structured settlement offers.

Produce Code: 0615 • Slide Calculator

Life and Worklife Expectancies, Second Edition

by Hugh Richards, M.S., and Michael Donaldson, Ph.D.

Now the information you need for determining life and worklife expectancies is in one complete volume right at your fingertips: smokers by education, many educational categories by race/Hispanic origin, persons with medical conditions, and more. Our brand new Life and Worklife Expectancies, Second Edition now features extensive life and worklife expectancy tables and figures in an easily accessible format.

Part I contains an overview of the methods and data sources used in life tables: differences between period and cohort life tables, properties of survival data, life expectancy by educational attainment, race/Hispanic origin, smoking status, relative mortality ratios for persons with medical risks, quality of care and life expectancy in cases of illness or disability, use of life annuities and structured settlements, calculation of retirement benefits, and more.

Part II addresses the main methods of determining duration of working life. Detailed tables for all methods and many educational, demographic, smoking status , occupational category, gender and race/Hispanic origin are provided. Biases are discussed and previous worklife estimates are corrected by including mortality rates by educational attainment. The increment-decrement model is carefully analyzed for correction of other potential biases. In addition, it discusses pros and cons of the various methods, for example worklife expectancies, Life-Participation-Employment (LPE) and Median Years to Retirement (MYR).

Part III contains comprehensive tables of life and worklife expectancies for the many demographics discussed in the text. This is the most complete overview of life and worklife expectancies for attorneys, insurance professionals, and forensic economists available anywhere.

Topics covered:

- Introduction to life tables and life expectancy
- Overview of life expectancies
- Cohort tables
- Current (period) tables
- Life expectancies for persons with medical risks
- Effects of cigarette smoking on life expectancy
- Life expectancy and the properties of survival data
- Bias and how to reduce or eliminate it
- Standard errors of estimates
- Introduction to estimates of working life

Produce Code: 5368 • ISBN: 978-1-933264-74-5 • Pages: 243 • Casebound • 8.5"×11"

The Plaintiff and Defense Attorney's Guide to Understanding Economic Damages

by Michael L. Brookshire, Ph.D., Frank Slesnick, Ph.D., and John O. Ward, Ph.D.

The Plaintiff and Defense Attorney's Guide to Understanding Economic Damages is an informative yet compact book pertaining to the use of economic damage testimony in trial or mediation. It will be a valuable part of your library as an attorney needing to understand the practical issues involved with retaining economic expert witnesses and using economic testimony in your upcoming trial or mediation. This is an essential resource for damages expert wishing to understand the legal perspective of their work.

Inside is a wealth of information on many important topics on understanding economic damages and using them to your benefit, whether you are the plaintiff or defense attorney. It covers estimation of wage and salary loss, fringe benefit loss, household services loss, estimating losses for adults and children, and understanding and retaining economic damage experts.

You'll also read about the roles of life care planners and vocational/rehabilitation experts and how they help determine economic damages. Special cases and issues-such as punitive damages, F.E.L.A. cases involving injured railroad workers, international issues, gender, age, ethnic background, and more-are covered in great depth. You'll also learn how to achieve a successful result in mediation and trial situations, on both the plaintiff and defense side. Structured settlements, and their advantages and disadvantages, are extensively covered.

The accompanying CD-ROM includes Internet sources with additional information, definitions of technical terminology, direct and cross-examination questions and answers, case studies, links to damage calculation sites, and more.

Topics Include:

- Understanding economic damage experts
- Daubert considerations
- Plaintiff attorney's considerations and perspectives
- Defense attorney's considerations and perspectives
- Estimating lost earnings

Produce Code: 4101 • ISBN: 978-1-933264-10-3 • Pages: 193 • Softbound • 6"×9"

Assessing Damages in Injuries and Deaths of Minor Children

by Thomas R. Ireland and John O. Ward

When you have a case that deals with the sad event of a death of a child, how do you determine how much the amount of damages should be? What statistics do you use, and how do you arrive at the final amount?

Assessing Damages in Injuries and Deaths of Minor Children's primary focus is to consider a wide range of topics that relate to how to assess damages or provide testimony in cases involving injuries or deaths of minor children.

Written with the forensic economic expert or attorneys specifically concerned with damages in mind, this book goes in depth on every approach to assessing damages in these cases. You will learn how to assess damages using the parental investment approach, how to determine a child's future earning capacity by taking into account the educational outcomes of the parents, and other ways to project a child's future earning capacity. You will read about the issues of wrongful birth and wrongful pregnancy. You will also find out by using the Child Support Guidelines how child support paid after a divorce can be factored into a damages assessment. Read about damages standards in various types of litigation involving personal injuries and wrongful deaths of children.

Be introduced to a variety of methodologies for projecting the lost earnings of a minor child, including the future financial support a decedent child might have provided to parents. Learn about the fundamental damages problem in the death of a minor child, which is that parents have losses of enormous value which they would have been willing to expend almost all financial resources to prevent, but standards for financial damages recovery tend to be very small.

Topics covered:

- Predicting educational attainment
- Parental effects on a child's educational attainment
- Parental influence on a child's future earnings
- Damages in wrongful pregnancy tort actions
- Damages in wrongful birth litigation
- Future economic contributions of a female child
- Using national opinion research data
- The parental investment approach
- U.S. Department of Agriculture estimates
- Saving rate estimates for single persons by income, age and sex
- Applying Cost Share
- Child Support Guidelines
- Using the Expenditures on Children report

Produce Code: 6184 • ISBN: 978-1-930056-18-3• Pages: 415 • Casebound • 6"×9"

Measuring Loss in Catastrophic Injury Cases

by Kevin S. Marshall, JD, Ph.D. and Thomas R. Ireland, Ph.D.

The measurement of loss in catastrophic injury cases is an interdisciplinary effort involving the participation of many specialists including economists, rehabilitation counselors and therapists, health care providers, life care planners, attorneys, and others, including the patient and his or her family. You will learn about the interdisciplinary nature of measuring loss, the role of the forensic economist in determining loss, working with life care planners and rehabilitation and vocational experts, impact of a reduced life expectancy, types of settlements including annuities, structured settlements and periodic payment judgments, and suggestions for building an expert damages team when working on this type of case. In this book, you'll find the information necessary to assess and derive a fair and accurate measurement that will, as fairly as possible, compensate the injured party and/or his or her family for his or her actual losses.

Topics covered:

- Interdisciplinary nature of measuring loss
- The role of the forensic economist
- The roles of vocational and rehabilitation experts
- Overview of life care planning
- What is needed from life care planning experts
- Impact of reduced life expectancy
- Annuity contracts
- Structured Settlements
- Periodic payment judgments
- Building an expert damages team

Produce Code: 4128 • ISBN: 978-1-933264-12-7 • Pages: 2726 • Softbound • 6"×9"